academy
317
338

PLATE I

ARTHUR CAYLEY
HEADLAM

Life and Letters of a Bishop

BY

RONALD JASPER

WITH A FOREWORD BY

THE DEAN OF S. PAUL'S

FAITH PRESS

7 Tufton Street London SW 1

MOREHOUSE-BARLOW INC. NEW YORK U.S.A.

PRINTED IN GREAT BRITAIN
in *11-pt. Baskerville type*
BY THE FAITH PRESS LTD
LEIGHTON BUZZARD

TO ALWYN WINTON

who has shown me unfailing
kindness in all my ventures with
the pen

FOREWORD

By the Dean of S. Paul's
the Very Revd W. R. Matthews

The invitation to write a foreword to Mr. Jasper's biography of Arthur Cayley Headlam came to me as a request to perform an act of almost filial piety, for it would be difficult to exaggerate the debt which I owe to him. He it was who gave me the opportunity to start on an academic career which led, to my enduring astonishment, to the chair of the Philosophy of Religion in the University of London and to the office of Dean of King's College, in which it was my privilege to try to carry on the work of the Theological Department of that College and the Faculty of Theology in the University of which he had been one of the principal founders. But perhaps even more, I am indebted to him for the gift of self-confidence. The fact that he believed in me helped me to believe in myself. More than once he said, 'You have not yet been fully expanded', and I remembered those words when difficult times came, for they seemed to indicate that, in the opinion of one whose judgment I trusted, there were potentialities in me still to be drawn out.

I dwell upon these autobiographical facts because they bring to light a side of Headlam's personality which was not generally known but was an essential element in his character. For I was not the only example of his interest in young men in whom he thought he discerned promise. In the midst of all his overwhelming work at King's College he was always on the look out for students who showed signs of 'intelligence' (his favourite word of approval). In my first term at King's College he set an essay for every theological student and he not only read and annotated the essays but discussed them with the writers. He was searching for intelligence, and it was my good fortune that he discerned some sparks in my immature production.

There was, I think, also another motive in Headlam's mind. No doubt he would have encouraged promising young men in any circumstances, but at the time when he became Principal of King's College, London, it was particularly important to show that the College and the University could produce graduates who had some real tincture of scholarship. The Theological Faculty had just been inaugurated in the University, not without criticism and heart-searching among those who were attached to the 'secular' tradition in London. It fell to my

FOREWORD

by the Dean of S. Paul's
the Very Revd. W. R. Matthews

THE invitation to write a foreword to Mr. Jasper's biography of Arthur Cayley Headlam came to me as a request to perform an act of almost filial piety, for it would be difficult to exaggerate the debt which I owe to him. He it was who gave me the opportunity to start on an academic career which led, to my enduring astonishment, to the chair of the Philosophy of Religion in the University of London and to the office of Dean of King's College, in which it was my privilege to try to carry on the work of the Theological Department of that College and the Faculty of Theology in the University of which he had been one of the principal founders. But perhaps even more I am indebted to him for the gift of self-confidence. The fact that he believed in me helped me to believe in myself. More than once he said, 'You have not yet been fully extended,' and I remembered those words when difficult times came, for they seemed to indicate that, in the opinion of one whose judgment I trusted, there were potentialities in me still to be drawn out.

I dwell upon these autobiographical facts because they bring to light a side of Headlam's personality which was not generally known but was an essential element in his character. For I was not the only example of his interest in young men in whom he thought he discerned promise. In the midst of all his overwhelming work at King's College he was always on the look out for students who showed signs of 'intelligence' (his favourite word of approval). In my first term at King's College he set an essay for every theological student and he not only read and annotated the essays but discussed them with the writers. He was searching for intelligence, and it was my good fortune that he discerned some sparks in my immature production.

There was, I think, also another motive in Headlam's mind. No doubt he would have encouraged promising young men in any circumstances, but at the time when he became Principal of King's College, London, it was particularly important to show that the College and the University could produce graduates who had some real tincture of scholarship. The Theological Faculty had just been inaugurated in the University, not without criticism and heart-searching among those who were attached to the 'secular' tradition in London. It fell to my

7

lot to be one of a small group who were the first to enter for the newly-established B.D. degree and Headlam keenly wished for our success.

This reminiscence leads me to comment on another aspect of his character of which perhaps only those who knew him well were aware —his passionate identification of himself with any institution for which he had responsibility. I suppose that when he was appointed Principal of King's College, London, he had no great knowledge of its past or of its ethos, but at once it became the object of his whole energies to solve its many problems and to place it on a firm foundation for the future without destroying its unique character. It is true that he lost his temper from time to time, and it would have been sometimes more politic to disguise his anger, but his wrath was always impersonal, in the sense that it was aroused by what he considered to be injustice to the College.

I have never known any one else who had such a capacity for hard and unremitting work. His incessant labours were possible only because he rationed his time and cut out unnecessary activities. This could sometimes have disconcerting results. I remember that I wrote to him once a letter expressing some thoughts on the study of theology. Probably they were of small value, but I was daunted to receive a brief note in reply, 'I have no time to write interesting letters.' On reflection, I concluded that this was not meant as a snub, but as a plain statement of fact.

Certainly Headlam was a formidable person. His piercing, blue grey eyes, which could strike apprehension when turned upon a timid student, and his directness of speech, combined with a complete inability to engage in polite but empty conversation, made him seem aloof; but I think he suffered from a shyness that inhibited easy personal contacts and did not consciously aim at being formidable. I noticed that he was specially tolerant to those who were not afraid of him and answered him firmly but courteously. Perhaps I am mistaken, but in my opinion Headlam was a man of deep emotions and affections which he scarcely ever allowed to express themselves in word or gesture. I know at least that he helped many in distress, concealing his acts of kindness from the world. When his wife died he came to spend a night with us and talked to my wife about her at length. Then he went abroad for some time and wrote, 'Do not be too sorry for me : after all, I have my work.' After that, so far as I remember, he never referred in conversation to her again. This, I think, is typical of the man; he was profoundly moved by the loss of one who had his whole affection, but he would not take the risk of even appearing to invite sympathy. I am allowed to quote a revealing sentence from a letter which he wrote to his niece, Miss Persis Wingfield, o.b.e. : 'People think me a hard man, and I suppose I have a rather hard exterior, but really I want affection very much and feel it.' He himself was evidently aware of the contrast between his external persona and his inner experience.

It has been said that a gentleman is one who is never rude except intentionally. This does not apply to Headlam. He could indeed be rude of set purpose. Towards the end of his life he came to see us at S. Paul's after a meeting of bishops at Lambeth and commented, 'I am getting deaf and that prevents me from being as rude as I should like to be!' But most often he was rude without intention. He had none of those innocent hypocrisies which smooth social intercourse, and if he did not like a person, or did not remember who he was, or was thinking about something else, he made no attempt to pretend to be glad to see him. I have known him to be really astonished when he was told that he had offended any one. This trait in his character was perhaps the obverse of what I regard as a virtue—he had no thirst for popularity, and I should be surprised to learn that he had ever asked himself whether he was liked or disliked. He pursued the policies which he believed to be right and said clearly what he believed to be true on any subject. There never was, I am sure, any one who had less of the art, or the temperament, of the rhetorician.

Having read through what I have written about Headlam's personality, I feel that I ought to add a note on the limitations of my opportunities of judging. The impression which I have tried to convey is mainly based upon the earlier period of his career; when he became a bishop, though I met him frequently, his activities were not under my daily observation and I can well believe that some who were closer to him are right when they assert that his consecration seemed to bring him greater ease in personal relations and enabled him to show in word and deed the good will and affection which had always been there. In particular, I am sure that his zeal for the cause of Christian unity brought a kind of release from inhibitions and helped him to acquire a graciousness of manner and sympathetic understanding in his personal relations with leaders of other Christian communions which surprised even his nearest friends. The witness of the late Revd. Philip Usher, who was his chaplain and trusted companion, is decisive on this point. After an international meeting, at which Headlam had played a prominent part, Usher wrote that on such occasions one came to a realization of Headlam's true greatness and that he seemed 'transfigured.'

Headlam was, in short, an intellectual whose religion, which was deep and sincere, took an intellectual shape. The lectures which he gave on Systematic Theology and on Biblical and Historical Theology

were truly systematic, surveying the whole field with admirable
lucidity. When he published the first volume of his book on Systematic
Theology, which was never completed, I recognized the lectures which
I had heard from him thirty years earlier, elaborated and enlarged,
but essentially unchanged. There was the same lucidity and the same
sense of the solemnity of the subject, and the same absence of emotion ;
indeed I doubt whether Headlam ever made an emotional appeal in
his life. That does not mean that he did not admit the importance of
the emotions ; they were there to be reckoned with ; but he dealt with
the doctrines of our faith in the dry light of scholarship, concerned
with historical facts, interpretation of Biblical texts and the development of ideas. He gave us the prose of Systematic Theology ; if one
wanted its poetry, one must look elsewhere. And yet this impression of
his theological attitude is probably misleading, for the great Commentary on Romans, in which he collaborated with Dr. Sanday, could
hardly have been written by one who had no sympathy for, or understanding of, the deeply emotional experience of S. Paul. Perhaps here
too the style was not the man.

   This is not the place for a considered estimate of Headlam's theological writings, but something should be said of this aspect of his life
work to which he gave so much attention even when he was a busy
diocesan bishop. The climate of theological discussion which now prevails would have seemed to him alien to his habits of thought and
indeed at the end of his career he was to some extent a representative
of the old guard opposition to modern tendencies. He was well aware
of this and it caused him no concern for he had no impulse urging
him to move with the times and was quite ready to believe that the
times were moving in the wrong direction. I think that he formed his
theology and his views of the Christian religion during his work on the
Epistle to the Romans and did not subsequently modify his views in
any fundamental way. He was critical of the theology of Liberal
Protestantism and out of sympathy with Harnack's presentation of the
essence of Christianity and his theory of the development of Christian
doctrine. When, however, the reaction against Liberal Protestantism
took place and the school of apocalyptic and eschatological interpretation of the New Testament came into the foreground, he found himself even more opposed to its principles and conclusions. He was not
of course alone in this attitude but it would not be an exaggeration to
say that the apocalyptic exegesis was so distasteful to him that he never
profoundly considered it. This does not mean that his writings on the
Gospels and the life of our Lord are without value. They are still
instructive, but one must regret that Headlam's powerful mind did not
treat more seriously the new light on the New Testament which came
from the study of apocalyptic literature.

In my opinion he has left us one great book which deserves to be read and pondered by all Christians who care for the future of the Church. In *The Doctrine of the Church and Reunion*, which was an expanded version of his Bampton Lectures for 1920, Headlam had a subject which was very near his heart and which his gifts qualified him to treat with wonderful cogency. His historical sense and knowledge enabled him to present his case fully documented and his orderly mind was at its best in the clear development of the argument through masses of detail. There was never any doubt about what Headlam was trying to say and his style though sometimes bald was effective when he had a reasoned thesis to expound. In this book the feeling of urgency gives the writing a warmth which is absent from most of his work. In reading this book one catches the undertone of exasperation that the unity of the Church should be impaired and hindered by scruples and prejudices which he regarded as 'unintelligent.'

Though no politician, Headlam had the outlook of a statesman, and his theology bears the mark of one who was fully conscious of the historical causes of the present situation and the probable results of present action, or inaction, in the future. His theology was not specu-lation apart from life; it was 'practical' in the sense that it was a theology of the Church and for the Church and always at the back of his mind was the thought of the Church as it was meant to be, as it is, and as it might become. The lectures are a reasoned thesis supported by scholarly criticism, but it would be a mistake to suppose that his conception of the Church was merely an intellectual construction. He had a vision of the Church which inspired him, an ideal which could be achieved not by faith and prayer alone, but by hard thinking on the meaning of the Body of Christ in the world. Though he thought much about the Ecumenical movement and the world-situation of our religion, his attention was directed first of all to the need for unity in the Christian witness to his native land.

Headlam has appeared to some to be primarily an aloof academic scholar and a formidable controversialist. This was a grievous mis-judgment and to refute it I will conclude by quoting the final para-graph of the Bampton Lectures :

'There is, I believe, in the country a strong desire for Christian Unity. Thoughtful men of every religious body recognize how much Christianity is weakened by our divisions. They feel that if all the power and earnestness which we at present display in strengthening our separate communities against one another were to be concentrated in preaching the Christian message to the world, Christian love and Christian faith would begin to abound. The world needs that we should strengthen spiritual principles against materialism and selfishness. To that end we must put aside self-will and self-assertion; we must be ready to listen and to learn, as well as to teach. Faith, humility and charity must be the weapons with which we attempt to recreate the sense of brotherhood and of divine things in the world.'

These simple words, as true now as they were in 1920, disclose the aspiration that was in the mind and heart of Arthur Cayley Headlam.

W. R. MATTHEWS

INTRODUCTION

SIR CHARLES OMAN's method of writing history was one of which Headlam fully approved. He spoke of it in his last public utterance—the Commemoration Sermon at All Souls on November 3, 1946. 'Oman was an historian in the truest sense. He had an intense interest in the past life of the world in both small and great things, and he told the story of the past with great knowledge and accuracy, without any pretension, without dwelling on its importance, without any desire to emphasize its lessons. History must be left to teach its own lessons. We learn from it by reading the true story and not by listening to the comments of the historian.' I have tried to adopt the same method in writing this biography.

It is still too early—only thirteen years after his death—to assess accurately Headlam's place in the history of the Church, and particularly his work for Christian unity. He was, of course, a controversial figure : but despite his critics—and they were many—he was absolutely unshakable in his own convictions. He was frequently heard to remark, 'People can say what they like about me now ; but in fifty years' time they will see that I was right.' Fifty years from his death will bring us to the turn of the twentieth century. It will then be interesting to see what path the Churches have taken in their search for unity, and where the Church of South India—the great monument to Headlam's œcumenical ideals—stands. But whatever future generations might think about Headlam, the fact will remain that in his own time he was a great ecclesiastical figure both at home and abroad—probably respected and loved more by foreign Churchmen than by those in this country.

This fact was revealed by the readiness with which his friends from all over the world supplied me with letters and reminiscences when I began to write this book. Those who have helped me have been so numerous that they must forgive me if I express my grateful thanks to them collectively rather than individually. If there are any who, quite unwittingly, I have quoted without their permission, I do hope that they will forgive me.

There are, however, a few who must be mentioned by name, for without their help and support the book would either have never been written or would have been even more inadequate than it already is. My debt is primarily due to Dr. Headlam's nephew and heir, Mr. Kenneth Headlam-Morley, and to his nieces and literary executors,

Professor Agnes Headlam-Morley and Miss Persis L. Wingfield, o.b.e. Apart from their own personal help they gave me complete freedom in the use of the great mass of documents and correspondence which the Bishop left at Whorlton. In addition Miss Wingfield allowed me the full use of the regular private correspondence which she had with the Bishop for something like thirty years. She was one of his few real confidantes and these letters revealed effectively the inner man. Then there was the late Miss Rose Headlam, the Bishop's redoubtable sister. Although of a great age when I first met her, she was blessed with a remarkable retentive memory; and she had also treasured some very early letters and papers which provided valuable documentary evidence for the early years of the Bishop's life. I visited her many times in her cottage at Whorlton and it was a great delight to 'give her her head' and let her talk of life and personalities of the Church in Durham in the second half of the nineteenth century.

The late Professor Claude Jenkins—friend and admirer of the Headlams for close on fifty years—also did me a great service. He rejoiced in the knowledge that the biography was being written and at the outset wrote a lengthy memorandum which was of the utmost value. (His handwriting in this, incidentally, was more than a match for Headlam's in illegibility!) His interest was constant and I frequently received letters with further pieces of information or suggestions of further people who might be approached. Equally helpful were Bishop John Hodson, former Bishop of Tewkesbury; the Revd. E. C. Prichard, Headlam's former domestic chaplain; and the Dean of S. Paul's (Dr. W. R. Matthews), who also wrote the Foreword. His Grace the Archbishop of Canterbury also very kindly gave me leave to use papers and reports both in the Lambeth Palace Library and in the files of the Council on Foreign (now Inter-Church) Relations.

I also owe a great debt to the Bishop of Winchester (Dr. A. T. P. Williams). From the beginning he has been an unfailing source of help and encouragement. He has lent me books, deciphered Professor Jenkins' notes, and read and commented upon every word that I have written. This is by no means the first occasion on which he has gladly given me such help; and as a small token of my gratitude I dedicate this book to him. Finally, a word of praise and thanks to my young daughter, Christine, who laboured valiantly at the onerous task of preparing the Index.

September 1960

CONTENTS

ILLUSTRATIONS

The Family

Early Years

THE origin of the Headlam family is obscure; but it possibly descends from the great Norman house of Roxel or Russell, from which the Bedfords trace their line. In 1909 Peter, the son of Jordan Russell, Seneschal of Durham, granted to his younger brother, Simon, all rights in certain lands including Headlam in Teesdale; and the latter is said to have taken the name 'de Headlam', by which the family was known from that time. Another tradition is that it descends from another famous Norman family, the Nevilles, who had been granted land at Staindrop (a mere stone's throw from Headlam) from the Prior of Durham in 1131. Whatever may be true, it was evidently of Norman origin and had long connections with the North East. Certainly by the fifteenth century there were Headlams in a number of widely-scattered places in Durham, from those engaged in sheep farming in upper Teesdale to those who built and sailed ships at the mouth of both Tees and Tyne.[1] The traditional conservatism of the Headlams manifested itself in the reign of Queen Elizabeth, when Brian Headlam of Sedgefield, near Stockton, opposed the Reformed ways of worship. In 1569 after the altar stone and holy water stoup had been removed from the parish church and hidden, he with others restored them to their rightful places. Nor was he without a puckish sense of humour; to the great amusement of the congregation—and not having God before his eyes, but stirred up with devilish contempt and irreverence, did . . . sit with his cap on his head, and being there of lawfully admonished, refused contemptuously to reform these defaults, or to pay 12d. to the churchwardens for the poore man's boxe, then demanded.'[2]

The family's regular line of descent began with Nicholas Headlam

[1] The Topographer and Genealogist, 1853, vol. 2, Article on Stockton families.
[2] Depositions and other Ecclesiastical Proceedings from the Court of Durham 1311 to the reign of Elizabeth, 1844, Surtees Society, vol. 31, pp. 11-12, 183-9.

CHAPTER ONE

The Family
Early Years

I

THE origin of the Headlam family is obscure; but it possibly descends from the great Norman house of Rozel or Russell, from which the Bedfords trace their line. In 1309 Peter, the son of Jordan Russell, Seneschal of Durham, granted to his younger brother, Simon, all rights in certain lands including Headlam in Teesdale; and the latter is said to have taken the name 'de Headlam,' by which the family was known from that time. Another tradition is that it descends from another famous Norman family—the Nevilles, who had been granted land at Staindrop (a mere stone's throw from Headlam) from the Prior of Durham in 1131. Whichever may be true, it was evidently of Norman origin and had long connections with the North East. Certainly by the fifteenth century there were Headlams in a number of widely-scattered places in Durham, from those engaged in sheep-farming in upper Teesdale to those who built and sailed ships at the mouth of both Tees and Tyne.[1] The traditional conservatism of the Headlams manifested itself in the reign of Queen Elizabeth, when Brian Headlam of Sedgefield, near Stockton, opposed the Reformed ways of worship. In 1569 after the altar stone and holy water stoup had been removed from the parish church and hidden, he with others restored them to their rightful places. Nor was he without a puckish sense of humour; for he disturbed divine service by making loud and facetious remarks—to the great amusement of the congregation—and, 'not having God before his eies, but stirred up with devilish contempt and irreverence, did . . . sit with his cap on his head, and being therof lawfully admonished, refused contemtuouslie to reforme these defaultes, or to pay 12d. to the churchwardens for the poore man's boxe, then demanded.'[2]

The family's regular line of descent began with Nicholas Headlam

---

[1] *The Topographer and Genealogist*, 1853, vol. 2. Article on Stockton families.
[2] *Depositions and other Ecclesiastical Proceedings from the Courts of Durham 1311 to the reign of Elizabeth*, 1844, Surtees Society, vol. 21, pp. 111–12, 187–8.

of Eggleston, who is recorded in the parish registers of Middleton-in-Teesdale as having married Grace Kipling of Carlton, near Stockton, in 1627. His son, Anthony, forsook farming in favour of shipbuilding on the Tyne, while his grandson, John, further extended the family fortunes by establishing a shipyard at Stockton. The reputation of the family in the industry must have been considerable, for when the latter's son moved back to Gateshead on the Tyne in the middle of the eighteenth century, it was said that the Corporation of Newcastle had induced him to do so by offering special privileges to his apprentices. Be that as it may, he made shipbuilding history in 1750 by launching a ship of thirty keels called 'The Russells.'

The wealth of the family must have now grown to considerable proportions, for in the next generation Thomas Emerson Headlam forsook shipbuilding and returned to upper Teesdale as squire of Gilmonby Hall, where in 1769 he married his cousin, Jane, daughter of the Revd. John Emerson, Rector of Winston and Middleton-in-Teesdale. Their eldest son, John, was born in the same year; and it is to him that his descendants looked with some pride as the real founder of their house. He followed in the steps of his maternal grandfather, took Holy Orders in 1793, and became Rector of Wycliffe, a tiny hamlet on the Yorkshire bank of the Tees near Winston, from which the famous John Wycliffe was reputed to have come. Here he stayed for the rest of his life, a man of considerable local importance : he was a magistrate for the county of Durham for over fifty years and for the North Riding of Yorkshire for over twenty : in 1826 he was appointed Archdeacon of Richmond, when the Archdeaconry was part of the diocese of Chester and spread over a vast area of Yorkshire, Lancashire, Cumberland and Westmorland. In 1836 its size was much reduced on becoming part of the reconstituted diocese of Ripon, but in the new diocese the Archdeacon was given further preferment by being appointed Chancellor. This handsome man with hooked nose and piercing eye had a reputation for tremendous mental and physical vigour. By religious conviction he was a staunch Evangelical and in politics a Tory, but throughout life he showed, as did many of his forbears, a sturdy independence of outlook. Sydney Smith scornfully held him to be a bigoted Tory, and it is said that in 1831 he led the North Riding landowners in a carriage and four to vote against the Reformers in the York election. On the other hand the Duke of Cleveland considered his views and actions at times to be dangerously Radical—as, for example, when he erected first a stone bridge and later a suspension bridge across the Tees at Whorlton : such ventures merely encouraged the lower classes to travel and this was a most undesirable thing.[3]

---

[3] Cecil Headlam, *Walter Headlam, Life and Poems,* 1910, pp. 9–11.

In 1806 he married Maria, daughter of the Revd. Thomas Wilson-Morley of Easby House, near Richmond, later Dean of Carlisle. This marriage was important, for it introduced the Bentley strain into the family : Maria was the great-great-granddaughter of Richard Bentley, the famous classical scholar and Master of Trinity College, Cambridge ; and from the Bentleys they could claim descent from Edward I. Both in his writing and in his College reforms Richard Bentley had shown himself to be of independent judgment, intrepid in thought and determined to attain what was right and just regardless of cost. Such characteristics—as well as the famous Bentley nose—came out in more than one Headlam descendant. Certainly the intellectual attainments of the Archdeacon's seven sons and five daughters were considerable. Of these Thomas Emerson was seventeenth Wrangler at Cambridge, M.P. for Newcastle for twenty-six years, a Privy Councillor and Judge Advocate General from 1859 to 1866 ; Edward was Bell Scholar at Cambridge, twelfth Wrangler and ninth Classic, and a Fellow of S. John's, later becoming Director of the Civil Service examinations ; John was twenty-first Wrangler and Tyrwhitt's Hebrew scholar ; Arthur was Scholar of Trinity, University Prizeman, twenty-ninth Wrangler and tenth Classic ; and Francis was Fellow and Bursar of University College, Oxford, and later Stipendiary Magistrate of Manchester. An illuminating estimate of these brothers has been given by Cecil Headlam, Edward's son :

'All left behind them a reputation of untarnished integrity, of unswerving devotion to duty, of serious and ungrudging work. Each in a different way attained a considerable position in his profession. Common to them all was a reserve and restraint, which in some sort sterilized the creative powers of their intellectual force. A spirit critical both of themselves and of others dominated and guided them. They demanded of themselves the same high standard as they applied to others. Their critical faculty seems to have dwarfed their imagination and the productive powers of their intellect. For a group of men who were so distinguished in their academic careers, and who were intellectually so capable, they were singularly lacking in literary enterprise, in the necessity or the ability of self-expression. On the whole one is left with the impression of a family of clever men, cultured and conscientious, but capable from a literary point of view of more than they performed.' [4]

This estimate did not apply, however, to the youngest daughter, Margaret Ann : this talented and cultured lady became a brilliant

[4] Ibid., p. 12.

French and Italian scholar and wrote a great deal of poetry—notably Italian sonnets—of a high order. She also showed her independence by becoming a devout Tractarian despite her strict Evangelical up-bringing, and in this she was followed by her brother Arthur. The other surviving children, Morley, Jane and Frances, although not so brilliant intellectually, nevertheless possessed charm and gaiety allied to sound common sense, which allowed them to make in their own way equally valuable contributions to the life of society. Jane and Frances married two brothers, John and Thomas Story Spedding of Mire-house, near Keswick, thereby coming into contact with a fascinating literary circle. Their brother-in-law, James Spedding, was the famous Baconian scholar, and through him Mirehouse became a constant meeting-place for literary men—Tennyson, James Anthony Froude, Thomas Carlyle, Edward Fitzgerald, Monckton Milnes and others.[5]

Morley and his younger brother, Arthur, settled on the Durham side of the Tees at Whorlton. Archdeacon Headlam, finding it impossible to extend his property at Wycliffe, had bought land in and around the village at Whorlton, and this passed to Morley and Arthur. At one end of the village Morley established himself at Whorlton Grange, while at the other, next to the church and overlooking the river, Arthur built Whorlton Hall. After leaving Cambridge, the latter had been ordained to the curacy of Knebworth, Hertfordshire; he returned home in 1853 to act as his father's curate and in the following year became Vicar of Whorlton. Here he opened a coaching establishment for students preparing for public examinations and the universities, ran his small country parish on Tractarian lines—Whorlton could boast of its surpliced choir as early as 1871—and indulged in his passion for gardening. In 1861 he married Agnes Sarah, daughter of Elizabeth and the late James Favell of Normanton.

The Favells were an old Yorkshire family from Craven who had entered the mining industry and held property and interests in both the West and the North Ridings. James Favell preferred to live away from his business and occupied in turn a series of country houses in more salubrious surroundings. It was probably at one of these, Derwent Lodge, near Keswick, that Arthur Headlam met Agnes Favell when visiting his sisters at Mirehouse; they were married at Crosthwaite Church on June 26, 1861. This marriage gave the Head-lams their Cayley connection, for Agnes was the only daughter of James Favell's second marriage to Ann Elizabeth Cayley in 1828. The Cayleys were also a Yorkshire family of long history, tracing their descent from the Plantagenets and the ancient Welsh kings, while one

---

[5] Ibid., p. 21. H. D. Rawnsley, *Literary Associations of the English Lakes,* 2 vols., Glasgow, 1894, vol. 1, pp. 170–80.

ancestor, Osborne de Cailly, had come to England with William of Normandy in 1066. In the course of their long history they could claim links not only with Oliver Cromwell but also with Peter the Great of Russia. In 1756 John Cayley, a merchant and British Consul General at St. Petersburg married Sarah Cozens, an attractive young lady of that city and daughter of Richard Cozens, natural son of Peter the Great : he had been born to Peter and a woman named Mary Cozens at Deptford when the Czar was in this country learning the art of shipbuilding; he had been taken back to Russia to win fame and position for his work in helping to create the Russian navy. John and Sarah Cayley's second son, Cornelius, returned to England to settle at Sowerby, near Thirsk, and in 1784 married Sarah Ward of London : to them was born in 1789 Ann Elizabeth, who became the wife of James Favell. Mention must also be made of Cornelius's third sister, Sally, who married another St. Petersburg merchant, Edward Moberly. As a result the Headlams were therefore related by marriage to George Moberly and his son-in-law, George Ridding, successive Headmasters of Winchester, and more distantly to Dean Church, who married George Moberly's step-sister.

Arthur and Agnes Headlam had five children : Arthur Cayley, born on August 2, 1862, James Wycliffe in 1863, Rose Gladys in 1864, Kenneth Francis in 1867 and Lionel William in 1870. They doubtless found their mother much more attractive than their father, for she was a jolly cheerful person who had inherited the gay charm of her great-grandmother. Their father was kind but reserved and to small children rather formidable : one of his nieces wrote later, 'We always felt we must be on our best behaviour when in his company.' He was a slight, distinguished looking man with side-whiskers and a Bentley nose; his gaunt appearance later earned for him in Durham the nickname 'Tin Ribs.' In his later years he mellowed a great deal and was remembered as a really handsome, courtly old gentleman. He was careless of dress, and had a habit—inherited by his eldest son—of standing with his back to the fire and staying there until his trousers were ruined with singe marks. In his work he was painstaking and conscientious [6]; and he expected a like standard from other people. Life at the Hall, both for family and for students, was governed by a rigorous discipline : in winter sufficient fire was provided to maintain just the necessary amount of warmth, but no more; food was plain and adequate, but there was no waste; there was plenty of hard work and little relaxation. There was, in fact, a great contrast between life at the Hall and life at the Grange, where his brother Morley brought up a large family of twelve children under a much more lighthearted and carefree régime.

[6] This was exemplified by his edition of the Parish Registers of S. Oswald's, Durham, which cover 331 closely printed folio pages.

Some idea of Arthur's interests as a boy is given in an old diary for 1873, which was found among his papers. It shows that from the earliest days he had his father's great passion for gardening and the country-side, while his favourite indoor hobby was the collecting of coins. These interests were shared by his sister and his brothers, and for some years they ran a museum. Its constitution was interesting : James was president and head of the departments of ornithology and philately; but Arthur was the effective leader as secretary, treasurer, and head of the departments of botany, conchology, minerology, numismatics and entymology; seemingly as an act of grace Rose was permitted to be clerk to the president and head of the department of miscellaneous objects, while Lionel as the junior was merely an honorary member. It is not surprising that as a senior at Winchester Arthur came to be called the 'General.' Yet although he was very much the master of Rose and Lionel, with James things were different : James was cast in a finer mould—less rugged and of greater charm than his elder brother. This was something which Arthur realized, even as a boy regarding him with something akin to respect and admiration as well as affection. Most of his holidays were spent at Keswick or at Cresswell in Northumberland, where he found ample opportunity to roam the country-side. Keswick was, of course, the home of his mother's three sisters, the Misses Favell, the eldest of whom had married the Revd. John Leefe, Vicar of Cresswell. Between him and these three aunts there was a great bond of affection—a bond which became all the stronger after his mother's death in 1871. The family had all suffered one loss in the previous year, when Kenneth Francis had died at the early age of three—a loss partly mitigated by the birth of Lionel William : but the untimely death of their mother—she was only just over forty—was a tremendous shock to the young children. They were all still under the age of ten, and she was obviously the dominating influence in their lives—so understanding and approachable and willing to share their interests. It was a relief that their father's talented and devout young sister, Aunt 'Mar,' was able to come and look after them : she was a great favourite and no one could have filled the gap more wonderfully.

In 1874 Mr. Headlam decided it was time to begin the serious business of schooling. Hitherto the elder boys had attended the village school, for Mr. Headlam firmly believed in the solid grounding which such a school could give : but now Arthur and James together with their cousin, John, from the Grange, were sent off to Reading School under the care of an old friend, the Revd. Dr. Thomas Stokoe.[7] The

[7] Dr. Stokoe had previously been Headmaster of Richmond Grammar School, Yorkshire, not many miles from Whorlton. He was a brilliant classical scholar, later becoming General Editor of the Revised Version of the Bible with marginal references 1898.

move was a sound one, and for the next two years Arthur proved himself a hard worker and a great reader; he was nearly always at the top of his form. Dr. Stokoe, in fact, complained of only one fault—he was hopelessly untidy. His passion for work and a lack of enthusiasm for games unfortunately but inevitably contributed nothing to his popularity with other boys : he once confessed to his father that he hated Sundays, when there was nothing to do, because 'the fellows do nothing but bully me all day.' During the holidays, however, he found happiness in his old haunts at Whorlton, Keswick and Cresswell, while every summer his father took him and James to the Continent. In 1876 they went to Lucerne and there—to the boys' great excitement— Mr. Headlam became engaged to Miss Ann Louisa Woodall, daughter of John Woodall of S. Nicholas House, Scarborough.

The Woodalls were an old and influential Scarborough family. John Woodall, of the banking firm of Woodall, Tindall, Cooke and Co., was a friend of Mr. Headlam and had sent his youngest son, Edward, to the coaching establishment at Whorlton. Louisa, his second daughter, was a devout Tractarian and an active Church and social worker, who later played a leading part in founding the Girls' Friendly Society. The wedding took place three months later, on November 8, 1876. Its effect on the children was unpredictable, particularly in view of Aunt Mar's popularity : but any doubts which may have existed were soon dispelled. The tall young lady had a sense of humour and she quickly found her way into their hearts. The question was settled beyond doubt when they discovered that she shared their passion for gardening.

1867 was a year of changes. Not only did Mr. Headlam remarry but he also left Whorlton for Durham. On January 22 the saintly Dr. J. B. Dykes, who had made S. Oswald's, Durham, one of the leading Tractarian churches in the north of England, died—worn out by his conflicts with Bishop Baring. The living was in the gift of the Dean and Chapter, but they were faced with the problem that the Bishop would not license any nominee whom he considered unsuitable. Mr. Headlam was suggested, and despite his Tractarian views he was accepted by the Bishop in virtue of his long and faithful service in the diocese. It says a great deal for his tact and sound judgment that he succeeded in restoring and maintaining peaceful relations with the Bishop and at the same time preserving all that Dr. Dykes had introduced—candles, surpliced choir, vestments and daily services. Arthur looked forward to the prospect of close contact with the Castle and the Cathedral, and some of the people he met there were destined to play an important part in his life, notably William Sanday and Archibald Robertson : but he was sorry to leave his beloved Teesdale.

Then again, 1876 saw his own move from Reading to Winchester. His father's proposal that he should try for an entrance scholarship at Winchester took him by surprise, for he rather fancied his chances of winning a scholarship at Reading and had already asked his father's permission to enter. The Winchester examination, however, put him in a 'fearful funk'; he felt sure he would fail—'I will, I expect, be kicked out the second day, or as soon as they can.' But to his great surprise he was not kicked out : instead he just scraped through, being eleventh of the thirteen scholars elected.

II

At this time Winchester was in the midst of a vast transformation under Dr. Ridding. Large extensions were being made to the buildings, the teaching staff had been increased, and proper courses in science had been introduced. A calmer and happier atmosphere pervaded the school too, caused partly by the abolition of excessive punishment meted out by the prefects,[8] and partly by the advent as Second Master of the Revd. George Richardson, the genial North-country mathematician, who with his wife earned universal respect and affection. Headlam found himself in brilliant company : among those boys more or less of his own age several were of unusual intellectual ability and later made a name for themselves. Of these D. S. Margoliouth, E. T. Cook, C. W. C. Oman, F. J. Haverfield, C. H. Turner, G. E. M. Skues and G. L. Morant were a little senior to him, while F. G. Kenyon, D. G. Hogarth, A. H. Cruickshank, F. L. Norris, H. W. Orange and H. A. L. Fisher were contemporaries.[9]

His early days were far from happy. As at Reading he was the victim of pestering and bullying, again partly no doubt due to his

[8] C. W. C. Oman, *Memorials of Victorian Oxford*, 1942, pp. 35–8.
[9] *D. S. Margoliouth*. Famous Arabic scholar ; Director and later President of the Royal Asiatic Society ; *E. T. Cook*. Journalist and author ; Editor successively of the *Pall Mall Gazette*, *Westminster Gazette*, and *Daily News* ; *C. W. C. Oman*. Chichele Professor of Modern History, Oxford ; M.P. Oxford University ; *F. J. Haverfield*. Archaeologist ; Camden Professor of Ancient History, Oxford ; *C. H. Turner*, Famous lay theologian ; Dean Ireland's Professor of Exegesis, Oxford ; *G. E. M. Skues*. Famous naturalist and fisherman ; *G. L. Morant*. Permanent Secretary to the Board of Education ; later Chairman of the Insurance Commission 1912 ; *F. G. Kenyon*, Director of the British Museum ; *D. G. Hogarth*. Explorer and archaeologist ; Director of the British School, Athens ; and Director of the Arab Bureau in Cairo during War 1914–18 ; *A. H. Cruickshank*. Professor of Greek and Canon Residentiary of Durham ; *F. L. Norris*. Missionary ; Bishop of North China ; *H. W. Orange*. Director General of Education in India ; *H. A. L. Fisher*. M.P. and historian ; Minister of Education 1916 ; British delegate to League of Nations 1920–2 ; Warden of New College, Oxford, 1925–40.

passion for work and his lack of interest in games; but mainly due to his temper, which made him fair bait for his tormentors. He was quite aware of this weakness, however, and he tried hard and not altogether unsuccessfully to control it. He wrote to his father in October 1877, 'My temper (which I feel is my weakest part) does not get tried so much by being bullied as it used, but sometimes I get angry about small things.' About the ordinary run of school life he did not complain : fagging was a necessity which he endured without comment, and, surprisingly enough, he quite enjoyed school food [10]; his pocket-money rarely went on tuck. He was, in fact, no spendthrift but careful to a point of meanness, keeping a detailed account of his finances down to the last halfpenny.

From the outset one bright spot in his school life was the Natural History Society, known as 'The Bug and Snail,' which had been founded by Dr. Ridding and owed much to his leadership. Here Headlam was quite in his element, and it was one of the few things on which he was willing to spend money.[11] Later two other societies also claimed his interest—the Shakespeare Society, in which he always read the female parts because of his high-pitched voice; and the Debating Society, which encouraged him to read widely and which he felt would help him 'to overcome the great difficulty to express myself as I wish.' As a senior, life became much more pleasant : his indifference towards games disappeared and he became a vigorous if not brilliant member of the College Fifteen ; his friendships developed ; and he was made a prefect. Indeed, so formidable and downright did he become that he earned the nickname of 'The General.' It was a joy, too, to sit at the feet of two men whom he admired intensely— Dr. Ridding himself and the Revd. W. A. Fearon, who more than any one else brought out his undoubted historical ability.

The religious life at Winchester meant a great deal to him. He followed sermons in chapel closely—his letters home often recounted them in detail—and some were a source of strength and comfort in time of trouble. He once wrote to his father, 'I have been brightened up very much to-night by a sermon of the Doctor's on Martha and Mary—being cumbered with much serving, in which he said nervousness rose through weakness and through caring too much about such things, which we could get over by putting before us as our aim, not slight successes here and afterwards, but our path of duty to do what

[10] Professor Oman considered it inadequate, bad and repulsive—an abominable diet, though he admitted that it improved later. Ibid., pp. 31-2, 39. Headlam's digestion was always hardy.

[11] He collected both butterflies and flowers, of which Dr. Ridding once wrote in his Report, 'A capital collection—except in neatness.' Every year he used to send his stepmother boxes of wild Spring flowers.

we have here and now, and to prepare ourselves for our future life.'
He was confirmed in December 1877. 'I am trying to think about my
Confirmation, but somehow can sometimes not understand it and at
other times I do not somehow seem fit for it. I do not think enough
about Heaven and I find it hard to imagine. . . . It is chiefly in small
things that I feel the greatest difficulty, as since I have been well
looked after and brought up at home, I never, I am thankful to say,
seem so tempted to do or say a thing as some do. I do not say this to
please myself. I have more given me, and therefore I must do more.
I think that many who do great faults are not so much to blame as I
am when I do a smaller thing, as many of them have not been
taught to think about it as I have.' Of the Confirmation service itself
he wrote, 'I do not think I can write to you as perhaps I ought, for I
never can properly express my feelings. I do not know how I feel
exactly; ever since yesterday it has seemed like a happy dream.'

It is obvious from all this that he was inclined to be introspective,
constantly worrying about himself and his work. He was not delicate
—far from it; but he simply could not stand the strain of really concentrated hard work for long. He became harassed and almost incapable of coherent thought; eyestrain and headaches developed; and
then he had to be sent off to bed. Dr. Ridding wrote to his father, 'He
soon gets distrait with over much exertion and then he blunders.' Then
again, he took some subjects in his stride—Mathematics and Natural
Science (the only subject in which he ever won a prize), and later
History, English and Divinity; but Latin and Greek were a nightmare
to him. Every report contained the same criticism—he was weak in
Classics, interested in principles but not in the grammatical form of
words and sentences. 'His handwriting,' wrote Dr. Ridding, 'which at
times lapses into wild illegibility, is sadly symbolic of his chaotic
blunders and shapelessness in all classical products.' His chances of
winning a university scholarship were therefore viewed with anxiety.
In December 1880 he was given a trial run in the examination for the
Goddard Scholarship and Divinity Prize. The results were true to
form, although not without promise : out of twenty candidates he was
placed fifth; in History he romped home an easy first with a brilliant
paper; in Divinity he was second with another paper which was highly
commended; in Classics he was almost last. It was thought best for
him to try for one of the six scholarships offered to Winchester by
New College rather than risk his chances in trying for an open
scholarship : he had a fair chance of success, if only. . . . He was placed
under strict orders not to overtax himself, and work not immediately
necessary for the examination had to be set aside. When the time
came, he rose to the occasion; his Classics had improved sufficiently

to be tolerable, while his other work was brilliant. Once again he scraped through, being placed fifth among the six scholars elected.

III

In 1881 New College, Oxford, had almost come to the end of a period of transition. One result of the University Commission of 1854–58 had been a revision of the College Statutes, and under the new order the Wykehamist monopoly was gradually becoming weaker. The number of fellowships had been reduced from seventy to thirty, of which only fifteen were open to Winchester men, while the obligation to take Holy Orders had been removed. Scholarships were also thrown open to general competition in the event of suitable candidates from Winchester not being available. Furthermore, the College itself had decided in 1861 to admit only commoners who were considered capable of reading for an honours degree. All these changes had now made themselves felt. The old generation of clerical Wykehamist fellows had all disappeared with the exception of the Warden, Dr. James Sewell, who, although disliking the changes, nevertheless conscientiously adhered to the new order. The number of undergraduates, too, had increased nearly tenfold, so that the College had grown from one of the smallest to the second largest in the University. Its contribution to the life of Oxford both socially and academically was now one of which it no longer need be ashamed. At the same time it had developed an outlook which was Liberal in politics and modernist in the sense that it opposed the old religious and Wykehamist traditions: it was an outlook to which Headlam was never reconciled and while he cannot be said to have been unhappy there, he never had that affection for the College which he had for Winchester and All Souls.

His introduction to university life was inauspicious. On the journey down from Durham he managed to catch the wrong trains and did not reach Oxford until a very late hour; he lost all his luggage: and then on his arrival he accidentally put all his money in the fire. He quickly settled down, however, to his new way of life. It was a great help to be surrounded by so many friends and acquaintances: apart from his five fellow scholars from Winchester—Cruickshank, Benn, Whitcombe, Fort and Vidal, there were other friends in the senior years—Margoliouth, Turner, Oman, Hardy and Cooper, while another new-comer from Eton—J. S. G. Pemberton—was a fellow-countryman from Durham. Then among the Fellows there was a great friend of his Keswick aunts, that delightful personality Dr. Archibald Spooner, to whom Headlam became firmly attached. Headlam's arrival was said to be responsible for one of Dr. Spooner's so-called 'occasional infelicities in verbal diction.' During the previous year the stair on which he had his rooms had been extremely noisy. Fortunately the rowdy element had departed, being replaced by more peaceful new-comers, among whom were Headlam and another man named Bell. The change was most gratifying and Dr. Spooner was credited with the remark that he had lived in peace since Hell and Bedlam had arrived. There were really only two things in these early days of which Headlam seems to have been critical; one was the high cost of living, the other the large number of ugly and badly dressed women who lived in Oxford.

At the very outset he was determined to make the most of university life. He wrote to his father, 'I am quite willing to admit the importance of getting a First; but if I could only get it by giving up other mental activity in the way of general reading or in the way of societies I should certainly not consider it worth the sacrifice, for in these must lie a great deal of the good I can get here.' The Shakespeare Reading Club and the Union were the first to claim his interest, but he found the latter rather disappointing—'It is astonishing how very seldom you hear a speech which in any way whatsoever attempts to convert; they only exasperate.' Later he was elected to the Phasmatological Society and to the New College Discussion and Essay Societies, and these three eventually absorbed most of his spare time and energy. He was introduced to the first by Hardy and Oman and here he met F. E. Brightman, who became an intimate and lifelong friend. The purpose of the society was to collect stories of supernatural experiences and to test and classify them after careful enquiry into groups—coincidences, hallucinations, natural causes, unexplained, and so on: it was an activity which provided valuable exercise for the critical faculties. The Discussion Society was rather a large and informal body which provided members of the College with opportunities for airing their views on current topics : the notes of two speeches which Headlam delivered still exist. They are most revealing. The first on Home Rule showed him to be a staunch Tory : retrenchment, reform, liberty, fraternity, equality and progress were all 'meaningless political catchwords which obscure the judgment, unsettle the mind, pervert the reasoning, hide the interests of the people, and are only worthy of being thrown upon the dunghill.' The second on the Rights of Women deplored any attempts by women to claim equality with men or to encroach upon male preserves : they were quite unsuitable for public and political life and it was their function in life to be men's helpmates and not their rivals.

The Essay Society was a smaller and rather exclusive body which was very much the centre of the College's intellectual life, and in which Margoliouth was the dominating figure. Members took turns to read essays, which were designed to lead to criticism and discussion. Here Headlam's activities led to a paternal rebuke. In January 1883 he elected to read an essay on the Oxford Movement : the subject gripped him, and so deeply did he become immersed in its study that his father was obliged to remind him rather sharply that he was dissipating his energies on an enterprise which, although not devoid of value and interest, was nevertheless not directly concerned with his main purpose in being at Oxford ; Moderations were in the offing, and the family had high hopes of his securing a First. They were hopes which Headlam did not share. He admitted frankly that he found much of his work unattractive—a continuation of things he had disliked at Winchester ; and he did not rank his own abilities as first-class. 'I have not, as so many people here, either composition or power of scholarship to fall back on ; experience has taught me that though perhaps not destitute of mental power, I am certainly not a born genius who can get on without work.' It would seem, too, that he did not take too kindly to the transition from school to university methods of teaching, for he complained bitterly of the lack of help with his studies. 'At school one has a good deal of direction—up here we have none. A great deal of my work during the last two years has been misdirected and useless either through being too vague or too minute.' [12] Nevertheless, his father's remarks were taken to heart. He restricted his outside activities ; he made no more prepared speeches at the Discussion and Essay Societies ; and he confined his reading to what was essential for the examinations. But his doubts were justified : his old weaknesses let him down and he was only awarded a Second. Although not surprised he was undoubtedly disappointed. He wrote to his father in very abject vein, 'I have been calculating how much you will have spent on my useless person in the last year. It is, I suppose, about the keep of five families and it is £100 more than the stipend of a curate. It makes me have cost you £194 during a time when your income has been reduced and when you have had to spend a good deal in other ways.[13] I must say I feel rather ashamed of myself and must only make up my mind to live much more economically next year. What makes me all the more uncomfortable is the doubt whether I am really worth such a good education in spite of all the trouble taken about me and which I have taken about myself. I have not been altogether successful.' His father brushed aside his misgivings, how-

[12] C. W. C. Oman made the same criticism about New College ; cf. *Memories of Victorian Oxford*, pp. 77–8, 92.
[13] His scholarship was worth £80 a year.

ever, reminded him that he and his brother James had cost him much less than they might have done in virtue of their scholarships,[14] assured him that they both deserved all the help they required, and sent him off to the Continent to spent the long vacation in Dresden.

In the following term he settled down to prepare for Greats much encouraged by the fact that the work was far more congenial, no longer involving what was 'alien to his mind.' His outside activities were drastically curtailed, and the Discussion Society was given up altogether. Most of his restricted leisure was given to Phas (the Phasmatological Society), of which he had just been elected Chairman. He also began to consider the future. It is difficult to say when he first thought of ordination : certainly his Tractarian interests indicated that religion had a leading place in his thoughts, and he was most assiduous in his attendance at College Chapel—a requirement which was quite voluntary. He also became closely attached to two men whose influence must have counted for a great deal. The first was William Sanday, who had left Durham in 1882 to become Dean Ireland's Professor of Exegesis, and who had promised his father to keep an eye on him. The second was Charles Gore, who had become a live force among young men at Oxford first as Vice-Principal of Cuddesdon Theological College and later as Principal of Pusey House. Certainly by November 1884 he had made up his mind to be ordained, and by the quickest and cheapest means. But when he suggested joining Bishop Lightfoot's Brotherhood at Auckland Castle in the autumn of 1885, his father demurred. It would be far better to stay at Oxford, read Theology and then go to Cuddesdon. 'I fully appreciate your wish to be at work, but I would rather that you should qualify yourself in the best way and have every previous advantage. As to your financial condition, let me know what you want, and when, and you shall have it.'

Meanwhile work for Greats continued, not without periods of strain and the inevitable spell in bed. In the examination, however, the papers were to his liking and his work was brilliant. This time he got his First—an easy First, well above the line. He was part of a Wykehamist intellectual triumph, for of the twenty-eight Firsts awarded five came from Winchester and seven from New College, which was a record.[15] Dr. Ridding, now Bishop of Southwell, wrote to congratulate him : 'I always hoped and expected that you would rise to great heights, and now I hope you are prepared to use your victory—that

---

[14] His brother James had won a scholarship to Eton from Reading School in 1877, and another to King's College, Cambridge, in 1882.

[15] It is also interesting to note that seven of the twenty-eight Firsts in Greats had been Seconds in Mods.

A. C. Headlam at Winchester

Family group *c.* 1883 at Durham
Back row: James Headlam, Mrs.
Headlam. A.C.H.
Front row: Lionel Headlam.
Miss E. Favel, Rev. A. W.
Headlam (father), Miss M.
Headlam (Aunt May)
In front: Rose Headlam

PLATE III

Principal of King's College,
London

Headlam being drilled by his
gardener at Whorlton in the
1914–18 war

is the mark of the real General.' How then was he to use it? It undoubtedly gave him confidence, and he was inspired to try for a fellowship. Admittedly his chances at New College were not bright for Cruickshank was also competing, and in Greats all the examiners had considered him to have been easily at the head of the list. Nevertheless he was determined to try. As was generally expected, Cruickshank was elected, with Headlam a close second. Not to be beaten, he immediately entered for the fellowships at All Souls, where two were offered—one in History and one in Law. His entry was something of a surprise and his chances of gaining so coveted a prize were regarded as meagre : but this time the critics were confounded. He completely outstripped his rivals to win the fellowship in History, while J. S. G. Pemberton was elected to the fellowship in Law—a double triumph both for New College and for Durham. Dr. Fearon wrote from Winchester, 'It was delightful to see the old love for History bearing its fruits and receiving due recognition. I have always said that Oman and yourself were two of the best historians I ever had under me ; and it is doubly gratifying therefore that the University should recognize the fact.' His family were overjoyed and his step-mother sent him a touching little note : 'I cannot help recalling to your mind a letter written in your boyish days to your father on this day nine years ago —our wedding day—in which you promised "to try to be good and affectionate and to do your best to please us both." You have indeed, my dear Arthur, kept that promise in the strength of Him who has guided and guarded you.' In the following year his younger brother, James, followed his example by winning a First and a fellowship at King's College, Cambridge. They had thus kept in step in a remarkable way : both had won scholarships to famous public schools, both had won university scholarships, both obtained Firsts, and both won fellowships. The Headlam reputation for intellectual brilliance was being safely upheld.

CHAPTER TWO

All Souls' College

I

At All Souls Headlam entered into a brilliant and unique society in which both scholars and men of affairs were united by the common bond of loyalty to and affection for Chichele's foundation. The usual midweek community of permanent residents was small—about half a dozen; but at weekends they were joined by a gathering of scholars, barristers, politicians, civil servants and business men in which seniors and juniors mingled in a most friendly and informal way. Headlam's first impression was, 'They are the best set of fellows in Oxford.' The dominant influence was the Warden, Sir William Anson. He was unmarried; and unlike other heads of houses who had family ties and interests, he regarded the College as his home and its residents as his family : his ready help, kindly advice and sound judgment were always available to them. Headlam came to regard him with real affection, and he was one of the few people to whom he was ready to unburden his soul. Of the other fellows who became his close friends there were H. O. Wakeman, C. R. L. Fletcher, A. V. Dicey, H. Reichel, and W. P. Ker [1]; Oman and Curzon had been elected two years previously and Hensley Henson the previous year. These, together with others outside the College—Gore, Turner, Brightman, Spooner and Sanday —helped to bring out the very best in him. His friendship with Henson was perhaps the most remarkable, for no two men were more dissimilar. Henson wrote in later life : 'Even before I came into personal contact with him when he was elected in 1885 to the All Souls' Fellowship, a year after my own election, I had, in a queer sort of way, met him, for he was rather conspicuous as an undergraduate, a big raw-boned North countryman, very fair but not handsome to look at and very angular. When we did meet, I felt that I knew him already.' [2]

---

[1] All these men distinguished themselves in their different spheres. Wakeman and Fletcher were noted historians; Dicey a noted jurist; Ker a man of letters who was elected Professor of Poetry at Oxford in 1920; and Reichel an educationist who became Vice-Chancellor of the University of Wales.

[2] *Letters of Herbert Hensley Henson,* edited by E. F. Braley, 1950, pp. 193-4.

'No two men could be more unlike in aspect, intellectual habit and ecclesiastical outlook, yet we drew together and have never gone apart. I used to describe him as a Brazil nut, concealing a generous character under a hard shell. He often tried me much, and I cannot doubt that I tried him more. But we were linked together in a friendship which was real and precious to us both.' [3] When Headlam was ordained in 1886, Henson wrote to him, 'I fear that in the future you and I will be rarely associated in any friendly way in our public conduct : I would venture—in the name of a very deep respect and affection for you—to hope that through the strife of parsons, the friendship of men may stand.' It was a hope that was fully realized : and the same was true of many other people too. In controversy Headlam spared no man in his defence of what he considered to be right, but he bore no malice and his friendship never suffered.

His first consideration was how to use the opportunities provided by his fellowship. 'I get £200 a year, rooms, and I believe an allowance towards dinner, for seven years. So that it practically means a competence and every opportunity just at that time which is most important.' An entry in one of his note-books from this period is revealing :

'Firstly, I must find some duty or profession in life in which I can both do my duty in my generation, and earn my bread ; for a man who cannot earn his bread has no right to live. To teach is what seems most open to me, and I must therefore endeavour to gain both a position in which I am to teach and the knowledge and ability to do so.

'Secondly I must strive in every way to form my character and my intellect so that I may be able to use my powers to the uttermost. I must especially learn how to write and to speak, both in public and in private, and I must gain the habits of self-control and industry.

'Particularly it is my duty as one whose intellect has been trained at great expense and trouble and as one who has a certain amount of the necessary leisure to engage in some way in the search of what is true.

'These are my duties, and must be my view.'

On Sanday's advice he decided to read Theology privately rather than for the Schools, and he drew up a scheme of work to include general theological reading and a detailed study of Eusebius and early Church History. In this he was influenced by Bishop Lightfoot's edition of Ignatius and Polycarp which had appeared in the previous year : its scholarly accuracy, scientific approach and sober judgment became the

[3] H. Henson, *Retrospect of an Unimportant Life*, 1942, vol. I, p. 22.

model on which he attempted to base all his own work, and for the rest of his life he remained a great admirer of Lightfoot. He wrote in 1932, 'For myself, as for Church History, the publication of Lightfoot's "Ignatius" represented a quite definite epoch. It was the definite assertion of the scientific method of study over the speculative for early Church history. . . . The real fact is that the scientific criticism which began with Lightfoot has attained almost as great an amount of certainty as is possible about the historical facts of early Christianity.'[4]

From the beginning he drove himself hard. His diary constantly noted the fact that his work was behind schedule and that he must work even harder; and it is not surprising that before long he had a recurrence of the old head troubles. But by the end of his first year he had begun to learn the lesson which he imparted so often to others in later life—the importance of discovering, not how much one can do, but how much one can neglect, in order to concentrate on what is really worth while. 'I must attempt somewhat to limit the number of things I devote some time to. After all no one can do everything.'

The question of ordination arose in 1887. R. L. Ottley, one of the Librarians at Pusey House, had left to become Vice-Principal of Cuddesdon; and Brightman, with Gore's permission, suggested to Headlam that he might like to take his place and be ordained to a librarianship. He declined the offer, however. Indeed, it is doubtful whether he would have been really happy in the atmosphere of Pusey House. He was finally ordained to his fellowship by the Bishop of Oxford at Michaelmas 1888. Of his sense of vocation there was no doubt : Henson wrote, 'The clerical office will be no burden to you : your vocation is clear in the minds of your friends.' Yet to many people his approach to religion seemed rather too intellectual and not sufficiently devotional. Brightman warned him, 'Forgive me for saying this. It is our danger now to give up being religious and devout, as the Tractarians were; the new generation of intellectual High Church people are not of the same tone as they used to be : and I ought to tell you that I said something like this to the Bishop when I wrote to him about you—that your devotional side wanted developing. But you do sometimes seem to me too "intellectual"—and affection ought to clear one's vision. Anyhow, we may try to help one another both ways, mayn't we? And work together too, to try even in details and down to the bottom "for their sakes to sanctify ourselves." You know how much and how really I wish for you all you need.' Headlam had, in fact, that element of reserve so evident in the earlier generations of his family : he was afraid of anything that smacked of sentimentality,

---

[4] Bishop Lightfoot's place as a historian, in *Lightfoot of Durham*, edited by G. R. Eden and F. C. Macdonald, Cambridge, 1932, pp. 136–40.

and he seemed incapable of giving any outward indication of what was in his heart. This had shown itself in another way only a short time before. He had fallen in love with a young lady in Oxford and had proposed to her—an action which took her completely by surprise, for he had not given her the slightest indication of what was in his heart and mind. He suit was rejected and he was extremely upset. Few people except his parents knew anything about it; but for the time being he found Oxford unbearable. His brother James was at the time studying in Berlin, so Headlam fled to him to seek solace and comfort in his calm and sympathetic ways : to the outside world he had gone abroad to study manuscripts.

His life was now a very busy one. He had taken up both golf and tennis, both of which he played with more energy than skill [5]; he was still a leading member of Phas; he frequently lectured at Oxford House in the east end of London—more so after Henson went there in 1887; he had become a member of Sanday's seminar on the Western Text; he had become a regular contributor to the *Church Quarterly Review*; and he had his own reading. To all this was added a great deal of clerical work. In Oxford he was found most frequently—and perhaps rather surprisingly—with F. J. Chavasse in the Evangelical stronghold of S. Peter-le-Bailey, where he preached his first sermon, while after Henson went to Barking in 1888 he often went there to help him. Then he became theological tutor at Oriel College in 1888 and at Queen's College in the following year. Finally he was also appointed Domestic Bursar of All Souls—an office which gave scope to his administrative abilities, and one which he undertook in a competent, vigorous and autocratic manner. Being himself a good trencherman, the College table was his especial pride and joy. A fellow once infuriated him by unwittingly but unwisely producing the old joke that the menu at lunch was more beautiful to the imagination than realizable to the palate : honour was not satisfied until a full apology had been given.

His membership of Sanday's seminar fostered his interest in Textual Criticism and Coptic. At this time Sanday was still engaged in that early stage of his life's work which he called lower criticism, or the study of texts. It was both a necessary and a fruitful field of study, and in his Inaugural Lecture as Dean Ireland's Professor of Exegesis in 1883 he had issued a plea on its behalf : 'The subject of all others in which youthful workers have a truly golden opportunity is Text. . . . I lay much stress on this particular subject, not because it is first in dignity, but because it is first in necessity, as a number of other subjects are being kept waiting for it, and also because it is a good subject

[5] His golf handicap was never lower than eighteen.

on which to make a beginning.' He himself concentrated his energies
on the recovery of the Western Text, and in this connection had
formed his seminar, which included such brilliant young men as
Margoliouth, Turner, Winfrid Burrows, R. H. Charles, C. Harris and
A. S. Peake. One important product of their labours was the *Appendices to the Oxford Greek Testament*, which appeared in 1889, containing a list of the texts and their whereabouts and a list of variant
readings. Headlam and Margoliouth produced what Sanday considered to be the most valuable part of the work—the Armenian and
Ethiopic readings, for which they were jointly responsible, and the
Memphitic readings, which were entirely Headlam's own work. These
few pages provided material which had hitherto been completely in-
accessible to the ordinary scholar.

Headlam's interest in Coptic had begun in 1886. It was a field of
study which had not attracted many men and a great deal of work
was open to be done. He became proficient in a remarkably short
space of time, and eminent Coptic scholars such as W. E. Crum,
G. W. Horner, and M. Amélineau came to regard his abilities with
respect. But his output of published work was small. Apart from his
work on the Appendices, he wrote two articles on the recently discovered Akhmim fragments of the Gospel and Apocalypse of S. Peter,
translated and emended an article by M. Amélineau on an unpub-
lished Coptic manuscript dealing with the Council of Ephesus,[6] and
added a summary of recent developments to Lightfoot's study of the
Coptic versions in the fourth edition of Scrivener's *Plain Introduction
to the Criticism of the New Testament*. He gave up serious work on
Coptic after leaving All Souls. It was perhaps a pity, for he could have
made his reputation in this field alone : but some things must be neglected. 'After all no one can do everything.'

Soon after going to All Souls Headlam began his connection with
The Church Quarterly Review. The editor at that time was C. Knight
Watson, grandson of the famous Latitudinarian Bishop Watson of
Llandaff, and himself a Tractarian layman of the old-fashioned
school. He was a friend of Headlam's father and his aunt, Miss
Augusta Woodall, while both his son and his nephew had been contemporaries of Headlam at Winchester. In 1886 he invited Headlam
to write, first employing him on short reviews. Here Headlam evinced
his ability to 'gut' books with remarkable speed : he had a quick,
incisive—even ruthless—mind, which sought instinctively for a prin-

---

[6] 'Recently Discovered Early Christian Documents, the Gospel and Apoca-
lypse of Peter.' *The Guardian*, December 1892, pp. 1883–4, 1929. 'The Akhmim
Fragments.' *The Classical Review*, vol. 7, pp. 458–63. 'The Council of
Ephesus.' *C.Q.R.*, vol. 33, pp. 91–115.

ciple and ignored details; he could often see the point while others were still floundering among the prolegomena. Unfortunately his mode of expression tended to give an impression of contemptuous intolerance which was apt to arouse resentment. In his first full-length article on Shelley in October 1887, for example, some of his strictures on the Shelley Society were quite violent : 'We think that the Shelley Society has drained the cup of silliness to the dregs. . . . With the mind of the most ill-educated stump-orator or a well-educated parrot, they imagine they are at the summit of the mental pyramid.' [7] He was, however, in these early days wise enough to accept frank and friendly criticism from the editor and his friends.[8] He soon moderated the violence of his tone and acquired the facility to express himself in clear, simple and forceful language, although never rising to the heights of what might be called masterly and distinguished prose. In 1888 and 1889 he wrote further articles—on Tudor's *Philosophy of Church Life,* Harnack's *History of Church Doctrine,* Mark Pattison, and Farrar's *Lives of the Fathers.* Then trouble came. It was almost inevitable; for Headlam and Watson were too much alike in temperament for them to agree indefinitely.[9] As an old-fashioned Tractarian Watson had the same feelings about Liberal Theology and Higher Criticism as Liddon felt about the views of Gore, and he began to express these feelings in his articles. Headlam, Turner and men of the younger school became increasingly conscious that the *Review* was becoming hopelessly retrograde in its attitude to people like Professor S. R. Driver, and matters came to a head after the publication of the controversial *Lux Mundi* under Gore's editorship. In May 1890 Headlam complained to Watson of his attitude towards the book, to which Watson replied (May 27) :

---

[7] *C.Q.R.*, vol. 25, p. 53.

[8] Three examples may be given.

(a) C. Knight Watson, 1886. 'Your articles bore traces of hurry and wanted touching up in sundry places in point of style. The English was in parts just a little too slipshod.'

(b) J. Spedding, 1887. 'Never try to be epigrammatic. You will be rough and crude where you mean to be pointed, and the result will be that you will *appear* self-asserting and dogmatic and will be set down as bumptious when nothing is farther from your intention. Enlarge your vocabulary as much as possible, and always write at first in language as simple and correct as you can.'

(c) F. E. Brightman, 1888. 'You know I haven't the persistence, and the power of acquisition, and the power of suppression that you have; but I want to criticize in one thing. I don't much like the beginning of your *Church Quarterly* Article. It "sarcs" too much, and I don't think we ought to encourage and contribute to that sort of thing.'

[9] Headlam had actually been warned by his father, 'It is a pity that he puts so little restraint on his tongue and his pen, as strangers don't understand him.'

'My dear Arthur,

'I am sorry we don't see eye to eye as regards *Lux Mundi*. That is a point on which we must agree to differ. I think however you will admit that *C.Q.R.* has said nothing that can be called acrimonious or denunciatory or unfair or wanting in consideration for the worth and character and piety of the writers. In spite of this difference, I hold and ever shall hold you very near to my heart. Let me be therefore now as ever,

Yours affectionately,

C. KNIGHT WATSON.'

At this juncture Headlam went to the Middle East for a year. During his absence Watson issued a pamphlet with the October number of the *Review* summarizing its work since its inception in 1875 and containing an unfortunate paragraph claiming credit for opposing the dangerous tendencies of *Lux Mundi*. On learning of this Headlam decided that it would be dishonest to continue writing for a journal which regarded views which he supported as being hostile to Christianity. He therefore notified Watson that he was severing his connections —a decision which no amount of pleading would induce him to alter.

Headlam's attitude towards *Lux Mundi* is shown in a letter which he wrote to his father refuting the suggestion that his journey abroad was a welcome relief from the disturbed state of the theological atmosphere of Oxford.

Athens, October 12, 1890.

'My dear Papa,

'You say that you feel glad that I should be removed from the disturbed state of the theological atmosphere. Now as my feelings were rather the other way, and as one reason which made me hesitate about going was a dislike to leave Oxford when an important controversy was going on in which I might do some good, or at any rate try to do so, I feel that I ought to explain my position to you.

'In the first place I do not think there is anything excited or unhealthy about the controversy. As long as religious life is healthy and real, there must be always controversies; for new questions arise to be settled. Nor do I think there would be a controversy on the whole conducted in a better spirit than the Oxford one. Not long before I came away Gore told me that after all one gained much more even from controversy when one learned every day to respect more and more the moral character of those from whom one differed : and when you see that it was Gore who was always with Liddon in his last illness, and that Gore and Paget were Liddon's literary executors, it brings out the character of the controversy.

'I often feel that you do not quite realize the altered condition of thought in which we live at Oxford—the new way of looking at things which science has introduced, still less literary and historical criticism. Now in secular matters one learns to ask always, Is this true? How do I know this is true? One learns to supply definite rules of evidence on subject matters in which it is possible to be unbiassed, and one learns above all things the faculty of judgment, which means not only to reject what is false, but to accept what is true.

'To explain my position is difficult. It was not so much that I had doubts or even difficulties, but I felt that I must ask myself the question, Is Christianity really true? I found soon that all the critical and historical training I had made me feel more sure of the historical character of all or most of the books of the New Testament and of the facts they narrated. I found that the different attacks made were often inconsistent and really less critical than the defence which was possible. All I have tried to do is to clear my judgment, as I had been taught, of preconceptions and to answer each question on its merits.

'I have satisfied myself that making every necessary concession to criticism the great miracle of the history of Israel remained, and the prophecy of the Messiah miraculously fulfilled in the coming of Jesus. Was it then true that our Lord had been mistaken about Israel's history and was not divine? That could not be, because all the evidence of history and criticism seemed to me to point to His divinity. The important factor to remember was the doctrine of the kenosis or divine self-humiliation of Christ. He laid aside His divine nature to come and live not only as a man but as a man of His own time and country. He used as a means of conveying truth the imperfect language, the imperfect philosophical, theological and scientific ideas of His day.

'If you read Holland's article on Liddon in the *Contemporary* (I think it is) you will see the position of younger men in Oxford well described, and my feelings in leaving Oxford for a year just at present were these. The new questions which had arisen caused to many undergraduates great difficulties. I have gone through the same difficulties as they feel and can thoroughly sympathize with them. I feel that I have worked out a solution which I believe to be honest and which is at any rate satisfactory to myself, and consequently I am sometimes able to help them.

'You must not imagine that we consider—any of us younger men— that our own views are infallible. All we feel bound to do is to explain them and defend them in controversy, in a spirit as befitting the subject as possible, in order that we may help to settle difficult questions. We hope to be quite willing to learn from those from whom we differ, and all we ask for is that older people may at any rate attempt to understand us, as for example the Dean of S. Paul's has done; and not to write in the dogmatic and inconsiderate way of so many of the writers in the *Guardian*. After all a former generation of High Churchmen ought not to forget how much they differed from their predecessors and how much they shocked the world, and yet looking back they must see how much after all they agreed with them in every great Christian truth.

Ever your affectionate son,

ARTHUR C. HEADLAM.'

Headlam had been able to express these views to a rather unusual audience in the previous August, when he had been invited to attend a conference of university men—mostly Scottish Presbyterians—at Bonskeid in Perthshire. The events leading up to this conference were interesting. In 1885 two famous Cambridge athletes, C. T. Studd the cricketer and Stanley Smith the oarsman, had conducted a series of meetings for students in Edinburgh before leaving for missionary work in China. They had created a great impression, and as a result Professor Henry Drummond had started his famous Sunday night meetings in the Oddfellows' Hall.[10] Among some of those who came to hear him week by week the conviction began to grow that the appeal of the Christian Gospel to students was hindered by the disunity and isolation of the various Christian bodies. This conviction finally crystallized in the decision to hold a conference between teachers and students of different denominations, at which the problem could be discussed. This was arranged by Drummond with the help of Dr. Hugh Barbour and Charles M. Douglas, founders of the Chalmers University Settlement in Edinburgh.

The conference was held in Dr. Barbour's home at Bonskeid, Pitlochry, in the summer vacation of 1889. Twenty-eight men from different universities and of different religious denominations attended, Scottish Presbyterians forming the largest element. The leaders were Professor Drummond, Dr. Whyte,[11] Dr. Barbour and his brother Robert, and Charles Douglas.[12] The precise details of the conference are not known, for no minutes or records of the papers and discussions

[10] G. A. Smith, *Life of Henry Drummond*, 1899, p. 297. Drummond was Professor of Natural Science at the Free Church College, Glasgow, and had been a leading figure in the Sankey and Moody Mission 1873–5.

[11] Minister of Free S. George's, Edinburgh; later Principal of New College, Edinburgh, 1909–18.

[12] Lecturer in Moral Philosophy, Edinburgh; M.P. and leading Scottish politician, 1899–1906.

were kept : there is a bare statement in Dr. Barbour's *Life of Dr. Whyte*—'At each session a paper was read on some question of theological restatement, or on the relation of the Churches to one another, or more especially on the problems of religious work in the Colleges.' [13] Headlam, however, left some notes on the two papers which he read, one on the Oxford Movement and another on the *Lux Mundi* situation : together they form something of a personal apologia. The Oxford Movement, as we have seen, had fascinated him since his undergraduate days and exercised a profound influence on his life. He wrote many years later, 'It is to the Oxford Movement, to its leaders and their works, that I owe (at any rate to a large extent) the beginnings of my theological beliefs. . . . I rarely find myself now believing exactly as they did—but yet I feel that the development of my mind has been truer to what they taught, and that I should not hold what I do so firmly and, as I venture, so healthily, if it were not for the beginnings, which I owe to my bringing up under the influence of the Tractarians.' [14] The Tractarian emphasis on the doctrine of the Church and the ideal of corporate Christianity, which became such an effective power in the cause of Christian unity was his theme, and it was one to which he returned time and time again. The second paper, which he called 'Religion and Intellectual Studies,' was largely a statement of the position he had set out in the letter to his father. Intellectual studies, he concluded, were of inestimable value in wrestling with the problems of disunity, for they disciplined the mind and produced a judicial temper. 'We must approach the subject with all the moral impulse of charity and with minds cultivated and disciplined to arrive at and discuss the truth on the truest grounds. If among all bodies alike there could be found a body of men united by common intellectual training, investigating questions by the same intellectual methods, and able by their mental power to grasp all subjects as a whole, they would work towards a common goal of Christian unity without indifference.'

The conference was so successful that it was decided to hold another on similar lines in the following year. Headlam was then abroad and unable to attend ; but it was equally fruitful. These two conferences, which never really received the notice they deserved, did a great deal for the cause of Christian unity. They brought added impetus to the work of the World's Student Christian Federation, and sowed some of the seed from which the British Student Christian Movement and the Mansfield House Settlement grew. [15] Certainly Headlam always

[13] G. F. Barbour, *The Life of Alexander Whyte*, 8th ed., 1925, pp. 257–8.
[14] *C.Q.R.*, vol. 116, pp. 167–8.
[15] Barbour, *Life of Whyte*, p. 257 ; Ruth Rouse, *World's Student Christian Federation*, 1948, p. 43.

regarded Bonskeid as of fundamental importance in the development
of his œcumenical interests : there he met a body of brilliant young
men discussing their religious differences—young men whose aspirations were fully awake, but whose intellectual sympathies were still
largely bounded by the limits of their own denominations. They were,
for the most part, tasting something new, and what they tasted they
found to be good.

II

In May 1890 Headlam left Oxford for a year to tour the Middle East
with Professor William Ramsay and D. G. Hogarth : on his return his
life at the University entered a new phase. Apart from his growing
interest in œcumenical work, he began to play an increasingly active
part in University politics—he was, in fact, considered to be one of
the 'coming men.' Dr. Ridding also appointed him an examining
chaplain, so it is not surprising to find that some of his former interests
were set aside. No more is heard of Phas, little is heard of Coptic, and
before long he retired from Sanday's seminar. Sanday regretted his
departure, but put no obstacles in his way : 'I have for some time felt
that I need not expect you to go on taking the trouble you have done
about the Seminar, and I am too grateful to you for what you have
done to think of putting the slightest obstacle in your way in that
respect. We cannot fill your place, but that is a secondary question.'
They had, of course, been friends for many years; their regard for
one another was high and they understood each other perfectly.
Sanday constantly turned to Headlam for help and advice : his
Bampton lectures on Inspiration in 1893, for example, were subjected
to Headlam's careful and searching criticism before being given. It is
also clear from his correspondence that Headlam made no decision
on matters of importance at this stage of his life without consulting
Sanday.

The monument to this great friendship was their joint *Commentary
on the Epistle to the Romans,* which appeared in 1895. Sanday had
been asked to undertake this work for the International Critical Commentary series in 1888 and had agreed to do so, prompted by the
conviction that as Dean Ireland's Professor of Exegesis he ought to
produce some exegetical work, even though his main interests were
then textual. He had secured permission from the editors of the series
to invite Headlam to collaborate; and this Headlam had gladly
agreed to do, for the work fitted in with his own studies in early
Church history. It was a rare compliment, for Headlam was still a

comparatively unknown young layman in his middle twenties. They divided the work fairly evenly between them; and, as they stated in their Preface, they went over each other's work with care and jointly accepted responsibility for the whole.[16] The scanty references to the *Commentary* among Headlam's papers give some idea of the way in which the work was done. Sanday undertook to write the notes and commentary on the first half of the Epistle and Headlam on the second half.[17] Headlam also wrote the introductory essay 'Rome in A.D. 58,' and took over some of Sanday's work when the latter was occupied with his Bampton lectures for 1893. When the book appeared in September 1895 it met with an enthusiastic reception both in England and in Germany. As may be expected, a strong point was its treatment of the text : it was typical of Sanday to write, 'Anything which throws new light on the history of the text will be found in the end to throw new light on the history of Christianity.'[18] Textual criticism was brought to bear in supporting the integrity of the Epistle and particularly of the last two chapters.[19] Their view that there was a recension in which the last two chapters were deleted and for which Marcion was responsible is now generally accepted. A noteworthy feature of the *Commentary* was its method of resolving the meanings of terms : these were decided, not by theological opinion but by a full consideration of their various uses and history. 'Faith' and 'righteousness' were notable examples : here a discrimination between the subtler varieties of their meanings was followed by a combination of them in a final synthesis of thought which was quite brilliant. Obviously with so many other commentaries on the Epistle already in existence, it was inevitable that the book contained much that was already well known. Nevertheless, its use of the latest discoveries and particularly the use of recent German works was excellent. Its appearance did much to establish Headlam's reputation as a scholar. *The Guardian* wrote, 'It is a volume which will bring credit to English scholarship, and while it is the crown of much good work in the past on the part of the elder editor, it gives promise of equally good work in the future from both.'[20] It was no surprise, therefore, when shortly afterwards Macmillan & Co. invited him to write a Commentary on the Acts of the Apostles as a companion volume to Lightfoot's Pauline commentaries.

16 W. Sanday and A. C. Headlam, *The Epistle to the Romans,* Edinburgh, 1895, p. viii.
17 Headlam was awarded the B.D. degree in 1895 for two of his Notes—the Punctuation of Romans 9 : 5 and the Argument of Chapters 9–11.
18 Ibid., p. lxxi.
19 Ibid., p. lxxxix.
20 *The Guardian,* November 6, 1895.

He accepted the invitation and actually started work, but lack of adequate leisure prevented him from ever finishing it.[21]

Headlam's regard for Sanday was further exemplified in 1895 when the Lady Margaret Chair of Divinity fell vacant. Sanday had confessed that it was his one serious object of ambition, and Headlam was determined to secure his election. Having secured Sanday's nomination as a candidate, he undertook an electioneering campaign with the utmost vigour. Under his direction a committee approached voters all over the country with ruthless persistence and efficiency : so telling was its effect that the other candidate, Dr. Wace, withdrew from the contest, leaving Sanday to be elected unopposed. It was an achievement to which Headlam often referred with both amusement and pride. He then almost immediately repeated the process to secure the election of Walter Lock, one of his friends in Sanday's seminar, to the Dean Ireland's chair which Sanday had just vacated. It was an interesting move, for many people felt that Headlam was almost certain to succeed Sanday himself : but he never appeared as a candidate, due doubtless to the fact that he was already feeling that it was time for him to seek pastures new.

By the beginning of 1896 he had made up his mind to leave All Souls and become—for a while, at least—a parish priest. The decision was not easily made, for his real interests were those of a scholar : he was impelled by a sense of duty rather than desire. The conflict is revealed in some notes which he made when he was offered the College living of Welwyn during the spring of that year.

REASONS FOR GOING TO WELWYN

'1. The very definite advantage of having parish experience. This advantage is twofold.

'(a) On the one hand there is the very real gain of being responsible for the spiritual well-being of people, of testing and applying in personal and pastoral work the principles and opinions which I have built up largely in the study, or on my own experience. There is the contact, and the necessary contact, with people of varying degrees of mental cultivation and religious interest, and the modifications and corrections which such contact must give to crude and perhaps unreal theories.

'(b) On the other side there is the gain and advantage of studying and becoming acquainted with the Church of England in the real circle of its work and administration.

'It is perfectly true that neither of these are absolutely neces-

[21] Much of this work appeared subsequently as articles in Hastings' *Dictionary of the Bible*.

sary, but no substitute may adequately replace the absolute sense of unreality which the personal responsibility of the parish priest must give.

'2. To these general reasons I must add a special one, which is connected with my own work and study. It seems to me that what is needed is the creation of a good sound school of what may be most clearly expressed as historical theology, for that I believe to represent the point of contact between the old Catholic school and the modern critical school. That is the idea in my mind in taking Welwyn, and forms a definite continuity between my work and my ideal at Oxford, and my work and my ideal in parish work.'

DISADVANTAGES IN WELWYN

'There would undoubtedly be one serious disadvantage in going to Welwyn. It would very seriously limit my hours of work—it might almost completely interrupt them. In any case I should only be able to get any time by a considerable exertion of will, and I might find that I had not the physical and mental strength to do more than what was required for my parochial work, and for keeping up such general reading as was necessary; and if I once fell behindhand, I might be unable ever to find myself again in a position to go on with the work I have definitely proposed to do.'

He consulted a number of friends, all of whom advised him to move. His father thought that it was absolutely right for him to go to Welwyn—it was an admirable place; he had known it in his younger days when curate of the neighbouring parish of Knebworth. Sir William Anson felt likewise, although he deplored his departure from All Souls—'I don't think any one in my recollection has done more to keep the College together, and that too in a time of poverty and depletion.' Sanday, too, considered the principle of leaving the University for a time in search of parochial experience to be a sound one, although he deplored the loss to Oxford and expressed a doubt whether a parish of the size and importance of Welwyn could be reconciled with his literary work. By June Headlam had made up his mind and accepted, only to be plunged immediately into further uncertainty. Mr. Gladstone, on the recommendation of Father Puller of Cowley, invited him to become the first Warden of the new Library and Hostel of S. Deiniol at Hawarden. It was a most attractive offer which his scholarly instincts urged him to accept. The College was very helpful : he was free to reconsider his former decision at leisure, and no objections would be raised if he wished to change his mind. His father advised him against Hawarden, however; and, as he admitted to

Sanday, his own sense of vocation urged him to do likewise. At the end of July he reaffirmed his acceptance of Welwyn. The move now took place with little delay, for the living had been vacant for many months. With characteristic vigour, he did not wait to be instituted but started work as curate-in-charge at the beginning of September. He was formally instituted as Vicar by the Bishop of St. Albans on September 28, 1896.

CHAPTER THREE

The Middle East
Early Œcumenical Work

BEFORE the end of 1889 Headlam's interests in Coptic, in the history of the early Church, and in the problems of Church relations impelled him to pay a lengthy visit to the Middle East. He approached his old friend of Winchester and New College days, D. G. Hogarth, who had already been to Asia Minor with Professor William Ramsay, with a view to joining them on another proposed expedition in 1890. Hogarth himself was perfectly agreeable but warned him of the difficulties. 'First (Ramsay) has always insisted that any one who accompanies him should absolutely subordinate any private object he had in going to the general ends of the expedition. Secondly I warn you that it is often very rough work. Bad food, bad water, rows with officials and natives and above all long weary rides in a blazing sun, wearier waits in filthy villages. It really requires some powers of physical endurance and a good deal of mental endurance. Thirdly you will find Ramsay an odd travelling companion, crotchety and exacting, though personally I have never failed to get on with him. The main work is inscription copying, mapping and planning.' Headlam was keen to go, however ; and Professor Ramsay accepted him 'so long as we are agreed to concentrate our entire mind and time on the work of the expedition.' He planned to be away for nine or ten months, visiting Greece, Egypt and Palestine by himself after the other two had returned home.

The three men left England for Smyrna in May 1890. From there they travelled up the railway along the great Roman road into the interior to its terminus at Dinari, the site of the ancient Apameia. Here they copied half a dozen new inscriptions, and then proceeded via Lake Egerdir into the wildest part of the Pisidian Taurus. Headlam described the difficult travelling conditions in a letter to his sister, Rose.

Konia, June 28, 1890.

'My dear Rose,

'We have two servants riding with us and two others in the cart with the luggage. . . . As both our servants are armed we seem to be a formidable party, but then every one in the country carries a gun or has a servant carrying a gun as a mark of etiquette and does not as a rule use it : in fact in view of the condition of the guns it is as well they should not.

'We get up generally between 4.30 and 5, and have a very hurried toilet to say the least; in fact it very often means a shake and nothing more; then the tents have to be taken down and packed, and the beds packed, and so on. We get off perhaps between 6 and 7. The Cusba or cart is sent on to the next place in order that the tents may be ready for us when we arrive, and we start on our day's journey. We go to visit all the various villages and ask whether they have "written stories" and so on. About 12 or 1 it begins to get very hot and we hope to reach a village. We go to the Oda or guest house—every Mohammedan village keeps a house which is given up for the accommodation of guests as hospitality is a religious duty. Then we lie down on (generally very dirty) cushions, and wait for food while all the population (i.e. male population) of the village comes and sits round and talks to us. The food when it comes varies : the most common things we get everywhere are bread—generally "yuk" bread—and "youghat." Yuk bread consists of very coarse flour with a good deal of dirt added and water; this is worked in very thin sheets and produces a substance of the consistency and appearance and largely the taste of coarse brown packing paper. Youghat is milk turned sour and curdled; it is very pleasant on a hot day; sometimes cheese made out of goat's milk, and sometimes a sort of boiled cream. We are the guests of the village and need not pay anything, but we generally do as we always ask for their best things. After this a sleep in the Oda and then more riding until we reach camp about 6 or 7, and dinner always after sunset about 8. Dinner is a very doubtful meal as meat of any sort is hard to procure, and it may resolve itself into a dish of rice. After that we are generally so tired that we are glad to tumble into bed.

'I find the tents fairly comfortable; but so far we have not used them much, as we went into the mountains for four nights where the Cusba could not go, and took practically nothing with us except a little food to fall back upon. I had a waterproof cloak to sleep on and a rug to wrap round me and slept fairly well. It was rather cold as we were some 4,000 feet above the sea. You said that you thought my boots would be a great bother to take off and put on. You were right; but the problem has been solved, for I did not take them off for four nights : they are excellent things to sleep in as they keep one's feet warm. Of course, there have been discomforts—first fleas, then the effects of riding an Asia Minor horse ten or twelve hours a day, then sleeping in the same room as your horse, then no washing. But these are mere trifles. . . . '

They finally arrived at Kara Bavlo, or Adada, in the very heart of the mountains some five thousand feet up and on the shortest route between Perga and Antioch. In a region of chiefly impassable mountains, it was road centre of vital importance. The ruins of Adada were striking both in extent and preservation, and they spent some time in making a survey. From Adada they had another rough journey through the mountains to the site of Lystra, or Khatyn Serai, their main purpose being to find proof of the existence of the temple of Jupiter before the city. In this they met with some success, for they established the probable site beside a pedestal dedicated to Augustus, standing on the south-east side of the city. Looking from the hill down the valley towards the open plain, this pedestal was clearly visible in front of the city, with the signs of concealed ruins beside it.[1] They were equally successful in their search for the site of Derbe; and Ramsay claimed proof of its existence on the mound at Gudelissin, three miles north-west of Zosta—a claim which has since been upheld.[2]

From Derbe they travelled over Taurus to Kestel, the site of the ancient city of Hierapolis, and then on to the ruins of Kodja Kalessi high up on the north-eastern slope of the Calycadnus valley. Here they found the important and well-preserved remains of a lonely monastery. Unique in design, and rich and elaborate in ornamentation, they were some of the most interesting fourth or fifth century ecclesiastical remains in existence. Ramsay identified them as the monastery of Apadna, built, according to Procopius, by Justinian in Isauria. They then travelled north to the coast at Corycos to see further inscriptions. The journey was difficult, their food was running low, they found the beach at Corycos swarming with mosquitoes, and the inscriptions were disappointing. The tempers of the party, which even in normal times were inclined to be fiery, were now unduly frayed by the unpleasant conditions, and there was a violent quarrel. Ramsay left Headlam and Hogarth, declaring that he would work with them no longer. Some days later, however, the three met again in cooler weather and under pleasanter conditions : tempers had cooled and they agreed to resume co-operation. Of this incident Ramsay was later heard to say, with a twinkle in his eye, 'During those days I had come to the firm decision that if at any future time I found it necessary, in the interests of archaeology, to travel with the Devil, I was prepared to do so; but

[1] W. Ramsay, *The Church in the Roman Empire,* 1897, p. 51.
[2] Ibid., pp. 54–5.

never again would I travel with two men who had been at Winchester and New College together.'

Finally by way of Eregli and Jorcez they reached Bor, where Headlam became seriously afflicted with boils—an illness not uncommon to travellers in Asia Minor. Although physically tough and strong, he was not used to the conditions as Ramsay and Hogarth were. He had been warned before leaving England to take things quietly at first and to remember that he was not like Hogarth—'made of leather and wood put together with wire and Canadian balsam'; or Ramsay, who seemed impervious to discomfort—an astonishing thing in a man who at home was notorious for habitually dining in bed. Apart from the hard conditions and hot weather, Headlam had disregarded good advice in the matter of food. The unaccustomed diet was too much for his digestion, and unlike many people he was not hindered from indulgence in it by feelings of repulsion. He became quite seriously ill; so his friends took him on to Kaisarieh, leaving him in the care of the American mission, while they went on to explore the Hittite monuments of the Anti-Taurus. Headlam was bitterly disappointed at being unable to accompany them on one of the most interesting parts of the expedition; but the fortnight's enforced inactivity was not unprofitable. In addition to recovering his health he was able to obtain first-hand information about the work of the Americans at Kaisarieh and gain some insight into Church relations. He eventually rejoined his friends near Nigdeh; and he and Hogarth decided to travel by the direct horse-road to the Cilician Gates—one of the ancient highways of Asia Minor, and then on to Smyrna. From there they went by ship to Constantinople, where they parted.

Headlam now joined A. H. Hardinge, another fellow of All Souls and one of the attachés at the Embassy, for a visit to the monasteries of Mount Athos. His intention to write an account of this expedition was never fulfilled through lack of time and opportunity; but one delightful episode was told later by Professor Kirsopp Lake which subsequently Headlam admitted he wasn't prepared to deny. At a much later date Professor Lake was staying at one of the monasteries and was served with a horrible vegetable soup which he found completely inedible. His hosts expressed surprise and concern, informing him that Kyrios Headlam had highly appreciated it and had left them its English name on a sheet of paper. Lake's curiosity was aroused and he requested that he might be allowed to see this document. His request was granted, and the monks proudly showed him a slip of paper bearing the letters 'DAMMUCK.'

October 1890 was spent on a sight-seeing tour of Greece, during which he wrote a confidential report on the interior of Asia Minor for the Legation at Athens—a work for which he received the thanks of the Foreign Office. Then in November he crossed the Mediterranean to Egypt to study the Coptic Church. After five weeks in Cairo he set out on Christmas Day for Maidoum, where he spent two days with Sir Flinders Petrie. From there he crossed the desert to Medinet in the Fayoum to explore monasteries and churches, interview the local clergy and visit the American mission. He then travelled slowly up the Nile to Luxor, visiting en route Tel el Amarna and more monasteries, including the famous Red and White Monasteries, near which the Akhmim Fragments of the Gospel and Revelation of S. Peter had been found in 1886-7. Luxor was the farthest point of his journey and there he enjoyed the luxury of a comfortable hotel for a week before return-ing to Assiut to have further talks with Coptic leaders and members of the American mission. He then travelled to Cairo by easy stages, reaching there by the middle of March after which he joined his parents in Palestine for a tour of the Holy Places. He arrived back in England in May 1891.

The archæological results of the expedition were considerable and were subsequently recorded—mainly by Ramsay—in a number of books and journals. Headlam's contribution to this literature was a Supplement to the Journal of Hellenic Studies for 1892, entitled *Ecclesiastical Sites in Isauria.* It contained a description of the remains at Koja Kalessi, correcting and amplifying Laborde's description of it written after his visit in 1826, together with notes on ecclesiastical remains in Asia Minor serving to indicate the work still remaining to be done, and an annotated list of the inscriptions they had copied.

In addition, however, he wrote a valuable report for the Archbishop of Canterbury on ecclesiastical conditions in Asia Minor, Egypt and Greece. He pointed out that in Asia Minor on the one hand the Turkish Government was trying to strengthen the Mohammedan character of the people, mainly by distributing waste lands to refugees from Christian countries; while on the other hand the development of trade and commerce attracted Christian Greeks and Armenians in search of financial gain, although they were Christians of somewhat doubtful character. He then discussed the work of the American Congregational missions centred at Kaisarieh. While accepting the value of their work in education, he was critical of their other activi-ties. They confined themselves entirely to the Christian population; and in attempting to bring about a reform of the Eastern Churches from within, they had unintentionally been instrumental in creating a schismatical body. Their personal integrity and conscientiousness was undoubted; but they showed a lack of understanding of local religious customs and beliefs. Nevertheless, their activities had tended to encourage the native churches to undertake much-needed reforms, and there had been a welcome advance in education among both Greeks and Armenians.

He then dealt with the Coptic Church in Egypt. The unfavourable representation of the Coptic character by Europeans was unfair : although admittedly not very attractive, the Copts compared favourably with the Mohammedans ; and in education, morality and ability, he considered them far superior to the rest of the population. Unfortunately the clergy were invariably uneducated, and the married parish clergy were very poor. The monks, on the other hand, from whom alone the bishops could be selected, held extensive property. The bishops were disappointing : though pious, they lacked knowledge and initiative, and being unsympathetic towards change, they were ill-fitted to meet the needs and difficulties of the time. The monasteries were well ordered but seemed deficient in piety and learning, with the exception of the desert monasteries of S. Anthony and S. Paul. In Church relations Headlam found the monophysite controversy was never regarded as a bar to union with other Christians, and cordial relations existed with the Orthodox Church of Lower Egypt, although attempts at union had been unsuccessful. Personal relations with the Church of England were friendly ; but the Patriarch, through timidity and ignorance, refused to enter into official relations. The American Presbyterian missions compared favourably with their Congregational counterparts in Asia Minor. They were more adaptable and tolerant and had a better conception of historical Christianity. Unfortunately their methods were also at fault and encouraged schism : but their work was not without some effect. They produced among Copts a dissatisfaction with the existing condition of their Church, although without any accompanying desire to leave it : this in its turn resulted in considerable and judicious attempts at reform. It was unfortunate that these efforts were hindered by the apathy of the superior clergy, the lack of perseverance in the people and their avariciousness, which prevented them from making sacrifices.

In Greece monasticism was seen at its best at Mount Athos, where moral and religious standards were high, but intellectual standards low. The monasteries tended to dissociate religious from practical life, thereby fostering formalism and lack of sympathy with the aspirations of the people. This was very obvious in their monopoly of appointments to the episcopate, which deprived the able parish priest of any legitimate hopes of advancement. The way in which the Church was bound up with the whole national and social life of the people was most striking : it had an immense hold on them and there were few dissenters. Its weakness was its failure to attract the more educated classes, due to the ignorance of the clergy and the divorce of religion from any intellectual basis.

Finally Headlam suggested two ways of helping the Eastern Churches. In the first place it would be helpful if some of their young priests and ordinands could come to England for theological study and training. Secondly the Church of England might send able men to the Middle East. Chaplaincies at such centres as Athens could be held by young scholars for limited periods; while teachers would be invaluable in key schools—the Coptic school in Cairo, for example, where some effort was being made to improve the educational standard of the priesthood.

This report, apart from its undoubted intrinsic value, revealed Headlam's growing interest in the life of other Churches. The Bonskeid Conference had made him alive to œcumenical affairs, and his recent travels had now given him a real and by no means uncritical interest in the Orthodox and other Churches of the East. The preparations had now been made for his entry into a field in which he was destined to play an increasingly prominent part in the years to come.

II

After his return home he found himself increasingly attracted to such men as Bishop John Wordsworth of Salisbury, Bishop Blyth of Jerusalem and W. J. Birkbeck, whose œcumenical interests were similar to his own. In January 1893 he acted as secretary of a small committee which undertook to revive the Eastern Church Association, founded by Professor George Williams in 1864 and now almost extinct. The surviving members of the Association and the Committee for the Defence of Church Principles in Palestine finally agreed to join forces with the Bishop of Reading (Dr. J. L. Randall) as chairman and Headlam as secretary. One of their objects was to publish books on the Eastern Churches. The first to appear was *The East Syrian Daily Offices* by A. J. Maclean in 1894, and this was followed by W. J. Birkbeck's *Russia and the English Church during the last Fifty Years*. In addition a number of occasional papers were issued, containing booklists, articles on various aspects of the life of the Eastern Churches and reports and documents on relations between them and the Church of England. In the summer of 1893 F. E. Brightman and S. A. Cooke were sent to the Middle East to survey the Eastern Churches and the work of the various missions in the area. As a result, Headlam, in the Annual Report of 1894, was able to put before the Association the possibilities of future work which lay before it.

'First there is a definite opening, and one which will not demand any large expenditure. What is required is that at three or four of the more important centres in the East, at Jerusalem, at Constantinople, in Egypt and in Cyprus, there should be one or more students who should be able to study the history and present condition of the Eastern Church and other Christian communities, and who should assist locally if occasion arises in organizing education and other similar work. Anything further must be the result of the action of the native Christians themselves. They are not in all cases very wealthy . . . but they would certainly be able with a little self-sacrifice and organization to manage their own schools. What they require is more assistance in organizing; and so far as European teachers might be necessary, some further help. The aim of all healthy work should be to develop the possibilities already existing, and not to impose an external system either in the sense of teaching Anglican theology and Western ways, or of paying with foreign money what should be provided in the country. Even slight and inadequate work done on right lines is better than much work done on wrong lines.

'A second point that the Association should keep before itself is that it should never attempt to do unauthorized work. Its representatives in the East must always go, not as representatives of a society, but directly or indirectly as the representatives of the Church. . . . (The Association's) agents must only remain there so long as they can commend themselves to and work harmoniously with the English Bishop there. Great evils in the East arise at the present day from unauthorized and independent action.

'The best scheme that can be suggested is that scholarships should be offered at the two Universities for men who have taken their degree and are prepared to be ordained, in order that they may devote themselves to the study of theology, and of an Eastern language or languages. They would have to undertake in return to go to the East for a number of years in the service of the Association.'

Finally the report pointed out the ultimate aim of all this work :

'The ultimate object which the Association holds before itself, that of Christian reunion, is beginning to occupy more and more a prominent place in men's minds. Our aim must be :

'(1). We must not attempt to move too rapidly in any direction.

'(2). The more friendly intercourse between members of different Churches and the more knowledge disseminated, the better. This should be the aim of the Association.

'(3). The possibility of Reunion will depend ultimately on the genuine desire for Reunion. If the constant work of some generations of Christians and of the best minds among us be devoted to discovering the points of difference, this will ultimately so foster and strengthen public opinion as to make Reunion a practical question.

'(4). Above all we must be unfailing in our prayers for Christian unity.' [3]

These suggestions were very much in line with Headlam's own report to the Archbishop three years previously, and the references to the imposition of external systems and unauthorized and independent action supported all he had then said about the work of the American missions. The schemes proposed were never fully realized; but in 1896 the Association did send the Revd. H. T. F. Duckworth to Cyprus, where for five years he did most valuable work in fostering closer relations between the Greek and Anglican Churches.

In October and November 1898 Headlam went to the Middle East with the Bishop of Salisbury, visiting Cairo, Jerusalem and Cyprus. During a very brief stay in Cairo they had a valuable meeting with the Coptic Patriarch and the new Coptic Bishop of Khartoum. Comparing it with his previous meeting eight years before, Headlam was favourably impressed. Then the Patriarch, though outwardly civil, had seemed suspicious—not so much unfriendly as frightened. Now there was a distinct change for the better: he seemed glad to see them and the attitude of suspicion had vanished. The outlook seemed to be distinctly promising. The Coptic Church had embarked upon a number of reforms: churches had been restored, schools had been established or improved, and some beginning had been made in the education of the clergy.[4] Bishop Wordsworth took the opportunity of securing the Patriarch's approval of the scheme for giving Bishop Blyth an assistant Bishop for Egypt: and on their return home Headlam took a leading part in launching the Appeal for £20,000 for the endowment of an Egyptian bishopric.[5]

From Cairo they went to Jerusalem, where Bishop Wordsworth consecrated the new Anglican Church of S. George. Headlam then went on alone to visit Mr. Duckworth in Cyprus. Here again, as in Egypt, signs were encouraging. Mr. Duckworth's work was highly thought of by the Government and his relations with the Greek Church were cordial. In the past twenty years nearly every church in the island had

---

[3] Eastern Church Association, *Annual Report for 1894*, pp. 9–12.
[4] Headlam's Confidential Report for the E.C.A.
[5] *Salisbury Diocesan Gazette*, vol. xi, pp. 249–50; vol. xii, pp. 29–30. *The Guardian*, January 1899, p. 107. The Appeal finally raised £14,995 5s. 6d. Llewellyn Henry Gwynne was consecrated first Bishop of Egypt and the Sudan on November 20, 1920.

been rebuilt and services were well attended. There was a creditable system of national education, while the Greeks themselves had established, with government help, a gymnasium for higher education. On the debit side the financial, intellectual and often the spiritual standards of the village clergy were low, while many of the higher clergy were incompetent; the monasteries were of little use; and ecclesiastical property was badly administered and distributed. Nevertheless, things were not so bad as they might seem. 'One or two capable Bishops, and the whole thing will work right.' In fact Headlam considered that the Eastern Church Association would be well advised to spend any money they had available on Cyprus rather than on Jerusalem, where he felt the atmosphere too artificial for any really useful œcumenical work.[6] Unfortunately these hopes of further improvement were soon dashed. The death of the Patriarch in May 1900 plunged the island into ecclesiastical turmoil, and conditions became so unfavourable that Mr. Duckworth was obliged to leave.[7]

On the literary side Headlam made two useful contributions to the understanding of the Eastern Churches in this country. The first was a pamphlet *The Teaching of the Russian Church*, which appeared in 1897, and the second was an article on 'The Church of England and the Eastern Churches,' which appeared in Hensley Henson's volume *Church Problems* in 1900. Both essays were subsequently reprinted in 1909 in Headlam's symposium *History, Authority and Theology*. They give a clear and sympathetic account of the Eastern Churches, and reveal Headlam's extensive knowledge and firm grasp of his subject. He had, in fact, learned sufficient Russian to enable him to consult Russian authorities in the original language. Surveying the relations between the English and Orthodox Churches since the Reformation, he showed that they had become increasingly friendly. The theological position of the two Churches was in many ways strikingly similar. Both appealed to Scripture and tradition; although the Eastern Church laid much more stress upon tradition than the Church of England, and was clearly confident that it possessed a true tradition.[8] In Eucharistic teaching too there was no essential difference : it was true that the Eastern Church believed in transubstantiation, but not in the Roman sense—the word was used to guard the doctrine of a real Sacramental Presence in the Eucharist and no more. Nor was there any real fundamental difference in teaching on the Sacraments.[9] Both Churches held that the standard of faith should be the Nicæno-

---

[6] Headlam's Confidential Report for the E.C.A.
[7] *The Guardian*, May 1901, p. 746.
[8] *History, Authority and Theology*, 1909, pp. 169, 196.
[9] Ibid., pp. 171-2, 198-202.

Constantinopolitan Creed, and although there was a difference of opinion on the filioque clause, it was a matter on which both Churches would be well advised not to lay too much emphasis. Admittedly the addition of the clause was irregular—the West was attempting to define a point which the Church had never defined, but it was equally wrong to condemn the West for heresy in doing so.[10]

Any movement towards reunion, however, found itself hampered by the uncompromising attitude of the Eastern Church. It had undergone long periods of isolation from the rest of Christendom; and although it had changed quite considerably, the changes had been so slow and gradual as to be almost imperceptible. It had never undergone any great transforming influence like Scholasticism, or the Reformation, or the Council of Trent; it had never been influenced, except in details, by the whole development of Western theology. Consequently it represented a natural and organic development. But as a result, the Eastern Church regarded itself as perfect and demanded absolute submission as a necessary condition of reunion. 'It thinks and says that it has never changed. It says that the Church is infallible and thinks that it is the Church. Until it will approach the points of difference between it and other communions in a different spirit . . . all real progress, anything beyond friendly intercourse . . . must be impossible.'[11]

This isolation and uncompromising attitude had also had a harmful effect on Christianity as a whole; for it had taken away any check that might have existed to the one-sided development of Western thought. The West had suffered by the introduction into theology, both Roman and Protestant, of hard legal ideas, a too rigid system, an exaggerated desire for construction, a banishment of mystery, and an attempt to solve by human reason problems which were quite inexplicable. 'An importation of philosophy into religious belief, and an attempt at precision in many questions where precision is impossible, has burdened us with creeds, and articles of religion which are treated as creeds, and which certainly subject all the different Churches to the anathema pronounced at the Council of Ephesus against those who added articles to the Christian faith.'[12]

The Eastern Church held a position of considerable importance and significance in Christendom. In the first place, it assisted in bearing vigorous witness against the uncatholic and unhistorical claims of the Roman Catholic Church. It was a great gain for the Church of England to be able to appeal to a Church whose claim to Catholicity and to an historical position could not be doubted, and which on funda-

[10] Ibid., pp. 169–70, 196.
[11] Ibid., pp. 180–3, 215.
[12] Ibid., pp. 215–16.

mental points was decisively on the side of the English Church.[13] Secondly, it supported the position of the Church of England as a National Church, holding to all that was essential to Christian unity, but having customs and worship corresponding with the genius of the English people. Eastern Christendom, too, was the home of National Churches, all of which had played a great part in their national life, providing their countries with an element of power and stability.[14] Thirdly, it provided valuable instruction in that it offered a very definite and distinct type of Christianity. Whereas Anglican theology was either Roman or developed in opposition to Rome, the Eastern Church looked at things from an older and different point of view. It was not troubled, for example, with the conflict between Scripture and tradition, for both alike were part of the teaching of the Church : the Bible was part of tradition, and tradition was in the Bible. Furthermore, it gave a corrective to rigid and mechanical theories of priesthood. The Holy Spirit worked through the whole Church—with clergy and laity ; and the Sacraments were in reality not accomplished by any single individual who was worthy of the mercy of God, but by the whole Church in the person of one individual, even though he be unworthy.[15] Finally, its refusal to meet any one except on its own terms taught a valuable lesson. The same phenomenon was evident in the Roman Church. The position in both was absolutely untenable and was a sad and ridiculous spectacle. It was an example for the English Church to avoid. 'Even if we cannot make other Churches be ready to learn from one another, we can at any rate attempt to learn ourselves.'[16]

Headlam considered the policy which the Church of England should adopt towards reunion would involve much patience. The method had to be one which worked without caring for the immediate results ; one which worked by the sober path of theological study, of mutual intercourse and charity, and of educating both ourselves and others. The more Christian bodies knew of one another, the less likely were they to preserve an attitude of bitterness. The spirit of charity could be evinced by offering assistance to Christians who were suffering from oppression, misgovernment or spiritual isolation. On the other hand, it should be clearly recognized that there was to be no attempt to proselytize : it was not the business of the English Church to weaken the influence of the Eastern Church or to attempt to convert its members.[17] 'We must learn to combine loyalty to our own Church

13 Ibid., pp. 183–5, 193.
14 Ibid., pp. 185–6, 217–18.
15 Ibid., pp. 186–7, 206, 216, 218.
16 Ibid., pp. 188–9, 220–1.
17 Ibid., pp. 189–91, 221–2.

with charity towards other Christian bodies. . . . Sober research, earnest work, loyalty, charity, prayer—these are the methods by which we can advance the reunion of Christendom.' [18]

On leaving Welwyn for London in 1903 Headlam felt obliged to resign his position as Secretary of the Eastern Church Association. It says much for his energy and influence that the Association's fortunes again began to wane after his departure; and finally in 1914 it was absorbed into the more progressive Anglican and Eastern Orthodox Churches Union, which had been founded in 1906.[19] This work had given him valuable experience in the œcumenical sphere, and through it he gained a reputation as an authority on relations with the Eastern Churches. When therefore the Lambeth Conference of 1908 requested the Archbishop of Canterbury to appoint a permanent Committee 'to take cognizance of all that concerns our relations with the Churches of the Orthodox East,' Headlam was one of those from whom Dr. Davidson sought advice as to the best way of implementing the resolution. He was consulted more than once on this subject during the next few years,[20] and it was almost inevitable when the Committee was ultimately appointed after the 1914–18 War that he should emerge as one of its leading members.

[18] Ibid., pp. 223–4.
[19] R. Rouse and S. C. Neill (editors), *A History of the Œcumenical Movement*, 1954, pp. 281, 649–50.
[20] e.g. Abp. Davidson to A. C. Headlam, March 17, 1909; Bp. E. S. Talbot to A. C. Headlam, May 24, 1913.

CHAPTER FOUR

Welwyn

I

HEADLAM was instituted as Rector of Welwyn on September 28, 1896.
Although the living was regarded as a good one he was faced with a
number of financial problems. The stipend was gradually decreasing
owing to the annual diminishing of the Tithe Rent Charge, he was
expected to pay the curate out of his own pocket, and his predecessor
claimed a pension out of the living. The Rectory with its avenue of
lime trees—it was here that the eighteenth-century Rector and poet,
Edward Young, had written his *Night Thoughts on Life, Death and
Immortality*—was a country house in all but name with extensive
grounds, and was expensive to maintain : and the former Rector,
Canon Wingfield, had warned Headlam that he might find it difficult
to maintain without private means. At that time the parish had a
population of just under two thousand. The occupation of the inhabi-
tants was mainly agricultural, although there were one or two small
industrial activities—the gravel pits at Danesbury and a small beehive
factory : at Woolmer Green, the principal hamlet, most of the men
were railway workers. There were also a large number of residential
families—for the most part very class conscious and not at all easy to
deal with. Most of these came to church and many were quite
generous, but very few condescended to take any share in the various
parochial activities. Among them there existed some violent differences
of theological opinion. Canon Wingfield had been a staunch Evangelical, and as such had had his supporters. On the other hand, there
were others who enthusiastically supported the English Church Union ;
and Headlam found them all rather trying as they solicited his favour,
endeavouring to make the church 'Higher' or 'Lower' according to
their several predilections. With a man of Headlam's temperament in
their midst, all the requisite elements for frequent and violent ex-
plosions were present. The parish was consequently not easy to run,
and matters had not been improved by the fact that his predecessor,
who had been there for twenty-five years, had for a long time been
hampered with ill-health.

Headlam set to work with vigour, making it clear that he would make changes if and when he thought them necessary, whether they were popular or not; and that he would stand no nonsense. People who disapproved of his actions were requested to come and see him personally, and they would receive an explanation of what he was doing.[1] In his first sermon he stated his Churchmanship : he was 'an historical churchman, true to the historical principles which have been exhibited through all ages, and true and loyal to the historic position of the Church of England.' If any of his parishioners did not realize the implications of this statement they were soon enlightened. A Choral Eucharist was introduced (though not every Sunday), the clergy wore coloured stoles, Holy Communion was celebrated on Saints' Days, and Morning Prayer was recited publicly every day at 8 a.m. The parish decided that the new Rector was 'rather High.'

Within three months there were abundant signs of his energy. Mothers' meetings and working parties had been instituted : schemes were set in hand to pay off the debts on the schools—a task which was achieved within two years : the parish finances were reorganized : a building fund was started for a new church at Woolmer Green : Bible classes were formed for both children and adults : and children were subjected to mid-week catechizing in church. Some of the intellectual meat which he provided at these classes and in his sermons was unquestionably strong : his Sunday School teachers, for example, were lectured on the problems of Textual Criticism, while his congregation were initiated into the mysteries of such subjects as Jewish life and thought in the immediate pre-Christian era, and the problems of early Church history. It must be admitted that neither his sermons nor his Bible Classes were striking. Their substance was undeniably good, but apart from so often being beyond his hearers, they were unattractively delivered. These were, however, faults which Headlam strove to eliminate, and gradually he acquired the ability to address humble congregations with simplicity.

He was singularly fortunate in his curates. The young man whom he had inherited from his predecessor did not stay long : he was rash enough to quarrel with Headlam and criticize severely his manner of reading the lessons. They parted company soon afterwards. He was succeeded by R. H. Cattell, a former captain of the English Rugby team, who stayed with Headlam for the whole of his time at Welwyn : he was blessed with tact and a sense of humour, and the two men worked together extremely well. In February 1897, finding living alone at the Rectory an impractical proposition, Headlam let it and went to

---

[1] *Welwyn Parish Magazine*, October 1896, no. 314.

live with Cattell at Hillside, a small house on the Hatfield road. Here they ran a successful bachelor establishment until Headlam married and returned to the Rectory in 1900. In 1900, owing to the pressure of his outside commitments, he acquired a second curate, and again he was fortunate in finding a wise and sympathetic helper in Wilfred Stubbs, son of the Bishop of Oxford.

Headlam proved himself a very capable and efficient parish priest, though he was never really popular. His hard work and conscientiousness were always marred by his overbearing manner. He said what he thought, regardless of the effect upon his hearers; and he was inclined to ride roughshod over people, which antagonized the upper classes and made the lower classes rather afraid of him. For example, when Queen Victoria died in February 1901, and general mourning was ordered throughout the country, all cathedrals and churches were draped. Despite this general practice, however, and against the wishes of his congregation, Headlam refused to drape his church and condemned the black hangings as both repulsive and unchristian. There was a storm of disapproval, but he believed himself to be right and absolutely refused to give way. He was therefore respected and obeyed but often disliked, except at Woolmer Green, where the people were simpler and less sophisticated. Woolmer Green had in fact a warm corner in his heart. In 1898 its population was estimated at some 400, and was infinitely more populous than most, if not all the surrounding parishes. Headlam decided that it should have its own church, and in less than two years had raised over half the £2,500 needed for the building. The foundation stone was laid in September 1899, and the main body of the church was consecrated in November 1900. Unfortunately it was another piece of work spoiled by his dictatorial manner. He insisted on employing as architect Mr. Weir Schultz, who, although possessed of unrivalled knowledge of archaeological remains in Greece and Asia Minor, made no claims to being an expert in contemporary church architecture. As a result, the plain red brick building, with a polygonal apse at the east end and a raised west end, showed no outstanding features. Headlam was said to be the only person who could raise any enthusiasm over its design. By general consent, however, the interior fittings were most beautiful, and towards these he himself contributed generously. He also took great pride and interest in the laying out of the grounds and churchyard: he drew up a series of designs for monuments which met with his approval, and every one who wished to erect a monument was compelled to accept one of these —a regulation which inevitably caused friction. But Woolmer Green was proud of the church and grateful to Headlam for his labours. They showed this, not only by keeping the building and its surroundings in excellent order, but also by attending services with commendable regularity—far more so than the people at Welwyn. They appreciated, too, Headlam's insistence on preaching himself at Woolmer Green at least once every Sunday, although the congregation at the parish church considered such assiduous attention rather unnecessary.

Headlam was probably quite unconscious of his dictatorial manner; he was simply confident that what he said and did was right and for the best. This was shown again in his determination to run his parish on democratic lines by setting up a Church Council many years before such institutions became generally established. The scheme was evolved with the help of Lord Hugh Cecil, who came over from Hatfield in May 1899 to speak about it. Headlam was convinced, however, that if left to themselves, the parishioners would elect all the wrong people; so in a most undemocratic way he arranged for the appointment of all its members himself. Inevitably the Council was never really popular. It is also not surprising that Headlam found it difficult to infect the congregation with any great enthusiasm. With some people, of course, it was simply not done to appear enthusiastic : but this lukewarmness in church affairs used to irritate him. He used to say, 'What can you expect when the church bells bear an inscription which means "Down with enthusiasm," and that message has been rung out every Sunday for generations?' Some of this coolness was due to party feeling : many people rather distrusted Headlam as being a High Churchman; although their suspicions were partly roused by his habit, which was quite unconscious, of suddenly and frequently bending his knees when at the altar—an act which many people interpreted as a form of genuflection. Actually no one could possibly have accused him of being advanced either in ritual or doctrine.

1900 was an eventful year. On September 18 he married Miss Evelyn Persis Wingfield of Wendover Lodge, Welwyn. She was a first cousin of Canon Wingfield, and the fourth child and eldest surviving daughter of the Revd. George Wingfield, formerly Rector of Tickencote, Rutland, and of Glatton. On his death in 1876, his widow had moved with her family to Wendover Lodge, and her two surviving daughters, Evelyn and May, had for many years done valuable work in the parish as district visitors, Sunday School teachers and leaders of various organizations. May died suddenly only three months before her sister's wedding. Evelyn, who was five years older than Headlam —she was 43 and he was 38—proved to be an ideal partner. They were completely devoted to each other; and throughout their married life, whenever he was away from home, he wrote to her at least once and sometimes twice a day—and in a way which would

c

have surprised those who thought him cold and aloof. Although never professing to be his intellectual equal or wishing to share in his academic pursuits, she played her full share in their social activities.

After their marriage they returned to live at the Rectory, where they were able to indulge in their common passion for gardening with the help of three full-time gardeners. Their primulas and irises became famous—Headlam used to claim that he and Sir Michael Foster [2] were the two best-known iris growers in Europe; and they were even known to import blue poppies from the Himalayas. These were interests, too, which they tried to share with the parish by holding botany classes both in the schools and in the Rectory gardens during the summer evenings.

Headlam did not confine his interest merely to ecclesiastical affairs in the parish. In the seventeenth century All Souls' College had acquired the manor and advowson of Welwyn; he therefore claimed that as Rector he was also Lord of the Manor, and as such interested himself in local affairs. With his love of tradition, he insisted on holding the court leet twice a year and presiding over it, while he took an active interest in such enterprises as the clothing and coal clubs, the Men's Institute, the provision of a new water supply for the parish, and the building of a cottage hospital. Nevertheless, from a pastoral point of view he did not find social relationships easy. With the agricultural worker he was at home, for he could understand his language : but with other ordinary working-class people he was lost. Many years later he wrote that it was not every one who could be a parish priest, and this was undoubtedly written in the light of his own experience. Although he worked hard and conscientiously, he was out of his element : but he considered it his duty to acquire some experience as a parish priest. Whether his heart was in it—and that is doubtful— he certainly did not regret it and he learnt much. It took him out of the rather artificial atmosphere of university life and for the first time brought him into real and continuous contact with the man in the street. He had to work among people who lived and thought on a level different from his own, and it was an experience which subsequent events proved to be valuable—not least when he became Bishop of Gloucester.

II

The extent of Headlam's activities outside the parish would have

---

[2] Famous biologist and physiologist. Professor of Physiology, Cambridge 1883–1903; Biological Secretary of the Royal Society 1881–1903.

caused most men to quail. He was secretary of the Eastern Church Association, examining chaplain to the Bishop of Southwell, member of the Council of Secondary Education appointed by the Convocation of Canterbury, and examiner for the School of Theology at Oxford : he was in much demand as a lecturer and preacher [3] : and over and above all this he still found time to read and write. One of his aims in going to Welwyn had been to help promote outside the University a sound study of historical theology, and with this in view he became leader of a society called 'The Clerical and Lay,' composed of local clergy and laymen who met in one another's houses to read papers and discuss theology. In this he was ably assisted by his neighbour, Alexander Nairne, Rector of Tewin and Professor of Hebrew at King's College, London, from 1900, destined to become a lifelong friend. An opportunity to extend this aim came in 1901, when he renewed his association with the *Church Quarterly Review*. The editor, Mr. Knight Watson, died on January 30. For some time there had been a sad deterioration in the general standard of the articles, and the circulation had declined in consequence. Furthermore, *The Journal of Theological Studies,* which had been founded in 1899 with Cuthbert Turner as editor, had already proved itself a serious rival. When Messrs. Spottiswoode and Co. offered Headlam the editorship in June 1901, the prospects were by no means bright. Many people urged him to accept, however. Lord Halifax, for example, told him that he had intended to give it up, but if he (Headlam) became editor, he would continue his subscription. Gore, too, had said that it would be best to strengthen *The Journal of Theological Studies* and let *The Church Quarterly* perish, but with Headlam in charge was quite prepared to change his mind. Henson also encouraged him to take it over : 'I think there is need of a responsible, learned and thoroughly independent journal which could give expression to the mind of Anglicanism.' Headlam therefore accepted, on the understanding that as editor he would be guaranteed full responsibility and complete freedom.

The magazine made what was virtually a new beginning. Headlam recruited a number of new contributors, mostly among his friends and acquaintances, and widened the journal's range of interests. Within a short space of time it had recovered its position as the representative of the intellectual and literary side of English Church life. Baron von Hügel expressed delight at the new régime (August 2, 1901) :

[3] e.g. He lectured at the Church Congress at Nottingham in 1897 ; he was Birkbeck Lecturer at Trinity College, Cambridge in 1898 ; and he was Select Preacher at Oxford 1899–1901.

'Let me say how very pleased I am to think of a man of your training, school, and temper of mind, becoming editor of the *C.Q.R.* I used often to be annoyed with that *Review*—I mean with things about it which I well knew and know to be in no sense bound up with Anglicanism : e.g. its (I think) quite unfair attitude towards George Eliot, its surely unnecessarily prominent anti-Roman polemics; and, I think above all, by its sort of Dean Burgon plus Archdeacon Denison anticlerical attitude in Biblical matters. Now I feel sure that in all these three classes of subjects, your becoming editor must and does mean the triumph of the wider, more generous and truly scientific temper and outlook, which we all want so much, and which, thank God, is, after all, infectious. I like so much to think of a collaborator of Canon Sanday's, a man of the most admirable perfection of self-less and generous temper, taking the place of that other, largely unattractive editorship.'

Headlam himself used the *Review* to good effect in the conflicts which raged round the controversial but comprehensive Education Act which the Conservative party effected in 1902. With a series of articles there and in *The Guardian* he emerged as a strong supporter of Church Schools, urging the Church to co-operate to the fullest extent in helping the Government to make the educational system of the country as sound and efficient as possible, in which denominational teaching was secured for those who desired it, and state and voluntary schools achieved equality in status.[4]

At the same time he continued his work on the history of the early Church. Towards the end of 1901 Cuthbert Turner suggested a new critical edition of Eusebius's *Ecclesiastical History* to replace Dr. Bright's edition, which was really a reprint of Valesius with an Introduction. He had already secured the promise of collaboration from H. N. Bate, Fellow of Magdalen College (later Dean of York); and he suggested that they should have a fourth collaborator in Claude Jenkins, a pupil of both Bate and himself. The plan received further impetus from Sanday, who reported that Dr. E. Schwartz was engaged on a similar task in Berlin, but it was doubtful whether he had the ability to do the work satisfactorily. Headlam agreed to help and work began, most of the collating abroad being done by Bate and Jenkins. In 1902 Headlam published a series of notes on the various texts and editions of Eusebius in *The Journal of Theological Studies,* which not

---

[4] He published three articles in the *C.Q.R.* (a) 'The Church and Education,' vol. 53, pp. 456–68. (b) 'The New Education Bill,' vol. 54, pp. 204–13. (c) 'Education and Religious Liberty,' vol. 55, pp. 169–99. A series of articles in *The Guardian* in December 1902 and January 1903 were eventually reprinted in pamphlet form under the title *The Education Act 1902. A Church Policy.*

only provided a summary of all the work that had been done hitherto but also served as a draft of the Prolegomena to the new edition. Its value lay in revealing that no really adequate edition of the History existed—'No collation of manuscripts can be trusted, and very little attempt has been made to construct a text on principles which have any pretence to be called scientific.'[5] Unfortunately the project ran into difficulties. In 1903 Headlam left Welwyn for King's College, London : he became heavily committed in other directions, and with the approval of Turner and Bate, Jenkins took over his share of the work. Before long these three were also faced with other more pressing demands on their time; and then other factors arose which resulted in the project being abandoned. Dr. Bright's edition was not exhausted as quickly as had been anticipated ; the Eusebius requirements from candidates in the Theology School at Oxford were modified ; and finally Dr. Schwartz's edition appeared and was found to be, despite inadequate and defective readings, a considerable advance on existing editions.

Another project was the commentary on the Acts of the Apostles. Lack of time prevented him from completing it, but much of the work which he did appeared in Dr. Hastings' *Dictionary of the Bible* between 1898 and 1902. He contributed articles on Acts of the Apostles, Gnosticism, Herod, Jubilees, Sergius Paulus, Prisca, Province, Rufus, Sceva, Simon Magus, Tertullus, Theatre, Theudas, Trypheana and the Unknown God. Some of these—notably the Acts of the Apostles, Gnosticism, Herod and Simon Magus—were masterpieces of compression and statement, while the first was a weighty contribution to the literature on the subject ; it was described for example, by the *Revue Biblique Internationale* as a model 'of clearness, of scientific precision, and of popularization.'[6] In this article and two others on the same subject in *The Church Quarterly Review*—'Criticism and the Acts of the Apostles' in October 1901 and 'The Credibility of the Acts of the Apostles' in January 1903 he firmly supported the traditional views on the date of the book and defended the author's historical accuracy. In particular he crossed swords with Professor Schmiedel of Zürich, the German Liberal Protestant, whose articles in *The Encyclopedia Biblica* were rousing such bitter criticism. Schmiedel denied that the 'we-passages' were by the same author as the other parts of the book and considered that the contradictions between Acts and Galatians were fatal to the historical character of the one or the other : the writer of Acts had invented the first person in the 'we-passages' for the sake of deception and he was certainly neither S. Luke

[5] *Journal of Theological Studies,* vol. 4, pp. 93–102.
[6] Quoted in *The Expository Times,* vol. x, p. 117.

nor a companion of S. Paul. He ascribed a late date to the book—105 to A.D. 130 and cast grave doubts on its historical accuracy. Headlam was critical of such views and dismissed Schmiedel as very self-confident—though acute and minute in his methods, he was not very formidable.[7]

This was not the only way in which Headlam registered his disapproval of Schmiedel's 'reduced Christianity.' As far back as 1895 the editors of *The Encyclopedia Biblica,* Professor Cheyne and Dr. Sutherland Black, had asked him to write the article on the Epistle to the Romans—a work which he had then agreed to do. But early in 1901, when the third volume of the *Encyclopedia* was almost complete, and Headlam's article had already been accepted, he felt he must object to the views which Schmiedel had expressed in the earlier volumes in 1899 and 1901. His feelings were further roused when Schmiedel attacked his old friend, Sir William Ramsay. He consulted Gore on the propriety of withdrawing his article at this eleventh hour. Gore encouraged him to be obstinate and to do so : 'I think the second volume passes the limit of what either sane people or Churchmen ought to be able to be associated with, and I think in the third volume it will be impossible to avoid responsibility for associations.' Headlam thereupon insisted on the return of his article, despite the most earnest pleadings from both Cheyne and Black.

He was in calmer waters, however, in his three essays on 'Christian Authority' in D. G. Hogarth's *Authority and Archaeology, Sacred and Profane* (1899), which discussed the relation of archaeological research to biblical and classical literature. Here he gave a valuable summary of the chief archaeological discoveries which affected the knowledge of the first three centuries of Christianity. It was a brilliant piece of work, and the third essay on the Catacombs at Rome was quite outstanding. It says much for his sober judgment that although his information is now dated in the matter of archaeological research, his conclusions still hold good, and require little change or correction. His first essay showed how the historical accuracy of the Gospel of S. Luke and the Acts of the Apostles was vindicated by archaeological evidence, while the evidence of local knowledge at Philippi and Thessalonica militated against the theory of a late date for Acts. The second essay, dealing with Phrygian inscriptions collected in Ramsay's *Cities and Bishoprics of Phrygia,* was a skilful demonstration of the way in which archaeology established the credibility of early Christian writers in questions of ecclesiastical organization, doctrine and practice. The third, on the Roman Catacombs, apart from providing valuable cor-

---

[7] *C.Q.R.,* vol. 56, pp. 1–22 ; ibid., vol. 55, pp. 388–404; cf. *Encyclopedia Biblica,* 1899, vol. 1, pp. 37–57.

roboration of the evidence of early Christian writers, gave a fascinating portrait of the life of the early Church, with its faith in the Resurrection, its devotion to Jesus Christ and the importance of the two Sacraments of Baptism and the Eucharist. Christian tradition could be trusted, and archaeology showed how the New Testament books and the writers of the early Church should be studied from the point of view of history : it translated, through what was often commonplace and unimportant, the history of early Christianity into life.[8]

All the work of this period was but grist to the historical mill, however, for Headlam had a real magnum opus in mind. Unfortunately the work was never completed, and to the very end of his life he regretted that he had never written what he called a really big book. It was to have been a history of the early Church, and by May 1898 he had gone far enough to have a preliminary understanding with Messrs. Macmillans about publication. The Prolegomena to this projected work was given as the Birkbeck Lectures at Trinity College, Cambridge, in January 1898 on 'Methods of Early Church History,' and Macmillans suggested that it might be a good advertisement for the book if these initial studies were first to appear independently in some journal. Headlam agreed, and the substance of both lectures appeared in *The English Historical Review* for January 1899. Here he surveyed all the critical work which had been done on the study of early Church history. In this Erasmus had played a notable part, and sober Church history had begun with him : he had realized that history was to be the teacher, and not the servant. Truth was to be gained by studying history, history was not to be learned in the defence of truth. In Erasmus' steps had come Casaubon, and ultimately their mantles had fallen on the shoulders of members of three schools in England, France and Germany, all of whom had developed historical methods to a very high degree—Lightfoot, Duchesne and Harnack. He then discussed the work done on the collection and publication of material and the criticism of documents, and finally the constructive work emerging from these two. The constructive work produced so far had been disappointing; and in spite of all the valuable preparation of the ground, no really authoritative history of the early Church had been written. It was to such a task that Headlam hoped to give himself. He was under no delusions—it would be a task of tremendous difficulty, requiring fairness of mind and freedom from prejudice.[9]

Plans for the fulfilment of such a task were shattered at the beginning of 1903, when Dr. Archibald Robertson, Principal of King's

[8] *Authority and Archaeology, Sacred and Profane* (edited by D. G. Hogarth), 1899, pp. 335–422.
[9] *History, Authority and Theology*, pp. 229–77.

College, London, and Headlam's close friend, was appointed Bishop of Exeter in place of Dr. Ryle. Cuthbert Turner suggested that he should apply for the vacancy, but Headlam at first refused. He had work on hand with which a move would sadly interfere; and in any case he was quite prepared to stay longer at Welwyn—he had plans to restore and enlarge the parish church, and he wanted to complete the church he had built at Woolmer Green. But it did not take him long to realize the advantages of such a move. He was at the height of his powers, in the prime of life, and possessed of immense vigour : his reputation as a scholar and a teacher was established : he was well known in ecclesiastical circles both at home and abroad : and administrative work at All Souls and at Welwyn had proved him a practical man of affairs with a firm grasp of detail. As he himself admitted to his parishioners, 'The post . . . of Principal of King's College, London . . . is one of a character which I believe I shall like, and for which I hope I may be suited, and is on the lines of all the experience and training of my earlier years; I cannot doubt therefore that you will understand that it would be natural when it was suggested to me . . . that I should in many ways look forward to what must be a wider and more important work.' [10] Finally, from seven candidates, Headlam was placed on the short list with two old friends of Winchester and Oxford days—Winfrid Burrows, Vicar of Holy Trinity, Leeds, and former Principal of Leeds Clergy School, and Llewellyn J. M. Bebb, Principal of S. David's College, Lampeter. Burrows had been invited to stand, but was not really attracted to the work and finally withdrew. Headlam was appointed and entered upon his next great task in May 1903.

[10] *Welwyn Parish Magazine*, April 1903.

CHAPTER FIVE

King's College, London: Incorporation and the Theological Department

AT King's College Headlam inherited a situation bristling with difficulties. In the first place the relations of the College with the University of London and with University College, London, were far from ideal, although they had undoubtedly improved under his predecessor. Secondly, the financial position of the College was precarious : for a quarter of a century its income had been hopelessly inadequate, permitting nothing more than a mere hand-to-mouth existence. Grants from the Government and the London County Council had alleviated some of the distress but even this help had been jeopardized when Dr. Wace had been Principal by his religious controversies and his intransigent attitude towards the abolition of religious tests. It had become apparent that if regular grants were to be expected, religious tests would have to go, and one of Dr. Robertson's last achievements before leaving in 1903 had been to secure their total abolition except in the Theological Department.[1] Nevertheless, financial problems still remained—money for vital improvements and extensions to the buildings was urgently needed; financial reserves were non-existent; and the staff was badly paid. In 1901–2 the average salary of professors and lecturers was £265 a year; and most of them were compelled to seek additional spare-time employment—an expedient hardly conducive to serious study and research. Finally, despite insufficient resources and inadequate accommodation, the College tried to maintain far too wide a range of educational activities. First there was the College itself, providing education of university character in various faculties; secondly, there was the Strand School and the Civil Service Department, which prepared candidates for the lower grades of the Civil Service—they had taken over premises in the basement of the College in 1897 previously occupied by King's College School, a grammar school which had been transferred to Wimbledon with the help of the Surrey

[1] F. J. C. Hearnshaw, *The Centenary History of King's College, London,* 1929, pp. 287–8, 341–2, 358–63, 400. The Bill actually received the Royal Assent on July 21, 1903, after Headlam had taken over.

County Council; then there was the King's College Hospital and Medical School in Portugal Street; and finally there was the Ladies' Department in Kensington Square, which since 1894 had both provided courses of lectures in subjects of general interest and prepared students for degrees and diplomas.[2]

Such then was Headlam's inheritance, offering obvious possibilities for a young man in his early forties with a determined will and a capacity for organization. As he saw it, his main task was to convert the College from an impoverished collection of incongruous elements into a single healthy institution for university education, capable of making a worthy contribution to the life and work of the University as a whole. In realization of this aim he was eminently successful, and his work throughout was governed by certain fundamental principles. He considered the primary purpose of a university was to supply the community with people who were fully trained to serve in any category demanding intellectual attainment; and to do this it should be an independent, self-governing corporation, devoted to the interests of learning, and free from political influence and governmental control.[3] The primary function of a university therefore consisted not in examining, but in teaching and in creating a vigorous intellectual life. The value of a degree lay in its being a sign, not that a certain examination had been passed, but that a proper course of instruction had been completed under competent teachers in a university environment. Such an environment demanded a unity of locality, and the idea of a federal university was a mistake.[4] On the other hand, universities should not be isolated units : they should form one great institution, both at home and overseas, with facilities for the interchange of personnel and the mutual recognition of entrance examinations and degrees. Headlam therefore wanted to make it possible for students at King's College to feel that they had taken part in a free and vigorous corporate life, to which social intercourse, the clash of intellectual conflict, and deep spiritual and intellectual emotions had all contributed their share : without a full participation in that life they would go out into the world inadequately equipped. 'If we are to make a real University for London, it will be necessary to make the world realize that we can provide not only university teaching but university life.'[5]

[2] Ibid., pp. 375, 377–8.
[3] *King's College Review*, June 1905, vol. 7, no. 3, pp. 5–7; *Universities and the Empire*, 1907, p. 6.
[4] He considered the creation of the separate Universities of Leeds, Liverpool and Manchester in place of the one combined Victoria University in 1903–4 a move in the right direction.
[5] *King's College Review*, December 1904, 'College and University Life.'

The first great practical step to attain all this was to secure the incorporation of King's College into the University of London, instead of trying to maintain it as an independent unit. Obviously there were problems to be faced, but they were not insuperable; and the advantages of incorporation were manifold, particularly in view of the recent similar action taken by University College and the proposed creation of the Imperial College of Science and Technology. His views on incorporation were set out in a letter to the Archbishop of Canterbury.

August 29, 1905.

'My Lord Archbishop,

'It will be better I think to look at the question at issue first from the University point of view. When in 1900 the University was reconstituted as a teaching university, it found itself compelled to deal with a situation in which the higher education of London was divided among a large number of institutions with little or no co-operation between them. Almost all these institutions were very inadequately endowed and there was a good deal of unnecessary rivalry. The University itself had no money at all to provide any teaching of its own. Most conspicuous was the fact that there were two university colleges each of them organized as small and inadequately endowed universities, each of them attempting to cover the whole field of learning. The first step that was made to alter this was the proposal for the incorporation of University College. This was first made soon after the University was reconstituted. After long negotiations a scheme was drawn up which received the sanction of Parliament during the last session. In about a year's time the incorporation of University College will become an actual fact.

'We have now to consider the situation as regards King's College. Up till now it has been a hard struggle to keep the College going, and if it had not been for the generosity of a single subscriber, it might very likely have come to an end : but the difficulty in the future will be infinitely greater—the College will have to compete not against University College but against the University of London, and although there is no reason to suspect any unfairness or injustice on the part of the University, it will be natural for it to consider that the first claim on its funds and interests belong to that College which is its own property. It is inevitable, as far as one can judge, that ultimately the College would be unable to continue the struggle. Then secondly the whole of our teachers will be put in an inferior position compared with those of University College. All the leading teachers at University College will be Professors in the University : those of King's College may have to struggle even to be recognized as teachers of the University at all. This inferior position combined with inadequate means will inevitably lead to our getting an inferior type of teacher. Then thirdly there is another consideration which must not be lost sight of. Your Grace will remember that under the last Radical Government the College was deprived of its grant as a university college. It is true that the principal reason for which this was done—the existence of theological tests—has been done away with; but it is, I think, very probable that after the incorporation of University College, a government which was unfavourable to the Church of England might propose to give the whole sum obtained by University and King's Colleges direct to the University of London. If that were done the University would be able to impose upon the College its own conditions. At present we are in the superior position in any negotiations because we have something to offer which will be of profound importance to the organization of the University and as long as we ourselves receive a Treasury grant we shall not negotiate at a disadvantage.

'Putting the matter as shortly as possible, there are two strong reasons for incorporation :

'1. So far as can be foreseen, if we do not make our terms with the University, we shall be embarked upon a hopeless struggle in which we shall ultimately fail.

'2. If we do incorporate, we shall take the most necessary step to make the University a strong and homogeneous body with the possibility of organizing the highest education efficiently. I think that there is no doubt that if we incorporate, other institutions will follow in the same steps very rapidly.

'Now as to the religious question. In the first place let us remember that the University of London is no longer a secular university although it is undenominational. It has a faculty of theology and recently the Senate of the University decided by a majority of more than six to one that religious education should be given at the Goldsmiths College at New Cross. Although the University would resent any attempt on the part of the Church of England to claim any privilege as against any other religious body, there is practically no hostility, and if we are careful to respect the principles of the University we may be certain of thoroughly friendly treatment. Under those circumstances I feel quite convinced that nothing will strengthen the position of the Church of England in the University as much as a friendly attitude on our part towards it. Then again there are two facts which we must remember. In the first place I cannot feel that the Church has done its duty towards King's College in the past. If during the seventy-three years of its existence adequate support had been given to it, it might now be a strong independent college able to hold its own; but this has never been done. Again and again appeals have been made to the public and especially to the Church public, asking for support for a definitely Church College but they have for the most part been unsuccessful. Of the amount subscribed within the last few years, more than £40,000 comes from a single donor. The College has practically no endowments and has never been out of debt since its foundation. Then secondly as a matter of fact under the new proposals religious teaching for the non-theological students will be in a far stronger position than it has ever been before. For the future the time of chapel services and one hour per week of religious instruction will be preserved free from any secular lectures, and all the dissatisfaction which is caused by the attempt very largely unsuccessful to make the chapel services compulsory will cease. By an arrangement which has prevailed until the present year divinity lectures for non-theological students have been pushed into the luncheon hour, and even then have often clashed with other lectures. Under these circumstances I do not believe that religious influence in the University will lose anything by the proposed incorporation. But there is a further consideration still. At present great efforts are being made to keep up on Church lines a complete college, and to give secular education which the University as a whole is prepared to give. In that way support is withdrawn from the theological faculty which it is the duty of the Church to keep up. By the proposed agreement, the theological faculty will be placed on a strong and secure basis, and the funds may be devoted to improving in every way the training of the clergy.

'I look forward to the time in the future when many of those in London who desire to be ordained will obtain a degree in Arts in London University studying at King's College under a religious influence which will come to them without any compulsion and without causing any irritation, and will then pass on to a two years' course in a theological faculty.

'What the aim of the Church should be is to improve the endowment of the theological professorships, to provide scholarships and exhibitions to enable future clergy to get a complete university training, and if possible a certain number of fellowships to encourage theological research. If we can do this we should do infinitely more for the cause of religion in London and London University, than by attempting to carry on inadequately a university college, and not throwing ourselves heartily into the full development of the University. . . .'

Headlam placed a memorandum on these lines before the College Council on June 22, 1904. He warned them, however, that incorporation involved disintegration. 'Although the multiplicity of interests connected with the College is in many ways attractive, I am sure that the dissipation of energy which is the result is a necessary source of weakness. The work of the College will be much more valuable if it is devoted only to the highest branches of education.' The financial problems involved were considerable. Apart from making good the loss of income of some £3,500 a year from the removal of the Strand School and the Civil Service Department, it would be necessary not only to build and possibly endow a new Hospital and Medical School, but also to meet outstanding debts on the College amounting to £35,000.

The Council agreed to proceed with the scheme and negotiations were opened with the Senate of the University. Agreement was reached before the end of 1906, but the necessary Parliamentary legislation had to be postponed until the College's financial obligations had been met. In February 1907 an appeal for £125,000 was issued; but the response was disappointing, only £32,000 being given. It was, however, almost sufficient to free the College from debt, and in August 1908 the King's College London Transfer Act became law. It provided for an arrangement very much on the lines Headlam had proposed; he was, in fact, one of its chief architects, playing a conspicuous part in the delicate and difficult negotiations. All the departments of the College engaged in university work except the Department of Theology became an incorporated college of the University with the title 'University of London King's College' under a Principal appointed by the Crown and a committee of the Senate known as the Delegacy. The Theological Department continued to be governed by the College Council and became a school of the University known as 'The Theological Department of King's College, London'; its head, appointed by the Council, was to be called the Dean. The site of the College and its buildings remained the property of the old corporation but were leased to the University at a nominal rent for 999 years, except certain parts of the buildings including the Chapel, which were retained for the use of the Theological Department. The Medical School and Hospital, the Women's Department and King's College School all became separate and independent institutions, while the Strand School and the Civil Service Department were only to remain with the College until the Council found them new accommodation elsewhere. The new administration actually came into operation on January 1, 1910.

By this Act the College was established on an entirely new and novel basis, becoming two institutions within one building with a common office and administration. The arrangement was made that during his time Headlam should combine the offices of Principal of the College,

Dean of the Theological Department, and Professor of Dogmatic Theology. He was the last Principal to be in holy orders and the only man to hold all three offices simultaneously. The new constitution seemed on paper to be so complicated that friction was almost inevitable; but experience proved it otherwise. It stood the test of time. Sir Ernest Barker, who was Principal from 1920 to 1927 wrote, 'Never at any rate was there such a complicated system of dualism : never in actual fact was there a greater and happier unity of feeling and co-operation.'[6] The arrangements for the property were an outstanding feature of Headlam's successful diplomacy; for the Senate had earnestly desired, as in the case of University College, that the site and buildings should also be transferred to the University. But Headlam stood firm. Whatever the University might do about the secular departments, the Theological Department was securely anchored to the Strand.

The process of disintegration may be told briefly. First there was the Hospital and the Medical School. It was already recognized when Headlam came that they would have to be moved : they stood in an area depopulated by slum clearance, with ten other large hospitals within a radius of a mile and a half. The obvious place to go was south of the Thames, where a large, quickly-growing working-class population were in desperate need of adequate hospital services. The matter was settled when the College Treasurer, the Hon. W. F. D. Smith, gave a twelve acre site for a hospital of six hundred beds on Denmark Hill. On October 12, 1903, the King's College Hospital Removal Fund Appeal for £300,000 was launched. To this both Headlam and his wife gave themselves unsparingly : their own personal donations were considerable, and they were constantly assisting with money-raising schemes. Mrs. Headlam, in particular, was a leading figure in three great efforts—the Elizabethan Fair in Lincoln's Inn Fields in May 1906, 'Ye Old Camberwell Fayre' revived after a lapse of fifty-two years in October 1907, and the carnival at Crystal Palace in July 1909—which alone raised nearly £12,000. When King George V opened the new hospital on July 26, 1913, £370,000 had been raised; but costs had increased as the work progressed. £150,000 was still needed and three of the eight ward blocks remained to be built. It was, however, considered to be the last word in hospital architecture and lay-out, and has since more than justified its removal. It became completely independent on September 1, 1909. In January 1910 Headlam persuaded the College Council to confer the Fellowship of King's College on the senior members of the Medical School staff—a gesture which was much appreciated.

[6] E. Barker, *Age and Youth*, 1953, p. 113.

Headlam had always supported the idea of an independent women's college, but the developments which took place after his time were vastly different from those which he had envisaged. He had hoped for an institution where women could study for university degrees and diplomas; but the new college, recommended by the Royal Commission of 1913 and created in 1915, provided for students in Household and Social Science only: the Arts and Science departments for women were transferred back to the Strand. The Strand School and the Civil Service Department caused Headlam some searching of heart, for they were of considerable financial benefit. At first he was inclined to identify the former with the College, but found the problem of accommodation a serious one. In 1905, however, the Board of Education forced the issue by condemning the accommodation and threatening to withdraw its grants unless new premises were found. The London County Council finally came to the rescue, provided new buildings in Elm Park, Brixton, and took over its management. As for the Civil Service Department, which provided mainly evening courses for adults, this was taken over by its Head, Mr. Bragington, and established as S. George's College in Kingsway and Red Lion Square in 1911. Finally there was King's College School: in 1909 it had a debt of nearly £40,000, caused largely by the move to its new quarters in Wimbledon. The transfer to the new governing body was therefore delayed until an appeal could be made and the debt reduced. More than £10,000 was paid off within a year, and the new governing body took over on January 1, 1911.

This whole process of incorporation and disintegration was a remarkable achievement, revealing in Headlam administrative and statesmanlike qualities of the highest order. Nothing had been lost. The impoverished collection of incongruous elements had been replaced by a flourishing institution for university education, while all the segrated elements were able to continue as healthy and independent units. In yet another sphere, Headlam had made his mark.

II

Inevitably the Theological Department occupied a dominating place in Headlam's interests, and here again he successfully undertook a programme of reorganization and expansion. The Transfer Act not only anchored the Department firmly to the buildings in the Strand; it also strengthened its financial position. Hitherto it had borne more than its fair share of the administrative costs of the whole College: but now, in addition to being able to use all its revenues for its own needs, it also received the rent of the rooms let to the incorporated secular departments. Headlam's arrival also coincided with the reception through the Ecclesiastical Commissioners of an annual grant from the funds of the City Parochial Charities of £1,500, which facilitated the increase of staff and the reduction of students' fees. A further grant of £500 from the same source also provided a fund for exhibitions.[7] The Department therefore began to enjoy a prosperity hitherto unknown. There was a welcome increase in the number of students reading for holy orders—rising from 85 in 1901 to 220 in 1909, and Headlam's new additions to the staff brought together a galaxy of theological talent which for brilliance was probably unequalled in the country.[8]

Among his reforms was the establishment of a tutorial system and essay classes—a work in which he himself played a full part, despite his other heavy commitments. For those students under his care, this could be a trying experience. Apart from being a silent, formidable person with no ability to put men at their ease, he was impatient of delays and devastating in his criticisms. On one occasion an unfortunate student was reading a rather indifferent essay when through sheer nervousness he dropped his papers on the floor: hurriedly gathering them up, he began to read again, but then stopped suddenly. There was a dreadful silence. 'Go *onnnnnnnnnn,*' said Headlam in characteristic fashion. 'Oh sir,' stammered the unhappy student, 'I'm afraid I have left out three pages by mistake'—only to be answered, 'Go *onnnnnnnnnn.* Go on anywhere. It will not make the slightest difference to your argument.' Headlam saw nothing wrong in such a remark, nor did he consider its possible harmful effect on the student; he was passing judgment, not on the young man himself, but on the piece of work presented to him; it would not have occurred to him to do otherwise. On the other hand, he respected a man who was prepared to stand up to him; and if he observed a pupil with the makings of a first-class brain, he spared no effort to help him. Such was the case of one young man whose brilliant career was unfortunately cut short by death in the 1914–18 War. He was reading an essay on the De Incarnatione of S. Athanasius, in which he ventured upon some very drastic criticisms of the author's theology. Headlam, evidently considering the approach rather too self-confident, said in icy tones, 'What is your age, Mr. X?,' to which the young man flashed the reply, 'One year older than Athanasius when he wrote this

---

[7] *King's College Calendar 1903–4,* p. 1.
[8] During Headlam's time the Theological staff included Alexander Nairne, H. C. Beeching, E. E. Watson, H. J. White, Clement Rogers, W. R. Matthews, J. P. Whitney, Claude Jenkins, G. H. Box, S. Kirshbaum, H. M. Relton, G. E. Newson and A. Caldecotte.

book, sir.' It was characteristic of Headlam that from that moment he took the keenest interest in the young man's career. It was his weakness that he found it more difficult than most people to suffer fools gladly; and it would be probably true to say that he was a little too ready to regard as fools those whose minds did not move on the same lines as his own. It was considered high praise from him to be regarded as intelligent, and 'unintelligent' was one of his favourite words of censure.

Another of Headlam's reforms was the revival of inaugural lectures by new professors, and in this he himself set the example. His inaugural lecture, on 'The Sources and Authority of Dogmatic Theology,' regarded by some as one of his best pieces of work, was a brief but masterly survey of the impact on theology of the developments in science, philosophy and biblical criticism. He gave two regular courses of lectures—one on systematic theology and another on biblical and historical theology. As a lecturer he had no graces of gesture or eloquence, and certain clichés of speech tended to repeat themselves with great regularity—as, for example, 'I pass on to ask myself,' with the strong north-country 'a' always in evidence. His voice was high but always audible, and he could hold his audience by his lucid thought and his ability to clarify deep doctrine. There was never any difficulty in following his argument; nor did he as a rule repeat himself. His appeal was constantly to the intelligence.

Another successful venture was the reorganization of divinity lectures for non-theological students. When religious tests were abolished in 1903, attendance at divinity lectures ceased to be compulsory for such people : but free lectures were provided for those who wished to attend and were normally held in the lunch-hour. In 1905 Headlam transferred these lectures to 10 a.m. on Wednesdays and suspended all other lectures throughout the College at that hour. This arrangement became statutory under the Transfer Act of 1908, and the A.K.C. diploma was restricted either to theological students or to graduates of other faculties who had attended these weekly lectures for three years and passed an examination at the end of each year. It was surprisingly popular, and at times there were as many as fifty members of other faculties taking the course. It not only provided a valuable link between the theological and secular departments, but it also helped to send out men into all walks of life with a definite religious background.[9]

Attendance at Chapel, too, was only compulsory for theological students after 1903; but Headlam effectively encouraged the whole College to make frequent and regular use of it. Services at the begin-

[9] Barker, op. cit., pp. 115, 127; Hearnshaw, op. cit., p. 437.

ning and the end of each term, corporate communions and College sermons were extremely well attended. He often preached himself, and his sermons were truly academic in the best sense of the word. Although he could not produce anything like the ordinary devotional address, he was not to be dismissed as an arid intellectual. On occasions, when he spoke on some such theme as the eighth chapter of Romans, he seemed to be inspired—his hearers could sense that he really felt and appreciated the religious basis of S. Paul's teaching: and what he said could be memorable and telling. Dr. W. R. Matthews, speaking of a Quiet Day which Headlam once took on the rather surprising theme, 'Wise as serpents and harmless as doves,' considered it at the time to be rather dull and disappointing; yet later, on looking back, he realized that it was the only Quiet Day that had really stayed in his memory.

An important adjunct to the life of the Theological Department, second only to the Chapel itself, was the Hostel. In 1903 a small establishment in Mecklenburgh Square was the only residential accommodation the College possessed. It had begun in October 1901 with one house and twelve students; just before Headlam's arrival a second house had been taken and the numbers had risen to twenty-three; later a third house was added, bringing the total accommodation up to thirty. Under the admirable supervision of the Revd. G. E. Newsom it was an unqualified success as a venture in corporate life, but was never free from financial difficulties, despite an annual grant of £100 by the Ecclesiastical Commissioners from the Parochial Charities Fund. The initial cost of some £1,600 was met by the end of 1905, but the building was uncomfortable and expensive to run. Headlam decided to replace it by something better and larger, and in January 1911 he submitted a scheme to the College Council: a generous offer was then made by the Ecclesiastical Commissioners of a site in Vincent Square, Westminster, for 999 years at an annual ground rent of £400—less than half of what might have been asked—on condition that it was accepted within six months. Finally, in October an appeal was launched for £50,000—half for a new Hostel for sixty students, and half for the further development of the Theological Department. At the end of the first year, when Headlam ceased to be Principal, £8,500 had been collected and building operations began. The Bishop of London opened the first section on February 26, 1914. Once again Headlam was a generous subscriber, and there is no doubt that the existence of the Vincent Square Hostel was largely due to his efforts.

Headlam considered the primary function of the Theological Department, in common with similar departments in other universities, was the training of men for the ministry—a task which could only be done by men who believed in the faith they had to teach. Students should be taught by teachers of their own religious denomination. This, of course, produced no problem at King's College, because it was an Anglican foundation; but it did produce a problem for the Theological Faculty of the University of London as a whole, which had to cater for students of various denominations. The solution which had been found met with Headlam's complete approval—not an undenominational faculty, which earned the confidence of no one, but the affiliation to the University of the different denominational colleges which were in the area. Of these there were six—two Anglican, two Congregationalist, one Wesleyan and one Baptist, and together they formed the Theological Faculty of the University.[10] The University recognized their teachers and ensured adequate tests before conferring degrees. The Colleges, too, derived the benefit of sharing in the life of the University and were saved from the dangers of isolation.[11] Headlam saw the advantages of having the co-operation of such outstanding Nonconformist theologians as Dr. A. E. Garvie, Dr. T. P. Forsyth and Dr. Wheeler Robinson and made full use of it, sending his own students to them for lectures when opportunity served. The arrangement worked extremely well. Dr. Garvie testified many years later that the Theological Faculty was known in the University as one of the most harmonious of the faculties, and relations between Anglicans and Nonconformists were of the happiest.[12]

The work of training ordinands at King's College during Headlam's time was carried on in an atmosphere of uncertainty and controversy, but his rocklike defence of principles which he considered to be right met with no small measure of success. When he arrived, all ordinands entering the Theological Department had to pass the Bishops' Central Entrance Examination and a special class existed to prepare them for it. This had been instituted in 1893, replacing the College's own entrance examination, and the change had been generally accepted as one for the worse. Many students sought the aid of special coaches and cramming institutions; and much of the work was learned by heart. Headlam found one candidate who had secured 80 per cent. of the total marks in Greek, but was later proved to be almost entirely ignorant of the language. Feeling this to be unsatisfactory, Headlam secured the assent of the Bishops on the College Council—the Bishops of London, Southwark and St. Albans—to institute a preliminary

---

[10] Anglican—King's College and S. John's College; Congregationalist—New College, Hampstead and Hackney College; Wesleyan—Richmond College; Baptist—Regent's Park College.

[11] 'The Church and the New Universities, *The University Review*, vol. 7, no. 39, pp. 168–9.

[12] A. E. Garvie, *Memories and Meanings of my Life*, 1938, p. 213.

year's course with an internal entrance examination,[13] followed by a two year course for the A.K.C. diploma, which was very much on the same lines as the course for the London B.D. Whenever possible students were encouraged to read for the latter; and candidates for both the diploma and the degree in fact attended many of the same lectures. This scheme proved to be wholly admirable, both from the academic and the spiritual point of view. Not only had the students the advantage of being under College discipline for a longer period, but it gave Headlam an opportunity of providing them with far more pastoral training than most ordinands were accustomed to receive.

The normal examination system for ordinands in other universities and colleges was rather different. For the university graduate nothing further was usually required beyond his degree than the bishop's private ordination examination. This varied with every diocese, although the lines of the Universities' Preliminary Examination were generally followed. The non-graduate was normally expected to pass the Bishops' Central Entrance Examination before going to a theological college for two years, after which he had to pass the Universities' Preliminary Examination. Headlam's opinion of the latter examination was almost as poor as his opinion of the former. Its influence upon theological colleges was bad; it stereotyped the subjects of teaching and its general effect was 'to destroy originality of outlook, to compel every one to work within a limited sphere, (and) to work not with the view of mastering theological problems but with the view of answering questions.'[14] From this system King's College was largely exempt, for its preliminary examination and A.K.C. diploma were accepted as adequate substitutes for the official examinations. But these concessions were threatened by new proposals of the Church authorities, and Headlam resolutely contested every inch of the way.

The first move was made in May 1906, when the Upper House of the Convocation of Canterbury endorsed a resolution submitted by Bishop Gore that the time had come to secure a more uniform and adequate standard of qualification and training for ordinands.[15] Although Gore emphasized that he was advocating no detailed plan, but merely a general principle for consideration, the idea gained ground that among other things a single compulsory external examina-

[13] It also provided the College with an opportunity for weeding out unsuitable candidates. For example, of forty-five candidates who entered in 1910–11, seven left voluntarily during the course of the year and one was sent down; in the examination at the end of the year four failed and were recommended to leave, ten were referred for a second year, three were referred in one subject, and twenty were passed. (*King's College Calendar 1911–12*, p. 537.)
[14] 'The Training and Examination of Candidates for Orders,' *C.Q.R.*, vol. 71, p. 125.
[15] *Chronicle of Convocation 1906*, pp. 258–67.

tion was contemplated. Such an examination would obviously invalidate the A.K.C. for ordination purposes, and Headlam wrote to Gore on March 18, 1907 :

'It seems to me, from the point of view of everything which is felt by those engaged in education and our experiences in London, to represent a thoroughly retrograde movement. All that you gain by having a general examination is that it will make it a little easier to keep out one or two weaker men, but it will do nothing to raise the standard of the majority. . . . (Here) the result would only be a great individual inconvenience. Any one who had passed our examination would immediately have to prepare for a second examination. This would interfere with his proper reading for orders, and would have a very disastrous effect on the education our students receive, if they were all generally adopted. . . . We should simply degenerate into preparing for examinations.'

The second proposal, passed by the Upper House of Canterbury Convocation in October 1909, and by the Upper House of York in 1912, was that after 1917 all ordinands should be required to possess a university degree. Headlam agreed with the general scope and purpose of the resolution, but felt that it was unpractical : not only was there no uniform standard of degrees throughout the universities, but also it was unfair to older men—many of whom came to King's College—and particularly at the moment when the Church urgently needed men.[16] What was really needed was the development of theological instruction in a university atmosphere. This could be done in a variety of ways. The older universities—Oxford and Cambridge— should provide a two-year course of post-graduate training for orders ; while the new universities should make provision for ordinands, first by establishing hostels with a Church connection where ordinands could live while studying for an arts degree, and secondly by co-operating with newly-established theological colleges in their area with a view to creating theological faculties. Developments on these lines could be facilitated by the formation of a Central Council to supervise and direct the training of men for the ministry, and in the event of such a scheme being established, bishops would then be able to dispense with the more academic portions of their own ordination examinations.[17] Headlam urged these views upon the annual conference of the Principals of theological colleges, and in January 1909 the conference passed two resolutions, urging first the creation of

[16] Ibid., p. 131.
[17] Ibid., pp. 133–9.

Diocesan Ordination Candidates' Councils to work in conjunction with a Central Council, and secondly the closest possible co-operation between the theological colleges and the new universities. In January 1910 the conference unanimously passed another resolution, deprecating the proposed requirement of a degree from all ordinands, and suggesting that for some men an adequate alternative course of general education should be recognized.

Headlam was determined to oppose anything that would weaken or destroy the ordination course at King's College. He therefore suggested that if the A.K.C. course could be recognized as an adequate preparation for orders, he would be prepared to extend it from two to three years and accept external examiners. If recognition was refused, however, not only would the effect on King's College be disastrous, but the supply of ordinands, especially for the dioceses of London, Southwark and St. Albans, would be seriously affected. Report reached him, however, that the Bishops were prepared to reject these suggestions ; so he wrote to the Archbishop of Canterbury on June 25, 1910, deploring the fact that such decisions were being reached without the College being given the slightest chance to defend itself : such treatment of the Professorial Board—a very distinguished body of men who comprised the main portion of the University Theological Faculty—had caused considerable bitterness and resentment. 'As a College we have been working hard year after year, improving to the best of our capacity the training of the large body of men who are coming to us, and we find that, instead of being assisted by the Bishops, generally—with the exception of those who know us— we are in danger at every turn by regulations which are being imposed on us.' The protest was effective, and the Archbishop invited Headlam to come and state his case. This matter had not been settled when Headlam resigned as Principal in 1912; but in January 1913 the Bishops definitely decided not to acknowledge the A.K.C. as the equivalent of a degree. This meant the virtual extinction of the Theological Department, while the suggestion that it should be converted into a coaching establishment for the degree of some other university where the requirements were not so exacting was bitterly resented. Headlam regarded the decision as something of a personal insult, for the A.K.C. course in its existing form was largely his own creation. In March 1913 he published an *Open Letter to the Archbishop of Canterbury on the Training of Candidates,* a document which was hailed with delight not only by theological colleges, but by some of the Bishops themselves—notably Dr. Burge, the Bishop of Southwark. At the same time the Theological Board of King's College and a number of theological colleges sent addresses of remonstrance to the Bishops.

The recently-created Central Advisory Council also considered the matter and urged moderation. As a result on May 21, 1913 the Bishops agreed to postpone the operation of the regulation demanding a degree of all ordinands until 1920, and to exempt from this regulation candidates over 26 years of age who undertook an approved three years' course at a college : the A.K.C. course was also referred to a special committee for consideration.

Headlam's *Open Letter* was a forthright document which received prominent and sympathetic notice in the press.[18] At the outset he vindicated his claim to speak on the subject with authority—he had taught in the Theological School at Oxford, he had been examining chaplain to the Bishop of Southwell for thirteen years and Principal of King's College for ten, and he was the only person in a position to attend the meetings of Principals of both theological colleges and university colleges. His experience had impressed upon him two things. The first was the advantage of men having a definite professional training—the following of an intelligent and carefully mapped out course, dealing with the principles of the profession they intended to follow, and carefully arranged so as to make them efficient in that profession. The second was the injury done to education by over-organization, by interference with the freedom of teaching, and by excessive devotion to examinations. The correct principle to follow in training ordinands was to make the existing system as efficient as possible and then suggest new developments, rather than destroy existing arrangements by enacting new regulations based on educational methods which had been condemned over and over again. The Bishops' proposals were based on the false assumption that clerical standards could be raised by means of examinations : in effect the only result would be to create an enormous system of cramming. The requirement of a degree was purely arbitrary : standards differed with every university ; and for older men with experience of life the training involved was not necessarily the best preparation for orders. Finally, if the proposal to demand attendance at a theological college was to be taken in its narrow sense of attendance at a residential theological college, it was a mistake. Whatever their advantages, such colleges were not without defects and ought not to be made the sole avenue of entry into the Ministry. They generally failed to provide intellectual stimulus and frequently covered students with a veneer of piety or ecclesiasticism without allowing it to get a deep hold.[19] He then

[18] *The Times, The Guardian, The Church Times, The Record* and *The Spectator* all gave it their support.

[19] Headlam called this 'seminarist education' and had the danger of divorcing religion from real learning, and producing an unintelligent religion. The bad effects of such a system were obvious in France. ('The Church and the New Universities,' *The University Review*, vol. 7, no. 39, pp. 165–7.)

formulated his own proposals. In the first place Oxford and Cambridge should establish post-graduate ordination courses : and if these could end with a diploma rather than a degree, graduate theological colleges might well be affiliated and avail themselves of them. Secondly, theological colleges should be created in connection with the new universities. Thirdly, the course for non-graduates should be extended to three years : for them an examination on the lines of the Universities Preliminary would still be necessary, but it should be flexible—as far as possible on the lines of an internal examination and involving some freedom of teaching, a situation which could be achieved by means of a close relationship between the teachers and the examining body. Finally, the claim of King's College for recognition of its own internal examination might well be justified on the grounds of the size and experience of its staff : the A.K.C. diploma was of the nature of a degree and should be recognized as such, particularly when the College was willing to extend the course to three years.

Apart from securing a reprieve of the King's College system, it is interesting to note how Headlam's action and policy influenced subsequent developments. Owing to problems due mainly to the War, it was found necessary to defer still further the regulation requiring all ordinands to obtain a degree, while investigations were made into the courses at King's College, Durham, Kelham and Lampeter. Both Oxford and Cambridge established post-graduate ordination courses after the War, and the Central Advisory Council explored the possibilities of establishing hostels for ordinands at the new universities. It also undertook to inspect theological colleges, discussed their courses with a view to improving the system of training, assumed control of examinations, and watched over the supply of ordination candidates as a whole, giving special attention to those who had received little early education. Headlam had laboured again with telling effect.

CHAPTER SIX

The Principal of King's College
Resignation and the War

I

HEADLAM fully extended himself in his threefold office of Principal, Dean and Professor, sacrificing his leisure and some of the pleasanter aspects of a scholar's life for the sake of the College. But just as he extended himself, so he made the same demands upon his staff. When he asked Claude Jenkins to join him as his secretary and sub-editor of *The Church Quarterly Review*, Dr. Kirsopp Lake remarked, 'I had rather be a galley slave.' Headlam, in fact, never seemed to realize just how hard his staff did work. His principle was to choose men as carefully as he could, give them as much work as they could take—often far more than they expected—and then trust them completely to get it done. His confidence in them was almost always justified, and in later life he was not slow to express appreciation of what had been achieved by his loyal and hard-working assistants at London. On the administrative side he owed a great debt to the College secretary and the College treasurer. The secretary, Mr. Walter Smith, who had had administrative experience in India, was most helpful and co-operative once he had secured from Headlam, as he had been compelled to do from Dr. Robertson before him, the recognition that the secretary of King's College was the servant of the College Council and not of the Principal, and that they were co-ordinate powers who had to work together. The treasurer, the Hon. W. F. D. Smith and later the second Lord Hambledon, was a brother Fellow of All Souls and a most generous benefactor to the College, on whose judgment Headlam greatly relied.

On the social side he owed a great deal to his wife, who sacrificed herself completely on his behalf, doing in a variety of ways what she could to conserve his time and energy. She faithfully guarded him from interruptions when she felt he ought not to be disturbed : no one was allowed to sit in his own particular chair ; and no one was allowed to touch *The Times* until he had read it. In the social life of the College she was a tower of strength. Headlam had few social graces, and almost no capacity for small talk; he saw no occasion to converse with anybody unless there was some direct reason for doing so; unconsciously therefore he often appeared rude. She did much to make up for these defects, however. She made a point of getting to know the wives of all the members of the staff, from professors to porters and visited them all in their homes, a task which at that time involved many long and tedious journeys into the suburbs or the country : and she made the Principal's house a social centre for the whole College, entertaining almost daily on an extensive scale. Commenting on her contribution to the life of the College, a friend wrote after her death in 1924 : 'Living as she did in the College and possessing a genius for hospitality and friendship, she was never happier than in her efforts to do what she could to overcome the barriers of merely official relationships. To convert a visit of ceremony into a pleasure is one of the most difficult as, if successful, it is one of the most worthy of social achievements. But Mrs. Headlam had the gift of putting people at their ease, of divining subjects in which they were interested or making them interested in things or people new to them; of enlisting the co-operation of everybody and forgetting no one. And the attraction was felt by every one, young and old, students and staff, as well as by many other friends, because it was exercised in a manner so natural and so entirely unstudied.' [1] Few people realized the cost of all this. The house was a most difficult one to run—there were some fifty stairs between each floor and a hundred between the kitchen and the drawing-room on the first floor : the strain upon Mrs. Headlam and her small domestic staff was considerable. When Headlam returned to Whorlton in 1913 she broke down with heart trouble and never fully recovered. One of her nieces wrote, 'King's College knew a tireless Grande Dame : after the War Oxford saw a tired, ageing woman.' That Headlam was not insensible to all these efforts on the part of his wife is evident in a letter which he wrote to her from London a few months after his resignation : 'I think they find at King's College that they can do very much better without me than without you.'

Many of the staff and students were also invited to house parties at Whorlton during the vacations. At these a rigid timetable was kept. During the mornings guests amused themselves while Headlam worked in his study; after lunch came visits to beauty spots in the district; then in the evening, after dinner, the party played whist until bedtime at ten o'clock prompt. With younger people both Headlam and his wife rather fancied themselves as matchmakers, but as often as not their efforts failed to produce the desired results, much to their chagrin. Nor were the children forgotten. He was very fond of them,

[1] *The Times*, March 26, 1924.

and it was one of the tragedies of his life that he and his wife never had any of their own. He was not the sort of person who would romp with them, but it gave him great delight to watch them enjoying themselves and to watch their pleasure at receiving presents. Two occasions in the year were red-letter days for the children of the staff. The first was at Christmas when he took large parties of them to the pantomime ; and the second was on the day of the Lord Mayor's Show when they thronged on to the great terrace outside the Principal's house, from which there was a grandstand view of the procession along the Embankment, after which they were entertained to a magnificent tea party.

Headlam also gave much time and thought to the social activities of the students. Not being a good mixer, and with his austere and seemingly unapproachable manner, he was never popular in the generally accepted sense of the word : but he took the trouble to see that the various athletic and social bodies of the College were well organized and financially sound. He was largely instrumental in acquiring some very fine playing fields in West London, which served the College well for many years; while it was to his credit that he assisted in the revival of the College Union Society, attending its meetings as often as he could and on occasions taking the chair. He also saw to it that all the societies had accommodation within the College, despite the lack of space. And just as he had the interests of the students as a whole at heart, so it was with the individual. To a man in trouble, financial or otherwise, he could be very kind : he had a sympathy which was awakened by real misfortune, and once he had championed a man's cause, he would stand by him to the end.

For his own relaxation Headlam had little time. It was a matter of regret that he had no garden ; but he began to collect Greek coins, a pastime at which he set out to make himself an expert. His collection was small but exceedingly beautiful, and one of which he became very proud. He loved to show them to his friends and to the staff, although the latter viewed them with mixed feelings; as one of them remarked, 'In view of our meagre salaries at that time, our interest in numismatics was in the collection of current rather than in ancient coinage.' Most of his collecting was a lunch-time activity. He would step across from King's College to Southeby's Auction Rooms, then in Waterloo Place and stay for half an hour at the sales, which began at 1.30 p.m., before returning to the afternoon's work at the College. He did little, if any, original research in this field, and his collection was not one of really first-class importance : but it was a very pleasant collection, chosen with the eye of a scholar and an historian. The historian's interest was obvious in the way in which he arranged his coins. Normally they were arranged geographically, a method which had the advantage of simplicity and custom, but was not founded on any scientific principle and did not exhibit the growth and development of coinage. Headlam arranged his coins historically, so that coins of the same period from different places lay together, illustrating in an interesting way political, social and artistic developments in Greek life. Obviously in such a collection of just under five hundred pieces, only the beginnings of such an arrangement could be attempted, but it was sufficient to show its advantages and warrant its use in larger collections. He wrote a short article on this method of arrangement in the *Numismatic Chronicle* for 1908.[2] After he returned to Whorlton and to his garden in 1913, however, his interest in numismatics waned, and he sold his collection at Southeby's in May 1916 at considerable loss.

II

Some idea of the development of the College under Headlam can be gathered from the figures in the Report of the Treasury's Quinquennial Inspection in 1906. Between 1901 and 1906 the total number of students in all categories rose from 5,145 to 6,897, while there was a significant increase in the number of people pursuing higher courses of study. In 1901–2 nearly all the degrees obtained were in Medicine : between 1901 and 1906 forty-eight students took degrees in Arts or Science, and in the single year 1906–7 there were forty Arts or Science degrees given. The number of post-graduate students also rose during the same period from thirty-two to one hundred and fifty-four, while the staff increased from seventy-seven to one hundred and ten.[3] Nor was Headlam content to have a larger staff under the old conditions : he had a high conception of their office and laboured hard to secure for them better salaries and conditions of service. By 1908 he had secured two substantial increases in salary and had started a pension scheme.[4] This not only relieved their financial anxieties ; it also went some way to removing the necessity for many of them to supplement their incomes by outside work, thereby enabling them to devote more time and energy to the College and their own research work.

The increase of staff and students raised problems of equipment,

---

[2] 'Some Notes on Sicilian Coins,' *The Numismatic Chronicle,* 4th series, vol. 8.
[3] *Calendar of King's College,* 1904–5, p. xlviii ; 1907–8, pp. xlviii–xlix.
[4] *Calendar,* 1905–6, p. xxxviii ; 1909–10, p. lxiv.

accommodation and income. The lack of accommodation was a serious matter. In the Theological Department, for example, there was only one regular lecture room available, while there were no private rooms at the disposal of the staff for tutorial work. Or again, in the Physics Department the apparatus of senior students had to be packed away to make room for the work of junior students, even though their experiments were not completed. Research work also had to be undertaken in the ordinary practical classrooms, where there was a maximum liability to accidents and disturbances; and in the one room reserved for research, there was inevitable crowding and inconvenience. Against all this, the College was poor, and stood on what was probably the most expensive site of any college in the country : the acquisition of adjacent property was therefore no light matter. Headlam faced the problem boldly, evolving schemes which utilized the existing space to the utmost, and in this he was helped by the departure of King's College School and the Civil Service Classes for new homes. The accommodation in the Chemistry and Physics Departments were nearly doubled; the Mechanical and Engineering workshops received large additions to their equipment; new laboratories for Zoology and Biology were provided; the Library was entirely refitted; and the Chapel was renovated.[5] But Headlam had even bolder schemes, involving if possible the acquisition of all the property to the north and east of the College bounded by the Strand and Surrey Street; and plans for a complete reorganization of the College were drawn up at considerable cost. These plans were prepared for exhibition to the visiting members of the Board of Education Grants Committee in 1912, but to Headlam's mortification, only one member deigned to inspect them, and then only for a few moments. It is significant, however, that Headlam's plans were not wasted; for not only were they at the basis of the reconstruction which was finally completed in 1952, but the College acquired nearly fifty years later a considerable portion of the property which Headlam had urged it to acquire and at vastly greater cost.

The problem of expansion was inevitably bound up with the problem of finance. The abolition of religious tests undoubtedly did much to free the restriction on grants; those from the Government rose from £2,200 in 1897 to £8,650 in 1907, and those from the London County Council rose from £1,500 to £3,500 during the same period. Nevertheless the demands on the College income were incessantly increasing, and Headlam felt that these grants, welcome though they were, were not commensurate with the enormous population for which the University had to provide, nor with the sums at the disposal of other

[5] Calendar, 1907–8, pp. xlix–l; *Annual Report 1906*, p. 389.

universities and colleges. Furthermore, he always feared that the acceptance of money from the Government might ultimately involve a loss of freedom and a measure of Government control. Admittedly, relations with the State had been good while grants had been in the hands of the Treasury; but when these were taken over by the Board of Education in 1910, he viewed the change with alarm, feeling that the dangers of interference had increased. Subsequent events proved his fears to be justified.

He hoped that some of the College's problems and difficulties might be solved when the appointment of a Royal Commission on University Education in London was announced on February 19, 1909, under the chairmanship of J. B. (later Lord) Haldane. Unfortunately its final Report, which did not appear until March 1913, the month Headlam ceased to be Principal, proved to be a bitter disappointment, and he considered its recommendations for King's College to be absolutely disastrous. In the first place, as we have seen, it suggested a complete reversal of his own policy for King's College for Women. He had constantly devoted his energies towards creating a comprehensive women's college. In 1910, when the question of a site was under consideration, he asked Lord Haldane whether they would not be well advised to defer further action until the Commission had issued its Report. Lord Haldane assured him, however, that there was no need for deferment and encouraged him to proceed with the scheme. This Headlam did, obtaining after considerable trouble and with the help of Sir Walter Phillimore a valuable site on Campden Hill. His feelings were therefore understandably bitter when the Commission's Report rejected all ideas of a comprehensive college and recommended that its activities should be confined to household science. Its second recommendation affected the Medical Department of the Faculty of Science, which was organized independently of the Hospital Medical School, and was recognized by the University as one of the official centres for preliminary and intermediate medical studies, three other hospitals—Westminster, S. George's and Charing Cross—all sending their students there for the first part of their medical training. The Commission suggested closing this flourishing department altogether. Thirdly, it recommended the removal of all the evening classes and the Day Training Department. Finally, it suggested that the College itself, reduced in size and status, should be removed from the Strand to a new site in Bloomsbury. The proposals were a 'devastating programme of dispersion, dissolution and migration,'[6] happily never fully implemented, but at the time of their publication more than enough to break Headlam's heart. The question of the transfer of the

[6] Hearnshaw, op. cit., p. 453.

College to a new site had in fact already arisen. In 1912, when the Board of Education had taken over control of the University grants from the Treasury, without consulting either the College or the University, it had condemned the buildings in the Strand and had announced that grants would be withheld in future unless a new site were found and a new College erected. To Headlam this meant that loss of freedom and independence which he had always feared. Only in December 1911 in his annual Report to the Senate he had commented on the transfer of the grants to the Board of Education : 'The result is to give the Board control over all university education, and to deprive the Universities of the position of independence which they formerly occupied. The Board also controls the distribution of the technical grants, and the grants for day training students. The result is to create opportunities for taking part in the internal affairs of universities and colleges in many directions.' This was one of the factors which prompted him to announce his resignation as Principal in October 1912.

Another factor was his relations with the Senate. Its composition was as follows : one third were University teachers, elected by their faculties; another third were graduates of the University, elected by Convocation; the final third were the heads of the Schools of the University, together with the nominees of the Board of Education, the County Council and other such bodies as the Inns of Court, the City Companies and the City Corporation. It was therefore a very mixed body, containing some very able and distinguished men : there were occasions, as Sir Ernest Barker has said, when a debate in the Senate could appear like a minor edition of a debate in the House of Lords.[7] But it suffered from its rivalries—between the internal and external sides of the University, between the various colleges, and between rival factions; and the whole situation was often embittered by personal animosities. It was galling for the heads of schools to find that they could be outvoted by a combination of teachers and graduates; and it was a hard fact for the head of a school to accept that relatively junior members of his own staff could be somebody and he virtually a nobody. 'The whole situation was somewhat parallel to an uneasy system of international relations : great powers stood at issue, massed their armaments, attempted a balance, and achieved a clash.'[8] It was inevitable that in such an assembly, particularly in the face of opposition and criticism, Headlam was never at his best; for it was too easy to make him angry. Being easily provoked, and being by nature a masterful and combatative man, he tended to excite a good

[7] Barker, *Age and Youth,* p. 134.
[8] Ibid., p. 135.

deal of opposition, and there were men on the Senate who were big enough to return as good as he gave. Those who disliked him or opposed him sometimes showed a malicious pleasure in provoking him, just to see him plunge his knuckles into his mouth and gnaw them—a well-known and sure sign of his rising anger.

A third factor was the friction between King's College and University College. There had always been an element of rivalry between the two; and here again Headlam's own temperament was not always helpful: but it was his constant complaint that his efforts at co-operation were not reciprocated. There was, for example, the scheme for inter-collegiate lectures—a scheme which not only facilitated contacts between the teachers and students of the different colleges, but also reduced the amount of lecturing to be done by the teachers. The scheme was tried in a number of faculties, but in every case there was friction and trouble between the two Colleges. To Headlam, University College represented ultra-academic influence, making a great parade of research. He often said that it wanted to confine the honours work of the whole University to itself, and to regard itself as THE University: in fact, its idea of co-operation was not co-operation but absorption.

Then again, Headlam was obviously working too hard. His activities covered an enormous field, and the pace was one which he could not possibly hope to maintain for long. Finally the call of his beloved Whorlton became ever stronger. In February 1909 came the death of his father, followed a year later by that of his step-mother. The family estate now became an added care, and as he had told his father before he died, 'I shall certainly look on the care of Whorlton for which you have made such full provision a religious duty, and one which I shall discharge with affection.'

On October 11, 1912, he submitted his resignation to the Chairman of the College Council. The letter was published in *The Times* on October 31.

'My dear Lord Bishop (of London),

'I am writing to you formally to announce to your Lordship what I have already intimated to you privately, that I propose shortly to resign my position as Principal and Dean of King's College, and to request you to inform the Council of my intention. You may be quite sure that I would not take such a step without the most serious consideration, and I feel it due to you and the Council which has always treated me with such uniform kindness that I should state at some length the reasons that have led me to this decision.

'My principal reason, and the one that has weighed with me most, is a personal one. I am anxious to obtain leisure for literary and theo-

D

logical work, and that I feel is quite impossible in my present position. I have reached an age when I cannot any longer hope to have the strength, if I have the ability, to do what I wish; if I wait any longer, I shall find myself too old for effective work.

'But there are other reasons which have weighed with me that I desire to have an opportunity of stating publicly. The Board of Education has recently, through the control of what was formerly the Treasury grant to universities and university colleges, obtained some authority over universities, and it has informed the College that its present site is inadequate and therefore that it will have to be removed. It seems to me most unfortunate that the Board should have initiated its control over universities by peremptory and arbitrary action, such as would not be possible in dealing with the smallest National School. Even ordinary courtesy should have demanded some preliminary conference with the College and with the University, which is now responsible for carrying it on. The Committee on whose advice the Board acted considered the most cursory visit to the College all that was necessary. A scheme for the improvement of the present buildings and the extension of the College on the present site has been worked out with great labour, and very great expense has been incurred in obtaining expert advice. Only one member of the Committee cared to examine the scheme, and he considered five minutes sufficient time to devote to it.

'It is admitted that the present site is confined, but its position makes it of the greatest value as a centre for university teaching; and while I have always kept in my mind the possibility of removing the College to another site, such a course would only be justified as part of a coherent and well thought out scheme for the unification of the University of London. There is no evidence that the Board of Education has formed any such scheme, and their whole action is an instance of arbitrary administrative interference of a character such as seriously interfered with those conditions of freedom and independence under which alone a university is able to perform its functions effectively.

'As regards myself I must honestly say that the position of Head of a College exposed to such methods of interference is not one which I desire or am qualified to hold; and it is clear also to me that in the interests of the College I should resign now unless I am prepared to continue as Principal for another ten years. A new policy will have to be formulated. That will mean either a long and difficult controversy with the Board of Education or the building of a new College. I do not feel that I should now care to embark on either : I must leave to others the carrying out of whatever scheme is decided upon, and I think that whoever has to carry out the future policy of the College should have a considerable voice in formulating it.

'A further reason that has prompted me in deciding to resign is that I do not feel that I could much longer stand the strain of my present office. In any case the combination of the three offices of Head of one of the largest University Colleges, Head of a Theological College, and Professor of Theology is too much for one person. Were it not for the loyal and ungrudging assistance that I have received from many members of the staff, it would have been impossible for me to have carried out my dutiees, and I am glad to think that my present work will in the interests of the College and of themselves be divided between at least two successors. But the strain of the position has been very materially increased during the period of nearly ten years that I have held it by the constant opposition to which the College has been exposed, and by what has been, in my opinion, the unfair treatment that it has received. Many difficulties have been brought before the Council or the Delegacy, but there are many others that have been dealt with privately, and I do not think that there is any one who quite realizes how great the opposition to be encountered has often been.

'The situation has been equally difficult in dealing both with outside bodies and with the Senate of the University. While some members of the Senate seem to consider that the well-being of the University is injured by the prosperity of its Colleges, there have been other and more serious causes of friction. All my experience has shewn me that the assistance of members of the professorial staff in the government of a university is essential to its well-being; but I am not equally convinced that it is desirable to place professors of one college in a position to interfere with the internal government of another college. Again and again schemes for the development of King's College— schemes which in some cases have been ultimately most successful— have needed the strenuous efforts to carry them through the Academic Council and the Senate. Looking back on the time that I have been connected with the College, I cannot help feeling astonished at the opposition which has been so often exhibited to see efforts made for its development, and I can honestly say that the strain that it has caused has been at times almost intolerable.

'In conclusion I am glad to have an opportunity of expressing my gratitude for the great kindness and consideration that have been shewn me throughout by the Council of the College, and for the continuous loyalty of the staff, for whose unselfish work in the service of the College I have always had the greatest admiration.

'As regards the time of my resignation I should of course be anxious to accommodate myself in every way to the convenience of the College.

My purpose at present is however to resign on December 31st of this year.

I am,

My Lord Bishop,

Yours very sincerely,

A. C. HEADLAM.'

The news came as a shock to the whole College, and expressions of regret were widespread. Archbishop Davidson wrote, 'I do feel that your going hence will be a very real disaster for King's College and it creates a sense of almost bewilderment in my mind.' Professor Nairne, who was able to see the situation from within, while regretting his departure, wrote, 'I am glad to think of your being freed from what has evidently become far worse than toil; only my gorge rises at the malignants who cause such trouble.' Professor W. B. Halliburton, of the Medical Faculty, wrote in *The College Review* of the wonderful way in which Headlam had served the interests of departments other than his own : 'When Dr. Headlam came here he entered on his duties with a reputation as a great scholar and literary man. We therefore fully anticipated that he would be familiar with the working of the literary and theological departments. It is superfluous to add that this anticipation has been fully realized, and that this aspect of College life and work has received a due share of the Principal's fostering care. What we did not foresee was the quick and ready brain and the businesslike acumen which enabled Dr. Headlam in a marvellously short space of time to grasp and understand the needs of the other departments of work with which he had hitherto been unfamiliar. He leaves us an expert on scientific and medical education, on hospital management and construction, on the training necessary for the engineer, the architect and the lawyer.' [9] Finally there was the opinion of the student : 'We received in (Dr. Robertson's) place a Principal of another kind, but one who has certainly not been less trusted, less loved, or less efficient. The crisis continues and still does continue, but too much has been accomplished during the last nine years to be easily reversed, and though Dr. Headlam has roughly disturbed any who might have been sleeping in a fool's paradise, his own high spirit has always been calmest in the storm and he has trained his officers not to be frightened.' [10] From many quarters he was urged to reconsider his decision. This he refused to do ; but he finally conceived the idea of maintaining his link with the College by retaining his Chair of Dogmatic Theology—a suggestion which met with the approval of the

[9] *King's College Review,* December 1912, vol. 14, no. 3, pp. 1–3.
[10] Ibid., pp. 3–4.

College authorities. He eventually handed over to his successor, Professor Burrows of Manchester University, in March 1913.

III

Headlam now settled at Whorlton with his books and his garden, coming up to London periodically to deliver his lectures. This more leisured existence was short-lived, however. At the end of 1913 he was invited to deliver the Moorhouse Lectures at Melbourne, Australia in the following May. These lectures had been recently founded by Dr. Clarke, Archbishop of Melbourne, in memory of Dr. Moorhouse, who had been bishop from 1876 until 1886; and an addition to the endowment by Dr. Moorhouse himself made it possible for distinguished scholars from England to be appointed from time to time. Headlam chose Miracles as his subject, and his lectures were subsequently published with additions under the title *The Miracles of the New Testament*. They were summed up by Dr. J. H. Bernard as a sane, well-balanced statement which would do much to bring out the true significance of the miraculous in the Creed. They were very critical of the rationalists, and very loyal to the great supernatural truths of the Christian faith.[11]

Headlam made the most of his time in Australia by undertaking a whirlwind tour, inspecting every conceivable institution, from the universities to sheep farms and gold mines, and even finding time to pay a flying visit to Tasmania to see members of the Headlam family who had settled there. He also delivered further lectures at Ballarat, Sydney, Newcastle and Brisbane, all of which were warmly welcomed by the local clergy, whose contacts with theological scholars were all too few; one clergyman even went so far as to describe his visit as that of an angel. His stay lasted a bare month, but during that short time he gathered a surprising amount of information about the life of the Church. On his return to England he contributed a series of articles on the Australian Church to *The Challenge,* providing a valuable portrait of a colonial church of the period not easily available elsewhere.[12] He was impressed with what he had seen and heard. The Church had a great deal more life than he had expected to find from reports in England : it was efficiently managed and services were better attended than in England. Its weaknesses seemed to be twofold. In the first place its hold on the intellectual life of the country appeared to be slight : the universities lacked theological faculties, there were few

[11] J. H. Bernard, 'Christian Miracles,' *C.Q.R.,* vol. 80, pp. 171–80.
[12] 'The Church in Australia,' *The Challenge,* July and August 1914.

graduates among the ordinands, and the average intellectual standard
of the clergy was not rising. Secondly, its impact on public life and
organized labour was not very effective—even less effective than in
England. Nevertheless, he formed a favourable impression of the
Church leaders he had met, and particularly of Bishop J. F. Stretch
of Newcastle, notwithstanding his deafness and unconventional behaviour—he was reputed to spend most of his time in pyjamas and to
swear with considerable vigour. Headlam finally sailed from Darwin
on June 2, sailing via the Philippines and China to Japan, where he
delivered further lectures. From Japan he returned home via Korea,
Manchuria, Russia and across Europe, arriving back on July 29, just
five days before the outbreak of war.

For Headlam the War to a large extent meant carrying on as usual,
as far as was possible. His work at King's College diminished with the
gradual absorption of students into the forces; and, of course, being
over military age, he was not required for active service. He did, however, join the Volunteer Force, and as Private Headlam drilled most
conscientiously both at London and at Whorlton, where the local
commander happened to be his own gardener. He regarded the discipline of being under orders as something essentially right and wholesome, although one might have expected him to chafe. 'I have been
doing an hour's military instruction this morning. The man who drilled
us was Regimental Sergeant Major of the Grenadier Guards. He was
very good, and he talked to me in a way that a schoolmaster would
not talk to a boy of six years old. It is extraordinary good for one to
stand to attention without moving a muscle (if you can) and be told
of all your faults relentlessly.' In spite of the fact, however, that his
life was disrupted less than that of most men, he was very much alive
to the trend of world events. Throughout the whole period he surveyed the war situation in successive numbers of *The Church Quarterly Review*—a work which benefited from the expert help and advice
on the political side of his brother James, who served in the
Propaganda and Information Departments, and on the military side
of his cousin, Major-General John Headlam, a distinguished soldier.
Nor was he a mere dispassionate armchair critic : he felt the tragedy
of the whole business and the waste of life very keenly. He wrote to
his wife from All Souls on November 2, 1917, 'We had our service
this morning. I do not think that I have ever felt the tragedy of the
War more—the chapel filled almost entirely with old men and the roll
of the killed and the feeling of sadness. At one point in the service a
great sob came from Wilkinson, whose son was killed : and I did not
know whether I should get through ; but just when I thought I might
fail I got stronger.' He felt that the War was a judgment from God,

bidding men to seek out their defects and consider how they might be remedied.[13] The country's principal defect was an intellectual sluggishness and an intentional blindness to facts: apathy had been evident for some years in politics, science, commerce and education. Nor had the Church been free from this defect: it had lacked 'an intellect on fire with the Spirit, an intellect full of eagerness, but an intellect controlled by reverence.'[14] Pastoral theology had hardly realized the situation, and there was a real want of capacity to interpret the problems of life. What the average Englishman wanted was a Church which would respond to his needs, teach a message which he could understand, and lift him up to a higher level of life: but this, somehow, was just what he never got.[15] A fundamental change was needed —a revived intellectual life which would mean the application of thought to everything instead of acquiescence in unmeaning customs or bad traditions; a grasp of Christianity in its completeness and its simplicity; a determination to be in living contact with people. It was, in fact, just the gift of the Spirit that was needed.[16] It was to this end that Headlam hoped some help would come from such things as the Archbishops' Commission on Church and State, the National Mission of Repentance and Hope, and the Life and Liberty movement. He never appeared as a leader of the latter, but he was sufficiently sympathetic to its aims to give two lectures under its auspices at S. Martin's-in-the-Fields in October 1917 on the revenues of the Church of England.

The administrative machinery of the Church was also inefficient. Admittedly financial efficiency would not make up for spiritual weakness; but it had to be recognized that the Church, no more than any other society, was not exempt from adapting itself to the conditions of the world and from using as instruments the necessary conditions of human life.[17] Both on a diocesan and on a parochial level reorganization was needed in the interests of greater pastoral efficiency and improved clerical incomes.[18] This would require money; so apart from the creation of a Sustentation Fund to help build up capital for future needs, the Ecclesiastical Commissioners should adopt a bolder financial policy, spending far more of their income on the immediate needs of the Church instead of reinvesting it. They should use their finances just as any other good business firm would do.[19] The first

[13] 'The National Mission: Where does the defect of the Church lie?,' *C.Q.R.*, vol. 83, p. 2.
[14] Ibid., p. 6.
[15] Ibid., p. 12.
[16] Ibid., pp. 18–19.
[17] *The Revenue of the Church of England*, 1917, p. 3.
[18] Ibid., pp. 19, 30.
[19] Ibid., pp. 55–6.

necessary action was to request Parliament for a Royal Commission to consider the whole problem : Headlam was quite convinced that the connections between Church and State should remain. He had no time for the reformers who demanded disestablishment : the benefits to be derived from it were for the most part illusory and could in fact be obtained just as well, or indeed in better form, without it. Establishment did in fact provide full religious liberty.[20]

It was just at this period that Headlam's own affairs underwent a change. In the same month—October 1917, Professor Caldecotte announced his intention of resigning as Dean of King's College at Christmas, and Headlam decided that it would be wise for him to resign at the same time. Apart from the inconvenience of the frequent long journeys to London, the emoluments he had received were small. His resignation would enable the new Dean to hold his Chair as well if he so desired, and he thought that this would be a very convenient arrangement. There was also the added attraction of greater freedom and leisure to pursue his own studies. It was therefore a great surprise to him when both the theological staff and the Governing Body of the College asked him to consider returning to the College as Dean, if not permanently, then at least until the end of the War. The work at the moment was not excessive, certainly not remotely comparable with that which he had faced as Principal; there was an income of £700 a year; and if he were to stay on after the War, when the College would be filled to capacity with returned Service ordinands, he would hold a position of considerable importance in the Church. In spite of its attractions, Headlam declined the invitation and resigned his Chair. He had nearly finished one book and had already started another; nor could his wife face London again. Another possibility, too, had just arisen. In December, Hensley Henson, then Dean of Durham, was offered and accepted nomination to the see of Hereford. There was some suggestion that Headlam should succeed him at Durham : it was a post which he, as a Durham man, would find congenial, with the comparative leisure of the Deanery and the close proximity of the University. Henson went so far as to suggest his name to the Prime Minister,[21] but nothing came of the matter. His next move was destined to be in another direction.

On March 17, 1918 Henry Scott Holland, Regius Professor of Divinity and Canon of Christ Church, Oxford, died. Bishop Gore immediately urged Archbishop Davidson that it would be a public scandal if any one other than Headlam were to succeed him, for he

[20] 'The Archbishops' Committee on Church and State,' *C.Q.R.*, vol. 83, p. 351 ; 'Church Reform : the Church and the Nation,' *C.Q.R.*, vol. 85, p. 287.
[21] H. Henson, *Retrospect*, vol. 1, p. 220.

was the one theologian the Church of England possessed with an international reputation.[22] The Archbishop, too, had also considered Headlam's retirement from public life to be no more than temporary. Shortly afterwards he was offered the Chair and Canonry, and this time the offer was irresistible. Apart from the attraction of returning to Oxford, he felt that the duties involved would not provide any serious obstacle to his other activities : he had, in fact, often said that Oxford Chairs were comfortable retiring places. Before the end of April he had accepted, and he went into residence in the following term without delay.

[22] Randall Cantuar to Headlam, November 19, 1919.

CHAPTER SEVEN

Literary Work at King's College
Controversial Topics

I

In spite of the burden of his work as Principal and Dean of King's College and the constant demands made upon him as a preacher and a lecturer, Headlam still found time to write—a work largely bound up with the fortunes of *The Church Quarterly Review*. The financial position of the *Review* had remained precarious, despite its new lease of life under his direction, and the owners were glad to sell it to him when he offered to buy it in 1907. He raised the money by creating a company among his friends. The change in ownership involved certain changes in policy. In the first place strict anonymity in the authorship of articles ceased. Hitherto utterances had been of the *Review* and not of the individual, with the result that some contributions made by experts had received nothing like the consideration they had deserved. In view of this and in deference to the wishes of many readers, Headlam permitted articles to be signed. Secondly, in order to encourage new subscribers, the price was halved—a bold venture, for the *Review* now needed at least three thousand subscribers to make it pay. The changes were amply justified, and ten years later Headlam revealed that the demand exceeded the supply.

With the appearance of signed articles it was interesting to see how much he relied on the help of his friends from Winchester and Oxford —Michael Sadler, Cuthbert Turner, Cruikshank, Spooner, Raleigh, Kenyon—and how extensive was his own writing. Few numbers of the *Review* appeared which did not contain at least one article from him and these were on a wide range of subjects. An essay on Newman, which appeared in 1912, was considered by Nairne to be a fine piece of writing.[1] Here he showed how Newman had confused authority and infallibility. Authority was the sum of the experience of past generations, providing a starting point for future investigation and knowledge : but once that authority was regarded as infallible, it became a means of stereotyping error. The Church, inspired by the

---

[1] 'John Henry Newman,' *C.Q.R.*, vol. 74, pp. 257–85.

Holy Spirit, had handed down the revelation of Jesus Christ, expanding it, applying it and interpreting it for each age, and employing in the process the highest gifts of the human intelligence. But the Church was not infallible; every age had to repeat the process of correction, expansion and interpretation. It was Newman's great mistake 'that he sought for the infallible, instead of being contented with a reasonable certitude, and the most pungent criticism upon that position is his own.' [2] Nevertheless, Newman's teaching was one of the inspiring influences of the great movement of French and Italian theologians to bring their Church into touch with the intellectual thought of the day. [3]

In this movement a notable figure was Alfred Loisy, who, in his efforts to reconcile Christianity with modern scientific criticism, found himself at variance with the Roman Catholic authorities. The trouble had started in 1892, when he had asserted in his review *Enseignement Biblique* that the Pentateuch in its existing form was not the work of Moses : for this he had been deposed from the Chair of Hebrew at the Institut Catholique in Paris, his review had been discontinued, and he had gone into semi-retirement. In spite of all this he had gone still further in his book *L'Evangile et L'Eglise* in 1902, claiming that the Church preached a truth which was not absolute but relative. The book had caused a tremendous uproar and had been condemned by Cardinal Richard, Archbishop of Paris. In the following year he had attempted to justify his position in a further work *Autour d'un petit livre,* thereby aggravating an already serious situation. Under pressure from Cardinal Richard, Pope Pius X had placed the last five of Loisy's works on the Index. Headlam had been kept informed of these developments by Loisy's close friend, Baron von Hügel, and it was largely at the latter's instigation that he intervened in January 1904 with three articles in *The Times Literary Supplement* under the title 'The Vatican and Abbé Loisy.' [4] Here he defended Loisy's ability to propound a criticism compatible with theology and also to demonstrate that if criticism should prove incompatible with revelation, either the former was wrong or the latter was incorrectly understood. Criticism was a science and must arrive at its conclusions by its own methods : if these conclusions were erroneous they would be proved so by further criticism. If the Church stood in the way of criticism, it would impede progress and would only succeed in making itself look ridiculous. False teaching should be proved erroneous, not condemned : and Loisy's condemnation was most unwise.

[2] Ibid., p. 281.
[3] Ibid., p. 285.
[4] *Times Literary Supplement,* January 15, 22, 29, 1904.

This attitude of Headlam towards freedom and authority was also evident in his review of *Foundations,* the controversial symposium of essays on Christian belief produced in 1912 by seven Oxford men— B. H. Streeter, R. Brook, A. E. J. Rawlinson, N. Talbot, R. G. Parsons, William Temple and W. Moberly. To him, these men had nothing of the tone or temper of heretics, as many held them to be. They were simply constructive theologians attempting the task facing each age of restating the traditional faith in the language of the day. It was right for them to make experiments on behalf of the Church, and Headlam felt that they had written with the modesty and courage of youth.[5] Admittedly some of their speculations were hazardous, but they had not exceeded the limits of legitimate experiment and adventure ; and it was certainly ill-advised to meet such speculations with ecclesiastical censure. Nevertheless it was precisely as 'Foundations' that it failed. The book was an attempt to build up a solid exposition of the Christian faith on principles or ideas which were in vogue at the time—Experience, Eschatology, Divine Immanence and the doctrine of the Absolute—and it was just in these foundations that Headlam saw a weakness.[6] It was one thing to take into account all the latest theories and forms of speculation ; but it was another to regard them as a final embodiment of truth to such an extent that the Christian faith might be reconstructed in harmony with them.[7]

Among these current ideas was one of which Headlam had been an early critic. He had discussed Eschatology in *The Church Quarterly Review* some time before England had received the full impact of what he called 'the brilliant but wild imaginings of Schweitzer' in the English translation of his book *The Quest of the Historical Jesus* in 1910. In his article 'The Christ of History' in January 1910, he agreed with Schweitzer that the work of the German Liberal Protestant school, which held Jesus to be no more than a great teacher, was of little or no value : but he also found Schweitzer's own views to be seriously defective. He was open to the same criticism which he himself had levelled against the Liberal Protestants—he only saw what suited his own theories. The eschatological element was admittedly a vital and a necessary one in the Christian religion, but it could not stand alone. Although it was true to say that apocalypses represented the current literature of our Lord's day, they certainly did not represent the sum total of current literature. The whole corpus of Old Testament literature had to be taken into consideration, and in His teaching Jesus Christ reflected all the current thoughts of His time.[8]

---

[5] 'Foundations,' *C.Q.R.,* vol. 76, pp. 1–31.
[6] Ibid., p. 27.
[7] Ibid., p. 10.
[8] 'The Christ of History,' *C.Q.R.,* vol. 69, pp. 257–81.

No religion composed simply of eschatological dreams could possibly have exercised such a universal influence as that which Jesus had created. Even judged by human standards, one who was able to do what our Lord had done must have been something more than a religious fanatic or dreamer, as Schweitzer would have Him to be.[9] The life of Jesus Christ had completely transformed the history of the world, and the Gospel narrative revealed a life and a teaching that was unquestionably divine.[10]

Headlam therefore had no sympathy for that critical attitude towards the earthly life of our Lord which deprived it of all supernatural content. This was evident from his criticism of the book *The Miracles in the New Testament* by the Revd. J. M. Thompson, Dean of Magdalen College, Oxford, which appeared in 1911. Thompson claimed that owing to the progress of critical studies and the exigencies of evidence, the miraculous element should be banished from the Gospels. The book made a considerable stir, and the Bishop of London and the publisher, John Murray, asked Headlam to write a reply. He was too busy to write a complete book, but in November 1911 he wrote two articles in *The Guardian* which later reappeared in *Miracles: Papers and Sermons contributed to the Guardian* edited by H. Scott Holland. He denied that the advances of Biblical criticism had done anything to refute the wealth of evidence for miracles contained in the Gospels. The other New Testament writings supported this : S. Paul believed in miracles and the early Church obviously possessed miraculous gifts.[11] Thompson's methods were fallacious—building up a theory, often interesting and ingeneous, on rather imperfect generalizations, and then adapting the remainder of the evidence to suit that theory : he was, in fact, so absorbed in his own point of view that he failed entirely to see how subjective it was, and how unsubstantial was much of the investigation which he called criticism.[12]

An even more devastating attack on liberal modernistic views was Headlam's criticism of the book *The New Theology*, produced in 1907 by Dr. R. J. Campbell, the famous Congregationalist minister of the City Temple, London. This book decried original sin and put man on such a pedestal that our Lord Himself suffered in consequence. Headlam considered Dr. Campbell to be strangely ignorant both of theology and philosophy [13] : he did 'not know enough about anything to use his knowledge properly, and he has not the sense of reverence

[9] Ibid., p. 273.
[10] Ibid., pp. 278–80.
[11] *The Guardian*, 1911, pp. 1460–1.
[12] Ibid., pp. 1500–1.
[13] 'The New Theology,' *C.Q.R.*, vol. 64, p. 410–11.

and respect for the thinkers who have preceded him to enable him to re-interpret the Gospel to the present day.'[14] When Dr. Campbell asked the questions, 'How can the Infinite become finite?' and 'How can God, who is all, create anything?' Headlam replied, 'The solution of the problems that Mr. Campbell raises will always be more adequate and true, the more the thinker is Catholic and not merely Protestant, reverent and not only critical, believing in the working of the Spirit of God in the Christian Society, rather than assuming that the place where God's Spirit works is everywhere but in the historic Church. The greater the unity of the Christian world, the more nearly it preaches the true ideal of the Christian Church, the sooner it will attain to Christian truth.'[15]

Headlam's own attempt to fulfil these words appeared in 1909 in a collection of eight essays, written over a period of twenty years, entitled *History, Authority and Theology*. He regarded them as 'fragments of an attempt deliberately to discover . . . whether, in any real sense of the word, what we know as Christianity is true; what Christianity is; what is the authority on which we receive it; how far can we trust that authority; how far we find it necessary to criticize, to restate, or to modify its teaching'; and then, 'how far do the existing religious bodies, or any of them, represent Christianity; which represents it most adequately; and which, if any, of the various churches or societies can claim to be the truest representative of that Church which Christ founded.'[16] After an introductory essay, he went on to discuss the sources and authority of dogmatic theology, the methods of early Church history, the Church of the Apostolic Fathers and the Athanasian Creed : he then surveyed the teaching of the Russian Church and the relations between the Church of England and the Eastern Churches, and concluded with his estimate of Dr. Campbell's *New Theology*. These essays served to illustrate his firm conviction that the Church of England was an adequate though not infallible representative of the Christian society, basing its standard of truth on the Bible as interpreted by Christian history and tradition : it was both Catholic and Reformed, representing a sound and healthy mean between the Roman and Protestant positions—a position closely akin to that which the Eastern Church had also preserved from primitive times.

II

Headlam's most important work during this period, however, was his

14 Ibid., p. 430.
15 Ibid., pp. 434–5.
16 *History, Authority and Theology*, 1909, pp. 3, 37.

essays on the Church and Ministry, for in them were the foundations
of his famous Bampton Lectures delivered in 1920. The subject had
been exercising his mind for twenty years or more : he had carefully
weighed the contributions of other eminent scholars—Hatch, Lightfoot, Hort, Harnack, Gore—and although he was obviously not in
agreement with all they had said, he had worked out his own ideas in
the consciousness of the ideas which they had expressed. Then again,
he had been an interested spectator of the discussions which had taken
place in 1895-6 under the inspiration of Lord Halifax and the Abbé
Portal on the question of the validity of Anglican Orders. The failure
of these discussions and the promulgation of the bull 'Apostolica
Curae' in 1896 condemning Anglican Orders, apart from creating in
him a profound distrust of the methods and theology of the Roman
Church, also encouraged him to probe the question of the Ministry
still further. His views were embodied in three groups of articles. The
first appeared in *The Church Quarterly Review* between 1904 and
1906 under the title 'The Christian Society' : the second was a course
of lectures delivered at Westminster Abbey in Advent 1908 on 'The
Church and Ministry'—these were not published, but the typescript is
extant among his papers : finally there were two articles on Apostolic
Succession and Episcopacy in *The Prayer Book Dictionary* which
appeared in 1912.

He began by pointing out that the Jews of the Old Testament had
considered themselves to be a people apart—they were a chosen race,
a peculiar people, a royal priesthood, an holy nation. This conception
was taken over by the Christian Church, the new Israel, and was
summed up in the word 'ecclesia,' thereby creating the technical term
for a religious society as apart from and opposed to all other forms of
association.[17] Here he was following lines already laid down by Hort.

'(Jesus) uses language which implies that it (the Kingdom of God) is
a Society, lays down for it a new code of laws, and suggests that He
foresees its future extension in the world. The preparation for such a
Society He Himself made by collecting around Him a body of disciples
bound by the closest of personal adherence, out of whom He selected
twelve who were to be in an especial way teachers and rulers. In other
words, He looked forward to and prepared for the founding of the
Church.' [18]

Furthermore, the two great institutions arising from our Lord's direct

[17] 'The Jewish Community,' *C.Q.R.*, vol. 59, pp. 30-8.
[18] Ibid., p. 275.

command—Baptism and the Eucharist—were clearly in their essence social rites implying the idea of a society.[19] Nevertheless it was not Jesus Christ Himself who directly founded the Church : all His actions were calculated to lead to that result, but the actual foundation was the work of the Apostles.[20] These men were the leaders of the new community ; they were the source of teaching ; they administered discipline ; they managed the finances ; in them dwelt the miraculous gifts of the Spirit.[21]

The first change in the constitution of the community came with the appointment of the 'Seven.' Here again Headlam followed Hort in claiming that it was an action undertaken to deal with an emergency, and not—as Lightfoot had believed—a deliberate institution of a new order. Nevertheless, it created a precedent, thereby forming the model on which the diaconate developed.[22] So these men became regular and necessary officers of the Church, selected by the community as men of good repute and 'full of the Spirit and of wisdom,' presented by them to the Apostles, and appointed to their office by prayer and the imposition of hands. Here were all the elements from which developed the normal ecclesiastical ordinations ; and here too was continuity with Old Testament practice, where the custom of the imposition of hands either for appointment to an office or as part of a formal blessing occurred in the appointment of elders.[23] In addition to the local ministry of presbyters and deacons, the Church possessed a missionary ministry of apostles, prophets, evangelists and teachers, although the latter gradually disappeared with the progress of organization. These men held definite office ; but they were ministers of the whole Church and not of a particular community, and they had received the gift of the Holy Spirit for their work in a special way.[24] In the local ministry, Headlam agreed with Lightfoot and Hort in identifying presbyters with bishops : the emergence of bishops arose from the need for a president of each college of presbyters, such as S. James had been at Jerusalem.[25] So there developed the threefold ministry of bishops, priests and deacons.

The authority of history and tradition was overwhelmingly in favour of episcopacy as against any other form of Church government, and history gave ample testimony to its value.[26] Nevertheless, it

[19] Ibid., p. 285.
[20] Ibid., p. 268 ; cf. Hort, *Christian Ecclesia*, pp. 19–20.
[21] 'The Earliest Christian Community,' *C.Q.R.*, vol. 60, pp. 325–6.
[22] 'The Development of the Church,' *C.Q.R.*, vol. 61, pp. 241–78 ; cf. Hort, *Christian Ecclesia*, pp. 52, 157–8 ; Lightfoot, *Ephesians*, p. 186.
[23] Westminster Lectures 3. 'Orders.'
[24] *C.Q.R.*, vol. 61, pp. 249–60 ; Westminster Lectures 2. 'The Episcopate.'
[25] Westminster Lectures 3 ; G. Harford and M. Stevenson (editors), *The Prayer Book Dictionary*, 1912, p. 314.
[26] *Prayer Book Dictionary*, p. 315.

was also quite clear that there was no command of Jesus Christ or of
the Apostles in favour of episcopacy : they merely handed on the idea
of ministry. There was nothing in the nature of things why the Church
should be episcopal, except that it was. The question was not whether
episcopacy was the only possible form of government, but whether it
was the form supported by the greatest amount of authority : and of
this there was no doubt.[27] 'Such an historic episcopate, linking the
Church at the present day with the past, supple, elastic, capable of
adapting itself to various circumstances, balancing authority and
freedom, is, more than any other system of Church government,
adapted to the needs of democratic civilization and fitted to form the
basis of Christian reunion.' [28]

With episcopacy was bound up the question of Apostolic Succession.
An analysis of the historical data showed that it was reasonably certain that the officials of the Church had from the beginning been
appointed by the laying-on of the hands of those who had been themselves so appointed. The fact of historical succession going back to the
Apostles or other 'men of repute' in the apostolic era was probably
true ; but it was not possible to prove a succession through monarchical
episcopacy.[29] There were four possible meanings of the idea of succession. First it could mean an orderly succession of officers, such as
that in a Roman province—a meaning pointed out by Hatch.[30]
Secondly it could mean a succession of Apostolic Commission—a
commission derived from the Apostles : this was the meaning in the
Epistle of Clement. From this there developed the third meaning of
continuity of function—bishops were successors of the Apostles in that
they performed the functions of the Apostles. Finally there was the
meaning of the transmission of grace—the meaning adopted by Gore
and Moberly. Of this meaning Headlam wrote :

'The Apostles gave the Holy Spirit to the bishops they ordained, and
they have handed it on in the Church ever since. It is through bishops
and bishops only that the Holy Spirit is given. This is the meaning
which is generally attached to Apostolical Succession at the present
time, and the form in which it is attacked by its opponents. But it is
not the meaning which ordinarily attaches to the term in the authoritative documents of the Church.' [31]

He claimed that both the Patristic theory of Orders and the Anglican

[27] Westminster Lectures 2.
[28] *Prayer Book Dictionary*, p. 316.
[29] Ibid., p. 41.
[30] E. Hatch, *The Organization of the Early Christian Churches*, 1881, p. 106.
[31] *Prayer Book Dictionary*, p. 41.

theory of Orders as given in Article XXIII and the Ordinal did not imply a transmission of grace from consecrator to consecrated : this was an idea which was additional and late, leading to a rigid and mechanical theory of the ministry.[32] Just as there had been no clear command of our Lord or of the Apostles in favour of episcopacy, so Headlam considered that there was nothing in the nature of things why a bishop only should have the right to ordain. There had been no command of our Lord or of the Apostles in its favour, and it had probably not even been a universal rule in the early days of the Church. Nevertheless there was the clear and unmistakable practice of the Church as a whole, and it was our duty to adhere to that practice until the Church as a whole changed its principles.[33]

Succession was concerned with the authoritative handing on of office. It was a fact, not a doctrine, representing an external connection with the first beginnings of Christianity of infinite value for the Church. The grace given depended, not on a mechanical transmission, but upon the authority of the Church. God's gift was freshly given at each ordination and granted to the Church through its authorized agents in answer to prayer. In this way ordination depended on the authority of the Church, and not the Church on ordination.[34]

'Apostolic Succession as an historical fact is of great force and power. It does assert that from the Apostles' time down to the present there has been a regular succession of ministers appointed in an orderly way, and that each of these ministers has been appointed by those themselves duly appointed with authority for ordaining. Thus there is a definite historical link between our own Bishops and the times of the Apostles. It is an external sign of that regular succession in the Church which has handed down to us the teaching and discipline and rule of the Apostolic age to the present time. It is the external sign of the solidarity of the Christian Society.' [35]

One part of the work of Christian reunion should therefore be the restoration of the links of succession through the Christian world ; although it had to be remembered that no rigidity or mechanical theory of Orders need compel the Church to deny divine grace to those separated from it.[36]

S. Paul had claimed that all Christians were baptized into one Body by the one Spirit. So Headlam considered that all the various Christian

[32] Westminster Lectures 3.
[33] Ibid.
[34] *Prayer Book Dictionary*, p. 42.
[35] Westminster Lectures 3.
[36] *Prayer Book Dictionary*, p. 42.

bodies composed of people who had been baptized were all imperfect parts of the one true Church. The Church was therefore divided inwardly by schisms : there was no case of the Church being a single visible communion, with all schisms outside it.[37] The Orders of non-episcopal bodies were within the Church, although they were not regular nor representative of the Catholic Church in its best and most complete form : their sacraments, too, though possibly irregular, were not necessarily invalid.[38] From a practical point of view Headlam considered there were three things which the Church of England could do to further reunion. First, it should do nothing to lose or to destroy what it already possessed : to do so would mean losing that which would make it worth while for other Churches to be united to it. Secondly, it should make no premature attempts at reunion : there would be no real progress through an excessive readiness to indulge in sentimental effusions, or an ignoring of differences which did in fact exist. Intercommunion was not a preparation for but the fulfilment of reunion. Thirdly, it should co-operate wherever co-operation was possible ; by discussing points of theological difference and learning to respect rather than to ignore them ; by sober learning and wise theology ; and by cultivating a true Christian spirit. Nor should the desire for unity ever be allowed to interfere with a loyalty to truth.

III

Headlam was convinced that the Church of England contained everything which the Catholic Church could mean potentially ; and he felt that the Lambeth Quadrilateral, although not defining the Church or explaining its rites and doctrine, did lay down a solid basis for reunion with other Christian bodies.[39] He therefore fully approved of the work of the Committee on Reunion at the Lambeth Conference of 1908. While retaining the principle of aiming at one organic society with a common faith, common worship, the Bible, and one organization based on an historic episcopate, it aimed at showing the greatest consideration for other Churches and at not pronouncing negatively on the value in God's sight of their ministries.[40] He fully concurred with the Committee's views on reunion with the Moravian Church, involving the participation of Anglican bishops in the consecration of Moravian bishops.[41] The same approach might also be made to the Scandinavian

[37] Westminster Lectures 1.
[38] Westminster Lectures 4.
[39] 'The Lambeth Conference and the Union of the Churches,' *C.Q.R.*, vol. 66, pp. 259–84.
[40] 'The Lambeth Conference,' *C.Q.R.*, vol. 67, pp. 16–17.
[41] Ibid., p. 19.

Churches; and in their case bishops of the Old Catholic Church, of whose valid consecration there was no doubt, might be persuaded to participate.[42] In the case of the Presbyterians, the Committee had expressed the view that some approach to reunion might be possible on the basis of consecrations to the episcopate on lines suggested by precedents such as those of 1610.[43] Headlam doubted whether much could be achieved on these lines at home at that moment but thought such a scheme might be worth consideration in Australia, where conditions were much freer and the need for reunion greater.[44] Nevertheless, although he felt that with the Presbyterians some new commissioning might be considered necessary by a proper and regular imposition of hands, this would be in no way a new or hypothetical ordination; it would be simply an extension and regularization of the commission already given.

Headlam himself furthered the cause of reunion by inviting scholars of different Christian bodies and schools of thought to contribute articles on the subject to *The Church Quarterly Review*. One of these, 'The Grace of Orders and Apostolic Succession' by Fr. F. W. Puller, s.s.j.e., had an interesting history, revealing the beginning of Headlam's long and considerable influence on the development of the Church of South India. After the World Missionary Conference at Edinburgh in 1910 Dr. J. R. Mott, the Chairman of the Continuation Committee, held a series of conferences in Asia in 1912–13. At one of these in Calcutta in December 1912 an address by Henry Whitehead, Bishop of Madras, aroused considerable interest. Whitehead's appointment to the see of Madras in 1899 had been viewed with some misgivings, for whereas the diocese was strongly Evangelical in outlook, he was known to be a staunch Tractarian. Such fears proved to be unfounded, however, for Whitehead developed a 'large-hearted œcumenicity' and came to play a leading part in the movement towards union in South India.[45] At a meeting between representatives of the Anglican Church and the South India United Church at Madras in 1910 Whitehead had pleaded that for the sake of peace and intercommunion, non-episcopal churches should accept the fact of the historic episcopate, without in any way committing themselves to any particular theory about it. The meeting had finally suggested a combination of the constitution of the South India United Church and

[42] *C.Q.R.*, vol. 66, p. 275.

[43] Episcopacy was reintroduced into Scotland in 1610 when three Scottish presbyters were consecrated by the Bishop of London and three other bishops without first being ordained priests according to the English Ordinal.

[44] *C.Q.R.*, vol. 67, pp. 20–2.

[45] Ruth Rouse and S. C. Neill (editors), *A History of the Ecumenical Movement 1517–1948*, 1954, p. 364; Bengt Sundkler, *Church of South India*, 1954, pp. 51–2.

the Lambeth Quadrilateral, with some modification of the latter—the two historic creeds were to be regarded as an 'adequate' rather than a 'sufficient' statement of the Christian faith, while the adoption of the article on the episcopate would not involve the acceptance of any particular theory or interpretation of it. This meeting had been unofficial; so the resolutions, though important, were in no way binding on the Churches concerned.[46] To Whitehead they represented the first step towards unity.

The second step occurred in Calcutta in December 1912. One evening at dinner, when representatives of all denominations were present, Dr. Mott suddenly asked Whitehead to speak on reunion. On the spur of the moment, and without any idea of making a formal pronouncement, Whitehead spoke in a conversational way on what he called 'the next step towards unity.' He had already had long conversations with Headlam on the subject at York during the previous year when home on furlough, and the substance of his remarks was in close agreement with Headlam's views. Both Headlam and W. H. Frere [47] were quoted as witnesses against the theory of Apostolic Succession as the transmission of an original gift from the Apostles: the historic episcopate did not presuppose a theory of Apostolic Succession, but expressed a fact in history. The acceptance of the historic episcopate was a necessary safeguard for unity, and what had been a safeguard from A.D. 150 to 1500 should form the basis of the new unity which the churches in India were trying to establish.[48] It was unfortunate that inaccurate reports of this speech appeared in the Indian press; and the Bombay paper *Dnyanodaya* represented Whitehead as quoting Headlam in support of the mutual recognition of the ministries of different churches. Fr. Maxwell, the Superior General of the Society of S. John the Evangelist, who was in India at the time, sent home a copy of this article to Fr. Puller, who asked Headlam whether he had ever made such a statement, or whether he had been misrepresented.[49] Headlam replied that although he and Whitehead were inclined to hold a conciliatory attitude, the article did misrepresent both what he had said and what he considered Whitehead to believe. His views were clearly stated in his two articles in *The Prayer Book Dictionary*.

'I think that your experience will make you understand the temper

---

[46] Sundkler, op. cit., pp. 61–5.
[47] Dr. Frere had approved of Headlam's view in an article in *C.Q.R.*, for October 1912—'The Reconstruction of Worship,' vol. 75, pp. 139–60.
[48] Whitehead to Headlam, October 14, 1913; Sundkler, op. cit., pp. 68–9.
[49] Puller to Headlam, January 20, 1913.

in which I would approach these questions. When you were engaged in the controversy as to Anglican Orders with the Church of Rome, you must have felt when Rome came down with its "Non possumus" what a terrible barrier it had made to reasonable approaches to reunion.[50] There is no doubt that everywhere there is great feeling in favour of reunion . . . but there are two or three stumbling blocks. The first I am confident in the Transmission Theory. People have felt that it is unreal and mechanical, and as I say, I am afraid has no authority for it. The second is that people are not prepared to take up an attitude which implies that they and their fathers before them have not received any sacramental grace or have been outside the fold of the Church. . . . The third point still remains—what should be the steps for reunion? Is there anything possible short of reordination? Might there be a possibility of mutual reordination? That is what I am pondering over now.'[51]

Fr. Puller strongly advised Headlam not to consider any proposals for mutual reordination : such an idea would rend the Church of England in pieces. Nor did he know of any Anglicans of weight who held what Headlam called the Transmission Theory : he had only read of it in dissenting works attempting to caricature the truly Catholic doctrine of Apostolic Succession.[52] Headlam, however, quoted both Haddon and Gore as representing the older and more modern schools who supported the mechanical theory of transmission; while Dr. Neale's translation of the Ember hymn, 'Christ is gone up' contained it in more popular form.[53] It would therefore seem essential that people of influence, and particularly those who could influence the High Church party, should provide some restatement of the doctrine of orders. As a step in this direction, he suggested that Fr. Puller himself might be willing to contribute something to *The Church Quarterly Review*.[54]

Fr. Puller had to admit that the passages from Haddon, Gore and Neale, if taken in their bald literality and without regard to the elementary teaching of all Catholic theologians that our Lord is the true baptizer, confirmer, ordainer and consecrator, did bear out

---

[50] Fr. Puller and Canon T. A. Lacey attended the Papal Commission of 1895–6 which enquired into the validity of Anglican Orders, and which resulted in the bull 'Apostolicae Curae.'
[51] Headlam to Puller, January 22, 1913.
[52] Puller to Headlam, January 23, 1913.
[53] A. W. Haddan, *Apostolical Succession in the Church of England,* 1869, p. 1 ; C. Gore, *The Ministry of the Christian Church,* 1889, pp. 70–1. The relevant lines in Neale's hymn are :

His twelve Apostles first he made	So age by age, and year by year,
His ministers of grace ;	His grace was handed on ;
And they their hands on others laid,	And still the holy Church is here,
To fill in turn their place.	Although her Lord is gone.

[54] Headlam to Puller, January 24, 1913.

Headlam's point. He also admitted that Dissenters, looking at these things, as it were, from the outside, might interpret them in a mechanical sense. He himself had used the word 'transmitted' to describe the action of consecrating bishops; yet at the same time he had realized that the gift of apostolic authority came down from our Lord. If he had been aware of the misapprehension of Dissenters, he might have used a different word; but he felt sure that neither Haddon nor Gore had meant to deny our Lord's direct bestowal of the gift.[55] The result of their correspondence is admirably summed up by Headlam in his final letter of February 4, 1913.

'My dear Puller,
  '. . . We both agreed that the Grace of Orders, if we are to use that term, was the direct gift from the risen Lord to His Church. That it was given in each individual case in answer to the prayers of the Church, and that the laying-on of hands of the Bishop was so to speak the instrument, or sign in the older sense, of the gift. The particular point on which we differed was the source of the authority or the commission of the Bishop. You would argue that he had an independent and apostolic commission, that he was appointed by those who themselves had been appointed by others right back to apostolic times, and that therefore ultimately his commission depended upon his succession. I on the contrary would believe that his commission depended on the authority of the Church as the guardian of the sacraments. That in order to give security and order, the Church had laid down that all ordinations should be by those who had authority in the Church for that purpose, and that the rule of the Church had been from very early times that those who were to receive this commission should be ordained by three who themselves had the commission. The result of that difference would be this; that whereas according to you the sacraments and therefore the Church depended upon the Succession, I should be inclined to believe that the Succession depended upon the authority of the Church. The one would make it primary and the other secondary in importance. Now as to which theory is the right one I really do not know. I doubt if the question was really considered in most periods of the Church's history, but judging by my own reading, I should feel that my view was the one that generally prevailed in early days, but in recent years your view has tended to prevail; but this is a matter on which you have, of course, a wider knowledge than I. You imply that the great advantage of your theory is the security that it gives. Are you quite certain that that is right? At the best the apostolic succession can only claim to be a very prob-

[55] Puller to Headlam, January 29, 1913.

able historical fact, and you are making that which is probable the basis of your security. I should feel the actual living voice and authority of the Church extending from generation to generation was the real living thing which gave us security for the whole Christian tradition, including the grace of the sacraments. . . .'

Fr. Puller's requested article 'The Grace of Orders and Apostolic Succession' did nothing to resolve their differences or answer Headlam's questions, for it was merely a detailed statement of the views he had already put forward. But Dr. H. Hamilton, the eminent Canadian theologian, contributed an article on 'The Essentials of a Valid Ministry' in October 1913 clearly favouring Headlam's line of approach. For him Apostolic Succession was a series of facts—there for all to see : but each generation saw in it something specially suited to its own needs ; and so it was doubtful whether any one theory about it could properly be called Catholic. Nor did he believe priesthood and sacrifice necessarily involved any such succession. Believing as he did that it was the Eucharist which had originally called the Ministry into being and maintained it in its three orders, he felt that if there had been no Eucharist, the Ministry would have taken a very different form, probably so different that it would have been impossible to speak of Apostolic Succession in at all the same sense. Succession depended upon the Church. A valid ministry was representative of the whole Church and had the authority of the whole Church. In ordination God bestowed the inner spiritual gift in answer to the prayer of the Church through the bishop; and the Church through the bishop bestowed authority to act in her name. Nor were these two wholly separate acts; for Jesus Christ was not removed at any great distance from the Church, but dwelt in her through the Holy Spirit.[56]

IV

Headlam's views on reunion were exemplified by his attitude towards the Kikuyu incident in British East Africa in June 1913. Some sixty missionaries of all denominations except the Roman Catholics drew up, under the chairmanship of Bishop Willis of Uganda, a scheme of federation with the creation of a united native East African Church in view. The basis of the federation was to be the acceptance of the Scriptures, the Apostles' and Nicene Creeds, and the two sacraments of Baptism and the Lord's Supper; the recognition of common membership between the various denominations; and a common form of

[56] 'The Essentials of a Valid Ministry,' *C.Q.R.*, vol. 77, pp. 388-404.

organization. Each society was to be autonomous within its own sphere of activity, and recognized ministers of one society would be welcomed as preachers in the churches of other societies but would not be permitted to administer the sacraments. All future native candidates for the Ministry from all the societies would be required to be set apart by lawful authority and by the imposition of hands. Baptism was to be the necessary condition of membership of the federated societies, and Holy Communion was to be confined to full members. Where the recognized members of one society were living temporarily in another society's district, permission would be given for them to communicate in the other society's churches. On the closing day of the conference Bishop Peel of Mombasa celebrated Holy Communion, at which all the delegates except the Quakers communicated. These proceedings aroused the opposition of Dr. Frank Weston, the Anglo-Catholic Bishop of the neighbouring diocese of Zanzibar. On September 30 he wrote to the Archbishop of Canterbury, demanding that if the Bishops of Mombasa and Uganda did not 'recant,' a Synodical Court should be appointed to try them; otherwise he would feel obliged to resign his see on the grounds that heresy had been condoned in the sight of the Missionary Churches in East Africa. He then published an Open Letter to the Bishop of St. Albans—*Ecclesia Anglicana*—citing Kikuyu as one of a number of indications that the Church of England, having regard to her chaotic system of Truth, was unfit to send missionaries to heathen or Mohammedan lands; and again appealing for the matter to be dealt with by the Archbishop of Canterbury and his comprovincial bishops.

The incident aroused considerable controversy. Some people defended the conference as a notable step towards reunion : others, like Weston, regarded it as wholly disastrous for the Church of England. Headlam entered the lists in support of Kikuyu, and his letter to *The Times* on December 31 earned the cordial thanks of Archbishop Davidson : 'Everybody is writing to the press and sometimes in a way which is doing untold mischief. The relief to me therefore is immense in reading your quite admirable letter in *The Times*—the first of all the published letters . . . to give me real satisfaction. Nothing could be better in substance or form, nothing at this juncture more useful. . . . I must not go into the fray, but let me, all the same, thank you most cordially for an utterance which cannot, I feel sure, fail to do good.'[57]

December 29, 1913.

'Sir,

'It is with some hesitation that I venture to write to you on the

[57] Archbishop of Canterbury to Headlam, December 31, 1913.

discussion which has arisen about the Kikuyu Conference. I do so only because it seems to me that the action of the Bishops of Uganda and Mombasa has been misjudged, especially by those who profess to support it. As it presents itself to me, judging from the report on the Conference and the Bishop's statesmanlike letter, it is an attempt carried as far as is possible under existing circumstances to build up a Church in East Africa on those fundamental Catholic principles which inspired the development of the whole Christian Church and have always been accepted by the Church of England. These principles were formulated for us at the Lambeth Conference of 1888 and are known as the Lambeth Quadrilateral. . . . They come to us with the authority of our own Church and of historical theology. May I venture to add that it is not likely that a wiser, more temperate or more comprehensive statement of fundamental Catholic principles is likely to be drawn up? Shortly it lays down for us that the fundamental principles of the Christian Church are the acceptance of the Holy Scriptures, the Apostles' and Nicene Creeds, the two Sacraments of Baptism and the Lord's Supper, and the historic Episcopate.

'Let us see how far these principles are being followed in laying the foundations for the East African Church :—

'(1). The condition of federation is "the loyal acceptance of the Holy Scriptures as our supreme rule of faith and practice; of the Apostles' and Nicene Creeds as a general expression of fundamental Christian beliefs." Surely it is of supreme importance from the point of view of Catholic Churchmanship that these principles should be accepted, and to have done so makes a long step forward towards unity.

'(2). It is insisted that Baptism should be recognized as the necessary condition of the membership of the Christian Church. The due matter and form of the Sacrament are to be observed. It must be in the name of the Trinity. The aim is to secure for the Sacrament of Baptism that recognized and paramount position which it already holds in our own Church. We may consider lay baptism irregular; we cannot hold it invalid.

'(3). Two fundamental points are thus, we believe, secured. As regards the other two the Conference goes as far as is possible at this stage. The Lord's Supper is to be regularly administered by outward signs, by the recognized ministers of the Church to full members of the Church only. The importance of the Sacrament is insisted on. I cannot hold that such celebrations would be regular; I do not care to use the word "invalid." Of them, I would rather say with Dr. Pusey that "God may make His own Sacrament efficacious even when irregularly administered."

'(4). We cannot expect that the historic Episcopate should be immediately accepted. What is possible is done. The ministry of every community is regularized. A minister is to be duly set apart by lawful authority and by the laying-on of hands. Care is, in fact, taken that in each community regularly appointed ministers shall regularly administer the Sacraments according to their own rules. I believe that this must inevitably lead to the question being asked, "How can our ministry and our Sacraments be made regular, not for each separate community, but for the whole Church?" And this must lead to the ultimate acceptance of this historic rule of the Church, episcopal ordination, as that which regularizes a ministry for the whole Church and guarantees a regular and valid celebration of Sacraments.

'Two points are fully secured. As regards the other two, the foundation is laid. I believe that a notable step forward has been made towards reunion on a sound basis. What concessions are asked of the Church? They are two. We are asked, when necessity demands, to admit baptized believing Christians who are full members of other communities to our Sacraments; that is, we have to waive our rule of discipline. I believe that that rule is a wise and healthy one, but it is not a Catholic principle. No one who has read the Bishop of Uganda's statement can doubt the supreme necessity of some relaxation under the conditions of East African life. Such relaxation is often allowed with full authority in the Church at home. I do not see why, when necessity arises, it should not be allowed in the Church of the mission field. That does not mean that the rule, which is a salutary one, should not be generally observed.

'The second concession we are asked to make is to allow regularly appointed ministers of other communities to preach in our churches in the position of a lay reader. This is a new proposal, but I would express the hope that under the particular circumstances the English Episcopate may concur in allowing this concession to be made. What is important to insist on is that it means a full recognition of the importance of episcopal ordination. If we say to the minister of another communion, "We recognize that you are adequately trained for preaching the Gospel—we shall admit you under certain regulations to preach in our churches, but because you have not received episcopal ordination we cannot allow you to administer the Sacraments," surely we are asserting in its most definite form the necessity for episcopacy for regular Sacraments.

'My aim has been to suggest that the action of the Conference has been misinterpreted; that, as Catholic Churchmen, we may accept the decisions that have been reached, and may look upon this as the beginning of an attempt to build up a Church in East Africa on those Catholic principles which the whole Church of England accepts. It does not complete the task, but it begins it well. I would deprecate most strongly the attempt to make this an occasion for provocative statements about the Protestant character of the English Church, or highly disputable and most irrelevant propositions about our relations to the Reformed Church of the Continent, or for exhibiting that strange idiosyncracy which condemns as illogical everything which is not extravagant. I would rather think at this moment of that great mass of unguided heathen suddenly exposed to the insidious attacks of civilization, of that little band of missionaries toiling to convert them in the isolation created by theological controversies long past, and of the splendid hope of building up, if we are wise and sober in our action, a united Church of East Africa.

ARTHUR C. HEADLAM. Whorlton.'

Headlam discussed the matter further in *The Church Quarterly Review* in January and April 1914. There he dealt with the Bishop of Zanzibar's objections to the scheme—the omission of references to the Athanasian Creed, Infant Baptism, Confirmation, Absolution and Episcopacy, and the absence of precise definition of the phrases 'one holy catholic and apostolic Church' and 'the Communion of Saints.' The credal requirements of the scheme were in agreement with the Lambeth Quadrilateral; and it could not be said that the Athanasian Creed commanded universal acceptance; while official interpretations of credal statements violated the principles of Catholicity.[58] Of Infant Baptism it could be said that no rule of the Universal Church required it; and as for the absence of Confirmation and Absolution from the scheme, they should be logical results of it, becoming essential and valuable elements of the Missionary Church.[59] Nor did the scheme really ignore Episcopacy; for some of the disciplinary questions at issue were directly concerned with it—as, for example, the regulations governing the celebration and reception of Holy Communion.[60] The Anglican Communion had in effect in the Lambeth Quadrilateral adhered to the necessity of Episcopacy for a united Church as part of the full Catholic tradition.[61]

Meanwhile the Archbishop of Canterbury, having interviewed Bishops Weston and Willis, refused to permit a trial of the latter and Bishop Peel on charges of heresy and schism, but summoned the Consultative Committee of the Lambeth Conference in July 1914 to

---

[58] 'Notes on Reunion: the Kikuyu Conference,' *C.Q.R.*, vol. 77, pp. 418–19; 'The Ecclesia Anglicana,' *C.Q.R.*, vol. 78, p. 147.
[59] Op. cit., vol. 77, pp. 418–19.
[60] Ibid., p. 149.
[61] Op. cit., vol. 78, p. 145.

enquire into the matter. With the outbreak of war in the following month, it was not until Easter 1915 that the Consultative Committee's findings and the Archbishop's answer—both of which were in substantial agreement—appeared. The Archbishop pointed out that the Anglican adherence to Episcopacy did not involve the belief that all non-episcopalians were extra ecclesiam : but federation, while falling short of corporate reunion, was certainly more than co-operation and as such seemed to require more than local sanction. It was a question which could be discussed at the next Lambeth Conference. He saw no objection to admitting non-episcopal ministers to Anglican pulpits, nor to admitting to Holy Communion devout unconfirmed Christians who were temporarily deprived of the ministrations of their own Church : but this did not imply that Anglicans might receive Communion from non-episcopally ordained ministers, and he could not recommend it. For the present, too, it would be wise to abstain from joint Communion services in view of possible misunderstandings.

This statement pleased neither side; but Headlam felt otherwise. He considered the accusations of timidity and love of compromise which were brought against the Archbishop to be singularly out of place : at such a moment it required far more courage to be soberminded than to be extreme.[62] If some attempt at co-operation were made on the suggested lines during the next four years, it would provide valuable experience which would be useful for the discussions at the next Lambeth Conference. The further accusation levelled against the Archbishop of rigidity for refusing to countenance corporate acts of communion was equally unacceptable. There was all the difference in the world between holding opinions in a charitable manner and denying them.[63] The fact that the Church of England did not deny that God could give grace apart from the sacraments did not remove the obligation from insisting that the sacraments were the proper means of grace and from making them a rule of the Anglican communion.[64] Corporate communion services should represent not the beginning of efforts for reunion, but their consummation.

[62] 'Kikuyu: the Archbishop of Canterbury's Statement,' *C.Q.R.*, vol. 80, pp. 330–1.
[63] Ibid., p. 342.
[64] Ibid., p. 343.

CHAPTER EIGHT

Regius Professor of Divinity, Oxford

I

WHEN Dr. T. B. Strong left Christ Church, Oxford, in 1920 to become
Bishop of Ripon, he said, 'There is no doubt that the old order of the
University and Colleges is now on trial. We have succeeded in resus-
citating it, more successfully, I think, than any element in the nation.'[1]
No one did more in this task of resuscitation than Headlam. He loved
tradition and he did his utmost to restore those elements of College
and University life which had tended to lapse and be forgotten during
the War years. The festivities of Eights Week, Commem, Encaenia
and the rest—all were taken very seriously. He would run along the
tow-path shouting 'House' and expect his visitors to do the same:
he would climb to the top of Magdalen Tower to greet the first of
May: he would be 'At Home' on Sunday afternoons. In all this, as
at London, hospitality played an important part, and he entertained
on a lavish scale that would have been impossible without private
means. Here again his wife, despite indifferent health, did much with
her natural attraction and friendliness to make up for his lack of social
graces. His well-meaning efforts to get in touch with junior members
of the University, for example, were always clumsy and never tended
to improve. It was said that he persistently opened what was meant to
be pleasant conversation with 'Do you go to many lectures?'; which
was, to put it mildly, not a particularly happy gambit. There was a
notable occasion when he and his wife held a ball: the orchestra was
composed of students from various colleges, and during the evening,
in a misguided attempt to show some interest in their activities, he
went to the piano and, leaning over the top without saying a word,
subjected the poor pianist to a long and ruthless stare of great interest
—as if watching some small insect at work through a microscope. The
young man was reduced to a state of confusion, and for a moment
musical chaos reigned.

In his work as Regius Professor, however, the note of reform was

[1] Harold Anson, *T. B. Strong*, 1949, p. 44.

sounded at the very outset. His Inaugural Lecture on 'The Study of Theology' was delivered on June 13. In it he declared that theology should be the interpretation of a deep and simple religious experience; and judged by this standard it was found wanting, being concerned too much with subordinate questions and not sufficiently with fundamentals—the being and nature of God, life, death and judgment. It required a recognition of the full stream of Christian tradition, an atmosphere of liberty, a willingness to learn from all Churches and a spirit of reverent criticism. The Oxford Faculty of Theology, in order to measure up to these requirements, was in need of reform : it was in fact curious, in view of its past history and influence, that it had not been reformed before. Certain tasks would therefore have to be undertaken.[2] The first was to create a school for the training of clergy. The Faculty of Theology, like those of Law and Medicine, should be mainly professional : it should provide the training necessary for a learned profession—it should train ministers. The second task was to reform the Divinity degrees, so that they should no longer be distinguished for their lack of merit, but should indicate a sound knowledge of theology, together with a capacity for independent thought and work. Then these degrees should be made available to those who were not in orders of the Church of England without endangering their essentially Christian character. Finally, in the University as a whole, the standard of all degrees—including even a pass degree—should be such, that no one could obtain a degree who had not learned the habits of work, who was not acquainted with modern habits of thought, who had not had his intellectual interests aroused, and who had not attained a fair measure of competency in the subjects he had studied.[3] Here then, was Headlam's programme; and it was one which he was largely successful in carrying through. His vigour and ruthless determination well-nigh guaranteed success : but, needless to say, the road to success was by no means always smooth and pleasant.

II

The institution of the Post-graduate Ordination Course at Oxford was in some measure a development from the National Mission of Repentance and Hope in 1916. One result of the Mission was the appointment of certain Committees of Enquiry on various aspects of the Church's work, and Headlam was asked to serve on that which considered the Teaching Office of the Church. Its Report was published in Lent 1918, and among its recommendations was the develop-

[2] *The Study of Theology,* 1918, pp. 3–24.
[3] Ibid., pp. 24–30.

ment of post-graduate schools of theology at Oxford and Cambridge, not only for the purposes of research, but also for the training of clergy, ordinands and religious teachers. Similar schools should also be created at the new universities, while all theological colleges should be associated as closely as possible with them. Furthermore, ordinands should receive longer and more adequate theological and practical training—two years for graduates and three for non-graduates. These recommendations had a familiar Headlam ring, and were in fact largely based on two Appendices to the Report which he himself had written, one on the teaching office of the Church in relation to the Universities, and another on the training of candidates for Holy Orders.[4]

In his first term as Regius Professor Headlam produced a memorandum on the training of ordinands at Oxford which was considered at the beginning of the Michaelmas term. Actually, he was not breaking entirely new ground; for his predecessor, Scott Holland, had set up a Committee in 1914 under the chairmanship of Professor Walter Lock to discuss the same question : but he now pursued his own course with vigour, proposing a scheme which he claimed to be consistent with the recommendations of the Archbishops' Committee of Enquiry. His plan was to provide a two year course for graduates and Service candidates, in which the key-note was to be work—'the best discipline of the clerical life is to have learnt to work with diligence and honour.' The standard of the examinations need not be high, but the amount of work required would be considerable, involving as much as fifteen lectures a week. He also proposed that the Divinity professors themselves should take part in the lecturing, for the benefit not only of the students but also of themselves. On the one hand the students would have the advantage of hearing lectures from experts, while on the other the professors would be given practice in the art of lecturing with lucidity to men who were not specialists. Although a certain amount of instruction might be given in elocution, music, education and pastoral theology, most of the practical side of ministerial training should come preferably in a parish after ordination. The best preparation, for example, which the University could provide in sermon construction, was to teach men to write and think clearly by means of essays and discussions. There should also be some devotional training—obligatory weekly devotional addresses on the lines of those given by Bishop Edward King,[5] and daily attendance at college chapel; men should

---

[4] *Report of the Archbishops' First Committee of Enquiry on the National Mission. The Teaching Office of the Church,* 1918, pp. 61–2, 86–90, 102–12.
[5] Bishop Edward King of Lincoln had been Regius Professor of Pastoral Theology at Oxford from 1873 to 1885. His spiritual influence had been immense.

PLATE IV

Working in the garden at Whorlton

A typical pose
A.C.H., Canon J. O. Hannay, (George A. Birmingham),
the Misses Horner at Mells. 1931

PLATE V

Distributing bibles from a farmcart

attend also services of differing types of churchmanship in order to help them form their own convictions.

There was, of course, opposition to the plan, not a little of which was due, not so much to its details as to Headlam's evident determination to model Oxford on King's College, London, lines. For this he made no excuse. The London course had been his creation and it had worked successfully : there was therefore nothing more to be said; what had been achieved at London would be achieved at Oxford. Another obvious objection was the heavy strain the scheme would impose on the college theological tutors, possibly with harmful effects on the work of the Theological Faculty itself. Furthermore, many people felt that such a course should still be supplemented by a period of residence at a theological college. There was much to be said on moral and spiritual grounds for a complete break with academic associations; and the discipline of theological college life was wholesome : a man could remain at university and still live in a very narrow circle, which might be even more deleterious than the 'seminarist' atmosphere which Headlam associated with theological colleges.[6]

In October 1918, however, the Central Advisory Council for the Training of the Ministry gave its approval to Headlam's scheme and to a similar scheme at Cambridge for all ordinands residing in halls or hostels inspected by the Council and recognized by the Bishops. The Bishops, too, accepted the scheme, although they felt that a man would be well advised to divide his two years' training, spending one year at Oxford and another at a theological college; this, however, was not insisted on. The course proved to be extremely valuable in training the large numbers of ordinands returning from the Forces after the War; but obviously its existence depended almost entirely on Headlam. It was not really popular, and after Headlam left Oxford for Gloucester in 1923, it lost its driving force and soon disappeared.[7]

In the reform of the Divinity degrees Headlam achieved a more lasting success. Before leaving Oxford for Welwyn he had pleaded for a revision of the regulations, but nothing had been done.[8] There was no question that the degrees had fallen into deep discredit : so much so that some able men preferred to take the degree of D.Litt instead.[9] No examination was necessary, and even the requirement of theses had become more or less formal : it was said that there had been

---

[6] Some objections to the scheme were published as 'Considerations' by an influential group which included G. B. Allen, C. M. Blagden, F. E. Brightman, R. G. Parsons, W. H. Hutton, G. L. Prestige, Leighton Pullan, A. E. J. Rawlinson, T. B. Strong, N. S. Talbot, W. Temple, C. H. Turner and N. P. Williams.

[7] Nominally the Course still exists.

[8] Headlam to Professor Ince, May 1894.

[9] Archbishop William Temple was a notable example.

E

instances in the past of theses being kept in college and passed from one candidate to another, with no pretence of their being original productions. This, of course, had been the almost inevitable result of the old statutes of some colleges—before the first University Commission—requiring their fellows in Holy Orders, as most of them were, to proceed to their B.D. and D.D. degrees on penalty of forfeiting their places on the foundation. Headlam was determined on a change, and at the same time desired to throw the degrees open to men of other religious denominations. Hitherto they had been confined to priests in Anglican orders. In 1913 Scott Holland had endeavoured to secure the removal of this restriction and he had been supported by all the Divinity professors and many of the leading clergy. The proposal had been carried by a considerable body in congregation but had been decisively rejected by Convocation after a stormy debate. The argument of the opposition had lain, not in any prejudice against Nonconformists, but in a refusal to support a scheme which involved the danger of the disappearance of the Christian character of the degrees. Theology might become a purely intellectual study, wherein the phenomena of one religion were considered to have no more intrinsic importance than those of another. Such fears had doubtless gained their strength from Scott Holland's lighthearted but tactless remarks about presenting a Buddhist for a divinity degree, and his later protestations that this was not meant seriously had not been sufficient to dispel every doubt. As Headlam himself had remarked at the time, there was a fear in some people's minds that a situation might arise where a person might be admitted to a divinity degree for writing a thesis which disproved the existence of God.[10] He had supported Scott Holland's proposal in an article in *The Church Quarterly Review* although urging at the same time that the Christian character of the degrees should be safeguarded.[11] He felt that they should be professional in character, indicating that their recipients were qualified to serve in the Christian Ministry as a whole, and not of just one particular denomination. He even went so far as to suggest that the leaders of the various Nonconformist bodies should be treated like bishops and receive a D.D. automatically : but it was one of their number, Dr. W. B. Selbie, Principal of Mansfield College, who earnestly and successfully persuaded him to refrain from seeking approval of such a plan.

Headlam's proposals for reform, which safeguarded the specifically Christian character of the degrees, were put forward in February 1920 and were carried without opposition. The new regulations

[10] A. C. Headlam, 'Divinity Degrees,' *C.Q.R.*, vol. 76, p. 358.
[11] Ibid., pp. 357–70.

required of candidates for the B.D. that they should first pass a qualifying examination, except in the case of those who had obtained a
first or second class in the Honours School of Theology and who were
excused part of the examination : a thesis was also required. Candidates for the D.D. were required to present either published work or
a thesis containing an original contribution to the study of Christian
Theology. One concession was granted : any one who had matricu-
lated before the Michaelmas term of 1909 was permitted to supplicate
for the B.D. and D.D. in accordance with the regulations then in force
at any time before the Michaelmas term of 1924—an arrangement of
which a number of men hurriedly took advantage.[12] Although these
degrees were now much more difficult to obtain, Headlam did in fact
show remarkable leniency towards hard-working parish priests who
tried to continue their theological studies in this way in the face of
difficulties. At the same time the degrees were no longer restricted to
Anglicans in priests' orders : and in June 1920, largely on Headlam's
recommendation, honorary doctorates were conferred on eminent
theologians of other denominations, both clerical and lay, among whom
were Baron von Hügel, Mgr. Batiffol, George Adam Smith,
A. S. Peake, James Cooper and John Skinner.

At the same time Headlam undertook a successful reform of the
Honours School of Theology. The existing curriculum had been in
existence for roughly a quarter of a century, following lines which he
had advocated when at All Souls. The basis was the Old Testament,
the New Testament and the formative period of Church History. All this
had provided a sound basis in the knowledge of Historical Theology,
and met the needs of the period. At the end of the nineteenth century
people were mainly concerned with such questions as the early history
of Church organization, the growth of the Canon and the authority
of the New Testament and the Creeds. Twenty years later, however,
although these questions were still a matter of interest, they were
regarded from a different point of view ; and the purely historical
element was no longer so dominating. Headlam considered four things
were necessary. The first was to reduce the amount of specialized Old
Testament studies, especially for the weaker student : the second was
to give greater emphasis to the religious teaching of the New Testament : the third was to broaden the basis of the study of Doctrine and
to connect it more directly with the needs of the day : and the fourth
was to make Christian Philosophy a necessary part of the curriculum.[13]
It was on these lines that Headlam submitted proposals in December
1921, and these were passed in the following February. An estimate

[12] *Oxford Examination Statutes*, 1922, pp. 279–86.
[13] *Theological Education at the Universities*, Oxford, 1921, pp. 18–19.

of Headlam's achievements in this field has been given by the late Professor D. C. Simpson :

'In the Theological Faculty reforms *were* needed, but the *means* and *methods* of achieving them! To some of us he seemed to be scrapping much of what *we* held dear in order to turn our Faculty into a replica of that of London University—more particularly the King's College colouring of it. I am inclined to think that it was his constant references to and laudation of the latter that put up our backs and made us his critics instead of (as we might otherwise have been) his allies. But looking back I realize the greatness of the debt we owe to Headlam, coming as he did after the long and latterly senile reign of Ince and then of Scott Holland, whose interests were wider—so wide and so practical as to leave him no time or energy in those latter days of his to reform the curriculum of the Faculty. It would, of course, have been in a far worse state (and in a way easier for Headlam to turn upside down) but for the devoted labours of Dr. Walter Lock, Warden of Keble, to whom for its maintenance in pre-Headlam days we owe as great a debt as we do to Headlam for the latter's reforms.'

His emphasis on Christian Philosophy was shown by his wholehearted support for Dr. Charles Nolloth of Oriel College in his design to found a Chair of the Philosophy of the Christian Religion, of which C. C. J. Webb became the first holder. Dr. Nolloth insisted that he should have the right of making the first appointment and that the person appointed should be a communicant member of the Church of England and a graduate from either Oxford or Cambridge—a limitation doubtless due to his conservative instincts. This limitation was modified, however, to include London—a concession attributed to Headlam out of loyalty to the University which he had served. Headlam was responsible for submitting this scheme and it was passed by Congregation and Convocation in February 1920 at the same time as the reform of the Divinity degrees.

III

Headlam's lack of sympathy with what he called the seminarist outlook was shown by his determination to provide students with opportunities for looking at religion from more than one point of view. In February 1920 the American scholar, Professor B. W. Bacon, came to give a course of lectures on 'Jesus and Paul' at Manchester College, the inter-denominational foundation. Notices of the course were sent to theological students at the different colleges, which caused resentment in some quarters. Headlam was approached and asked to remonstrate with the Principal, Dr. L. P. Jacks, on the grounds that Professor Bacon was considered to be unorthodox in his views and might lead students astray. He refused to take any action, however, and later indicated his appreciation of Professor Bacon as a scholar by proposing that he should be given the honorary degree of D.Litt.

More notable was his attitude to the Revd. H. D. A. Major, a leading Modernist. In 1919 Ripon Clergy College was transferred to Oxford becoming Ripon Hall, with Mr. Major as Principal. Headlam welcomed the arrangement and said to him, 'We have two other kinds of Churchmanship here in Oxford and we shall welcome you : but don't think that I agree with you, for I don't.' But despite disagreeing with Major's outlook, he did not hesitate to send him students to tutor. Two years later came the noted charge of heresy. The Modern Churchmen's Conference, held at Girton College, Cambridge, in August 1921, considered the subject 'Christ and the Creeds', and papers which had been read—some of which contained statements of a highly controversial nature—were printed in the September issue of *The Modern Churchman*. One of these statements, dealing with the Resurrection, had been made by Mr. Major : 'The form which the doctrine assumes in my mind is the survival of death by a personality which has shed its physical integument for ever.' On September 10 the Revd. C. E. Douglas formally delated Mr. Major to the Bishop of Oxford on a charge of heresy, accusing him of teaching a doctrine concerning the Resurrection contrary to the Christian faith as set forth in the Creeds and in Holy Scripture.[14] Mr. Major denied the charge, submitting to the Bishop a lengthy reply. Dr. Burge then submitted the case to four Theological professors—Headlam, Lock, Watson and Turner, asking them to advise what further action should be taken. For various reasons Turner demurred at giving an opinion; but the other three agreed that there was no sufficient cause for proceeding with a more formal enquiry. The Bishop therefore rejected the charge of heresy and decided to take no further action.[15] Headlam felt that many things had been said at Cambridge with which he disagreed but the papers undoubtedly represented considerable ability and theological learning and great religious earnestness.[16] His view of the situation was summed up in a letter to the Archbishop of Canterbury on April 28, 1922, deploring the action of the English Church Union in asking the Convocation of Canterbury to condemn certain statements

[14] H. M. Burge, *The Doctrine of the Resurrection of the Body*, 1922, p. 1.
[15] Ibid., pp.2–61, 63–70.
[16] 'The Modernist Christology,' *C.Q.R.*, vol. 93, pp. 203–7.

expressed at the Conference as subversive to the Christian religion :

'As far as I can judge the whole tendency of the work of the writers of *The Modern Churchman* is definitely constructive. The attacks upon them come from a body of men who seem entirely blind to the many religious difficulties which are aroused at the present day, and who seem not to understand the points at issue in these discussions. I doubt if any of the statements made in *The Modern Churchman* are definitely heretical ; but some of them are undoubtedly precarious and many of them half thought out : but if the members of the E.C.U. are anxious to test that question, they ought to bring a definite accusation of heresy before the proper courts, stating the particular passages complained of and the actual doctrines which are denied. If they do that, a proper trial might ensue before the competent courts with an appeal, of course, to the secular authorities. If they are not prepared to do that, they should meet erroneous doctrines such as they assert are being put forward by the methods of reverent criticism.'

Archbishop Davidson was very much in agreement, and largely because of this he was reluctant to accede to the demands for the appointment of a Commission on Doctrine. He only did so after considerable hesitation in December 1922.[17]

IV

Two other features of Headlam's work at Oxford which merit attention were his interest in the Serbian students and his relations with the Governing Body at Christ Church.

At the end of 1915, after eighteen months of heroic resistance, Serbia fell before the attacks of the Austro-German and Bulgarian armies. Many people fled through Albania to avoid capture, among them the remnants of the Theological Seminary at Belgrade. They eventually reached Corfu and began to work as best they could, until a telegram from the Archbishop of Canterbury arrived, inviting them to come and train in England. A number of them went to Cuddesdon and Dorchester Theological Colleges, and some went to S. Stephen's House, Oxford, to read for a degree. On his return to Oxford in 1918 Headlam took a great interest in them, becoming Chairman of the Committee which supervised their academic training and general welfare. When the Serbian leader, Father Nicolai Velimirovic, later Bishop of Ochrida, thanked him for his help, he replied, 'You can find any

17 Cf. G. K. A. Bell, *Randall Davidson*, 2nd ed. 1938, pp. 1134–50.

number of charitable persons, even without me, to help in some kind
of charity; which, of course, is important. But I myself would like to
help in a more lasting and constructive work for the future of your
people and your Church. In my opinion, this work should be to pick
the best of your boys now in England and to give them the best education we are able to give them here.' This in effect helped to answer
what Father Nicolai considered to be one of Serbia's greatest needs—
the creation of a well-educated clergy to revitalize and reorganize the
life of the Church.

By 1920 S. Stephen's House was no longer available, so the
Serbians found a temporary home in Parks Road, which became
known as the Hostel of S. Sava and S. George. Headlam hoped that
this might develop into a permanent college for Eastern Orthodox
students; unfortunately financial difficulties never made this possible.
In all this work Headlam took a deep and kindly interest in the men
as individuals. He endeavoured to make a real personal contact with
them; he was untiring in his efforts for their welfare; and he did all
he could to bring them into the general life of the University. The
men on their side thoroughly appreciated all this and acquired for
him a deep and lasting affection. Many wrote to him regularly for the
rest of their lives and they feted him during his visits to Jugo-slavia
in 1926 and 1936. The Serbian authorities showed their appreciation
of his work by conferring upon him the Order of S. Sava, 4th Class,
in 1919.

His relations with the Governing Body of Christ Church were less
cordial. He himself stated quite openly, 'The Governing Body was
without exception the most disagreeable body of which I have ever
been a member—more disagreeable even than the Senate of the
University of London.' [18] This, of course, was saying a great deal; but
it was a view by no means shared by all his fellow-members.[19]
Admittedly there was some heritage of resentment from the past on
the part of the Governing Body at the way in which, until after the
middle of the nineteenth century, the clerical element had held a
dominating position in both Cathedral and College affairs. But the
real reason for Headlam's adverse opinion went deeper. King's
College, London, had also possessed a dual constitution, for which he
himself had been responsible and which had worked efficiently and
amicably—far more so than the dual system at Christ Church: but
whereas at King's College Headlam had been at the head of affairs
and in a dominating position, at Christ Church he was not at the head
of affairs and was much less able to get his own way. Other members

[18] Anson, *T. B. Strong*, p. 32.
[19] Ibid., p. 33.

of the Governing Body were equally determined and pugnacious and not in the least overawed by his formidable manner. Consequently meetings were often stormy. Headlam's temper was quickly frayed : he found opposition from men of like ability and stature quite unpalatable ; and it drew out the worst in him. The Chapter Fund was a typical cause of strife. It was the first charge on Christ Church revenues ; and one of the leading senior lay members had only to utter the acid, but true remark that the Canons held preference shares in the House for Headlam to get simply furious. Or again, when Professor White succeeded Dr. Strong as Dean, the question arose as to whether the Chapter or the Governing Body were responsible for the renovation of the Deanery. During the controversy Headlam wrote to one lay member of the Governing Body, 'That members of the Governing Body should be still brooding over grievances sixty years old which are really no grievances at all, simply amazes me. . . . I came here with an eager desire not merely to fulfil the duties of my Chair but to throw myself into the life of the College as I have thrown myself into the life of every other institution I have been connected with. I find myself thwarted in every direction. I find a Governing Body which seems to love to nurse old grievances and quarrels and grudges, which takes a narrow, illiberal view of almost every question, which tries to keep all authority in the hands of a clique of College tutors. I can assure you that, coming here with every desire to be as great a help to the College and as friendly as possible, the impression that has been created upon me has been most unfortunate.' Protests that no sense of grievance did in fact exist in the Governing Body left him quite unconvinced. Despite these differences Headlam found life congenial and had no great desire to leave Oxford. His official duties were not onerous, but he was never idle. It was during this period that he emerged as a dominating figure in the œcumenical movement, and so extensive did his work become that in the summer of 1921 he felt obliged to relinquish the editorship of *The Church Quarterly Review* to 'Members of the Faculty of Theology, King's College London,' which meant in practice Dr. W. R. Matthews, the Revd. R. P. Hanson and Claude Jenkins.

When Headlam was made a Companion of Honour—a rare distinction—in the Birthday Honours List of June 1921, some people said rather unkindly that it was a consolation prize instead of a bishopric : but at that time he had no real wish to become a bishop. In the autumn of that year the sees of Bath and Wells and Salisbury both fell vacant, and he confessed to his wife that he really dreaded the prospect of being offered either of them : although Henson did in fact urge his claims on the Prime Minister. Archbishop Davidson had long made up his mind, however, that Headlam was a leader whose learning and

driving power were needed on the episcopal bench, and whose qualities far outweighed the disadvantages of his brusque manner. When
therefore Dr. Gibson resigned the see of Gloucester in the autumn of
1922, he urged the new Prime Minister, Mr. Bonar Law, to appoint
Headlam as his successor. Henson, who knew the Archbishop's mind,
warned Headlam and advised him to accept if the offer were made.

October 28, 1922.

'My dear Headlam,

'It is, of course, very futile to discuss personal futures, one's own or
another's : but we are old friends, and neither of us is, in any unworthy
sense, an ambitious man : therefore I shall allow myself to say this.

'If you are offered the Bishoprick of Gloucester, *take it.* Your doing
so will not prejudice, and probably would facilitate, your going to
London, or to one of the Primacies. It is to be remembered that these
greater sees are generally filled by translation, and that there is a
strong tradition to follow that policy in Downing Street. Indeed, if
translation be allowed at all, it could hardly be otherwise. Moreover,
you are now sixty years old, and, as men think now, that is a fairly
advanced age for appointment to a bishoprick.

'Great as is the importance of your present position, and wide as is
your influence, I have come to the conclusion that *you could do your
best work now as a Bishop.*

'The Church of England needs a strong man with knowledge and
a considerable backing of public confidence *on the Bench.* In some
ways a comparatively light see like Gloucester would be better than an
absorbingly heavy see like London. No one who has not an inside
knowledge of episcopal counsels can realize how greatly the Church
needs strength and independence *there.* Therefore, I do beg of you,
if the offer is made, to regard it as the call, and to obey. . . .'

The offer was duly made; and in early December Headlam accepted
—a decision which the Archbishop of Canterbury received with intense
satisfaction.

December 5, 1922.

'My dear Headlam,

'At last after several days of expectation and anxiety I learn to-night
from Downing Street that you have accepted the call which I was
determined should, if I could bring it about, be made to you.

'I am quite sure of the gain to our episcopal counsels from your
participation therein, and of the added weight which will attach to
utterances of a joint kind which are sometimes inevitable. . . .

'My own time of active work cannot, I imagine, be long prolonged and I am the more anxious to know that in the coming years the reins will be in hands which I, for one, can trust as regards the great things —the things that really matter. . . .'

Headlam's departure from Oxford was not long delayed. His appointment was announced on December 9, and he was consecrated in Westminster Abbey on the Feast of the Conversion of S. Paul— January 25, 1923—together with Dr. J. H. B. Masterman, suffragan Bishop of Plymouth.

v

On the day of his consecration his book *The Life and Teaching of Jesus the Christ* was published, aptly described as a parting gift from the Regius Professor. Much of it had been delivered as lectures at King's College, London, and at Oxford, and he had been working on it intermittently since 1918. The scope of the book was limited, dealing only with the Gospel sources and our Lord's life and teaching as far as the Transfiguration : but it was only the first part of an attempt 'to put the case of the New Testament leading to a belief in a Divine Christ merely on the grounds of true history.' [20] Inevitably it was critical of those who denied the historicity of Jesus and those Form-critics who regarded the Gospels, not as sources for the life and teaching of our Lord, but as expositions of what the early Church thought about Him. The views of scholars such as Professor J. Wellhausen, Dr. Foakes-Jackson and Dr. Kirsopp Lake therefore came under fire [21]; although rather surprisingly he made no mention of three German writers—M. Dibelius, K. L. Schmidt and R. Bultmann— whose works on Form Criticism had created such a stir after the War.[22]

The book was an important piece of historical work, written in the scientific Lightfoot tradition. Yet it was written with clarity and simplicity, acceptable both to the theologian and to the thoughtful layman. It was truly popular, not only running into a second edition within a matter of weeks in this country, but also meriting special American and German editions. Cuthbert Turner's comment is worth recording :

[20] Headlam to Fr. Rickaby s.j., March 9, 1923.
[21] *The Life and Teaching of Jesus the Christ*, 1923, pp. 30-2, 42.
[22] M. Dibelius, *Die Formgeschichte des Evangeliums*, 1919; K. L. Schmidt, *Der Rahmen der Geschichte Jesu*, 1919; R. Bultmann, *Die Geschichte der synoptischen Tradition*, 1921.

'We do enormously need to popularize the results of sane and sober criticism, and yet to show that they leave the centre and core of the Gospels untouched. And the best way of doing that is not by arguing, but by telling the story itself. Now that the whole is done, you must let me say how much, as a whole, I admire and welcome it. It has been a great pleasure, perhaps also a little bit of a surprise, to find how nearly, in this central subject, our views, critical, historical, theological, coincide. Perhaps the younger generation would call us "late Victorian" just as I call Sanday "mid-Victorian." But, unless I am much mistaken, your book will fill a real gap; the thing wanted doing and it is exactly what your gifts fitted you, more perhaps than any of the rest of us, to do.' [23]

[23] C. Turner to Headlam, October 4, 1922.

CHAPTER NINE

The Bampton Lectures and the Lambeth Conference 1920

I

HEADLAM'S election as Bampton Lecturer for 1920 saw the fulfilment of a design which had been in his mind ever since the Bonskeid Conference of 1889—a study of the growth and development of the Christian Church and its relation to the problem of reunion. The lectures, delivered during the Hilary and Trinity terms, unquestionably had a profound influence on the Lambeth Conference, which began in July. They were published by John Murray with unprecedented speed; and the book *The Doctrine of the Church and Christian Reunion* appeared on June 7—the day after the delivery of the final lecture and one month before the opening of the Conference. It immediately aroused considerable interest and the first edition was quickly exhausted. Much of the book was not new, for Headlam made considerable use of his earlier writings on the subject : but here, for the first time, he presented to the world a full and masterly statement of his position. It was a position which he maintained for the rest of his life, completely unshaken by all criticism. Throughout it conveyed the impression of confidence and finality : his mind was made up and his last word had been spoken. Cuthbert Turner wrote, 'One who finds it extraordinarily difficult to clarify his ideas and state them in a form which shall express in due balance and proportion the elements which he dimly seems to see must be preserved in juxtaposition with one another, may well lay down Dr. Headlam's Bampton Lectures with a sigh of envy, for here we have a writer for whom all these difficulties, in so far as they exist for him at all, have been satisfactorily solved. In some three hundred and twenty pages the whole course of Christian history is surveyed : . . . what seems to be the most prominent characteristics of each period, and the most fundamental problems in each group of documents, are described in outline; differences are discussed and objections are dismissed; the argument marches relentlessly over ground strewn with the debris of eighteen centuries of debate to its inevitable and triumphant close.' [1]

[1] C. H. Turner, 'The Doctrine of the Church and Christian Reunion, *C.Q.R.*, vol. xc, p. 330.

Almost inevitably its reception was mixed. Professor Nairne rightly wrote, 'Of course plain men and scholars and sober and saintly church-men will find plenty to question, to criticize, to disagree with. . . . These Lectures may or may not win assent. As in all reasonings of man, so here there must be defects.'[2] At more than one point Head-lam's interpretation of evidence was questioned, both publicly and privately. Dr. Darwell Stone, for example, was so deeply concerned at his treatment of Apostolic Succession that he submitted a criticism of it to the Archbishop of Canterbury for distribution to members of the Lambeth Conference.[3] Or again, Brightman, Gore and Turner all remonstrated with him for his reading of a passage from S. Augustine, Brightman even going so far as to describe it as 'monstrous, and such as would disgrace a Fourth Form schoolboy'[4] : but Headlam was impervious to their criticisms. In the Preface to the second edition he wrote, 'I have confined myself to making some corrections almost entirely verbal. I have seen no reason for making larger changes.'[5]

Admittedly Headlam was entitled to adhere to his own opinions if he felt convinced that they were right, but in so doing he appar-ently and sometimes quite inexplicably failed to take into considera-tion other points of view on a number of really important issues. Perhaps pressure of work and lack of time may have been largely to blame; but particularly in those sections of the book where earlier work was incorporated, the more recent studies of eminent scholars were ignored. For example, portions of his chapter on 'The Origins of the Church' were taken verbatim from articles which he had written fifteen years previously and no reference was made to anything which had been written during the intervening period: the eschatological interpretation of the Kingdom of God was given the most summary treatment and Schweitzer was not even considered worthy of a reference. Again, although he asserted quite emphatically that episco-pacy could not claim apostolic authority, even though it had its origin in the apostolic Church, he made no mention of Dr. Armitage Robinson's weighty arguments to the contrary which had appeared in 1917 in *Essays on the Early History of the Church and the Ministry.*[6] Or again, when discussing the question of non-episcopal

[2] A. Nairne, op. cit., p. 356.
[3] F. L. Cross, *Darwell Stone*, 1943, p. 142.
[4] *The Doctrine of the Church and Christian Reunion*, 1920, pp. 159–60. Headlam asserted S. Augustine as stating that priesthood and episcopacy were not necessary for salvation, whereas the others insisted that S. Augustine meant that a person could be saved without being a bishop, but could not be saved without being a Christian.
[5] Ibid., 2nd ed., Preface, p. xxi.
[6] Ibid., pp. 105–6, 131 ; cf. H. B. Swete (editor), *Essays on the Early History of the Church and the Ministry*, 1917, pp. 57–92.

ordinations in the second and third centuries, he referred to Gore's treatment of the subject in his *The Church and Ministry*, describing it as 'the fullest discussion of the problem that I know'; but he ignored Turner's massive essay on 'The Organization of the Church' in the first volume of *The Cambridge Mediaeval History*.[7]

In the same way he refused to discuss or perhaps even to accept the problems involved in the question of the nature of the Church. For him it was all perfectly clear and simple. The Church consisted of all baptized Christians who believed in the Lord Jesus Christ : it was the purpose of God that all these people should be united in one body—a unity which did not in fact exist owing to sin : a reunited Church of such people could be built on the basis of the Lambeth Quadrilateral —the Scriptures as contained in the Old and New Testaments, the Nicene Creed, the two Sacraments of Baptism and Holy Communion, and the historic Episcopate.[8] But Headlam did not or would not realize that this scheme of things depended absolutely upon an agreement as to the nature of the Church : and it was upon this very point that opinions were in fact so strongly divided and continued to be so.[9] Seventeen years later, after a period of tremendous activity in the œcumenical field, Archbishop Temple pointed out that men were still prone to take the Church itself for granted and to concentrate upon its various functions and relationships, whereas the main subject of difference was the nature of the Church and all other differences flowed from it.[10] Dr. Armitage Robinson did in fact write to Headlam pointing out the difficulties involved in the doctrine of the Church. There would be no general agreement on the assertion that the different denominations as such were within the Church or were integral parts of it : both the Baptists and the Independents, for example, had deliberately left the Church to set up what they considered to be a truer Church, so to speak. They would have repudiated the view that they and the Anglican Church which they had left were groups within the same Church : and Scottish Presbyterians

[7] Ibid., p. 102 ; cf. *The Cambridge Mediaeval History*, vol. 1, pp. 143–82.
[8] Ibid., pp. 209, 231, 280.
[9] The whole question was aired in a little book which Darwell Stone and Fr. F. W. Puller produced in 1921 entitled, *Who are Members of the Church?* Later Professor O. C. Quick expressed it with admirable succinctness : 'The . . . doctrine of the Church's nature . . . depends upon the answer to the question : What is the essential relation between that outward structure which makes the Church an organized society in the view of the world at large, and the spiritual reality which all agree to be, in the deepest and most ultimate sense, the Church itself? Or, more particularly, do any outward unity and continuity of organization in any way *constitute* the unity of the Church, or are they *outward* even in the sense of being external to that unity?' (O. C. Quick, *Doctrines of the Creed*, 1938, p. 330.)
[10] L. Hodgson (editor), *Faith and Order, Edinburgh 1937*, 1937, p. 64.

would have said the same. It was all very well to quote S. Augustine as saying that Christian unity meant Christian charity, that outside the Church there was no charity, and that no one could possess it unless he loved unity : but both the Presbyterians and the Congregationalists had been willing to sacrifice unity in order to gain something they valued more highly.[11] Headlam, however, was not to be moved.

Another feature which not only gave rise to controversy but was also far-reaching in its consequences was Headlam's interpretation of the Lambeth Quadrilateral. In its original form, as propounded at Chicago at the Convention of the American Episcopal Church in 1886, it had stated that Christian unity could only be restored by the return of all Christian Communions to 'the principles of unity exemplified by the undivided Church during the first ages of its existence.' These principles were 'the substantial deposit of Christian Faith and Order committed by Christ and His Apostles to the Church unto the end of the world, and therefore incapable of compromise or surrender by those who have been ordained to be its stewards and trustees for the common and equal benefit of all men.' As inherent parts of this sacred deposit and therefore essential to the restoration of unity among the divided branches of Christendom were the Holy Scriptures of the Old and New Testament, the Nicene Creed, the two Sacraments of Baptism and the Lord's Supper and the historic Episcopate. Two years later the 1888 Lambeth Conference Committee on Home Reunion had accepted the Quadrilateral in a revised form, involving the addition of the Apostles' Creed, as 'a basis on which approach may be, under God's blessing, made towards Home Reunion.' The four Articles, instead of being 'inherent parts of the sacred deposit,' had now become 'a basis upon which approach may be made' : but in both forms they were clearly the starting point—'a *terminus a quo* from which there could be no dispensation, but from which, when accepted, one might proceed to the discussion of other matters in dispute.' [12] Headlam, however, now took these four points and regarded them as a sufficient basis for reunion itself ; no further agreement was necessary. 'The necessary elements of the Christian faith are few, and it is the right and wise course to insist on them only. If you really mean reunion, it is only possible if you reduce what you demand from others to things which you feel that you can rightly insist on. . . . What the fullest and richest religious life demands is, on the one hand, a firm and simple faith ; on the other, the widest intellectual freedom.' [13]

[11] Cf. *Bampton Lectures*, p. 145.
[12] Rouse and Neil (editors), *A History of the Ecumenical Movement*, pp. 264–5.
[13] *Bampton Lectures*, pp. 280–2.

Consistent with this demand for intellectual freedom, Headlam was unwilling to attach any specific interpretation to Creeds or Sacraments. 'It will always be right and necessary that the same document should be held by different persons in different ways. To impose any particular interpretation on the Creed is the same as to put forth a new and additional Creed.' [14] As for the Sacraments, Christ ordained them as rules of life and devotion, and not as articles of belief. 'What is essential is that, by our manner of celebrating them, we should make clear that we intend to fulfil His will. We should have no necessary rule of faith about the Eucharist any more than the Church for the first 1,200 years of its history. Many of the evils of disunion have come from an attempt to define what cannot be defined.' [15] Here again, Headlam was treading upon delicate ground, approaching perilously near the primitive conception that private beliefs did not matter provided correct procedure was followed. The Roman Empire, for example, had required no more than the fulfilment of the external demands of state worship; and it was in fact for external nonconformity rather than for theological conviction that the early Christians had found themselves in trouble. The impossibility of divorcing faith from cultus has been stated admirably by the late Professor O. C. Quick: 'The whole point of the Gospel is that it is essentially a message concerning certain historical facts and their meaning in relation to God and man. The Church exists to declare that message to men and to manifest the new life of freedom and fellowship which belief in it makes possible. . . . Creeds and dogmas are but formulated statements which are needed as visible signs of the continuity and permanence of the witness of the truth of the Gospel. Apart from the interpretation given to them by living minds which they guide, they could have no authority and indeed no significance at all. . . . Creeds express faith in God and in what through Christ He has both revealed and done, not assent to a certain number of propositions. They are standard expressions of the Church's faith, not test-formulae to be imposed on people for their assent.' [16]

Headlam also took the same liberal line with regard to Orders. 'All those who . . . appoint their ministers as His Apostles did with prayer and the laying on of hands, must be held to have valid Sacraments and Orders.' [17] This meant that he was prepared not only to accept the validity of non-episcopal ministries, provided they were appointed with prayer and the laying on of hands, but also to dispense with

---

[14] Ibid., pp. 237–8.
[15] Ibid., p. 281.
[16] Quick, *Doctrines of the Creed*, pp. 319–20.
[17] *Bampton Lectures*, p. 280.

reordination in a reunited Church. What was required was a mutual recognition of all orders and the granting of a new commission to all ministers to work under the new conditions, with the clear understanding that all future ministers in such a Church should be episcopally ordained.[19] His mind had, of course, been moving in this direction for some years—in 1913 he had asked Fr. Puller, 'In a reunited Church is there anything possible short of reordination?' But this was the first time that he had publicly stated this bold and extremely contentious proposal. Precedent could be found in the action of S. Augustine and the African Church in healing the schism with the Donatists by recognizing their Orders and Sacraments; although, of course, the Donatists possessed an episcopal organization as traditional as that of the African Church itself. 'On every point of Church organization they were one with the Catholic party. They had the same hierarchy and the same sacraments.'[20] It was clearly a case of schism and not heresy. In undertaking this charitable action, however, Headlam considered S. Augustine to have committed himself to a theory which was neither Scriptural nor Catholic—the theory of the indelibility of orders.[21] Headlam maintained that all patristic passages prior to S. Augustine referring to episcopal succession from the Apostles supported the idea of serial succession only. In its early struggles with Gnosticism the early Church regarded Apostolic Succession as an external guarantee of the identity of the Faith with that taught by the Apostles : the doctrinal validity of the Faith was guaranteed by the succession of bishops in each see—a succession of office. The authority of the bishops was derived from the Church, and had not been inherited by sacramental transmission from the Apostles.[22] That was why it had been generally assumed before S. Augustine that heretical and schismatical orders were null and void and ordination bestowed no indelible character. The idea of indelibility had been S. Augustine's invention to facilitate the restoration of the Donatists to the Church.

On this question of Apostolic Succession Headlam refused to be liberal—a striking contrast to his attitude towards the Creed and Sacraments. It had one rigid, precise meaning; and there was no evidence for any other in the early Church. Many people tried to persuade him against this rigid interpretation, but in vain. He triumphantly quoted Cuthbert Turner as supporting his point of view in his essay on Apostolic Succession in *Essays on the Early History of*

---

[19] Ibid., pp. 306–7 ; cf. pp. 254, 268, 311.
[20] Ibid., p. 142.
[21] Ibid., pp. 161–2.
[22] Ibid., pp. 124–33.

the Church and the Ministry [23] ; but Turner's essay was really concerned with the word διαδοχή—succession—and not with the effect
and significance of ordination. Turner did actually believe Apostolic
Succession to have a wider, transmissional meaning, but felt that the
two ideas were by no means incompatible.[24] There was really nothing
to be gained by an insistence on a primary and grammatically correct
meaning of Apostolic Succession : the idea of transmission did not need
the exact use of the word—it could be implied; and it was the
implication of the transmissional idea that was claimed by Turner and
others. To this Headlam retorted, 'Surely if we once begin to give up
taking words in their ordinary and common meaning, and assume that
the statements that we read in ancient authors are quite different from
what they say, we had better give up writing history at all.' [25] This
was rather unfair, for he himself had admitted in his article on
Apostolic Succession in *The Prayer Book Dictionary* that a passage
from Hippolytus in *Refutatio omnium haeresium* might bear this
implicit meaning of transmission [26]; while in his references to the
Eucharist in the *Bampton Lectures* he claimed that we were not
expected to accept any words in a particular way.[27] On this issue
Claude Jenkins wrote to him, 'In regard to the fact of Apostolic
Succession you have more than once seemed to try to establish a
negative inference from the evidence when the most that is warranted
is a suspense of judgment. The establishment of such a negative inference could of course be fatal to the theory you set yourself to dis-
prove, but it is not necessary to the disproof, and if its establishment
were necessary to your conclusions they would seem to me to rest on
a highly precarious foundation.'

Despite its shortcomings, however, the book was a fine, courageous
piece of work. Appearing when the œcumenical movement as it is
known to-day was still in its infancy, it was a brave pioneering effort.
As Professor Nairne remarked, Headlam had looked facts in the
face and had shaped a policy.[28] Its influence was profound—perhaps
even more so abroad than at home ; and subsequent events proved it
to be a major factor in shaping the course of movements towards
reunion for the next twenty years. The judgment of Professor Flögstrup
of Denmark was significant : 'We have many of us seen visions and
dreamed dreams, but here ideals which seemed remote and unreal are

---

[23] Ibid., p. 124.
[24] H. N. Bate (editor), *Catholic and Apostolic*, 1931, pp. 36–8; *C.Q.R.*,
vol. xc, p. 336.
[25] *Bampton Lectures*, p. xii.
[26] *The Prayer Book Dictionary*, p. 41.
[27] *Bampton Lectures*, p. 272.
[28] *C.Q.R.*, vol. xc, p. 355.

brought near to us. They appear to be not Utopian but practicable. I should think your proposals would be the very best basis for future deliberations and practical attempts.' [29]

II

Headlam's influence on the Lambeth Conference was by no means confined to his Bampton Lectures. He also conceived the idea of gathering valuable data on reunion problems from professional theologians, and he summoned a conference of some fifty scholars for that purpose in Oxford on June 25–30, 1920. It was an impressive assembly —the cream of scholarship from the various schools of thought in the Church of England and in all the other principal religious bodies except the Roman Catholics in England and Scotland. It was fortunate that this conference followed the third conference between representatives of the Anglican and Free Churches at Mansfield College, for it was possible to avoid the mistakes which had been made there. The Mansfield conference, apart from being strongly Protestant in flavour, had conveyed the impression of being in too great a hurry —its announced intention had been 'not merely to promote, but to secure reunion.' Its manifesto, emphasizing the fundamental equality of both Anglican and Free Churches within the Church of Christ and the efficacy of all their ministries, had urged the interchange of pulpits, mutual admission to Holy Communion, and the authorization of ministers who desired it to minister fully and freely in the churches of other denominations—such authorization not being regarded as reordination or involving a repudiation of their previous ministry. This document had found critics among both Anglicans and Free Churchmen ; and Dr. B. J. Kidd voiced the feelings of many in his remark to Headlam that the conference had not fully thought out the implications of the language it had used.

It was not surprising, therefore, that Headlam sounded a note of caution at the very outset of his own conference. No immediate results should be expected from such meetings : if the various churches were to overcome their difficulties, they must get behind their differences of belief. The conference then proceeded to examine the nature of the Church, the Ministry and Sacraments, and the place of the Creed in a reunited Church. As might be expected from a body of experts, the discussion throughout was closely reasoned, revealing at times not so much contradictions, but something which perhaps was even worse— parallel lines of thought which apparently could only end in infinity. On the question of the Church there was general agreement that it

[29] Professor Flögstrup to Headlam, October 2, 1920.

consisted of all who professed the faith of Christ and had been baptized into His Name. The only dissent came from a few extreme Anglo-Catholics led by Dr. Darwell Stone, who desired Confirmation rather than Baptism as the necessary condition of membership. The Creed, too, caused little difficulty, most delegates being prepared to accept the Nicene Creed as the right expression of the religious unity of the Church. Nor did the Ministry prove to be as thorny a problem as might have been expected. Dr. Darwell Stone again was prepared to go to almost any lengths to preserve the rigid transmission theory of Apostolic Succession, but he found little support. Here the Church of Scotland delegates made a valuable contribution in stressing that our Lord had never renounced His own ministry and that it was He Himself who set the ordinand before the Church and ordained him : the Ministry was the ministry of Jesus Christ.

The conference devoted most of its attention to the question of the validity of sacraments. The Anglicans unanimously conceded to the Free Church delegates that validity was not the same as efficacy and did not deny the efficacy of Nonconformist sacraments. The Revd. O. C. Quick distinguished between two conceptions of validity : one was the due performance of the sign appointed by Christ, the other was the due authorization to administer the sacrament. According to the first conception, Headlam and those who agreed with him could maintain that Nonconformist sacraments were valid : but that was not sufficient to serve as a basis for a reunited Church, which demanded the second conception. This latter conception regarded validity as a matter of degree ; and it was one which many of the delegates found attractive. On the question of non-episcopal orders, there was little enthusiasm for reordination for its own sake ; but many delegates—both Anglican and otherwise—were willing to be reordained provided there was no implication of a slur on their existing orders. Others considered reordination to be ridiculous and unnecessary, however. This led almost inevitably to the *via media* suggested by Headlam—the mutual recognition of orders and a regularization of all future ordinations. Here he noticed a significant development : whereas the Nonconformists had hitherto laid little stress on ordination and the validity of orders, they were now becoming increasingly 'ordination conscious.' A final problem which the conference had no opportunity to discuss and which Headlam considered important was that of safeguards for an achieved unity. Supposing reunion were achieved upon some agreed basis, how long would it be before the various elements dissolved once more into their component parts?

The conference then passed two resolutions which Headlam sent to the Archbishop of Canterbury together with a report of the proceedings. The first, noting the large measure of agreement which had been attained, urged the desirability of continuing such discussions and of making use of every available opportunity for intercourse and co-operation. The second urged the creation of a council, representative of as much of Christendom as possible, to promote the rule of God among men. In the light of the Mansfield manifesto these resolutions seemed disappointing. Headlam was satisfied, however. Though modest, they were constructive and did not create as many problems as they attempted to solve, while the very fact that such a conference had been possible at all was sufficient reward in itself.

III

A further contribution which Headlam made to the work of the Lambeth Conference was a Memorandum, drawn up at the request of Archbishop Davidson, on the relations of the Church of England with other episcopal Churches. He first referred to the Roman Catholic Church. Here there was little prospect of further immediate progress, although evidence was not lacking of a much less rigid tone and temperament which might well produce a different situation in the future. In the Eastern Orthodox Church there had been many recent signs of improved relations. This was due partly to political causes brought about by Allied co-operation during the Great War, and partly to the more enlightened bishops and clergy realizing the necessity of keeping in touch with modern thought if they were to retain their hold on an educated laity. The recent conferences with the Orthodox delegations at Oxford and London had also revealed a much more accommodating spirit on the part of some members of the Eastern Church, although a considerable body of Orthodox opinion would still tend to be rather conservative. Although he was not hopeful of immediate doctrinal agreement, prospects for the future were encouraging. Evidence for the desire for friendly relations with the Church of England was provided by the Encyclical Letter from the Patriarchate of Constantinople to the Christian Churches throughout the world issued in January 1920.[30]

The Scandinavian Churches too were becoming increasingly friendly, although with Nonconformists rather than with the Church of England. They were episcopal in constitution, but Lutheran in tendency.

---

[30] Bell, *Documents on Christian Unity*, ser. 1, pp. 44–8. This letter outlined a scheme of practical measures for co-operation, involving the acceptance of a uniform calendar, closer intercourse, mutual respect of customs and usages, mutual facilities for burials, settlement of the question of mixed marriages, etc.

They were in communion with non-episcopal Lutheran Churches and had no intention of departing from that position. The Swedish Church claimed to possess Apostolic Succession, the Norwegian and Danish Churches did not. Nevertheless, Sweden did not consider it necessary for valid orders and sacraments, and therefore regarded those of Denmark, Norway and the Lutheran Churches to be valid. Headlam thought that Sweden would probably feel it an advantage for all the Scandinavian Churches to have the Succession restored to them, although many people in Denmark and Norway might consider it to be a Romanizing tendency.

When the Lambeth Conference was over and its Report published, Headlam's influence on its deliberations was obvious. Professor Nairne wrote to him, 'How good it was to see the Bishops at Lambeth following you so faithfully; that hopeful Appeal must be considered your work.' In the Report on Reunion, the sections on the Roman Catholic Church, the Eastern Orthodox Church and the Swedish Church reproduce most of what he had written in his Memorandum. The Appeal to all Christian People also reproduced the essential features of his policy for reunion. On one essential point, however, the Appeal did not go as far : whereas he favoured a mutual recognition of ministries and a mutual conferring of a commission under the new conditions—an expedient which did not require the laying on of hands, the Appeal suggested that the ministries of non-episcopal bodies should receive this commission by means of episcopal ordination; although it was careful to point out that no one would thereby be taken to have repudiated his past ministry.[31] Conferences with other denominations with a view to reunion were to be encouraged, but general schemes of inter-communion and the exchange of pulpits were not approved. Nevertheless, both these restrictions might be relaxed on occasions and under proper safeguards.

This Appeal, owing so much to Headlam's influence, evoked an immediate response from the Free Churches in this country. Their Federal Council issued a provisional statement in September 1920, expressing a willingness to discuss its proposals; and this was followed by a more detailed statement in March 1921, entitled 'The Free Churches and the Lambeth Appeal.'[32] As a result twenty-five delegates from the Free Churches met the two Archbishops and nine diocesan bishops (later ten) at Lambeth on November 30, 1921, to inaugurate a series of discussions lasting over a period of ten years, the like of which had not been held since the Savoy Conference of 1661. The main work was done by a sub-committee, composed of six

---

[31] *Report of the Lambeth Conference 1920*, p. 142.
[32] Bell, *Documents*, ser. 1, pp. 118–41.

members from each side. Archbishop Lang was chairman, and on the Anglican side were the Bishops of Gloucester, Peterborough, Salisbury and Ripon together with Dr. W. H. Frere and Headlam, who were included as acknowledged experts on reunion. Dr. P. Carnegie Simpson (Presbyterian) was appointed convener of the Free Church delegates, and with him were Dr. Scott Lidgett (Wesleyan), Dr. A. E. Garvie (Congregationalist), Dr. J. H. Shakespeare (Baptist), Dr. J. D. Jones (Congregationalist) and Professor A. S. Peake (Primitive Methodist). Their first report, on which there was remarkable unanimity, was accepted by the whole Conference in May 1922.[33] It affirmed a general endorsement of the terms of the Quadrilateral, including an acceptance of episcopacy in a united Church, provided that the elements of presbyteral and congregational order were also maintained. This was favourably received by the Free Church Federal Council in September 1922; but questions were raised as to the status of the existing Free Church ministry. The sub-committee therefore turned its attention to this problem. The Free Churchmen conceded that after reunion all ministers should be episcopally ordained but could not assent to the re-ordination of non-episcopally ordained ministers. The Anglicans then agreed to prepare a statement on the question. The ground was prepared by Headlam at the request of Archbishop Lang. His memorandum expressed agreement with the Free Church position—their orders were real and valid, and their refusal to be reordained was justified. On the other hand, the view of many Anglicans that it was unacceptable for non-episcopally ordained ministers to celebrate in Anglican churches was also reasonable. Conditional re-ordination was no solution to this problem; for it suggested that the first ordination was no ordination at all, so there would in fact be no *re*-ordination. If, however, Free Church ordinations could not be regarded as invalid, although they might be irregular, a mutual recognition of orders was all that was necessary. The fact of reunion and the meeting of two separate bodies in the unity of one Church would do away with any irregularity. The concession could still be made that such recognition did not imply a right of inter-celebration. Bishop Gibson (now succeeded by Headlam as Bishop of Gloucester) was not prepared to accept this, however, insisting that all ministers in a united Church should submit to episcopal ordination.[34] Archbishop Lang, too, felt that Headlam's suggestion exceeded their terms of reference :

'I ought to point out that whatever may be said on grounds of theology

[33] Ibid., pp. 143–51.
[34] Bell, *Randall Davidson*, p. 1119.

or history in favour of accepting some at least of the ministers of non-episcopal bodies without any further ordination, that definitely goes beyond what is contemplated and indeed laid down by the Lambeth Conference in its Appeal, and in the Resolutions which it adopted; and I do not think it is competent for our Committee to come formally to any conclusion which goes beyond the Lambeth Appeal. (The Appeal specifically mentioned that it was hoped that the longing for unity "would lead ministers who have not received it to accept a commission through episcopal ordination, as obtaining for them a ministry throughout the whole fellowship." Appeal, sc. 8, Lambeth Report 1920, p. 135.) You will remember that the Committee was appointed at the request of the Federal Council of the Evangelical Free Churches in order to elucidate matters arising from the Lambeth Appeal. The Committee was therefore one of Bishops who had the responsibility for the issue of the Appeal. Only, you and Frere was added at a later stage in order to give advice as eminent theologians. Thus in my judgment, though we may be free to discuss the whole question, I do not think we are free to go behind, or, if you prefer, to advance beyond what the Lambeth Appeal laid down.' [35]

After further discussion the Anglican statement finally submitted to the sub-committee was not as Headlam would have wished; but he agreed to support it in order to ensure the progress of the discussions. Those non-episcopal ministries which rested upon long established order, and which had been conferred by some solemn and authoritative act implying ordination to the Ministry of the Universal Church, and which were regarded as involving a lifelong vocation, were held within their several spheres as real ministries of Christ's Word and Sacraments within the Universal Church—although they might in varying degrees be irregular and defective: in Anglican eyes they were certainly so as lacking episcopal ordination. But if, in the future, any of the Free Churches and the Anglican Church agreed to unite on the basis of episcopacy, ministers of both should be recognized as of equal status in the councils of the United Church. And if, during the transitional period, ministers wished to exercise a full ministry in the United Church, bishops and clergy of the Church of England would be willing to accept 'authorization'—whatever form it might take, provided Free Church ministers would accept an Anglican 'authorization' in the form of episcopal ordination.

The full joint conference considered this memorandum on July 6, 1923. The Free Church members were undoubtedly impressed—Dr. Carnegie Simpson described it as 'the most notable thing which

[35] Archbishop Lang to Headlam, March 14, 1923.

Lambeth has said to any non-episcopal Church since the time of, say, Bancroft or Laud.'[36] Finally they added a note to the effect that 'while recognizing that the responsibility for this answer must rest with the Anglican members, the representatives of the Federal Council desire to record their opinion that the document contains statements of such importance as amply to justify their hope that the Federal Council will reappoint the committee to unite with the representatives of the Church of England in further discussions of the many points that still remain to be considered.'[37]

The committee was accordingly reappointed, but before long ran into difficulties. On October 31 Dr. Carnegie Simpson submitted to the sub-committee some comments on the Anglican statement. While admitting the difference between intercelebration and intercommunion, he failed to see why intercommunion was not generally possible if it were already accepted that Free Church ministries were real ministries of Christ's Word and Sacraments. Christ's Sacrament was always and everywhere Christ's Sacrament : it could not be more or less than itself. To admit that another Church had Christ's Sacrament and then to refuse to participate with them in it was both a logical and a religious impossibility. As for the Free Church ministries, Anglicans considered them to lack due authorization to exercise their functions within the Anglican Church. But surely ordination would not remedy this, for ordination in any true and adequate sense had nothing to do with matters of interior jurisdiction. The South India proposals for a 'mutual recognition for a wider ministry,' which had been accepted by the Anglicans there—involved a form of commission clearly less than ordination.[38] Why then could not something be done on these lines at home?

Archbishop Lang was not prepared to accept that the Word and Sacraments could always be regarded as in perfect accord with Christ's mind and will. There were many degrees and grounds of imperfection. A Church could not accept a mere intention—however sincere—to preach the Word as Christ's Word or to administer the Sacraments as Christ's Sacraments as sufficient without any further questions. Again, spiritual efficacy was one thing, but due authority was another : the latter was not involved in the former. 'We regard this bestowal of the authority of the whole body to the ministry by episcopal ordination not merely as something which is desirable for the united Church of the future, but as something which "from the Apostles' time" has always been provided for the Church.' There were two possible suggestions for overcoming the difficulties of the transitional period—

[36] P. Carnegie Simpson, *Recollections,* 1943, p. 78.
[37] Bell, *Documents,* ser. 1, pp. 156–63.
[38] Ibid., pp. 313–14.

both tentative and made without authority. The first was some form
of commission to Free Church ministers by the laying on of hands by
a bishop, which would in no way repudiate their past ministry, but
would publicly and formally seek additional recognition of a new call
to a wider service in the united Church. It had the disadvantage of
being ambiguous. Some people might regard the formula used in the
sense of conferring order; others might regard it in the sense of conferring jurisdiction. The second suggestion—conditional reordination
—was preferable. Here all ministers would submit to episcopal ordination; but it would be prefaced and governed by a condition expressed
by some formula as 'If thou art not already ordained.'

Headlam considered this to be most unsatisfactory. He was convinced that the Free Churches would never accept conditional
reordination, and he had no desire to associate himself with any statement proposing it. He therefore made another attempt to persuade
Archbishop Lang to consider his own proposal. Surely the answer to
the problem was the mutual recognition of existing orders with intercommunion but no intercelebration. Such a scheme violated no rule
of the Anglican Church, while it fully recognized the position and
importance of the Free Church orders and services.[39] The Archbishop
would still not agree, however. He reminded Headlam that he had
already expressed his willingness to recognize the limitations of
Clause 8 of the Appeal, and he refused to open up the whole discussion again. Nevertheless, when the sub-committee met on September 25, 1925, the reaction of the Free Church delegates to conditional
reordination was just as Headlam had feared. While recognizing it as
a sincere effort to solve a difficult and crucial problem, they felt bound
to say that they could hold out no prospect that the Free Church
Federal Council would regard it as adequate or acceptable. Their own
solution to the problem lay along the lines of a mutually extended
commission. These questions needed careful consideration, however;
and it would be neither wise nor desirable to accept an immediate
decision.[40]

The conversations were now drawing to a close. The Federal
Council had suggested in September 1924 that it was not in the
interests of the reunion movement to prolong the conferences indefinitely, and that the various Churches should now consider the results
which had been reached.[41] The meeting of the full conference on
June 19, 1925, was therefore the last of the series. Here the Free
Church members took the same line as their delegates had done—the

[39] Headlam to Archbishop Lang, February 12, 1925.
[40] Bell, *Documents*, ser. 2, pp. 77–86.
[41] Ibid., pp. 72–3.

idea of conditional reordination was unconvincing and unpromising.[42] The final outcome of the discussions seemed therefore to be disappointing and rather inconclusive. Nevertheless, the conference declared, 'In a field of inevitable controversy we have, by the Blessing of God, attained a much larger measure of agreement than was thought by most people to be possible,' and expressed the hope that the discussions would be resumed.[43] This was is fact done after the Lambeth Conference of 1930. Here, then, were the first-fruits of Headlam's Bampton Lectures : and there was no need for him to feel dissatisfied.

[42] Ibid., pp. 98–107.
[43] Ibid., pp. 73–7.

CHAPTER TEN

The Eastern Orthodox Church
1918-26

I

In 1918 Archbishop Meletios Mataxakis, the new Metropolitan of Athens, visited America and England with a view to promoting closer relations between the Greek Church and the Anglican Communion. He was young, vigorous, an ardent reformer, a champion of Christian unity and a strong supporter of M. Venizelos, the pro-Allied Greek leader. The Archbishop of Canterbury viewed his impending visit with some misgivings and expressed his doubts to Headlam. How would other parts of the Eastern Church—Russia, Constantinople, Alexandria—view Meletios' action? How far was he independent of such co-operation and control? Lord Robert Cecil was strongly urging the importance of not committing the Church of England in any way that would possibly alienate other branches of the Eastern Church.[1] Headlam had no such doubts, however, and welcomed the visit. His views were publicly expressed in an article which he wrote for *The Quarterly Review* entitled 'Eastern Christianity : Reform and Reunion.' The desire for reform, which was in evidence in so many parts of the Orthodox Church, was most prominent in Greece and was due largely to the work of Archbishop Meletios. In learning, education, administration and finance, despite interruptions due to the War, the Greek Church had improved. At the same time there had been a growing interest in England and a desire to promote friendly relations with her. The world was looking forward to the establishment of a system of International Law and a League of Nations, but this should have a spiritual basis : commercial, economic and political union should be accompanied by religious union.[2]

The Metropolitan, accompanied by Professor Chrysostom Papadopoulos and Professor Alivisatos, met members of the American Episcopal Church at the General Theological Seminary, New York, at the end of October. The conference discussed the questions of orders

[1] Randall Cantuar to Headlam, August 5, 1918.
[2] 'Eastern Christianity: Reform and Reunion,' *The Quarterly Review*, no. 458, pp. 112–26.

and the Filioque Clause, but lack of time prevented any consideration of other points. Full details were therefore sent to England, so that time might not be wasted in covering the same ground at the meetings in London.[3] In preparation for these Headlam arranged two preliminary conferences at Oxford to consider the American reports and to draw up an agenda. The first, held on October 30–31, was attended mostly by university teachers and professors. They were generally agreed that reunion, implying a good deal of corporate solidarity, was impossible; but there was no serious bar to intercommunion. This view was endorsed by two Orthodox priests, Fr. Iordachesco of Roumania and Fr. Yanic of Serbia, who attended a second session. On the Filioque Clause the formula reached at the Old Catholic-Orthodox conversations at Bonn in 1874 and the view taken by Fr. Puller in his discussions with the Russian Church in 1912 were considered to be entirely satisfactory.[4] They were also quite satisfied with Anglican orders and undertook to try and secure their recognition in the Orthodox Church.

The second conference took place on November 30 when Archbishop Meletios was visiting Oxford to receive an honorary degree. He was accompanied by M. Gennadios, Fr. Callinicos and Professor Alivisatos. Since the American discussions had dealt with orders and the Filioque Clause, they confined their attentions to Baptism and Confirmation. No difficulties seemed to arise over the former, although the Greeks regarded immersion as the proper form: they were prepared to accept affusion, however, and the Metropolitan clearly affirmed that in his opinion the differences between the two Churches on Baptism would be no bar to reunion. Confirmation proved to be much more difficult. The Metropolitan appreciated Anglican practice and saw its advantages, but traditional Eastern theology was too strong for him to act against it. Possibly in time English Confirmation might be recognized; but the existing Greek rule was to administer chrism in all cases, whether there had been an imposition of hands or not. Some of the Anglican delegates deprecated the practice of their own Church, suggesting that the separation of Baptism from Confirmation in the West was a mere accident, and that the Eastern practice was undoubtedly correct. Headlam disagreed with this point of view, however, and checked those who favoured it in no uncertain terms. Time for discussion was unfortunately limited, and the Metropolitan showed a propensity to hold the floor. Nevertheless,

---

[3] *The Christian East*, vol. 1, no. 3, pp. 163–4; *6th Report of the Anglican and Eastern Association 1914–21*, pp. 81–2.

[4] It had been agreed that the clause had been inserted irregularly, and that it was desirable to find a way by which the original form of the Creed could be restored without compromising the truth expressed in the article.

Headlam felt it wise to let him talk and regarded the conference as well worth while.

Reports of both these conferences were sent to the Archbishops of Canterbury and York and to the Bishop of Winchester (Dr. Talbot), who was in charge of the official conference at the Jerusalem Chamber on December 2. At this Headlam was again present and the Orthodox were represented by the Metropolitan, Professor Chrysostom Papadopoulos, Dr. Alexander Papadopoulos and Professor Alivisatos. No time was wasted on going over the ground which had already been covered in America and at Oxford, and the conference discussed the Seventh Œcumenical Council and Icons. Once again there was a considerable measure of agreement. On the Council the Anglicans stated that its decisions would present no difficulty for Anglican acceptance; while on Icons the Metropolitan was strongly opposed to ascribing certain virtues and vices to them; he had written against the practice and the Holy Synod of Greece had issued directions against it.[5]

Throughout the whole series of discussions there had been a significant advance towards mutual understanding and agreement, and Headlam's contribution had been considerable. Archbishop Davidson wrote to him on December 19:

'I want to take this opportunity of thanking you with all my heart for the very great trouble you took and the splendid influence you exercised in regard to the recent visit of the Metropolitan of Athens and the discussions which that visit made possible. Your presence and aid, with the introduction thereby of so much knowledge and authority, made all the difference to these deliberations, and I have heard on all sides expressions of what we owe to you. This refers both to the preliminary conferences and those at which the Metropolitan was present. You have rendered to the Church of England many great services at different times. In this case you have rendered a service which may turn out to have momentous consequences for good not to the Church of England only but to the Churches of the East.'

The Archbishop was now moved to take the step which had been proposed by the Lambeth Conference of 1908. In November 1919 he appointed the Eastern Churches Committee under the chairmanship of Bishop Gore.[6] Headlam was an obvious choice, and at the very outset he and Brightman were given the task of preparing a statement

[5] *The Christian East*, vol. 1, no. 3, pp. 164–5; *6th Report of the Anglican and Eastern Association 1914–21*, pp. 84–5.
[6] Shortly afterwards the Holy Synod of Greece instituted a similar permanent Committee.

of terms on which intercommunion with the Orthodox Church might be proposed. The Committee made only minor changes to their draft statement and the 'Suggested Terms of Intercommunion' were published in 1921.

These Terms were composed of thirteen propositions and two appendices. They declared that the Christian Faith was enshrined in the Scriptures, the Nicene Creed and the decisions of the Œcumenical Councils. The Canon of Scripture was that defined by S. Athanasius in his Festal Letter. Tradition was to be accepted as a guide to the right understanding of Scripture, for the right administration of the Sacraments, and for the preservation of sacred rites and ceremonies in the purity of their original intention. The Exposition of the Faith promulgated by the Council of Chalcedon was accepted as an explanation of the Creed and it was considered unlawful for a Church to demand any further statement of faith as a necessary condition of intercommunion. On the doctrine of the Holy Spirit it was admitted that the addition of the Filioque Clause by the West had not been done in an ecclesiastically regular manner, and in assemblies of Eastern and Western Christians the Creed should be recited without it : nevertheless the clause was used in an orthodox sense and could so be used by Churches which had received the Creed in that form. There would be general recognition of those customs possessing the authority of our Lord, of Scripture and of the Universal Church : otherwise each Church should retain its own customs. On the Sacraments it was stated that their number had never been fixed either by tradition from the Apostles or by the decision of an Œcumenical Council, but two— Baptism and Holy Communion—were recognized as pre-eminent, ordained by Christ Himself and generally necessary to salvation. Ordination, Penance, Confirmation, Marriage and Unction might also be considered sacraments, possessing outward and visible signs, and conveying inward and spiritual grace. The presence of Christ in the Eucharist was a divine mystery transcending human understanding : but the doctrine of the Eucharist as taught by the liturgies of the Orthodox Church, the Anglican Church and those Churches in communion with her were regarded as adequate and sufficient. The orders and forms of ordination of both Churches were also regarded as adequate and sufficient. On the question of images and icons both Churches were to have liberty to preserve their own customs; but neither should accuse the other of idolatry or false teaching. The first Appendix gave the propositions on the procession of the Holy Spirit adopted by the Bonn Conference; the second gave the formulae of ordination in the Orthodox and Anglican Churches.[7]

[7] Bell, *Documents,* ser. 1, pp. 77–89.

These Terms were of course on the lines of suggestions Headlam had made in his Bampton Lectures. There was the recognition that neither Church could claim to be infallible, and that variety both in interpretation and custom was permissible, provided some fundamental, agreed basis of Christian thought and action could be found. Doubts were expressed, however, even within the Eastern Churches Committee, whether the Terms had much hope of success. The Revd. J. A. Douglas, for example, confessed to Headlam that although he considered them to be a fine and courageous piece of work, he did not feel that they went far enough to win acceptance from the Orthodox Church. It was a grave error to present them with any such formal propositions. He wrote a little later :

'When (Dr. Headlam) suggests that there is a possibility of (the Eastern Churches) entering into Union with the Anglican Churches as they are, or with the totality of the United Non-Papalist Christianity of England simply on the basis of the Creed with provisos of an agreement as to the Filioque, of the mutual recognition of Orders and of mutual liberty as to the doctrine of the Eucharistic Presence, he is holding out an expectation which, as things are, is altogether illusory. . . . On the other hand, the Eastern Orthodox have made it plain, and that repeatedly, in the last three and a half centuries, that the only basis of Reunion which they can conceive, is that of the Faith of the Undivided Church of the first nine centuries. . . . In its history, whether its record be a record of slavery and disaster or a record of freedom and prosperity, devotion to the Faith of the Church of the Œcumenical Councils has been above everything its controlling inspiration and the most cherished of its glories.'[8]

These doubts were supported by the Archimandrite Athenaz Carradas in London, to whom Headlam had sent the 'Suggested Terms' for comment. He wrote on July 20, 1921 :

'Although I am anxiously looking forward to take advantage of the opportunity to give further explanations on the Greek point of view, I would say that I am afraid that no success is to be hoped. I assure you I am the most zealot partisan of union and for that I would with great pleasure suggest to my country your point of view which I personally admire : but by experience I am sure also that this point of view should find many difficulties and very strong obstacles in the Orthodox Church.'

[8] Cf. Headlam, *Bampton Lectures*, pp. 297–8 ; J. A. Douglas, *The Relations of the Anglican Churches with the Eastern Orthodox*, 1921, pp. 18–22.

Headlam refused to accept this pessimistic point of view, however. 'I am perfectly well aware that all his (Douglas') statements can be paralleled in Eastern theologians, but I am also quite convinced that there are many Easterns who recognize that such an attitude is an impossible one, and are not prepared to adhere to it.' [9] In the light of these conflicting opinions it was interesting to read the official report of the Orthodox delegation from the Patriarchate of Constantinople to the Lambeth Conference of 1920 [10]; for the leader, Archbishop Philaret of Demotika, was considered to be much more conservative than Archbishop Meletios. The delegation had been deeply and favourably impressed by their reception in England, and they had appreciated the Anglican desire for reunion; but as an indisputable condition of dogmatic union, agreement on certain points was essential. They could not accept the validity of Baptism administered by Anglican priests either simpliciter or by economy, and they wished that Anglicans would practice immersion rather than affusion. Here, as with Confirmation and Holy Communion, much depended on the validity of Anglican orders, and upon this question the delegation did not feel that they should express an opinion. They desired that the Anglicans should make some definition of the Eucharist as a Sacrifice and a Propitiation and insert an Epiklesis in the Prayer of Consecration. They also desired that there should be some formulation of the Anglican category of sacraments, while they felt that the cause of reunion would be advanced by the abolition—or at least—the revision of the Thirty-nine Articles. The acceptance of the Seventh Œcumenical Council was also regarded as indispensable. Finally there came the significant statement, 'The Orthodox Church does not as yet accept those who do not belong to it as forming a part of the Church in the true and proper sense of the word.' [11] This, then, was the other side of the Orthodox picture from that given in Headlam's preliminary conferences; and whatever might be said about the Lambeth delegation's sense of sacred duty to continue to do all they could to further the cause of reunion, their report undoubtedly gave support to Douglas' point of view.

Douglas was most emphatic that both reunion and intercommunion were impossible without full dogmatic union. The first step was the economic recognition of Anglican orders by the Orthodox Church, and he felt that this might be secured if a large body of Anglican clergy could give satisfactory statements on the four questions of

[9] A. C. Headlam, 'Union with the Orthodox Church,' *The Christian East*, vol. 2, no. 2, p. 95.
[10] An English translation appeared in *The Christian East* for March 1922. Headlam seemingly had little or no dealings with this delegation.
[11] Cf. Bell, *Documents*, ser. 1, pp. 52–76.

F

Sacraments, Confession, Eucharist and Œcumenical Councils. He had, therefore, collaborated with members of the Society of the Faith in drafting a declaration, which, if sufficient signatures could be obtained, they hoped to send to the Œcumenical Patriarchate and which would dispose Orthodox theologians to decide that 'not only the historico-canonicity of Anglican orders but also their purpose, are adequate, especially with Roman Catholics, for *economic* recognition. In its composition we have been studious, as far as possible, to use terms which would be used by the Eastern Orthodox and to avoid making it an Anglican party document.' [12] This declaration appeared in the Church newspapers on May 26, 1922, claiming to be a joint undertaking by various Catholic Societies within the Church of England, and differing from the 'Suggested Terms' on a number of fundamental points. It declared that an Œcumenical Council was the supreme tribunal of the Church and its dogmatic decrees were incontrovertible and binding on all Christians : to such decrees the Church of England was loyal. The number of sacraments were specified as seven and the 'transmission' theory of Apostolic Succession was accepted. The doctrine of the Real Presence was affirmed; and although the declaration declined to state the manner of the change or mode of the presence, it asserted the belief that 'Christ thus present is to be adored.' It agreed with the Orthodox Church that honour should be given to the Virgin Mary and to the Departed Saints and that requests for the benefit of their intercession were permissible. Finally, the Thirty-nine Articles were stated to be of secondary importance concerned with local sixteenth century controversies and should be interpreted according to the faith of the Undivided Church.

This declaration was published only four days after the Report of the Anglican-Free Church Conferences on Church Unity. The two documents were so different, both in tone and content, that it must have seemed incredible to many people—not least to the Orthodox Church—that both could come from the Church of England at the same time. Headlam disapproved of the declaration and was surprised to find that the list of signatures was headed by that of Bishop Gore and included the names of Pullan, Douglas and Fynes Clinton—all members of the Eastern Churches Committee. He therefore wrote to Archbishop Davidson on June 1 denouncing the declaration as inconsistent with Anglican teaching. It was 'a travesty of the English Church dressed up in the clothes of the Eastern Church.' Catholic principle had been violated by a body of people within the Church making an independent approach to the Œcumenical Patriarch. It was an added complication for the list of signatures to be headed by

[12] Douglas, op. cit., pp. 89–90.

Bishop Gore, who, as Chairman of the Archbishops' Eastern Churches Committee, was responsible for official negotiations with the Eastern Church. It might well convey to Eastern minds the impression that the declaration was an official statement; and it certainly prejudiced the position of members of the Archbishops' Committee. He therefore offered his resignation from the Eastern Churches Committee, and announced his intention of publishing his reasons for doing so. Bishop Robertson followed suit and the Archbishop was very distressed. He urged them both not to resign : it might involve the break-up of the Committee and an end to all their efforts towards reunion in that direction.

Gore and his three co-signators were approached without delay and evidently to good effect. On June 9 Bishop Robertson wrote to Headlam, 'I think the people who need a timely caution have received it and will lay it to heart.' Gore actually professed that he had known nothing of the declaration until he had seen it in print, nor had he known who had written it. He refused to withdraw his signature but he would direct his name to be removed from the head of the list. His statement satisfied the Archbishop, who thereupon asked Headlam if he was willing to withdraw his resignation. Headlam finally agreed to do so, although he was by no means completely satisfied with Gore's explanation.[13]

The declaration actually aroused considerable opposition, and the Orthodox authorities wasted little time in taking action. On July 1, the Revd. G. K. A. Bell, the Archbishop's chaplain, wrote to Headlam :

'Communications have just been received from Constantinople to the effect that as the Orthodox authorities have heard of the *controversy* in England with regard to the declaration, they can no longer treat it as having significance for the purpose of what is described as "Economic Intercommunion." They could not, in view of what had happened regard the declaration as representing a main stream of opinion in the Church of England, but only the views of a section . . . I gather from Douglas that signatures may continue to be accumulated and that the declaration may be actually despatched to the Patriarch, but with the intimation that no importance attaches to it. . . . The attitude adopted by the Orthodox authorities gives considerably more importance to the Suggested Terms of Intercommunion which were drawn up by the Sub-Committee of the Eastern Churches Committee.'

[13] Randall Cantuar to Headlam, June 12 and 19, 1922; Headlam to Randall Cantuar June 15, 1922.

Signatures did in fact continue to be collected and early in July Headlam wrote to *The Church Times* and *The Guardian* on lines similar to his letter to the Archbishop, encouraging people not to sign. Douglas in reply claimed that the declaration had never been intended as more than a sectional document and there was no danger of it being taken otherwise in the East. Its simple object was to demonstrate that there exists a large section of Anglican clergy who account themselves to be priests in the sense in which the Eastern Church accounts its priests to be priests. Such a declaration would prove a weighty consideration when Constantinople came to decide on the acceptance of Anglican orders. Therefore, even if people like Headlam could not support it, at least they might extend a 'sympathetic confidence' to its promoters.

The die was already cast, however. Orthodox theologians had been investigating the question of Anglican orders for many years, and in the same month Professor Commenos of Halki produced the first volume of his *Contribution towards Reunion*. Here he concluded that Anglican orders bore scrutiny on the grounds of rite, intention and succession no less than Roman orders. He therefore advocated their acceptance and the recognition of all Anglican sacraments, at the same time urging the establishment of economic emergency intercommunion.[14] On July 28 the Patriarch of Constantinople informed the Archbishop of Canterbury that his Holy Synod had declared that Anglican orders possessed the same validity as those of the Roman, Old Catholic and Armenian Churches.[15] This decision was then sent to other parts of the Orthodox Church, inviting them to consider and communicate their views on the matter.[16] Favourable replies were received from the Patriarch of Jerusalem in February 1923 and the Archbishop of Cyprus in the following month.[17]

This was a welcome though limited step.[18] Not all the Orthodox Churches had as yet spoken their mind, nor did this limited recognition mean that intercommunion had been established. Nevertheless, the way was open for further advance. Headlam now approached the Archbishop on the use which could be made of the 'Suggested Terms,' and on May 16 approval was given for the Eastern Churches Committee to use them as a basis for discussions with the Orthodox Church.[19] In the autumn they were sent to the Œcumenical Patriarch of Constantinople for consideration. From the Anglican point of view

[14] *The Christian East,* vol. 2, no. 2, p. 91 ; vol. 2, no. 3, p. 107.
[15] Bell, *Documents,* ser. 1, pp. 93–4.
[16] Ibid., pp. 94–6.
[17] Ibid., pp. 97–9.
[18] *Chronicle of Convocation 1923,* pp. 69–77.
[19] Headlam to Gore, May 18, 1923.

the outlook appeared promising. Unfortunately the Patriarchate of Constantinople was experiencing serious difficulties due to the unfriendly attitude of the Turkish Government; and no further developments in this direction took place until the Orthodox delegation attended the next Lambeth Conference in 1930.[20]

II

In the spring of 1926 Headlam paid his first visit to Jugo-slavia. Accompanied by his niece, Miss Persis Wingfield, he set out immediately after Easter, and after a hair-raising journey on the Stamboul express—he would insist on leaving the train to go sight-seeing every time it stopped—they were received at Belgrade with extraordinary kindness. The Government provided them with free first-class railway passes throughout the country and placed a motor-car at their disposal; the Church authorities detailed Mr. Kosta Lukovic, the secretary to the Patriarch, to look after them; and his old students defrayed all their expenses. The whole visit cost him nothing; and it was made clear that this was being done as a token of gratitude for all his services to the country after the War. There was only one snag. The Orthodox Easter was a month later than in England : he therefore had to start observing Lent all over again, and far more rigorously than he had done at home.

After a short stay in Belgrade he visited the Patriarch at Sremski-Karlovci, for over two hundred years the seat of the Serbian Patriarchate. Their talks were friendly and valuable. Like many other Orthodox churchmen, the Patriarch found it difficult to understand the Anglican attitude towards the Free Churches; but he felt that Anglican orders should be recognized by the Orthodox Church. Headlam then returned to Belgrade to lecture to the University on Anglican-Orthodox relations, after which he went south to Nish to meet Bishop Dositi, one of the leading members of the Church, a great Anglophil, and bishop of the largest diocese in the country. From here he visited the Macedonian district which had been only recently emancipated from the Turk. This district contained the dioceses of Bitolj, better known as Monastir, and Ochrid. Their bishops, Bishop Joseph and Bishop Nikolai, had both known Headlam in England and he considered that they with Bishop Dositi were the three ablest leaders the Serbian Church possessed. Bishop Joseph, a small, vigorous man, had been a crack sharp-shooter in the Serbian army : he had come to England as head of the Serbian theological

[20] *Lambeth Occasional Reports 1931–8*, p. 96.

students at Oxford. On returning home he had, with Bishop Nikolai, founded a theological seminary at Bitolj; some three hundred men were now there preparing for ordination. Headlam was most impressed to see how Mohammedans as well as Christians held him in high esteem. It was the same with Bishop Nikolai at Ochrid : but he was cast in a different mould from the other two. Headlam regarded them as bishops who would meet every requirement of the Life and Liberty Movement, but not so Bishop Nikolai. His outlook was that of a mystic and his desire for ecclesiastical reform was confined to a desire to see his clergy become more earnest and devout. Ochrid was very poor, and its poverty was exemplified by his palace, which was extremely dilapidated. Money which his people had given him for repairs had been spent either on the poor or on the monastery of S. Naum. Headlam spent the first part of Holy Week in this lovely spot, with its wonderful lake and woods against a background of snow-capped Albanian mountains. The eve of Palm Sunday was a children's festival, when the resurrection of Lazarus was commemorated. The children were given palms and went in procession with the priests to the springs of Ochrid. Headlam was completely captivated and refused to go in procession with the Bishop, but walked along surrounded by children : to use his own understatement, 'It was very pleasant.' Bishop Nikolai wrote from America nearly thirty years later, 'As if I should need reminding ! It was an unforgettable visit !' From Ochrid Headlam travelled north to the village of Kosjerici near the Bosnian frontier, where another old student was the parish priest. It was a district which represented old Serbian life in its most characteristic form and it gave Headlam a valuable insight into the life of a country parish. At the end of April he returned to England via Belgrade.

Apart from short accounts of his visit which he wrote for his *Diocesan Magazine* and for *The Christian East* [21] Headlam prepared a longer report for the Archbishop of Canterbury and the Eastern Churches Committee. He felt that the first great problem facing the Church in Jugo-slavia was that of organization. Before the War Serbia had been for all practical purposes a homogeneous country with a uniform faith and a single Church : but the addition to the country of Croatia, parts of Dalmatia, Montenegro and a large part of Macedonia had involved the addition of a number of separately organized Churches and a considerable Roman Catholic population. This had called for the creation of a new single Church with a uniform organization. What had already been accomplished in this direction constituted a very considerable achievement. The Roman Catholics presented a difficult problem : directly after the War

[21] *The Christian East*, vol. 7, no. 2, pp. 49–55.

relations with them had been fairly good; but this had now changed, and a system of proselytizing had begun. Negotiations with the Vatican in 1925 for a Concordat had failed.

Another problem facing the Church was its changing position in the life of the nation. Before the War the Church had been the centre of national life and aspirations : the village priest had preserved the consciousness of race through five hundred years of Turkish rule, and he had been the local leader both in war and in insurrection. With the creation of a new united state, however, national life was now represented by the government and the army. In future the Church would have to confine itself almost entirely to spiritual functions. Unfortunately standard of clerical life, particularly among the elder clergy, were not high; although some of the younger men did something to redeem the situation. The real weakness of the Church was its lack of appeal to the intellectual element of the nation. With the exception of men like Nikolai, Dositi, Joseph and Popovic, few could answer the criticisms levelled by the state University at Belgrade at the Church's intellectual failings. It had to be remembered, however, that hitherto the Church had been occupied solely with filling the gaps in the priesthood and had not yet had an opportunity to turn to advanced theological study. Here Headlam himself endeavoured to help : deploring the recent publication of a Serbian translation of Renan's Liberal *Vie de Jésu,* he arranged with another old student, Professor D. Maric, for the publication of a Serbian edition of his *Jesus Christ in History and Faith* at his own expense. This appeared in the autumn of 1927, and Maric wrote to Headlam, 'Your book has made the best impression upon the minds of our people; especially is interested in it our priesthood. The other day Bishop Joseph ordered about a hundred copies for the pupils of our seminary at Bitolj. Your book will mean a new starting point in reorientation of our educated people towards Jesus Christ.' A welcome sign of improvement had been the opening of four new theological seminaries : nor did there seem to be any shortage of ordination candidates. What was needed was a drastic overhaul of the ordination course, so that real encouragement was given to men's intellectual interests.

The work of the Y.M.C.A. shed interesting light on Church relations. The Association was anxious to found an institution in the University of Belgrade, but it was viewed by many members of the Orthodox Church with suspicion. In the past its representatives had not always been Anglicans; and it had been argued that if a man did not belong to his national Church he should be regarded with caution, if not suspicion. In Jugoslavia, where the Church had been for so long the centre of nationalism, Nonconformity was likely to lay one's patriotism open to suspicion. It was fortunate that the existing representatives, Mr. and Mrs. Sitters, were Anglicans and had done much to dispel doubts. Finally Headlam spoke highly of the people themselves. Despite their volubility and lack of organizing capacity, they were kindly, hard-working and hospitable. With good leadership they were capable of great things, and it was indeed remarkable what they had done since the War.

Obviously Headlam's short visit produced no spectacular results : but it was none the less valuable. He had always believed that the correct approach to reunion involved patience, without regard for immediate results. The cultivation of knowledge, and particularly personal knowledge, in a friendly spirit, was most important. Narrow isolationism and bitterness of spirit could not possibly survive in the face of friendly and charitable relations. In Jugoslavia he had done a great deal to foster such relations, and it was a service which many people in that country never forgot. One of them remarked many years later, 'I was touched by his liking for my countrymen, though he had, perhaps, a rather higher opinion of them than they deserved.'

CHAPTER ELEVEN

The Early Episcopate

I

HEADLAM was enthroned at Gloucester on Tuesday, February 13, 1923. The ceremony began with an impressive display of episcopal strength and vigour. On his arrival at the Cathedral to demand admission, he struck the West Door three lusty blows with his pastoral staff. The final blow was so violent that the tip of his staff became embedded in the panel, and as he pulled it free, a voice from the crowd was heard to remark, 'The bishop ain't 'alf vaccinated that door!' No less vigorous were his enthronement addresses to the clergy and laity, in which he outlined the tasks which confronted them. To the clergy he pointed out that during the past hundred years the Church, although by no means lethargic or inactive, had failed to hold the intellectual life of the country : it must therefore learn to speak with real authority to convince men that the Christian message was true. To the laity he emphasized three things. First there was the need for administrative efficiency and an adequately paid clergy. His predecessor had grappled with both these problems effectively, having created a Diocesan Board of Finance and raised the average of clerical stipends from £140 to £300 a year : but there was still more to be done, 'If you are not prepared to give your clergy a sufficient income to enable them to live properly and to do their duty, you must not expect to have the sort of clergy you desire. . . . If you send them to live in poverty and inefficiency, unable to do their work, they will not come to you.' Secondly there was the need to promote Christian unity throughout the world : it was of supreme importance and he conceived it to be his duty to further this work in every way he could. Thirdly there was the task of religious education, in which the moral and spiritual training of the rising generation should be integrated with their intellectual training : this task was far more important than social reform, political reconstruction or economic stability. As for Headlam himself, he too had a threefold task—his work as a scholar, as a diocesan bishop, and as a bishop of the whole Church—and he made it perfectly clear that he intended to divide his time and energy between them; the diocese could not expect to monopolize him. To these three activities he might have added a fourth—his gardening, which he regarded as of equal importance; for the effectiveness of his work in the other three fields depended in large measure on the complete relaxation he could obtain from time to time in his garden at Whorlton.

Headlam again referred to his own work as a bishop in his address to the Diocesan Conference later in the year.[1] A bishop had three main functions, but whether his position was regarded as administrative, intellectual or spiritual, in no case could he fill it better by taking upon himself work which could be done better by others. The most able administrator was not the man who did everything himself, but one who so organized his work that every one else fulfilled their function properly, while he himself was free from attention to detail. The man who would aim at being an intellectual leader was not one who devoted his time to continuous lecturing and teaching, but one who by his own studies and thought was able to speak and write in a way which influenced a great body of teachers. So also with regard to spiritual things: spiritual influence did not depend entirely on personal contact—it was often the recluse rather than the active evangelist who exercised the greatest force and power. He should exercise spiritual influence by making his people feel that there was always a real spiritual power behind the administrative work. The bishop should be a leader and commander, not a regimental officer. 'My own ideal is that I should be not the manager of my clergy but the leader of free men of independent position. . . . We do not want our clergy to be all of one mould; we do not want them to march at the word of command like a well-drilled army; we want them to be guided by the great ideals of Christianity and by loyalty to our own Church; but we want them to walk independently to their goal, to seek and explore new paths and to make our English Church rich by the fertile activities of many minds. So I value the independence which the freehold of the clergy gives.'[2]

Gloucester saw in its new bishop a man who was able, scholarly and vigorous: but what was he like as a person? Bishop Gibson had also been an able scholar and administrator: but above all he had been a well-beloved Father-in-God, inspiring the very atmosphere of holiness. If reports were to be believed, however, Headlam was set in no such mould as this. His reputation for outspokenness and brusqueness had preceded him. Sir Charles Oman's jocular remark at a farewell dinner in Oxford—'We are sorry to lose you, but we are also sorry for the

[1] Cf. 'Little Bishoprics,' *C.Q.R.*, vol. 193, pp. 146–63.
[2] Presidential Address, Gloucester Diocesan Conference 1923.

clergy you are going to rule'—had already reached the diocese. Nevertheless, many people—if not all—were agreeably surprised. The Revd. J. Outram Smith, who acted as his chaplain for a short while soon after his arrival, said that it was surprising to find the patience and humour which Headlam showed to humbler folk : his brusqueness seemed to be reserved for those whom he considered to be his equals. The fact is that in this predominantly rural diocese he soon found himself at home with country folk. A countryman himself, he could speak their language and genuinely share their interests. People soon found, too, that he was essentially just, straightforward and trustworthy : where matters of right principle were involved he was completely steadfast, no matter the cost. There was, however, one factor which did more than anything else to bind the diocese to him in those early days—the death of his wife.

She had always dreaded the possibility of Headlam becoming a bishop : apart from the conviction that all bishops killed themselves with overwork, she could not see herself performing the public duties expected of a bishop's wife. She had never been really well since the King's College days, and in June 1923—soon after moving into the Palace—she became seriously ill. Recovery was slow, and it was not until the following spring that there appeared to be any real signs of progress. The improvement was only temporary, however, and she was then found to be suffering from an incurable cancer. Both she and Headlam knew that she had not long to live, and to those near to them, their love for one another during the last few weeks was most moving. She died on March 17, 1924. Her death was a terrible blow to him, for although undemonstrative by nature, his feelings for her were deep. The Rector of Cheltenham (the Revd. H. A. Wilson)[3] recalled having dinner with them on one occasion. On the table was a small vase filled with some rather pretty and unusual wild flowers. When he remarked on their beauty, Mrs. Headlam replied, 'To-day is my birthday and these are my favourite flowers. The Bishop had heard that they were in bloom and he went out early this morning searching the Cotswolds to find them for me.' It was typical of him, and few others except the Rector of Cheltenham would have known about it. The nearest approach to a public indication of his feelings was his letter in the April issue of the *Diocesan Magazine* :

'My wife and I had nearly 24 happy and interesting years together, and we had, I think, even more than our share of good fortune. There are, I am glad to think, many who know how it brightens the work and alleviates the troubles of life always to look forward to coming

[3] Later Bishop of Chelmsford.

back to a happy home, and that has been in an exceptional degree my lot. At King's College she never spared herself. In the life of a College there should always be something more than good administration and efficiency—personal friendship, the giving and receiving of a simple and kindly hospitality, something of home life. To securing this she gave herself up and I think the strain was a little too much. She was extraordinarily happy in her life there, but she was never really strong afterwards. She was always diffident about her life at Gloucester, I thought unnecessarily so. It was a real grief to her that she was so much prevented by illness from making friends of clergy and laity alike. She did what she could, often at great effort to herself, and when she was able to exercise some hospitality she never allowed herself to fail in brightness or thoughtfulness, and I do not doubt that if she had had life and strength granted to her, many would have found in her a friend. I should like to say how much during her last illness the prayers and sympathy of so many helped her, and how brave and peaceful she was.'

His reserve was such that he could not show his feelings : but he was deeply touched by the sympathy and kindness which the diocese showered upon him, for he was lonely and yearned for affection. He was very glad, for example, although he did not admit it, to join in the family life of the vicarages for an hour or so, as he went around the diocese : there he could share in something which he could not possibly get at the Palace. With his clergy and their families he was able to experience and enjoy friendship naturally and unobtrusively ; and since he enjoyed good food, clergy wives found real pleasure in giving him a good meal. All this meant far more to him than most people ever realized.

Immediately after his wife's death he attempted to carry on his work as usual, but found it impossible. Finally his doctor sent him off in the company of Canon Maynard Smith and his brother Outram to Ravenna, where he found relief in striding about the mountains and in gardening. He persuaded the hotel manager to give him the use of a small piece of ground, in which he planted all sorts of specimens—to the Smith brothers mere weeds—found during his ramblings : these he watered and tended assiduously, eventually sending them back to Whorlton. In the early summer he returned to Gloucester to start life anew. At first his cousin, Maud Headlam, who had recently returned from teaching in New Zealand, came to keep house for him. It was no easy task ; for the Palace was a large, barrack-like Victorian mansion, in which Bishop Gibson had employed a large staff of servants. Headlam found it impossible to maintain his household on an equally lavish scale, but at the same time he considered it to be part of his function as bishop to be given to hospitality. Men of affairs, officials, scholars, foreign churchmen, clergy, ordinands, friends —all came and went in a steady stream, adding to domestic problems which he did not really appreciate. There was, for example, an occasion some years later, after his sister Rose had taken over the housekeeping from Maud, when on his own initiative he rashly gave the whole domestic staff a day's holiday sending them off before all the essential chores were done. Rose failed to appreciate this magnanimous gesture and enquired how he proposed to deal with such things as the washing of dishes and making of beds, apart from the preparation of meals; to which he replied that he would help her. Rose, who could be as redoubtable as he was, knowing that his idea of help might mean little more than wandering into the conservatory to water a few plants, thereupon suggested that he might make a start by making his own bed—a suggestion with which he meekly complied. Actually he never really liked the Palace: he merely made the best of it and after his wife's death regarded it as little more than a *pied-à-terre*. He felt, too, that it was not the ideal arrangement for a bishop to live in his cathedral city and he would have liked to move away from Gloucester—for preference to Prinknash—but never succeeded in doing so. Whorlton, of course, was his real home, and nowhere else could ever possibly take its place.

Normally the Palace was run with clockwork precision, for Headlam lived an ordered life. He was always in his study by 8 a.m. to do a good hour's theological work—real 'work'—after which came Morning Chapel at 9 a.m. This was followed by breakfast and five minutes with *The Times*, and at 10 a.m. he returned to the study to attend to business and correspondence, which had already been sorted by his staff. Usually this went on until 12.30 p.m. without a break: outside morning engagements were rare. He then went for a walk with his dog until lunch time at 1 p.m. Afternoons were taken up with work in the diocese, and whenever possible he contrived to be back in time for dinner. Then came a further spell of study, Evening Chapel at 9.45, a few minutes' relaxation with a detective novel and bed at 10.30 p.m.

His ordered life, vitality, and powers of concentration enabled him to get through an enormous amount of work; but his very able staff counted for a great deal. First there were his domestic chaplains— notably Edward Prichard and later Philip Usher—both brilliant young men whom he had known at Oxford and who were devoted to him. Then there was G. H. W. Jones, his secretary from 1923 until his death in 1944, who had previously served Bishop Gore. Finally there was Sister Lavinia Smith, who had attended his lectures at King's College, London and subsequently had met him frequently at theological discussions in Oxford. After some years in a religious community serious intellectual differences had compelled her to seek her release. Headlam then asked her to come and help him with those important but unspectacular tasks which are part of the life of any administrator or scholar—digging out information, compiling lists, checking references and so on. To these people and to the administrative staff of the diocese he owed a great debt : but he recognized their worth and trusted them completely. Miss G. le Bailly, who was secretary of the Diocesan Board of Finance from 1918 to 1945, wrote :

'Apart from his constructive work for the diocese, he was a most conscientious and careful administrator at all times. He never went away without coming into the office to find out if there were any things he ought to see to, was always careful to leave his address, and had a regular time each day when at home when I could go and see him on any important business that might have arisen, apart from pre-arranged interviews. He was ideal to do business with, clear-headed on any of the various matters to be discussed, considerate, and above all unhurried. He might say he had only six minutes or whatever it might be, but for that time his attention was wholly given to the business in hand as if nothing else existed, nor would he leave it unfinished. If need really was, the next matter had to wait, whoever or whatever it might be.'

II

Soon after his enthronement he announced his intention of visiting every parish in the diocese. With these visits he was most painstaking, enquiring closely into parochial activities and examining every church and parsonage house. By the end of his first year he had visited ninety-three parishes in this way—no mean achievement in view of his other commitments : it was a task, he told the diocese, which had given him much satisfaction and great enjoyment. His first official Visitation took place in the spring of 1924. This was interrupted by the illness and death of his wife and only parts of his Charge were delivered : the whole work was published, however, under the title *The Church of England* and every clergyman in the diocese was given a copy. Much of its contents had appeared elsewhere in earlier books and articles, but here Headlam succeeded in showing his people what he thought of the Church of England as a whole—its history, its life and its mission: questions of faith, worship, organization and reunion—all were surveyed with clarity and succinctness, and the diocese was left in no doubt as to where its bishop stood. On matters of worship, for example, Headlam's directions were clear-cut. Although variety in forms of worship and vesture were permissible, no clergyman should undertake changes in his parish without the goodwill and co-operation of his people.[4] On Sundays he himself had a personal preference for mattins as the main morning service, but he had no objections to a choral eucharist provided some provision was made for mattins and non-communicating attendance was not made obligatory.[5] The practice of private confession was most desirable—every clergyman should be ready and able to exercise this ministry: but he did not approve of compulsory or habitual confession, although there might possibly be some cases where the latter could be helpful and desirable.[6] Then there was the question of his own episcopal dress. In the diocese he wore rochet and chimere on all occasions, claiming that there was a simple dignity about them which harmonized better with the instincts of the British people and gave no cause for offence, as vestments might well do.[7] Like his predecessor he wore a cope in the Cathedral, but never a mitre, which he regarded as rather a ridiculous head dress.

The section of the Charge dealing with the Cathedral was of particular interest, for the Visitation had there met with opposition. The Cathedral had not been visited for some 250 years; and Headlam's decision to do so by reason of his statutory position as Visitor was questioned by the Dean, Dr. Gee, who claimed that the charter upon which these visitatorial rights were based had been superseded by the statutes of the New Cathedral Foundations. Headlam, after consultation with his Chancellor (Mr. E. W. Hansell), refused to accept this claim, and the Dean only gave way after further protest. Headlam then asked for the honorary canons to be summoned, but the Dean again objected, claiming that there was no provision for them in the statutes. This time Dr. Gee remained absolutely adamant, despite an episcopal rebuke for his lack of co-operation, and the honorary canons were finally summoned by Headlam through the Diocesan Registrar.

In the course of his Charge Headlam pointed out that according to ancient custom it was usual for a bishop at the time of his Visitation to visit first the cathedral and then the diocese. It was a misfortune that this custom had fallen so much into abeyance, for a number of reasons.[8] In the first place it provided a means of solving those prob-

---

[4] A. C. Headlam, *The Church of England*, 1924, pp. 79–80.
[5] Ibid., pp. 92–4.　　　　　[7] Ibid., p. 88.
[6] Ibid., pp. 97–9.　　　　　[8] Ibid., p. 206.

lems created by the growth of customs which had superseded the statutes, thereby rendering their legal observance difficult : secondly it was helpful in meeting the criticisms levelled against the constitution and management of cathedrals : and thirdly it provided a means of finding the best way of using cathedrals and their resources.[9] He then went on to criticize the Dean and Chapter for their attitude. By the Foundation Charter of the bishopric the Cathedral was clearly the Bishop's church, and he had complete episcopal authority in it both ordinary and extraordinary. Their contention that the statutes of the New Foundation Cathedrals defined and limited his authority appeared to him to be incorrect. These statutes were concerned with the powers of the Dean and Chapter and not with the Bishop at all; they not only took him for granted but in fact extended his power, for they gave him the position of Visitor. The Cathedral was the Bishop's church, by tradition, by custom and by charter : it was therefore pre-eminently the church in which he should officiate. Although with the passage of time the Bishop's duties had extended and much of his work had devolved upon the Dean and Chapter, this did not take away the potentiality of the Bishop's action. There was necessarily inherent in the Bishop's office a right to preach and celebrate in his own cathedral, and the Dean had no authority over him.[10] Then there was this question of the honorary canons. As Visitor he had the right to hold his Visitation Court in the Chapter House, to which he summoned all those over whom he exercised jurisdiction. The honorary canons had been duly instituted and had sworn canonical obedience to the Bishop : they must therefore attend when he summoned them. Furthermore their position had been settled by Act of Parliament, and by it they had been made members of the Cathedral Body.[11] Finally he suggested a number of reforms. First he hoped that their statutes might be revised and adapted to the needs of the times. He hoped too for an improvement in their financial position, with adequate, fixed stipends for the Dean and Chapter and sufficient money to maintain the fabric and the services. He also wanted to see the Cathedral develop stronger diocesan links; its chapels could be associated more closely with the religious and secular activities of the diocese; the honorary canons could be given a greater share in its activities; and prominent laymen could be given closer ties by the appointment of honorary lay canons. On the other hand he did not approve of the residentiary canons being given official diocesan responsibilities. They should be left free to develop their work along their own lines— writing, preaching, or whatever it might be.[12] Finally he reminded

[9] Ibid., pp. 212–14.
[10] Ibid., pp. 217–21.

[11] Ibid., pp. 221–2.
[12] Ibid., pp. 224–35.

them that the Cathedral should be the parish church of the whole diocese. 'The demand in this diocese, and I think in all dioceses, for close association with the cathedral by all those interested in our religious life is increasing. The appeal cathedrals and their services make, if those services are adapted to the needs and outlook of the present day, is not less than it was but greater. It is diffused over far more classes of the population, and I am sure that if the Dean and Chapter are prepared to go forward and adapt the cathedral more and more to the conditions of the present day and needs of the people, they will have the hearty support of the whole diocese.' [13]

Such then was Headlam's Primary Charge—'the most noteworthy episcopal pronouncement that we have had for many years,' wrote Dean Inge.[14] It reached a public far beyond the borders of the diocese; indeed the hope was expressed in *The Modern Churchman* that the clergy and churchwardens of the entire provinces of Canterbury and York might digest it.[15] Certainly it would be true to say that Gloucester accepted it loyally and under Headlam's leadership was a well-run, trouble-free and prosperous diocese. His episcopate was later regarded as great and memorable [16]; but he was the first to acknowledge the part the diocese played, and at its close he expressed the hope that *between them* they had done something for the kingdom of God in their generation.

III

Within a few months of the Visitation Headlam made a ten-week tour of Canada and the United States. The initial invitation to come and lecture had been sent by McGill University, Montreal; but once his projected visit became known further invitations poured in from both countries. It was then arranged through Archbishop Davidson that he should preach the opening sermon of the triennial General Synod of the Church of Canada in London, Ontario, on September 24, and this was his first engagement. At the Synod he was impressed by the vigour, earnestness and business capacity of many of the members, but thought the speeches on the whole were eloquent rather than good and certainly inferior to those heard in the Church Assembly. There was, however, some excuse for the desire to talk too much: if a delegate had travelled a very long way, he could hardly be expected

13 Ibid., pp. 220, 239.
14 *The Edinburgh Review*, vol. 241, p. 17.
15 *The Modern Churchman*, April–May 1925, p. 57.
16 The Bishop of Tewkesbury, January 24, 1947.

to go home again without wishing to say something. Some of them, too, had come enormous distances: those from the Pacific coast had travelled two thousand miles, the Bishop of the Yukon had set out from his diocese as early as June, and one representative had come from within the Arctic circle. It was an example which people in Gloucester might well take to heart, as Headlam hinted rather heavily in *The Diocesan Magazine.*[17]

During his stay he also preached or lectured in the Cathedral, the University of Western Ontario and Huron College, apart from what he called 'a certain amount of miscellaneous talking.' Then, after a flying visit to the Anglican University of Bishop's College, Lennoxville, to receive an honorary degree, there followed a busy week in Montreal—four lectures on the life and teaching of Jesus Christ at McGill University, sermons in the Cathedral and the principal churches, and the inevitable round of meetings and social gatherings. He was most hospitably entertained and there was only one complaint: it was so hard to find something decent to drink. 'The Province of Quebec has government control in liquor, and one occasionally gets something to drink; although as the clergy are mostly abstainers, this is not often. But Ontario was quite dry. I hate a temperance regime. Temperance drinks give me a feeling of nausea, and drinking the King's health in iced water gives me colic.'[18] From Montreal he went to Toronto for another week of lectures, sermons and meetings. It was a particularly interesting and enjoyable week: he was entertained at Government House; he met among other prominent people the Prince of Wales and the Prime Minister; and he himself gave a luncheon party for a family from Whorlton who had settled in Canada; it added to his delight to find that the waitress who served them was also a native of his own part of Durham.

The Canadian portion of his tour was now over. After a short rest at Niagara Falls there followed another full week of lectures on reunion in New York. Then came a typically American hustle—flying visits to Lehigh, Philadelphia, Gloucester, Washington and Baltimore —and so to Boston, where he gave the Noble Lectures on the life and teaching of Jesus Christ at Harvard University in addition to the usual heavy round of sermons and meetings, but he enjoyed it: 'It was rather exhilarating to expound the merits of episcopacy to the descendants of the Pilgrim Fathers and receive a very considerable amount of assent.'

Here the tour ended and Headlam returned to England during the first week in December. His impressions of American church life were

[17] *The Diocesan Magazine,* November 1924.
[18] Headlam to Miss P. L. Wingfield, October 21, 1924.

in some respects not too favourable. There was undeniable evidence of religious earnestness, vigour and administrative ability—the Church was growing in numbers and influence, and its members were very generous—but he doubted whether it had the capacity to rise to its opportunities. Very few of the bishops were first-class men and there was a general weakness in theological learning : very few universities had theological faculties, while much of the teaching given was poor and inadequate. Theology was in fact overshadowed by the practical and business side of religion, resulting in the prevalence of fundamentalism on the one hand and a somewhat insipid modernism on the other : there were not many signs of a sober Catholic tradition. In the United States, too, the outlook of the Church was fundamentally congregational, and there was little real conception of corporate life in the Church. Few people had any real vision of the Church Catholic, with the result that much of the existing desire for reunion was based, not on theological conviction but on a reaction against the waste and inefficiency of the number of half-filled churches in any given community. Headlam had sensed that his lectures and discussions on reunion had not made the impact he had hoped for. He confessed to Canon Maynard Smith, 'They did not like my speaking very much, but a great many of them thought they ought to like it.' There was, in short, too much business and hustle and not enough intelligence.

These were impressions which, of course, Headlam made no attempt to gloss over or hide—it would have been quite foreign to his nature to have done so. They caused resentment in some quarters in Canada and in the United States, but it must not be thought that his tour failed to do any good. His Noble Lectures, for example, were extremely well received and American scholars welcomed the new and healthy stimulus to theological study which he provided. Many of them were well aware of their own theological weaknesses and were most grateful to him, not only for his inspiration but also for his generous gifts of books which he later sent to colleges in both countries. Others, too, were genuinely interested in the theological issues of reunion, and he was able to meet some, at least, of those who later played an important part in the Faith and Order movement. The tour had been interesting and instructive, and he fully appreciated the extraordinary kindness with which he had been received : but he was glad to get back to Gloucester. The affection and pride with which he had already come to regard the diocese were clearly revealed in his Diocesan Magazine for January 1925 :

'It is always pleasant to get back to England, and however hard I may have been worked, I have to remember that, although a bishop is a bishop of the Church as a whole and therefore has obligations outside his diocese, his diocese is his special care; and work in his diocese is not only his first duty but is also the most pleasant and the most profitable.

'First of all I must thank every one for the way in which the work of the diocese has gone on while I have been away. In particular I must thank the Archdeacon for carrying on everything so well that I hardly feel as if there were any arrears to make up. Then I must thank the clergy for the patience they have shown in postponing things until my return; and I must thank the laity, and particularly the Diocesan Board of Finance, for having solved so many problems in my absence. It is pleasant to find things when one returns better, as far as one can see, than when one went away.' [19]

[19] *The Diocesan Magazine*, January 1925.

CHAPTER TWELVE

Prayer Book Revision

IT was not until Headlam became Bishop of Gloucester that he played any active part in the work connected with the revision of the Prayer Book. At that particular time in 1923 the Church Assembly was considering the document N.A. 84, which embodied the answers of the Convocations to the Royal Letters of Business as accepted or amended by a joint committee of the three Houses of the Church Assembly. Comment, advice and criticism poured in from all quarters, and Headlam contributed to this literature with a letter to *The Times* on November 15, 1923, opposing any alternative Canon for the Communion Service—a policy which he considered to be supported by some ninety per cent of Churchmen. In the following spring he set out his position more fully in his primary Visitation Charge. He had no sympathy with the view that Revision was necessary in the interests of order and discipline, but he felt that it was desirable to bring the Prayer Book into line with the customs and needs of the day. Those elements which were unedifying needed to be changed, and a greater variety of services and prayers was required : but whatever variations might be permitted, there should be no variety in the Canon of the Communion Service :

'As regards the Canon of the Communion Office there should, I think, be no variety. It is the central office of the Church and the most essential rite. . . . As regards the present Canon . . . it is, I think, quite adequate and sufficient, but it might quite well be enriched and enlarged. . . . Personally, I should like to see the Canon in the Communion Office enriched by an invocation of the Holy Spirit in some form, by a commemoration not only of the death and Passion of our Lord but of the other great events of His life, and by the solemn oblation of the Church as giving the intention of the sacrifice in the service.' [1]

These words clearly stated his position—no alternative Canon, but

---

[1] *The Church of England*, pp. 108–9.

no objection to the enrichment of the existing Canon. Nor was this a position which he had taken up in a hurry; for he had expressed the same opinion to Archbishop Davidson some years previously.[2] It was therefore something of a surprise to find him accepting the invitation of Dr. Pollock, Bishop of Norwich, to join his group of 'No change' bishops in May 1925. On June 13 this group—nine in number—presented a Memorial to the Archbishop of Canterbury, declaring that they were 'definitely opposed at the present time to any change being made in the Order of Administration of the Holy Communion after the Creed, or to any alternative form of service.'[3] Headlam was evidently not happy about the line he had adopted, for six days later he wrote to the Archbishop, explaining that although he was firmly opposed to the 'No Alternative' policy, his attitude towards 'No change at all' was much less rigid. He was opposed to the idea of an alternative Canon because he considered it to be contrary to every Catholic principle and harmful to the cause of reunion : but he would not oppose an enrichment of the existing Canon if it were acceptable to all the leading parties in the Church. It was his hope, therefore, that it would be possible to divide the Prayer Book Measure into two portions. The first, containing uncontroversial material and not the service of Holy Communion, should be brought to the Assembly as soon as possible. The second, dealing with Holy Communion, should be referred to a committee of experts representative of different views; and until they could agree on changes of which the great body of Church people would approve, the Holy Communion office should remain unchanged.

Headlam's apparent hesitancy on the question may have been due to the feeling that the chances of effecting changes which would meet with general approval were remote; but it may also have been partly due to the fact that at the moment he had little real enthusiasm for the business of Revision. When the Bishops met in October to revise N.A. 84, Dr. Pollock did in fact propose that Revision should be undertaken in two stages, the uncontroversial matter being dealt with first; but he was defeated by 24 votes to 9.[4] Little progress was made at these meetings and Headlam thought them very unsatisfactory. He wrote later : 'The discussions were often irrelevant, and whenever we got to a difficult point we postponed it. By the end of

---

[2] Headlam to Randall Cantuar, November 19, 1919.
[3] Bell, *Randall Davidson*, p. 1330. Other members of the group were Dr. Pollock (Norwich), Dr. Thornton-Duesbury (Sodor and Man), Lord W. Cecil (Exeter), Dr. Pearce (Worcester), Dr. Barnes (Birmingham), Dr. Whittingham (St. Edmundsbury and Ipswich), Dr. Perowne (Bradford) and Dr. Nickson (Bristol).
[4] Ibid.

the third day it had become quite clear to me that if we were to continue in the present process, we should none of us be alive when the Revision was complete.' The Bishops were due to meet again in January 1926, and so little had been achieved that Headlam was exasperated. 'The result will be to disturb, at any rate, all my Christmas holidays, and to prevent me, as far as I can see, doing any intelligent work.' [5]

That was just it. Revision did not come into the category of 'intelligent work' and therefore had not received his wholehearted attention. The ineffectiveness of their deliberations constituted a serious challenge, however; and Headlam made up his mind that it was something to which he must devote time and energy. The first essential was to brief himself. It was perfectly clear that, with the exception of Dr. Frere, Bishop of Truro, the Episcopal Bench was sadly lacking in liturgical knowledge; so for many months he got up early each day to study the subject and at the same time sought the advice of experts both at home and overseas. As a result his views underwent a modification; and when the Bishops divided on the amended form of the alternative Canon in N.A. 84 in June 1926, Headlam voted in its favour. The Canon was accepted by 29 votes to 5.[6] The Bishop of Norwich pleaded with him for his continued support, but he felt that he must refuse.

'. . . (The present Canon) eliminates the element of prayer; it eliminates the work of the Holy Spirit; it is most jejune in its memorial of the Gospel story and the basis of Evangelical truth. It is capable of a purely Zwinglian interpretation, but if we avoid that it almost reads like a magical formula. There is not the same criticism possible for either the American or the Scottish Prayer Book, nor of course for the first Prayer Book of Edward VI. In these circumstances I think it is most desirable that we should have a revised Canon. I should be glad if we could possibly postpone it for a little time, and then carry it as an agreed measure, and I am prepared to support any further proposal for a division of the Measure and some postponement of this part; but I am not prepared entirely to leave out this revision of the Communion Service. If it is passed I shall put quite definitely and strongly to my diocese that I look upon it as a very great improvement, and I shall use all the pressure I can to make it generally and if possible universally used. I am prepared, that is to say, as a transitional but only a transitional measure, to allow an alternative use.' [7]

Headlam now emerged as a strong supporter of the new Prayer Book

---

[5] Headlam to Canon Maynard Smith, October 23, 1925.
[6] R. C. D. Jasper, *Walter Howard Frere*, 1954, p. 106.
[7] Headlam to the Bishop of Norwich, September 22, 1926.

and he wrote a number of letters to the Press urging its acceptance. By the beginning of 1927 he had acquired quite a reputation, a correspondent in *The Record* calling him 'the episcopal protagonist of the Composite Book.' This change of view was, of course, too good for opponents to miss, and the same paper did not hesitate to remind its readers that whereas in *The Morning Post* on March 7, 1927, Headlam belittled the opposition to the Book and represented the majority of Churchmen as welcoming it, on November 15, 1923, he had asserted the opposite.[8] The Bishop of Norwich also reminded him of the same fact shortly afterwards when a joint sitting of the Convocations of Canterbury and York on March 30 debated whether to submit the Book and the Measure to the Church Assembly. Headlam admitted quite frankly that he had changed his mind, but he was now convinced that the Church would benefit by the new Book. It was consistent with Anglican doctrine : it was Catholic, Evangelical and in harmony with modern thought; and as such it would help the cause of reunion.[9]

He stated his position at length in his second Visitation Charge, delivered in April 1927, and subsequently published under the title *The New Prayer Book*. Here again he admitted the change in his point of view but 'no one has ever been ashamed to change his opinion in the face of arguments which he recognized were sound.'[10] In uncontroversial parts of the Prayer Book he thought the changes presented a great improvement on the old services. 'I have some acquaintance with the revisions of the Book of Common Prayer which have been made in other parts of the Anglican Communion, and I do not hesitate to say that this Revision is better and bolder than any other.'[11] As for the Communion Service, he personally felt a preference for one rite only, but there was precedent for an alternative use and indeed it was inevitable in view of the pledge given that the old Prayer Book should remain in use for those who desired it.[12] He had no doubts, however, as to the superiority of the new rite. The new Canon was better, richer, more Catholic and Evangelical, and entirely loyal to the theological traditions both of the Catholic Church and the Church of England.[13] Whereas the 1662 Prayer of Consecration was quite compatible with Roman theology, the new Prayer forbade it, following the traditions of the Eastern liturgies and probably also the earlier forms of the Western.[14] He also defended the provisions

[8] *The Record*, March 24, 1927.
[9] *Chronicle of Convocation*, 1927, pp. 84, 126–31.
[10] *The New Prayer Book*, 1927, p. 17.
[11] Ibid., pp. 41–2.
[12] Ibid., pp. 43–4.
[13] Ibid., pp. 45–6.
[14] Ibid., pp. 75–6.

made for Reservation. In parishes with many sick people it was necessary and there was no doctrinal reason against it.[15] As for extra-
liturgical devotions it was impossible to prevent them unless it could
be shown that they were theologically unsound : they were certainly
not Catholic, being unknown in the Eastern Church and for more
than a thousand years in the Western Church.[16] 'The new Prayer
Book gives quite legally and without any difficult or doubtful interpretations very wide latitude in the Church of England. It is a tolerant
and comprehensive measure, and as such harmonizes with the characteristics of the present day. But if we accept that latitude, it must
mean also loyalty.'[17] It was interesting to note that the Diocesan
Conference at Gloucester had approved of every point of importance
in the new Book except the provision of the alternative Communion
Office. Headlam admitted that he could sympathize with such an
attitude : he still felt that alternative forms, either of Holy Communion, Baptism or Confirmation, were a mistake : but the pledge
had been given and the policy accepted. They must therefore accept
the situation, deriving comfort at least from the fact that all the new
forms were better than the old.[18]

He followed this with an article in *The Church Quarterly Review*
for July 1927, 'A Defence of the New Prayer Book,' pointing out that
the mounting evidence of Diocesan and Ruri-decanal Conferences and
Parochial Church Councils throughout the country seemed to indicate
that the new Book was becoming increasingly acceptable.[19] This
acceptance was broken in three directions : first by a group of the
more extreme Evangelicals led by Bishop Knox and Sir William
Joynson-Hicks, who attacked it with violence and persistence but
without much intelligence ; secondly by a small knot of extreme High
Churchmen, led by Dr. Darwell Stone ; and thirdly by 'a small number
of academical faddists who may be expected to be a little too clever
to acquiesce in a too commonplace solution and who are anxious to
defend some novel or almost paradoxical point of view.'[20] Headlam
agreed that there was undoubtedly a Romanism against which protest
should be made, but he felt that the extreme Evangelical party had
done harm to the cause of true Protestantism and to the Christian
faith by putting forward a purely negative view of Christianity and
by devoting their energies to denouncing what they considered to be
the errors of almost every section of the Christian Church, instead of

[15] Ibid., pp. 84–5.
[16] Ibid., pp. 86–7.
[17] Ibid., p. 101.
[18] Ibid., pp. 94–5.
[19] 'A Defence of the New Prayer Book,' *C.Q.R.*, vol. 104, p. 200.
[20] Ibid., p. 201.

preaching Evangelical truth.[21] As for Dr. Darwell Stone, who seemed
to complain that the Prayer Book had not been revised in accordance
with his own particular views, did he not understand that the very
essence of association together in a Christian society was that men
should subordinate their own desires to the teaching of that society?
His attitude was destructive to that corporate unity of the Christian
Church for which Catholics stood.[22]

Unfortunately for Headlam his advocacy of the Book was damaged
by the famous article of Dr. F. E. Brightman 'The New Prayer Book
Examined' which appeared in the same number of *The Church
Quarterly Review*. Brightman was no lover of the Book and was
severely critical. 'On almost every page I find something irritating,
something inexact or untidy or superfluous or ill-considered or
unreal.' [23] The essay, enlivened by flashes of caustic wit, succeeded in
making the new Book appear rather ridiculous and Headlam was
annoyed. Brightman was rebuked: such an article was hardly fair
when he had been approached, as a liturgical expert, to give advice
during the course of the Revision; surely he could have done something to improve the Book on these occasions? Brightman's reply was
revealing. The original draft of his article had been even more severe,
and the whole thing had caused him much unhappiness.

June 23, 1927.

'My dear Bishop,

'Thank you very much for your letter. . . . The article itself I did
not offer, but only did it at Maynard Smith's desire, and I supposed
at yours.[24] . . . You seem to forget that more than a year and a half
ago, by the desire of the Archbishop of York, I annotated throughout
—or almost throughout, for there was little time—and also the Canon,
so far as I remember, was not then in a condition to be dealt with—
the three column book on which, I understood, the bishops were to
work: and a good deal of what my article contains simply reproduces
what I said there and was made no use of.

'I sat throughout on the Advisory Committee—how, when, or why
it came to an end I don't know—and spent a good deal of time over
it; but we were told more than once that it was not our business to
make proposals, but to answer questions—including a whole day spent
in the attempt to turn what was submitted to us into English; and
some of my present criticisms were made in that Committee some
fifteen years or more ago. So that when you say I was "consulted,"

[21] Ibid., p. 208.
[22] Ibid., pp. 215–18.
[23] F. E. Brightman, 'The New Prayer Book Examined,' *C.Q.R.*, vol. 104,
p. 222.
[24] Canon Maynard Smith was then editor of *C.Q.R.*

that is all that it has amounted to, except that I answered two questions of your own some months ago—and all you told me was that you had decided to do nothing.

'It remains that I detest the Book; but I have spent two days almost in endeavouring to blunt some of my remarks in proof. It remains also that I am quite miserable about it and would gladly suppress the article, if I could. I shall ask Maynard Smith to show you the proof, if you will read it; and if you think that it will do harm—harm, I mean, from your point of view, not mine—I hope you will suppress it. I dare say Maynard Smith has something he could substitute for it to make up his number. But anyhow I have said less and not more than I mean.

Yours ever,

F. E. BRIGHTMAN.'

It says a great deal for Headlam's courage and honesty that he made no attempt to take advantage of Brightman's permission to suppress it, nor did he withdraw from his own position in the face of such damaging criticism. He spoke strongly in favour of the new Book in the final debate of the Church Assembly on July 6 before final approval was given to the Measure [25] and he pleaded earnestly for Parliament to pass it in another letter to *The Times* on October 7. The new Prayer Book possessed the full authority of the Church expressed in a constitutional way. He deplored the activity of a determined minority, defeated both in votes and by argument, to influence M.P.s and to secure Nonconformist support. The latter had withdrawn their allegiance to the established Church and therefore had precluded themselves from a right to control its affairs: they would have been most indignant if Roman Catholics had intervened in the same way, yet they had every right to do so. It was incorrect for the Bishop of Norwich to say that the rejection of the new Book would help the cause of reunion: if Nonconformist influence proved a telling factor in its rejection, the bitterness caused would throw back the hopes of reunion for fifty years. The new Book on the other hand implied toleration and comprehension, preparing the way for a reconciliation with Nonconformity, while it would give just that ordered liberty which the Church of England needed. At the same time he wrote to all the members of both Houses of Parliament in his diocese asking for their support and pointing out that the Diocesan Conference had just shown itself overwhelmingly in favour of the Book by 423 votes to 51.

Such efforts were of little avail, however. Although the Lords passed

[25] *Church Assembly Proceedings,* vol. viii, pp. 148–51, 196.

the Measure by 241 votes to 88, the Commons rejected it by 247 votes to 205 on December 15.[26] Headlam was annoyed : it was a tiresome setback. He wrote to Sister Lavinia Smith :

'I suppose it is because of my excessive worldliness but I do not feel unhappy, or despondent, or anything of the sort. Some of the Bishops are very worried and upset. I am only angry. But I am really very much annoyed at this—that all this controversy wastes so much time. *We want to get on with the things that really matter.* I shall have to waste more time over the Prayer Book, when we all thought that we could put that behind us and get on. However, we must try and get good out of evil.'

The Bishops discussed the situation on December 19, and it was decided to reintroduce the Measure into the Church Assembly as soon as possible with changes which would tend to remove apprehensions and clarify its intentions and limitations. The Alternative Canon was obviously one of the crucial points of issue. Headlam sounded Dr. Frere on the possibility of solving a difficulty by following the example of the Alexandrian rite and having two Epicleses, one before and one after the Words of Institution : supporters of the new Canon could hardly object to it, while it might also find acceptance with the Anglo-Catholics.[27] Frere, however, was not enthusiastic : he felt that it would play into the hands of those who accused them of following Eastern tradition, whereas they were trying to maintain a non-Roman Western position; nor would it be acceptable to those who wanted to have no Epiclesis at all. After further consideration Headlam also came round to the conclusion that such an alteration would after all be unwise. He wrote to Frere on December 30 :

'I have been thinking about things and also talking to people, and I am certain now that we had better give up the idea of doing anything to improve the new Prayer Book. If we send it back to the Commons, it must be with a minimum of alterations, and we must not distract people with subordinate issues. The question is one now of spiritual independence of the Church, and the more we confine people's atten-tion to the one issue the better. After all, any improvement which we made in one direction would be considered harmful in another direc-tion, and so I think we had better quite clearly make up our minds not to attempt alteration, and our policy should be the minimum change possible.'[28]

---

[26] Jasper, *Frere,* p. 138.
[27] Ibid., p. 139. [28] Ibid., p. 144.

The new Book in its revised form, despite acceptance by the Convocations and the Church Assembly—although with reduced majorities—was again rejected by the House of Commons on June 13th by 266 votes to 220. Archbishop Davidson pleaded for charity in the face of a difficult situation; and although Headlam agreed with him that it was undesirable to indulge in recriminations against the opponents of the Book, he did feel that it should be made perfectly clear to them that their action was strongly resented.[29] He expressed his own resentment in characteristic fashion to Dr. Darwell Stone on September 18. It is sufficient to say that he did not mince his words and left no possible hope of future co-operation in that particular sphere.

It appeared to him that there were three main reasons why the new Prayer Book had again failed to gain acceptance. In the first place there had been a lack of religious appeal in the debate in the House of Commons. Apart from Lord Hugh Cecil's peroration, the speeches in support of the Book had failed to touch the hearts of the House. Secondly, there had been a lack of corporate consciousness. Despite the fact that the new Book had the authority of the Houses of both Convocations, the Church Assembly and every Diocesan Conference except one, certain people had refused to accept that authority and had obtained their way by soliciting the support of members of the House of Commons who neither belonged to the Church of England nor even resided in the country. Thirdly, the Church had failed to teach its people properly; the issues and theological problems at stake had never been really adequately explained. The rejection of the Book reflected not upon the Book itself, but upon the Church; the Church was obviously not ready for it, nor would it have been good for the Church to have had it.[30]

Headlam's considered judgment on the situation was expressed in his Presidential Address to the Church Congress at Cheltenham in October 1928. He pointed out that a union between Church and State for the well-being of a community had been common in history and, if established on sound lines, beneficial : but if the one had encroached upon the other, the result had been disastrous. The present dilemma fully exemplified this; the spiritual independence of the Church was injured. It was, and it had always been recognized to be, the function of the Church to formulate its own faith and regulate its own worship. Each successive revision of the Prayer Book had been the work of the Church, and it had only been the desire for a State-enforced uniformity that had made the authority of Parliament necessary. What

[29] Headlam to Archbishop Davidson, June 19, 1928.
[30] *Gloucester Diocesan Magazine,* July 1928.

was now needed was the repeal of the Act of Uniformity, so that the spiritual independence of the Church might be restored. Certainly while this Parliamentary authority in spiritual matters existed, any reunion at home was impossible. The belief in the spiritual autonomy of the Church was not merely a fad of High Churchmen; it was a fundamental belief of all Free Churchmen. He would regret Disestablishment as a solution to the problem; but some way might be found on the lines of the Church of Scotland Act of 1921, whereby that Church had been given full spiritual independence. Such a solution might need patience, however; for the Church of Scotland had been forced to wait for seventy-eight years to attain its freedom and to pass through great and serious crises. It would also need statesmanship, for it would involve having a clear policy and a determination not to be deflected from it. The most serious element in the situation, of course, had been the rejection of the Book by the House of Commons, for it had involved an appeal to Parliament against the corporate voice of the Church. A better instance could not be given of the perversion and exaggeration of party spirit, which was the real cause of the difficulties within the Church and of the conditions which had caused disunion among Christians. The evil which the new Prayer Book had been intended to cure had in effect been the very means of securing its rejection. The Church was now faced with the task of strengthening its corporate life, and strengthening it against party tendencies. This could be done in the first place by laying greater emphasis on the corporate organization of the Church; and in this respect great progress had been made in recent years by the creation of the Church Assembly and the granting to it of legislative power. The Church as a whole should summon its members to take part in conferences and receive instruction, in the rural deanery, in the diocese and even on a wider basis. 'Party' Conferences, however, in which there was no opposition, were fruitful nurseries of error. The second thing which could be done was the regulation of worship by the bishops acting in harmony with their clergy through the diocesan synods. During the last century the publication of various directories of worship had been the work of private enterprise : as a result, the relations between clergymen and their bishops in matters of worship had changed. Instead of regarding the bishop as the obvious person to consult when variations or improvements in services were felt to be needed, clergy had come to regard him as one who wished to prevent them from doing things and to restrain excessive zeal and enthusiasm. All this needed changing : the function of the bishops should be a positive one—to help and encourage clergy to do what is right.[31]

[31] H. A. Wilson (editor), *The Anglican Communion*, 1929, pp. 3-35.

Headlam held a synod of his clergy on October 18 and explained the situation to them. They endorsed by a large majority the statement of the Bishops asserting the inalienable right of the Church, in the last resort and once its mind had been fully ascertained, to formulate its Faith and to arrange the expression of it in its forms of worship.[32] The final act came a year later. The Bishops had announced to the Convocations in July 1929 that 'during the present emergency and until further order be taken' they would not regard as inconsistent with loyalty to the principles of the Church of England the use of such additions or deviations as fell within the limits of the proposals embodied in the 1928 Book. At his Diocesan Conference in October Headlam issued his directions. Nothing should be done which was not in accordance with either the 1662 Book or the 1928 Book without his permission : in the case of the Occasional Offices the use of the 1928 forms would need the permission of the parochial church council and the interested parties : the use of the 1928 Communion Service after the Nicene Creed would require his special permission ; and finally Reservation would only be permitted in parishes where there was a special need and where the application was endorsed by the parochial church council.[33]

Headlam had no serious trouble with opponents of the new Book in the diocese. Of the relatively few extremists he considered the Protestants to be stupid rather than disloyal. He took the trouble to make a careful investigation of their reasons for opposition and found that hardly any of them had ever read the Book or knew in the least what it contained. On the other side there were no really extreme Anglo-Catholics to cause serious trouble. So far as he was concerned, the situation left him and his fellow-bishops with the task of exercising their due prerogatives in matters of worship. But the whole business had been very tiresome. They had wasted a great deal of time and energy which might have been used to greater advantage on far more important issues.

---

[32] *Gloucester Diocesan Magazine*, November 1928.
[33] Ibid., November 1929.

CHAPTER THIRTEEN

Faith and Order:
Lausanne 1927

THE idea of the Faith and Order movement came from the Edinburgh Missionary Conference of 1910 : in the words of Bishop Brent, 'It was the sense of God's presence at that Conference, and the wonderful and immediate results, that led some of us to believe that a similar Conference on matters of Faith and Order might be productive of good.'[1] The Protestant Episcopal Church of America undertook the necessary arrangements and, after a delay caused by the 1914–18 War, summoned a preliminary meeting at Geneva in 1920. Here the representatives of some forty nations and seventy churches agreed to hold the first Conference of Faith and Order at Lausanne in August 1927. The direction of the movement was placed in the hands of a Continuation Committee, while a Subjects Committee guided preparatory study by issuing lists of questions for discussion. Some indication of the position in the theological field was given in a pamphlet issued in 1936—*Statements by the Subjects Committee*— summarizing the agreements and disagreements of the various Churches on these questions; and from all this there emerged the final list of seven subjects which the Conference undertook to consider—the Call to Unity, the Gospel, the Nature of the Church, the Church's common Confession of Faith, the Church's Ministry, the Sacraments, and the Unity of Christendom and the place of the different Churches in it. This preliminary work provided at least one indication of the influence exerted by Headlam's Bampton Lectures. To the questions on the Ministry of a reunited Church the Danish Lutheran Church group gave no detailed answers but merely declared that they held the same view 'Which is expressed in the book of Dr. Headlam about the doctrine of the Church and Reunion.'

The Conference finally met on August 3, 1927, with just over four hundred delegates representing 108 different Christian bodies throughout the world. The Roman Catholics were the only notable

[1] H. N. Bate (editor), *Faith and Order: Lausanne 1927*, p. vii.

absentees. Headlam, who felt some misgivings about the whole venture, was among the Anglican delegation of twelve, which included Gore, Temple, Quick and Tissington Tatlow. He was obviously expected to play a prominent part in the proceedings, for in addition to being assigned to Section Four on the Creeds, he was also appointed Chairman of Section Five on the Ministry and an official speaker in Section Seven on the Unity of Christendom. The early discussions in Section Four did nothing to dispel his sceptical mood. Two apparently irreconcilable groups emerged. On the one hand Professor Zankov of Bulgaria, one of the Orthodox delegates, stated, 'If Christendom of to-day is not ripe to accept the Nicene Creed as a common confession of faith, then this same Christendom is far less ripe for the attempt to draw up, and secure acceptance for, a new common creed.' On the other hand Professor Wobbermin, a German Evangelical Lutheran, considered it to be an open question whether the formulae in the Creeds represented a satisfactory expression of the Christian faith : a Creed might be extremely desirable, but it was not an absolute necessity—'The intellectual formulae in which a belief is stated cannot be unreservedly identified with the underlying Christian conviction.' [2] Headlam then intervened. Admittedly Churches could not be united merely by formulae—the spirit of unity was necessary : but it was equally true that Churches could not be united without some concrete expression of faith. He felt that the time had now come for someone to be so bold as to try and express what they had come to, in a way that might be agreed upon. He therefore proposed a formula for their consideration : 'We accept the faith of Christ as it has been taught us by the Holy Scriptures, and as it has been handed down to us in the Creed of the Catholic Church set forth at the Council of Chalcedon, and in the Apostles' Creed.' The words had been carefully chosen. He deliberately used the expression 'Faith of Christ'—not 'Creed' : it was the faith not the Creed upon which they were united—something deeper, broader and fuller than any Creed could express, although it might be well expressed by the Creed. Secondly, he put in the forefront the Holy Scriptures as the source of their knowledge of the faith of Christ. Thirdly, the great Œcumenical Creed was the almost universal authority of the ancient Church, was agreed upon by East and West and was accepted by almost all the modern Churches. The Apostles' Creed could perhaps be added as a simpler expression of the same thing. 'I venture to think that on those words it may be possible for us to unite with the great majority (at any rate) of the Churches.' [3]

The speech made a profound impression. 'There was a buzz of

---

[2] Ibid., pp. 176–81, 190–6.
[3] Ibid., pp. 202–3.

H

intent and animated conversation on the Bishop's proposals as members of the Conference trooped away to *déjeuner* in their hotels, and
members of the Creeds Section felt they had been given an interesting
and substantial addition to the material which their group would have
to digest.'[4] Now came the difficult task of hammering out a Report.
Not only was the time allotted all too short but, as the Section Convener, Dr. Tissington Tatlow pointed out, he had to deal with one
hundred and twenty delegates who were the most talkative people in
the world, for each one was a leader in his own Church, and was
accustomed to talk. The Section therefore divided into five groups,
each of which prepared a statement, and from these group statements
a small sub-committee under Headlam then produced a final Report.
It was a task demanding firmness and patience—last-minute differences between German Lutheran and Eastern Orthodox delegates, for
example, involved a great deal of private discussion : but Headlam
made an excellent chairman—'just the kind of one needed for the
occasion, good-humoured and bluntly determined to get the work
done.'[5] The Report was accepted *nem. con.* by the full Conference in
the record time of five minutes.

Headlam sent an interesting account of the proceedings to Canon
Maynard Smith, revealing that his initial scepticism had soon been
dispelled.

'Really the world is very strange—but I think there is a good deal
which is extraordinarily satisfactory about the Conference.

'In the first place there is a real agreement in the Christian Faith. I
have not heard a single speech which has denied what one might call
orthodox Christianity. I mean the Trinity and Incarnation. Some
religious bodies have creeds and some do not, but they all maintain
that they believe what the Creed teaches.

'Secondly the great majority are prepared to accept the Nicene and
Apostles' Creeds and we have found a formula which will rope in the
more intelligent Congregationalists and others who have no creed. A
few members of the "Disciples of Christ"—a body founded to unite
Christianity as a simple Gospel, and therefore doing everything it can
to keep it disunited, are very difficult. But in spite of all there is really
a remarkable agreement here too.

'So you might think we could do something; but for the last two
days as Chairman of a small sub-section founded that we might get
to grips with our Report, I have had every sort of difficulty to meet.
They have all come from three or four Germans who, I believe, are

[4] Canon E. S. Woods, *Lausanne 1927,* 1927, p. 77.
[5] Ibid., p. 83.

angry at being asked to agree to anything which any one else has drawn up. First of all two or three of them have made a determined effort to introduce the Athanasian Creed : and they were extraordinarily persistent. And so some of the other Germans went for them tooth and nail. Then when I proposed a straightforward statement in favour of the supremacy of Scripture, some of the Lutherans would not accept it, and they all shouted at one another and got excited. You may imagine the difficulty of getting any decision at all, and really every one was agreed ! I pointed out that after three hours we could not get a form of words for accepting what we had all agreed upon.

'It will be very interesting to see what comes out of it all. But there is the fact that we all from Orthodox to Baptists do really believe in the same Christianity. I have no time to do anything except our work, but we see a lot of people and dine together, and it is quite interesting.'

The Report clearly bore the imprint of Headlam's original formula. 'Notwithstanding the difference in doctrine among us, we are united in a common Christian Faith which is proclaimed in the Holy Scriptures and is witnessed to and safeguarded in the Ecumenical Creed, commonly called the Nicene, and in the Apostles' Creed, which Faith is continuously confirmed in the spiritual experience of the Church of Christ.' It went on to express the truths of revelation in other forms as might be demanded by new problems, while no external or written standards could suffice without an inward and personal experience of union with God in Christ. Two notes were appended : the Orthodox Church only accepted the Nicene Creed without the Filioque clause, while other Churches which had their own Confessions of Faith would continue to use them and could not regard the use of the Creeds as obligatory.[6] This document was a notable achievement. William Temple wrote later, 'The agreement registered was most remarkable when the divergence between the bodies represented is remembered.' It was something of a personal triumph for Headlam and his position at the Conference was soon enhanced by further weighty contributions to the work of other Sections.

On August 12 work began on Section Five, dealing with the crucial question of the Ministry. 'Here, it was felt, if anywhere, would come the breaking point. Agreement beyond the expectation of the most sanguine had been reached in regard to the message of the Gospel, the Creeds, and even in large measure as to the nature of the Church. . . . Could the one Spirit lead the one Body into agreement here ? Or

---

[6] *Faith and Order: Lausanne 1927*, pp. 466–7.

is there a limit to miracle?' [7] The introductory paper by Bishop Palmer of Bombay boded ill. Contrary to expectation, he made a controversial speech from an uncompromising Anglo-Catholic point of view. Dr. Bulgakov of the Orthodox Theological Institute, Paris, was equally uncompromising : and other speakers only tended to emphasize differing views of the Ministry. Dr. Dibelius of Berlin, an Evangelical Lutheran, seemed to endorse the apparent impossibility of progress by suggesting that there could be no question of finding a formula on which all might agree : the most they could hope for was to secure respect for the ministries of other Churches by those who did not consider them to be valid.[8]

It was at this juncture that Headlam again intervened to save the situation. In the process of outlining his own view of the Ministry, which differed so much from that of Bishop Palmer, he was able to demonstrate the extent of the Church of England, maintaining contact with both Catholic and Protestant traditions. It was a contribution of 'lucidity, sanity and practical statesmanship. . . . No paper had elicited such reiterated and long-continued applause.' [9] It put new heart into the Section, and Headlam's appointment as Chairman for its study sessions was most welcome. 'He discovered to our section the sub-conscious preference of human kind for monarchical government, sketching for us in five minutes the order we were to follow instead of allowing us to spend weary and priceless hours in the discussion of procedure. Oh, the huge relief of all of us ! The preliminary discussion at this meeting revealed a widespread readiness to consider with an open mind even the thorniest of the questions which confronted us.' [10] In presenting the first draft of their Report to the Conference Headlam explained the lines on which they had worked. 'Our purpose was to explore lines of unity and to submit suggestions for the consideration of the Churches, so that this Report does not give exactly what each person thinks, but gives what we all think ought to be put before the Church as lines of investigation.' No essential changes were made to this draft Report and it was received unanimously by the whole Conference in its final form on August 20—an achievement regarded by some as perhaps the most notable and significant of the whole Conference.[11]

Again Headlam was the chief architect; and he gave himself to the task unsparingly. 'It has really been extraordinarily hard work : one

[7] Woods, op. cit., p. 87.
[8] *Faith and Order: Lausanne 1927*, pp. 233–82.
[9] Woods, op. cit., p. 93.
[10] The Revd. W. E. S. Holland, quoted ibid., p. 93.
[11] Cf. ibid., p. 98.

night I got to bed at 1.30 and was up the next morning at 6.' [12] The Report began with certain propositions on the nature of the Ministry with which the members of the Conference found themselves in 'substantial accord.' The Ministry was a gift of God through Christ to His Church; it was essential to the being and the well-being of the Church, and it was authorized and made effective through Christ and His Spirit. Its purpose was to impart to men the saving and sanctifying benefits of Christ through pastoral service, preaching of the Gospel and the administration of the Sacraments. It was entrusted with the government and discipline of the Church in whole or in part; and ministers were called by the Spirit, accepted by the Church and commissioned by the laying-on of hands and of prayer. Then the difficulties of the situation were considered—the authority of the various forms of ministry, the number of orders, the nature of ordination and the questions of episcopacy and apostolic succession. Finally, certain suggestions involving the accommodation of episcopal, presbyteral and congregational elements in the life of a reunited Church were commended to the Churches for their consideration. It was to be understood, however, that the acceptance of any special form of ordination was not to be interpreted as implying the acceptance of any particular theory of orders or of casting doubts on the validity of other existing orders.[13]

Headlam's third great contribution to the Conference was made in Section Seven on 'The Unity of Christendom and the relation thereto of existing Churches.' This subject was not considered until the last week. Inevitably by its very nature it had to come at the end; but by that time the effects of the previous strenuous fortnight were beginning to tell. Difficulties arose, too, over the subject itself. Emphasis had been laid more than once on the fact that it was not the purpose of the Conference to formulate a scheme of reunion : but the subject proved extremely difficult to handle without involving some consideration of a reunited Church. Headlam pointed out that it was difficult to decide what the relation of existing Churches to a future united Church should be until they had decided on what lines the unity of Christendom was to be attained. He believed the ideal to be a unity possessing the greatest possible diversity : not a federation for the sake of efficiency, but a spiritual unity—a unity of faith, a unity in the sacraments, and a unity in the ministry. Unity of faith had already been expressed in the Report on Section Four—the faith of Christ as taught in Holy Scriptures and handed down in the Apostles' and Nicene Creeds : this did not commit them to any particular theory of Inspira-

---

[12] Headlam to Canon Maynard Smith.
[13] *Faith and Order: Lausanne 1927*, pp. 467–72.

tion nor did it regard the Creeds as anything more than the traditional expression of the faith in Christ. Again, sacramental unity meant the acceptance of the fact of the sacraments and not of any particular teaching about them. Finally, unity in the ministry meant, for him at least, the acceptance of episcopacy and episcopal ordination : he did not propose to discuss how it might be achieved, but he did believe that all existing orders were in some measure irregular because the Church was divided. The fundamental postulate of their united Christianity must be freedom and toleration.[14]

His speech was well received. Dr. R. F. Barbour described it as a masterly address, with its courageous plunge into prophecy and wealth of concrete suggestion.[15] Certainly it was largely instrumental in safeguarding the subsequent discussion from degenerating into a succession of platitudes and airy generalizations, and the Section met with no great difficulties in drafting a Report under the direction of Archbishop Söderblom, Archbishop D'Arcy of Armagh and Dr. Dibelius. First came a statement on fellowship in Life and Work, whereby Christians could act together as a body without prejudicing theological principles : then followed a statement on fellowship in Faith and Order, envisaging a united Church with certain characteristics—a common Faith, Baptism as the rite of incorporation, Holy Communion as expressing the corporate life of the Church, freedom of interpretation about sacramental grace and ministerial order and authority, and provision for the exercise of the prophetic gift.[16] Finally, all Christian bodies were asked to learn more about each other and the differences which separated them. Hasty measures for reunion and ambiguous statements were to be deplored, and intercommunion was to be regarded as the seal of completed fellowship in the Church.[17]

The Conference's reception of the Report on August 18 was generally favourable : and despite Bishop Gore's criticism that its terms made it difficult for any one of Catholic outlook to remain in the Faith and Order movement, it showed no radical changes when the Archbishop of Armagh presented it in its final form two days later. It therefore came as something of a surprise when an objection was raised against the first paragraph on fellowship in Life and Work. Dr. F. C. Morehouse of the American Protestant Episcopal Church felt that with the Report in its existing form, there was a serious danger of inter-Church collaboration proceeding at the expense of Faith and Order ; he therefore proposed that it be referred to the Continuation Committee. On

14 Ibid., pp. 331–42.
15 Woods, op. cit., p. 136.
16 A note on this point was inserted on behalf of the Orthodox Church, which could not agree with what was said on the liberty of interpretation.
17 *Faith and Order: Lausanne 1927*, pp. 397–9.

this development Archbishop Söderblom wrote to Headlam, 'The opposition seems to have been made by a few, I dare say rather sectarian members of the American Episcopal Church who call themselves Anglo-Catholics—say rather Americano-Catholics—and who must have felt some of their illusions crushed by the entire Conference, since they concentrated their discontent on that last Report.' [18] Headlam, however, had some sympathy with this opposition. He wrote to Bishop Slattery of Boston :

'Some of your extremer people put the backs of the Conference up on the last day over the final Report on the steps to promote Christian unity. . . . As regards the grounds of their opposition, there was a good deal to be said for it. They were frightened that the Report was one which would support a vague federation. As regards their manner, it was not altogether happy. After all, it is difficult to assert yourself in an unpopular way in a becoming manner, but it was the point on which fundamental differences came out between those who were in favour of the sort of vague federalism which is typified by Lutheranism. The one lays stress on the Ministry, the other ignores it : and this is really the great difficulty we have to surmount.' [19]

The Report, of course, did not go undefended. Dr. Tingfang Lew of China,[20] for example, said that if it were not accepted, he would feel obliged to withdraw his vote in support of the other Reports—an action which the Chairman reminded him was constitutionally impossible. It was clear, however, that there was no chance of the Report being accepted *nem. con.*; and finally the Conference agreed to a motion by the President, Bishop Brent, that the Report should be received by the Conference in the same way as the other Reports, but on the understanding that it should be referred to the Continuation Committee for their consideration and that it should not be transmitted to the Churches.

During the Conference the Continuation Committee had been reconstituted and Headlam had become a member. His first task as such was to redraft Report Seven with the help of two Americans, Professor Adams Brown and Bishop Perry of Rhode Island. Their work was completed by the end of October. The Business Committee of the Continuation Committee accepted it with very minor amendments on December 21 and agreed to circulate it with a brief intro-

[18] Archbishop Söderblom to Headlam, September 5, 1927.
[19] Headlam to Bishop Slattery, September 20, 1927.
[20] *Faith and Order: Lausanne 1927*, pp. 435–9 ; Rouse and Neill, *A History of the Ecumenical Movement*, pp. 421–2.

ductory statement as an appendix to the full Lausanne Report. The Conference Secretary, Mr. R. W. M. Brown, wrote to Headlam, 'I am sure we are all much in your debt for the work you have done in carrying this somewhat delicate and responsible piece of work to so satisfactory a conclusion.' The Report now began with a brief statement registering the degree of unity attained by the Conference in Reports Two to Six in the conception of a united Church. It then went on to discuss the implications of unity : it implied a unity in faith and order, but not uniformity; there should be room for diversity of expression and liberty of interpretation within the limits of the accepted faith. To this Headlam added a note suggested by Archbishop Germanos on the Orthodox limitations to the acceptance of diversity in matters of faith and order. The third section referred to the statement in Report Five concerning the possibility of Churches uniting in 'activities of brotherly service.' It pointed out that some council might be evolved to further this practical work, but differences of opinion existed as to the form it should take : some believed such a council should include both 'Life and Work' and 'Faith and Order,' while others believed that the two should be separate. It was agreed, however, that ultimately life, work, faith and order were all expressions of an existing spiritual unity. The Churches should therefore consider what steps should be taken. The fourth section then outlined three suggestions which the Conference had not been able to discuss adequately. In the first place Churches should seek more intimate knowledge of each other : secondly they should study their relations one with another and consider the place they might hold in an undivided Church : finally there was the continuation and expansion of movements for practical co-operation along social, evangelistic and other lines : experience showed that they could be continued with mutual profit and without surrender of principle. To this section Headlam added a note on 'federation' suggested by Professor Adams Brown. Section Five, dealing with the mission field, noted with gratitude the increase of effective co-operation in this sphere. Here more than anywhere else unity was essential. The missionary Churches pleaded for greater freedom of action : 'their hopes of unity should not be frustrated by the long continual acquiescence in disunion at home which makes it difficult to recognize how fatal disunion is to the new indigenous Churches.' The final section affirmed that intercommunion was the goal and not the means of reunion. Reunion should be approached with prayer and care : 'ambiguous statements and hasty measures may hinder rather than hasten the work of unification.' The Report ended with a plea to all churches for daily prayer in the cause of unity.[21]

[21] Bell, *Documents on Christian Unity* (2nd series), 1930, pp. 17–23.

The Report was an excellent, temperate piece of work. Headlam pointed out that it did not commit them to anything which the Conference had not agreed to; it avoided any possible criticism of outlining a scheme for reunion; and it also avoided the danger of envisaging programmes of practical collaboration without safeguards to faith and order. The document was, moreover, fully in accord with Headlam's own views and was a fitting conclusion to his work at the Conference. He came to Lausanne with an undoubted reputation as a scholar, but at the same time not possessing the standing in the field of church relations of such people as Archbishop Söderblom, Bishop Brent or John R. Mott. That was now changed. To be primarily responsible for three out of the seven reports produced by the Conference was no mean achievement, and he emerged from Lausanne as a dominating figure in the Faith and Order movement.

Headlam had approached the Conference rather uncertain as to what to expect, and perhaps not even expecting very much; but after it was all over he was quite emphatic that it had been a success—not because of what had been accomplished, but because of the friendly and co-operative attitude displayed by the delegates. Most people had really tried to understand one another, to see how far they could agree, and to express clearly their differences. He deplored any suggestion that the Conference had accepted ambiguous formularies : it was quite untrue and members had not concealed their real opinions. There had been a real desire for unity and a real unity of spirit : that had come out markedly in the Report on the Gospel—the Church's Message to the World, which had been fully endorsed by the whole Conference, including the delegates of the Orthodox Church. It indicated sufficiently and conclusively that all the essential elements of the Christian Faith were believed by the great body of Christians throughout the world. The great difficulty, of course, lay in the difference between those people who recognized the force and importance of questions of faith and order and who wanted to get to the bottom of them and arrive at some solution, and those people who had no interests in that direction. The latter, he thought, were largely recruited from a section of the Liberal Protestants in America, 'who think themselves far superior to the limitations and superstitions of the Old World. All questions of ministry, sacraments, church order, etc. they propose to scrap ; and they wish to create a sort of loose federation of Christian bodies on an enormous output of hot air, and they are very indignant with what they think is the obstructiveness of us old-fashioned people in Europe.' [22] A further difficulty lay within the sphere of faith and order itself over the question of episcopacy. 'The great body of

[22] Headlam to Monsignor Batiffol, November 3, 1927.

Anglican representatives would feel, I think, that although as regards the theory of the ministry and the interim period, we may be able to do much to meet the Nonconformists; yet we cannot compromise on this question of episcopacy in the interests not only of our own theories but of any substantial church union. Many representatives of Nonconformity are prepared to recognize that, but it is very difficult for them; and of course some of our people are inclined to demand not only the historical episcopate but the full doctrine of apostolical succession, and that at once imposes a barrier.' [23]

On August 18 the Eastern Orthodox delegation had created a stir by presenting a Manifesto to the Conference. While expressing gratitude for being invited, they regretted that the bases assumed for the foundation of the Reports to be submitted to the vote of the Conference were inconsistent with the principles of the Orthodox Church. They would therefore vote for the Report on the Gospel but on the others they would abstain.[24] Headlam's comment was characteristic. 'As they had always believed exactly the same thing, and as what they believed was the truth and nothing else was true; and as the only basis of union was to agree exactly with them, therefore they would not agree to anything that we did.' [25] He did not think that the Manifesto should be taken too seriously. Many of the higher Orthodox clergy were well educated and liberal minded men who wanted to be friendly and who understood the limitations of their position and the necessity of approximating to the conditions of the modern world. Most of their brethren, on the other hand, were both uneducated and unsympathetic towards such an attitude. There had been a real danger, therefore, of the progressive Orthodox delegates at the Conference being repudiated by their brethren. The Manifesto had been in the nature of a diplomatic necessity : but it had caused some distress—'Archbishop Germanos, who had to read it, went back to his seat half-crying.' Headlam concluded cryptically, 'The methods were oriental but perhaps intelligent.' [26]

No such problems were experienced with the American delegates. 'The Americans have been for the most part very nice. They are, of course, very emotional, and after singing 'The Church's one foundation' two or three times will accept most things ! But most of them did really want to get somewhere and do something.' The Germans too had been 'infinitely nicer than they used to be' : they had been friendly and nice-mannered ; and although they had been more puzzled than

23 Headlam to Bishop Slattery, September 20, 1927.
24 Rouse and Neil, op. cit., pp. 423–4.
25 Headlam to Canon Maynard Smith, August 19, 1927.
26 Ibid. ; Headlam to Mgr. Batiffol, November 3, 1927.

any one else, they had come into line in an extraordinary way.[27]

Finally, Headlam thought that the Conference had produced one great practical result: it had gone a long way towards endorsing the principles expounded in the Appeal to All Christian People. He said later to the London Diocesan Conference, 'I cannot but think, reviewing all the findings and realizing the many different Churches whose representatives accepted them, that there is greater unity amongst Christians than we sometimes believe. They really adopted in a tentative way—and could you expect anything else—the four points of what has sometimes been called the Lambeth Quadrilateral, the union of the Churches on the basis of the Scriptures, the Creeds, Episcopacy and the Sacraments.' It was an achievement, from which he himself might derive considerable satisfaction: for both Lambeth and Lausanne had demonstrated in a remarkable way the power and influence of his own Bampton Lectures.

[27] Headlam to Canon Maynard Smith, August 19, 1927.

CHAPTER FOURTEEN

The Lambeth Conference
1930

THE underlying theme of the Lambeth Conference of 1930 was *witness*—the natural outcome of that *fellowship* which had been the theme in 1920 : but 'if Christian witness is to be fully effective, it must be borne by nothing short of the whole body of Christian people.'[1] Christian unity was therefore again one of the major questions to be considered; and here Headlam was in his element. The Committee on the Unity of the Church was under the chairmanship of Archbishop Temple; but Headlam was appointed Chairman of a sub-committee of fourteen members to deal specifically with the relations of the Anglican Communion to episcopal Churches—a task involving discussions with delegations from the Eastern Orthodox Church, the Old Catholic Church, the Armenian Church, the Church of Sweden and the Moravian Church. The Committee as a whole had discussions with delegations from the Church of Scotland and the English Free Churches.

At the very outset the treatment of some of these delegations caused some resentment which Headlam felt could have been easily avoided. He had suggested to the Archbishop of Canterbury before the Conference that all the delegations might be invited to attend the opening service in S. Paul's Cathedral on July 6 and then officially welcomed : but this was not done, and only the Orthodox delegation attended S. Paul's. The Free Churchmen felt hurt and Headlam could sympathize with them. He wrote later to Bishop Palmer, 'I understand the Nonconformists are very sore about Lambeth. I think they have a good deal to complain of in the way they were received. I always thought it would be much better if all the deputations were received formally by the Conference : it would only have taken an hour for the whole lot : and if they had all been asked to S. Paul's to occupy prominent places. A certain amount of ceremonial courtesy counts for a good deal.'[2]

[1] *Report of the Lambeth Conference of 1930*, p. 18.
[2] Headlam to Bishop E. J. Palmer, September 13, 1930.

Archbishop Temple preached on the sovereignty of God at the opening service on the Sunday morning, and Headlam followed with an inspired plea for unity at Evensong. He pointed out that this was the day on which Lutherans commemorated the promulgation of the Confession of Augsbourg, a document designed as a document of unity. Its fundamental thesis of justification by faith was, of course, an essential part of Christian doctrine, but it was only one element of S. Paul's teaching : against it should be set his emphasis on the significance of corporate Christianity. It was this unity which they needed to restore. Fundamentally all Christians had a common faith —they all believed in God, Jesus Christ, the Incarnation, the Resurrection, the Holy Spirit : and against this differences on the sacraments and the ministry seemed disproportionate.

The general agreement on fundamentals had, of course, been emphasized at Lausanne in 'The Church's Message to the World—the Gospel,' and the Lambeth Conference was reminded of this fact by a Report on the Lausanne findings prepared by a Committee under Headlam's chairmanship. But it was equally evident that much more consideration would now have to be given to the questions of the Church and Ministry.[3] Headlam reminded the Conference of his own views in a small book *Christian Unity* which appeared in May 1930 reiterating in briefer and simpler form the substance of his Bampton Lectures. He was now able to add weight to his arguments by referring to Lausanne and the South India Scheme; and he quoted the Bulgarian theologian, Professor S. Zankov, in claiming that Orthodox views on the Church were less rigid than many people realized :

'One opinion holds that only the Orthodox Church is *the* Church, and that all the others do not belong. . . . This opinion has its supporters among hierarchs and theologians. It is still occasionally expressed in official statements of local orthodox churches. But this opinion is not consistently maintained, at least in practice, because its supporters do not oppose the present more liberal attitude of the Orthodox Church at large.

'The second opinion holds that the Orthodox Church is the Church of Christ, but that the great historical non-orthodox churches are not to be considered as completely fallen away or separated from the Church of Christ. This position . . . has never been precisely formulated or supported in detail. . . . In general one has the impression that this opinion is essentially as follows : the Church is *one*, and it

[3] *Proceedings of the Church Assembly,* vol. 9, pp. 260–1 ; L. Hodgson, *Convictions,* 1934, pp. 174–94.

embraces all who have been baptized in Christ. . . . And just as single members may be ill, so whole groups may be erring or ailing members of the Church. Divisions have been made, chiefly for pedagogical and moral reasons, which form two general sections of the Church, an inner and an outer. But the boundaries of these sections are not absolute, hence the divisions they represent are not absolute. The walls of partition between us do not reach as high as heaven; they do not extend as high as Christ our Head, or as deep as the heart, the Holy Spirit. . . . This is the general content of the second opinion which is held by many prominent Church leaders, many theologians and very many simple orthodox Christians, among whom I dare to count myself.' [4]

In addition he wrote an article 'The Christian Ministry' in *The Church Quarterly Review* for April 1930 in which he examined—and demolished—the conflicting views and criticisms which had appeared in recent books and pamphlets on the subject. He was quite sure that he was on the right lines.

'The aim of all my writings has been to defend the inherited Catholic order that it can be accepted at the present day, and become the Church order of the united Church. . . . Since (the Bampton Lectures) I have seen little to modify the views that I have expressed, although possibly I might feel that in some cases I had been a little too favourable to the traditional view. I have read most of the literature which has appeared since and such criticisms of my book as have appeared; and it has become clearer, in my opinion, that most of the modern attempts to restate the old view of the Apostolic Succession have had the fatal attempts to fit a dogmatic theory into historical facts which are inconsistent with it. I do not claim any infallibility and am always reviewing my own conclusions, but I do not think that the tendency of recent investigation has made these conclusions more precarious. I really think that the opinions that I have formed have been the inevitable result of the evidence.' [5]

His efforts were not in vain. Hensley Henson wrote on July 9—the third day of the Conference, 'It is plain that his books have been read, and have impressed the bishops, and certainly he counts as one of the weightiest factors in the Conference.' [6]

On that day Headlam was one of the official speakers on reunion.

[4] S. Zankov, *The Eastern Orthodox Church* quoted in A. C. Headlam, *Christian Unity*, 1930, pp. 61–2.
[5] 'The Christian Ministry,' *C.Q.R.*, vol. 110, pp. 39–40.
[6] Henson, *Retrospect of an Unimportant Life*, vol. 2, p. 261.

Henson remarked that he spoke well and was well received, although his speech lent itself to much hostile criticism and could have been torn to ribbons by a competent opponent.[7] He was referring to Headlam's suggestion that reunion with the Orthodox Church and reunion with the Free Churches could go hand in hand. To many people this appeared to be sheer nonsense—the Orthodox and Free Church approaches to questions of Faith and Order were so completely different : but Headlam saw nothing outrageous in it, possibly for two reasons. In the first place his conception of the requirements laid down by the Lambeth Quadrilateral was extremely liberal : and secondly his relations with Orthodox and Free Church theologians had been largely confined to men who were also liberal in outlook, and in the case of the former to men who knew England well and could appreciate the Anglican mind. He was, in fact, much more hopeful of success with them than he was with the Free Churchmen. This was obvious from his reactions to the disappointing conversation with the Free Church delegation on July 15. The Congregationalist, Dr. Carnegie Simpson, made a particularly damaging speech, pressing the point which he had made in 1923 in the Anglican-Free Church discussions : if they possessed real ministries of the Word and Sacraments, what further could they gain from episcopal ordination? No progress was made ; and in its Report the Committee on Unity, instead of endorsing the Memorandum on Existing Ministries accepted during those discussions, simply fell back on the statement in the Appeal to All Christian People referring to their spiritual efficacy.[8] Headlam wrote, 'The only conversation which was a real failure was that with the Nonconformists. Two or three of our people made foolish or irritating speeches and Carnegie Simpson on their side was very truculent. I do not think things were advanced, but I believe it was right ; for the difficulty is that with one or two exceptions like Garvie and Selbie the Nonconformists don't want reunion. They want us to recognize their orders and then that they should go on being separated. They want us to be sort of honorary members of the Federation of Free Churches.'[9]

The discussions with the Orthodox delegation were far more fruitful. Their leader, Meletios, now Patriarch of Alexandria, was of course no stranger to Headlam : and with him were Archbishop Germanos of Thyateira and representatives from Roumania, Jugoslavia, Antioch, Jerusalem, Greece, Cyprus and Poland. On questions of doctrine Headlam and Meletios more or less had the field to themselves : the discussions of the first two days read almost like a dialogue in the report

[7] Ibid.
[8] *Lambeth Report*, p. 116.
[9] Headlam to Miss P. L. Wingfield, August 3, 1930.

written by Canon Douglas. It was recognized that the present Conference did not permit a full examination of the outstanding theological problems between the two Churches, so it was agreed that a Joint Theological Commission should be appointed to undertake this task. Meanwhile they turned their attention to Orders and the Eucharist. Headlam was asked to explain the attitude of 'The Appeal to all Christian People' towards non-episcopal ministries. He pointed out that the Church of England did not deny the spiritual reality of such ministries, and for the sake of reunion and on the principle of 'economy' they could be given some temporary recognition. Meletios then referred to the current practice of reordaining a Nonconformist minister who became an Anglican. Was he right in assuming that if all Nonconformist ministers became Anglicans to-morrow, that they would all be reordained? Headlam replied that Nonconformists becoming Anglicans and the reunion of Nonconformists and Anglicans were two different things : he believed that in the event of corporate reunion the reordination of Nonconformists would not be necessary; for an interim period there would have to be certain economical arrangements. On the question of economy, which he defined as the turning aside from the strict law—subject to the general spirit of the Church, Meletios was cautious. Although agreeing that from the Orthodox point of view it might be used in the cause of unity and charity provided that it did not involve a clash with the fundamental grounds of faith, he was careful not to state specifically that it might be applied to the recognition of non-episcopal ministries. The subject was a delicate one, and Meletios was undoubtedly relieved not to be pressed further. On the Eucharist the Orthodox delegation expressed satisfaction at the Anglican definitions of the Real Presence and the Eucharistic Sacrifice. It was then agreed that sacramental ministrations to the Orthodox by Anglican priests where no Orthodox priest was available—in America, for example—might continue until the question could be settled by the Pro-Synod of the Orthodox Church : but it was emphasized that regular intercommunion was the sign and seal of full union, which did not exist.[10]

It is interesting to compare Headlam's views on these discussions with those of Meletios. Headlam wrote to his niece, Miss P. L. Wingfield :

'The discussions with the Orthodox were most interesting. I was in the Chair and had to carry on the whole thing. The Committees were extraordinarily good—the best Committees I have ever worked with. They never spoke unnecessarily but only when they could help matters

[10] *Lambeth Report*, pp. 131–40 ; Headlam's private account.

out. The point was to get an agreed statement of belief on Orders and the Eucharist, which should contain nothing which should be difficult for an Evangelical. Then I had to explain all our efforts with Nonconformists and South India to them, and put a sort of modified approach, so that it would be no longer possible to say that South India would make Union with the Orthodox impossible. I always took care to explain carefully anything which represented another point of view from theirs, so that there might be nothing conceded.

'Meletios was very helpful. He wanted to come to terms, so he put his questions in a way that was easy to answer them. They had a good many conferences together and had a good deal of trouble with one or two of their people. The Roumanian Archbishop was inclined not to be conciliatory; the Roumanians are unlike the others—not Philo-Anglican—and are a good deal under Romanist intrigues. If we had had one or two more days it would have been completely satisfactory.' [11]

Meletios was less optimistic in the brief report which he drew up for the Holy Synod of his Patriarchate.[12] Here he revealed the tensions which existed among the Orthodox delegates : they were all eager to take part in the discussions, but none appeared to expect any concrete results. Some came with the intention of appearing as champions of Orthodox purity, almost as if they suspected some of their brethren to be making concessions. He also made it clear that any easy optimism over the use of the principle of economy in the South India Scheme was misplaced : in the proposed arrangements for the South India ministry 'it was made plain that the proposed act of economy has no precedent in the history of the Orthodox Church.'

This cautious statement seemed to convey an impression different from that given in Headlam's letter and certainly less favourable than that given at the Conference : but in fact Meletios was being careful not to commit himself in either direction. His remarks on economy at the Conference and his statement in the Report were both perfectly true, but both were capable of different interpretations—an important point to remember in view of their respective audiences. There is not the slightest doubt that Meletios himself was ready for a considerable advance on the lines of economy and earnestly desired closer relations between the Anglican and Orthodox Churches. Headlam was well aware of his liberal outlook—not only from the Conference in 1919, but also from private talks which they had had before the present

---

[11] Headlam to Miss P. L. Wingfield, August 3, 1930.
[12] Canon Douglas had received a copy of this report and had sent it to Headlam.

Conference had begun. It was therefore quite natural for Meletios to give the Anglicans as much encouragement as he could. On the other hand among other members of the Orthodox delegation and certainly in his own Synod there were certainly people much more conservative in outlook who needed reassurance that the Orthodox position had not been compromised. It was yet another instance of the difficulties involved when an ecclesiastical leader was in advance of the Church which he represented.

On July 18 Headlam's sub-committee also began their discussions with the Old Catholic delegation, composed of the Archbishop of Utrecht and the Bishops of Haarlem and Deventer. The Old Catholic Churches of Holland, Germany, Switzerland and Austria had been in contact with the Church of England for some fifty years : only the Dutch had had any doubts about Anglican orders, and in June 1925 they too had accepted their validity—a decision which was ratified by the Conference of Old Catholic bishops in the following September. This Conference had also expressed a desire for 'a future more intimate and powerful contact' with the Church of England, and the present delegation to Lambeth had been the result. They first discussed the doctrine position of the Old Catholics as laid down in the Declaration of Utrecht and agreed that it contained nothing to impede union between the two Churches. The Archbishop of Utrecht welcomed the proposal for a Joint Commission on doctrine, suggesting that if closer intercommunion could be achieved, the mutual consecration of bishops would be possible. At Headlam's suggestion they then went on to discuss the Terms of Intercommunion with the Orthodox and the question of non-episcopal ministries. Headlam defined the Anglican position—a firm belief in episcopacy together with a recognition of the spiritual value of non-episcopal orders and sacraments : the proposals for the Church of South India represented an interim arrangement, in which the consciences of individual congregations would be respected. He supported this with a liberal interpretation of Meletios's statement—the Orthodox delegation had considered this to be an instance of justifiable economy. He hoped that the time would come when the Old Catholic Church would be faced with the same problem, as they looked forward to reunion with their non-episcopal neighbours. The Archbishop of Utrecht finally expressed the hope that both the Orthodox and the Anglican Churches would come to discuss the question of reunion at the next International Old Catholic Congress to be held in Vienna in 1931 : meanwhile it would be helpful if the proposed Joint Commission on Doctrine could meet before then.[13]

[13] *Lambeth Report*, pp. 141–2 ; *Lambeth Occasional Reports 1931–8*, pp. 30–6.

The sub-committee also had single meetings with the Armenian, Moravian and Swedish delegations. In the case of the first political conditions prevented any immediate progress in church relations, but Headlam felt that everything possible should be done to help this ancient and sorely-persecuted church.[14] In the case of the second—a small but very missionary-minded Church, which desired closer contacts with the Church of England, a resumption of the negotiations which had been dropped in 1924 was recommended.[15] Finally there was the meeting with the Swedish delegate, Bishop Rohde of Lund. Relations between the Anglican and Swedish Churches were already close, and the discussion now centred on the other Scandinavian Churches with whom relations were not so intimate. Among these was the Church of Finland, which Headlam had visited in 1927; and Bishop Rohde agreed that the Church of England might well look forward to closer ties with it; a little later on, a proposal from the Archbishop of Canterbury for a Joint Commission on Doctrine would undoubtedly be welcome.[16]

This concluded the work of the sub-committee. The discussions had been strenuous, but undeniably fruitful; and it was the sort of undertaking at which Headlam undoubtedly excelled. He proved to be equally effective when the whole Committee discussed the South India Scheme. His able defence was testified by Henson :

'The most interesting episode in the proceedings at Lambeth (July 22) were vehement speeches against the South Indian Scheme from the Bishops of Indiana and Kootenay; but the first was effectively answered by Headlam, and the last was not very successful. He has certainly made a considerable figure both as a theologian and as a negotiator with the Easterns. He has also "cut in" on behalf of the South Indian Scheme very effectively. His attitude on episcopacy has been greatly modified since the days when he used to "correct" my use of Lightfoot's "Dissertation." He is apt to intervene too often, and, perhaps, with too pontifical a manner. There is always a bludgeon up his sleeve; and he is a hesitating speaker, but it must be admitted that he has done well.' [17]

The South India question was, in fact, managed much more satisfac-

[14] *Lambeth Report,* pp. 145–6.
[15] Ibid., pp. 149–50.
[16] Ibid., pp. 148–9. The present Archbishop of Finland, apart from being a rigid Conservative, was old and very frail. It was thought advisable to wait until his successor was appointed before making any approach.
[17] Henson, *Retrospect,* vol. 2, p. 269.

torily than was expected, and Headlam was full of praise for the
efforts of Bishop Palmer, Bishop Waller of Madras and Bishop Shedden
of Nassau in bringing people together.

On July 31 the Report on Unity came before the whole Conference.
The fact that Temple and Headlam piloted it through in half the time
allowed was for them a personal triumph. Certainly Headlam was
most satisfied.

'Then came the Resolutions. Mine came first and I persuaded them
to accept three important statements with very little difficulty. Then
in the afternoon the Archbishop of York introduced the South India
Resolutions, and they all went through without a division and unanimous. Then we all stood up and sang the Doxology. People afterwards
were extraordinarily complimentary, especially the American Bishops.
They said that we had got the Conference into such a state that they
would have passed anything. I had seemed to myself not to be speaking very well, but somehow I got hold of them. Somehow or other I
seem to reassure them, and the fact that the agreement with the
Orthodox and the Old Catholics was got through helped them to
accept South India. Anyhow it was really very wonderful, and one
hopes very much it may lead to a great deal in the future.' [18]

He was not, of course, unaware of the serious problems involved in
attempting to reconcile negotiations with the Orthodox and the proposals for South India but he was quite convinced that the policy
was right.

'It is quite easy to make fun of the South Indian Scheme, or any such
proposal, but if you had heard what is actually happening, and have
any care for the building up of a Catholic Church, you would have
found it difficult to oppose either the Orthodox resolutions or the
South Indian. . . . We have still, of course, to make what we have
done effective, and that may be more difficult than we think : but as
to the rightness of our attitude throughout, I have no doubt.' [19]

His impressions of the whole Conference appeared in an article in the
Church Quarterly Review entitled 'The Lambeth Conference and
Reunion.' [20] He considered that the most important piece of work
achieved by the Conference was the Report on the Christian Doctrine
of God. It reminded men of the fundamental Christian belief, the

---

[18] Headlam to Miss P. L. Wingfield, August 3, 1930.
[19] Headlam to Canon Maynard Smith, September 9, 1930.
[20] 'The Lambeth Conference and Reunion,' *C.Q.R.*, vol. 111, pp. 205–26.

revelation of God in Christ, which must be the basis of all religious life. If men were to concentrate more than they did on fundamentals, they would be less inclined to argue about subordinate matters, interesting and even important though they might be. This had to be borne in mind in any consideration of the ideal which the Conference had set before the Anglican Communion—which was nothing less than the Catholic Church in its entirety. This meant something more than a federation of Churches : it meant a united Church possessing a universally recognized ministry which connected it with the Church of Apostolic times. Such a ministry was the historic episcopate, and this had been accepted at the 1921–5 discussions with the Free Churches and also, although less definitely—as was natural—at Lausanne. This certainly did not imply, however, that no orders and sacraments were efficacious except those which came through the Apostolic Succession. The present Lambeth Conference, like its predecessor in 1920, recognized the efficacy of non-episcopal orders and sacraments, although it refrained from declaring them 'valid' because the word was used so ambiguously.

Headlam was perfectly candid about the Free Churches. They were not justified in thinking that the Conference had taken an unfriendly attitude towards them. Dr. Carnegie Simpson seemed to desire an arrangement whereby intercommunion and possibly an interchange of ministries would be accepted : but this was just not possible. Intercommunion was refused not on any grounds of orders and sacraments : it would also be refused in the case of Roman Catholics, whose orders and sacraments the Church of England had never doubted. The will and intention of Christians to perpetuate separately organized Churches made it inconsistent in principle for them to come before our Lord to be united as one body by the sacrament of His own Body and Blood. The general rule of the Church of England must be held to exclude indiscriminate intercommunion, or any such intercommunion as expressed acquiescence in the continuance of separately organized churches. Intercommunion was the goal of reunion not a means towards it.

The South India Scheme which had been endorsed by the Conference surely gave Nonconformists an idea of the line to be taken. There, too, a further definite step towards unity had been made : for the idea of any form of reordination or commissioning such as had been propounded by the Lambeth Conference of 1920 had been given up. There would be a union of the traditions of all the uniting bodies subject to the Pledge, that the convictions of existing congregations would be respected. It had been suggested that the acceptance of the South India Scheme by the Conference would cause a schism in the

Church of England : but the Conference had accepted the Scheme unanimously. Many objections had disappeared when it became clear that the object was to create an autonomous branch of the Catholic Church and not another province of the Anglican Communion.

As for the Orthodox delegation—the most important that had ever come to any Church—and the other delegations, nothing final or effective had been accomplished, nor had been expected : but substantial agreement had been attained in matters of Faith and Order, and it was reasonable to look forward to much closer relations with other Churches.

In its work for Christian Unity the Conference had given Headlam cause for considerable satisfaction and matters had gone very much as he had hoped. Henson regarded him as one of the four most potent figures in the Conference, and his comment on Lang, Temple, Palmer and Headlam is worth recording.

'A striking feature of this Conference to those who know the previous history of the persons concerned, is the solidarity created by their academic experience. Lang, Palmer and Temple are Balliol men, Lang and Headlam have been All Souls' Fellows, Headlam as Regius Professor of Theology had been the official chief and colleague of Temple. It is ever the sway of unperceived and unacknowledged personal forces which determines the courses of public affairs. These four men—Lang, Temple, Palmer, and Headlam—have been the most potent figures in the Conference, and the fact is not *solely* due to their official positions and personal ability, though these of course are very considerable. The habit of personal association and common loyalty to institutions have counted for much.' [21]

---

[21] Henson, *Retrospect*, vol. 2, p. 276.

CHAPTER FIFTEEN

The Old Catholic Church

I

IN accordance with the wishes of the Archbishop of Utrecht arrangements were made for an Anglican-Old Catholic Commission to meet in July 1931, two months before the Old Catholic Synod at Vienna. Headlam was again asked to lead the Anglican delegation, consisting of the Bishop of Fulham (the Rt. Revd. S. Batty), the Dean of Chichester (the Very Revd. A. S. Duncan Jones), Dr. N. P. Williams (Lady Margaret Professor of Divinity, Oxford), Canon J. A. Douglas, the Revd. G. F. Graham-Brown (Principal of Wycliffe Hall, Oxford), and the Revds. C. L. Gage-Brown, C. B. Moss and P. Usher. The Old Catholics were represented by the Bishop of Deventer (Mgr. J. J. Berends), the Bishop of Berne (Dr. A. Küry), the Bishop of Bonn (Dr. G. Moog), Professor E. Gaugler of Berne and Professor A. Rinkel of Amersfoort.[1] Bonn was chosen as the place of meeting, not only because of its geographical convenience, but also because of its close associations with the reunion movement. It was there that Dr. Döllinger had held his conferences between members of the Eastern Orthodox, Old Catholic and Anglican Churches in 1874 and 1875. These meetings had been quite unofficial but they had done much to promote friendly relations between Eastern and Western Christianity. They were of particular interest to Headlam, for fifty-six years previously on one of his earliest visits to the Continent, he had met Canon Liddon coming away from the Conference of 1875. 'It is rather interesting,' he wrote, 'to think that we are finishing now the work that was then begun.'

The Conference, which met on July 2, lasted exactly one day. Indeed, Mr. Moss has said that but for certain difficulties involving the Evangelicals, the work might have been completed in half an hour or less, for there were no fundamental differences of belief.[2] The two

---

[1] The Revd. P. Usher and Professor Gaugler did not attend the Conference: Mr. Usher was in Greece and Professor Gaugler was ill.

[2] C. B. Moss, *The Old Catholic Movement. Its Origins and History*, 1948, p. 342.

key members of the Anglican delegation were Headlam and Mr. Graham-Brown. Headlam was elected Chairman of the Conference and it was he who was primarily responsible for providing the explanations required by the Old Catholics : Mr. Graham-Brown was the Evangelical 'watchdog,' alert to safeguard the interests of those whom he represented. The morning session was devoted to elucidating points of difficulty, in the course of which Headlam spoke on the position of the Lambeth Conference in the Anglican Communion, the various 'parties' within the Church of England, the Thirty-nine Articles, and the Anglican doctrine of Orders—all to the satisfaction of the Old Catholics.[3] There were, in fact, only three crucial points of discussion —the position of the Evangelicals in the Church of England, the authority of Scripture and the doctrine of the Eucharist.

The question of the Evangelicals arose in a discussion on intercommunion. The Old Catholics wanted to know with what Churches the Anglicans were already in communion and whether such arrangements would commit them too. Headlam referred to Anglican relations with the Church of Sweden and assured the Old Catholics that they were not bound by them in any way. He then gave them a statement on intercommunion prepared by Mr. Graham-Brown which most though not necessarily all Evangelicals would have been prepared to accept. It asserted that reunion on a basis of identity of doctrine was simply not possible : it was clear that the doctrine of the Church of England and that of the Old Catholic Church were not identical : if, therefore, identity of doctrine were a condition of union, such a union could only be effected by a change of doctrine by one or the other. Intercommunion, however, should require no such identity—a common allegiance to our Lord should be sufficient. On such terms, therefore, Evangelicals might be prepared to agree that there was nothing in the terms of the Declaration of Utrecht which might be an impediment to intercommunion between the Church of England and the Old Catholic Church.[4] The Bishop of Deventer then asked whether the Evangelicals regarded the Church of England as identical with the pre-Reformation Church, and Mr. Graham-Brown assured him that they did. The Old Catholics were very relieved to hear this. If his answer had been otherwise, they would have been faced with the same serious problem as confronted them in their relations with the Dutch Reformed Church ; for the latter denied any such continuity.[5]

The Old Catholics then dealt with Anglican difficulties, pointing out first that the Declaration of Utrecht was by no means a complete

[3] *Lambeth Occasional Reports 1931–8*, pp. 14–18.
[4] Ibid., p. 19.
[5] Ibid., pp. 18–20 ; Moss, op. cit., pp. 344–5.

statement of their beliefs. It merely defined their position with regard to Rome. On the authority of Scripture, to which the Declaration made no reference, they were in complete agreement with Anglican doctrine, being perfectly prepared to accept Articles Six and Twenty.[6] They also regarded the fourth Lateran Council and the Council of Trent as local councils whose decrees were not binding. Assurances were then given on eucharistic teaching : the Declaration was meant to exclude Transubstantiation in its mediaeval sense and the word was not used in their teaching : nor was the Eucharist regarded as a propitiatory sacrifice in the sense of a repetition of the sacrifice once offered—this was a mistaken impression arising from the mistranslation of the word *Versöhnungs*. All this was eminently satisfactory to the Anglicans, for all the points on which the Evangelicals had misgivings were now cleared up.[7]

The second session of the Conference was devoted to drawing up the terms on which intercommunion might be recommended to the two Churches. A draft document drawn up by Mr. Graham-Brown and Dr. N. P. Williams, served as a basis for discussion. Bishop Küry made the point that it would not do to produce anything which might be regarded as a new confession of faith, and a brief statement, devoid of all doctrinal references, was agreed upon.

'1. Each Communion recognizes the catholicity and independence of the other, and maintains its own.

'2. Each Communion agrees to admit members of the other Communion to participate in the Sacraments.

'3. Intercommunion does not require from either Communion the acceptance of all doctrinal opinion, sacramental devotion, or liturgical practice characteristic of the other, but implies that each believes the other to hold all the essentials of the Christian Faith.'[8]

Headlam was most satisfied with the result. It had been a 'very pleasant' Conference and 'successful in the very best way'[9] : the Agreement—brief, clear and flexible—was admirable, providing an ideal model for use in negotiations elsewhere. It expressed just that principle for which he had always pleaded. If two Churches could agree on the essentials of doctrine and order, even wide divergences in interpretation and practice ought not to keep them apart; full agreement in every detail was not a necessary precondition of inter-

---

[6] Article 6—Of the Sufficiency of the Holy Scriptures for salvation. Article 20—Of the Authority of the Church—It is not lawful for the Church to ordain any thing that is contrary to God's Word written. . . .
[7] *Lambeth Occasional Reports*, pp. 10, 21–3 ; Moss, op. cit., pp. 345–6.
[8] *Lambeth Occasional Reports*, pp. 25–7 ; Bell, *Documents*, ser. 3, p. 60.
[9] *Diocesan Magazine*, November 1931.

communion. In this particular case, too, the Agreement achieved something more than just intercommunion : it also 'bridged the Reformation,' establishing close relations between a Church which had passed through the Reformation and one which had not. Finally it gave the Church of England a link with two great movements which stood for the cause of religious truth. The first of these was Jansenism, with its assertion of moral sincerity and religious devotion : when its adherents, as a result of their attempts to reform the Church of Rome, had been condemned, they had found a welcome refuge in Holland and their treasures were still carefully preserved in the Old Catholic seminary at Amersfoort. The second was, of course, that associated with Dr. Döllinger, representing loyalty to traditional Catholic Church order while denying modern Roman claims.

II

The Bonn Agreement was ratified by the Episcopal Synod of the Old Catholic Churches at Vienna on September 7, 1931, and by the Convocation of Canterbury in the following year. Headlam secured the unanimous approval of the Upper House of Canterbury on January 20 after a very short debate. He wrote to his niece, 'I think that was partly due to the excellence of the tactics I adopted. I read a very long speech which set their Lordships into a comfortable sleep, and they were in such an excellent temper in consequence that they were prepared to accept the motion almost without discussion !' [10] He dwelt at length on the history of the Old Catholic Church, emphasizing that it represented the tradition of the two great movements for religious liberty in the Roman Church during the past three hundred years associated with Pascal and Döllinger. Formed by the union of the Old Church of Holland and the separated Churches of Germany and Switzerland its growth had been significant : the five bishops in 1889 had now risen to fourteen ; national churches had come into being in Austria, Czecho-slovakia and Jugoslavia and there were about one hundred thousand members in America. Admittedly it was still not a large Church but a Church's importance did not depend entirely upon its size. For the Church of England the Agreement meant the end of centuries of ecclesiastical isolation—for the first time she was entering into formal relations with another Church. The Agreement was also an admirable model for other attempts at intercommunion. He could not agree that approaches to the Old Catholic Church or the Eastern Orthodox Church would jeopardize approaches to the Nonconformists

[10] Headlam to Miss P. L. Wingfield, January 23, 1932.

or to the Continental Reformed Churches. If anything like real Christian unity was desired, the Church must look in both directions. It seemed to him that every step taken towards reunion had a tendency to make further steps easier and more desirable.[11]

During the debate the Archbishop of Canterbury paid a gracious tribute to Headlam's efforts : 'It is perhaps only someone like myself who has been able to watch these negotiations from beginning to end, who has been in correspondence with the authorities of the Old Catholic Church, and who has had the confidence of the Bishop of Gloucester, who realizes what an immense amount of patient and constructive labour the Bishop has put into these long negotiations. . . . If I may say so in his presence, it is difficult to realize with what extraordinary width of mind and sympathy and what infinite patience the Bishop of Gloucester has continued on his way. If it be a remarkable stage in our history that we should have this Resolution before us, let us not forget where a large measure of the credit is due.'[12]

The Lower House of Canterbury expressed its approval two days later. Mr. Graham-Brown, seconding the motion of the Dean of Chichester, also paid tribute to Headlam's work. The point of view which he (Graham-Brown) happened to hold with conviction and belief was received with the greatest possible patience, especially by the Bishop of Gloucester, who showed every consideration, and made the position much more easy than he ever expected. He also fully endorsed Headlam's contention that the Agreement would not jeopardize approaches to other Christian bodies on the Evangelical side.[13] He had, in fact, consulted privately the leaders of the Free Churches in this country and had received their reassurances on this very point.

At the same time both Houses of York Convocation ratified the Agreement, and in the ensuing years nearly all the other Churches and Provinces of the Anglican Communion followed suit.[14] One immediate result was the beginning of the practice of the mutual consecration of bishops. The Bishop of Haarlem came to England to take part in the consecration of the Bishop in Jerusalem [15] and the Bishop of Kensington in 1932, while the Bishop of Deventer assisted in the consecration of the new Bishop of Gibraltar and the Assistant Bishop on the Niger in 1933. In 1937 Headlam and the Bishop of Fulham went to Holland to assist in the consecration of Dr. Rinkel as Arch-

---

[11] *Canterbury Chronicle of Convocation,* January 1932, pp. 19–28.
[12] Ibid., p. 33.
[13] Ibid., pp. 164–8.
[14] *Report of the Lambeth Conference 1958,* pp. 252–3.
[15] The Revd. G. F. Graham-Brown. It was fitting that he should be the first bishop to receive mutual consecration under the terms of the Agreement.

bishop of Utrecht, and other similar acts have taken place since. These mutual consecrations might well have considerable significance in the future, for Old Catholic consecrations and ordinations are regarded as valid by the Church of Rome. The possession of the Old Catholic succession by Anglican bishops therefore provides a possible point of contact if conversations with Rome ever materialized.

Headlam's visit to Utrecht with the Bishop of Fulham in June 1937 was a fitting climax to his work with the Old Catholics, for this was the first occasion on which Anglican bishops had shared in an Old Catholic consecration. The service was historic for another reason : Headlam wore a mitre for the first time. When the Old Catholics first asked him to wear one, he was inclined to refuse, but the Bishop of Fulham advised him that it would be a gracious act to accede to the request. When the Bishop of Deventer had taken part in Anglican consecrations in 1933 he had worn choir habit instead of a cope and mitre purely and simply to oblige his hosts ; Headlam could therefore hardly do other than reciprocate. Reluctantly he had to agree. The lesson went home, however. The rather long and complicated service was followed by a great dinner, with many toasts and speeches, during the course of which the Anglican chaplain at Utrecht, the Revd. T. A. Coulson, was called upon to speak for English Church people in Holland. He was quite unprepared and had scarce spoken five words in English when Headlam commanded, 'Say it in Dutch, Coulson!' The poor man had never before made an after-dinner speech in Dutch and now found himself compelled to do so impromptu before a distinguished audience. He stuck to his task manfully ; and afterwards Headlam congratulated him, saying, 'I hope you did not mind my interruption : but all these Old Catholics seemed to be speaking a lot of English for our sakes, and I felt someone ought to do something about it—not least for the prestige of the Church of England !'

Two years later, in November 1939—after war had already broken out—Headlam again went to Utrecht accompanied by the Bishop of Fulham, Douglas and Usher for the commemoration of the twelfth centenary of S. Willibrord, the Yorkshireman who had become the Apostle of the Netherlands. On the eve of the official celebrations— November 6—he preached at Solemn Vespers in the Old Catholic Cathedral of S. Gertrude. Speaking of the life and work of S. Willibrord, he pointed out that he had linked the Netherlands and England in a close spiritual union. Nor had all the benefits come from England : she had every reason to be grateful for such gifts as the life and work of Erasmus and Thomas à Kempis' *Imitatio Christi*. The two Churches now enjoyed intercommunion, but that should not be the limit of their aspirations. They should strive to break down the isolationism of other Christian bodies and follow S. Willibrord's example in spreading the Gospel that God's will might prevail throughout the world.

A glimpse of the fundamental religious unity of all Christian people was seen in the national celebrations on the following day, and Headlam was most impressed. The commemoration took place in the ancient Cathedral, formerly the seat of prince bishops, and now belonging to the Dutch Reformed Church. It was now filled by people of every religious persuasion to hear three addresses—one by a Roman Catholic, one by an Old Catholic and one by a Liberal Protestant. On his return home, Headlam wrote to the Burgomaster of Utrecht:

'I should like to congratulate you personally on the success of your national celebration. It seems to us to have been a remarkable achievement on your part to have succeeded in bringing together representatives of every religious body and every part in your country to commemorate the conversion of your land to Christianity and the beginnings of your religious life. It was a great pleasure to us from England to take part in these celebrations and I hope that it will mean the strengthening of the friendship between our countries.'

CHAPTER SIXTEEN

The Eastern Orthodox Church
1930-40

I

THE Orthodox delegation to the Lambeth Conference had intimated that relations with the Anglican Communion would be discussed at their forthcoming Pro-Synod in the summer of 1931. The appointment of the proposed Joint Doctrinal Commission was therefore a matter of some urgency if its work was to be completed in time. By November 1930 the Archbishop of Canterbury had appointed the Anglican members and Canon Douglas had set out for the Near East to make the necessary arrangements. Headlam was asked to be chairman and with him were the Archbishop of Dublin (Dr. J. A. F. Gregg), the Bishop of Gibraltar (Dr. F. C. N. Hicks), the Bishop of Fulham (the Rt. Revd. B. S. Batty), the Bishop of Northern Indiana (Dr. C. Gray), Dr. Goudge (Regius Professor of Divinity, Oxford), Dr. Grensted (Nolloth Professor of the Philosophy of the Christian Religion, Oxford), Canon Douglas and the Revd. P. Usher. It was a carefully chosen team. The Bishops of Gibraltar, Fulham and Northern Indiana all had first-hand experience of the Orthodox Church in their own dioceses; the Archbishop of Dublin and Professor Grensted were representatives of the Evangelicals, and Professor Goudge and Canon Douglas of the Anglo-Catholics; while Headlam, Douglas and Usher were all acknowledged experts on Orthodox affairs.

The appointment of the Orthodox members was not such a simple matter. The Œcumenical Patriarch did not nominate them himself but invited the various autocephalous Churches to choose their own representatives—a method involving difficulties and delay. Eventually eight delegates were named representing the Churches of Constantinople, Jerusalem, Alexandria, Antioch, Serbia, Roumania, Cyprus, Greece and Poland, and led by Mgr. Germanos, Metropolitan of Thyateira and Exarch of Northern and Western Europe. Two Churches were not represented: the Bulgarian Church was in a state of schism and was not invited, while it was found quite impossible to obtain any one from Russia. By the time these preliminaries were completed the Pro-Synod had been postponed until Whitsun 1932, and it was at the Œcumenical Patriarch's suggestion that the Commission finally met in London from October 15–20, 1931.

The whole business was viewed by the Evangelicals with some apprehension, for they had been far from satisfied with the Résumé of the Lambeth Anglican-Orthodox discussions to which the Bishops had given their assent. Headlam was well aware that these Evangelical anxieties should not be ignored. With his approval, therefore, Professor Grensted drew up a memorandum on the Evangelical attitude towards intercommunion with the Orthodox Church. This expressed doubt as to whether the Lambeth Résumé did in fact contain the 'sufficient account' of Anglican teaching which it claimed. For example, the phrase 'a special charisma' used of Ordination was too mechanical, and the term 'mysterion' or 'sacrament' should only be used of the two dominical sacraments of Baptism and Holy Communion. Again, the statement that 'the meaning of the Thirty-nine Articles must be interpreted in accordance with the Book of Common Prayer' was one-sided : the converse was equally true. Nor again would Evangelicals agree either that 'after Communion the consecrated elements remaining are regarded sacramentally as the Body and Blood of Christ,' or that 'in the offering of the Eucharistic Sacrifice' the Anglican Church included in its intercessions 'the whole company of faithful people, living and departed.' The memorandum then went on to point out that Evangelicals would clearly insist on Scripture being the sole and absolute authority in matters of Faith—Tradition could not be regarded as its equal. As to the scope and meaning of intercommunion, the Report and Resolutions of the Bonn Conference were quite admirable.

It was well that these points were clearly before the Commission for they were focal points of discussion. The Commission did not consider the Lambeth Résumé, regarding that as outside their province, but based their deliberations on the Suggested Terms of Intercommunion. The results of five days' deliberations were frankly unspectacular and no progress was made on some of the most controversial issues. For Headlam there was some cause for personal satisfaction, however, for most of the Suggested Terms, which were so largely his work, were endorsed by the Commission : in a number of cases they were included verbatim in the Report. The two important questions of Orders and the Eucharist were not included : the best the Commission could do was to refer the Résumé and Précis of the Lambeth discussions to the consideration of their Churches. On two other difficult points the Report was far from satisfactory. The Anglicans were quite determined to maintain the Sufficiency of Scripture, but the Orthodox fought equally hard on behalf of Tradition. The Report therefore included first an Anglican statement asserting that 'Holy Scripture containeth all things necessary to salvation' : this was followed by an Orthodox statement, 'We believe that the Holy Scripture is completed, explained and interpreted by the Holy Tradition.' Then came an agreed paragraph which was manifestly unsatisfactory, 'Everything necessary for salvation can be founded upon Holy Scripture as completed, explained, interpreted, and understood in the Holy Tradition, by the guidance of the Holy Spirit residing in the Church. . . . We agree that nothing contained in Tradition is contrary to the Scriptures.' [1] The same method was adopted on the Sacraments. First came the Orthodox belief—while accepting Baptism and the Holy Eucharist as pre-eminent, the other five were not of secondary importance as Sacraments nor were they unnecessary to the spiritual life of the Christian : the Anglicans then affirmed that the Prayer Book only called Baptism and Holy Communion by the word Sacraments; but other rites could be considered to have the character of Sacraments and were commonly called Sacraments.[2] In their conclusion the Commission expressed the hope that the discussions might be continued at a subsequent meeting. They also agreed that the basis of intercommunion should be a union of Faith, but they did not feel that it was their function to determine what measure of divergence might be considered legitimate. Finally the Orthodox delegation undertook to lay the Report and Resolutions of the Bonn Conference before their Pro-Synod.[3]

It had not been an easy Conference; and it was evident from the Report that Headlam had done what he could to safeguard the Evangelical point of view, although he doubted whether the result was entirely satisfactory. The difficulties he encountered can be appreciated from an account which he sent to his niece. But he was not enthusiastic : what they had done would just 'keep things going.'

ACH to PL Wingfield.　　　　　*Lambeth Palace. October 21, 1931.*

'My dear Persis,

'. . . We began our Conference on Thursday and went on until Tuesday morning. It was by far the most difficult Conference I have had. Germanos (the Bishop of Thyateira) was their Chairman. He was a Greek, a Professor and a rigid Orthodox. He bullied all his own people, did all the talking, laid down the law and did not seem to

---

[1] *Lambeth Occasional Reports 1931–8,* pp. 50–2.
[2] Ibid., pp. 54–6.
[3] Ibid., pp. 56–8.

realize you cannot conduct a conference by imposing your will on the other side. The Metropolitan of Bukovina (Nectarios)—a Roumanian—was pleasant and good natured but he only spoke German, and could not assert himself. Germanos was supported by Leontios, Archbishop of Paphos in Cyprus, who made blunders in his theology. Germanos also had the support of the Archimandrite Constantinides who is at the Greek Church in London. He had a fluent command of English and Greek, acted as interpreter, and had therefore a great deal of influence. He was on in place of the Archbishop of Jordan, who had to stay in Palestine. There were no Russians and no Bulgarians.

'All the others were in different ways friendly and easy to get on with. Polycarpos, Bishop of Trikkes, was a genial cheerful prelate with considerable theological knowledge. Ireney, Bishop of Novi-Sad is one of the most delightful of men, but does not assert himself in debate; Theodosios, Bishop of Tyre and Sidon, who represented the Patriarch of Antioch, was a delightful little man, an Arab, who spoke French— extremely friendly but snubbed by Germanos. Arseniev—the lay Professor—who represented the Church of Poland nearly came to blows with Germanos. The Russian point of view is fundamentally different from the Greek.

'Our own people were excellent—worked thoroughly well together, and gave no difficulties. While the differences of the Orthodox were conspicuous and serious, we presented a united Anglican front. Goudge argued extraordinarily well for the supremacy of Scripture, and Grensted backed us up excellently. According to Grensted if his Protestant friends could have heard us, it would have united the Church of England!

'We managed to produce a fairly satisfactory Report which will keep things going, and the discussions made it clear that the desire for a Christian unity which does not wish to trouble about theological minutiae is very widespread. As Nectarios said, we had far too much theology. You see Germanos was head of a theological college and had got into the habit of laying down the law, and he did not think any one could be right who differed from him.

'We got on very pleasantly really. The domestic staff at Lambeth got a great deal of amusement out of it. Their hilarity became very great when they discovered that some of the Orthodox Prelates wore hairpins. . . .

Your affectionate uncle, A. C. GLOUCESTR :'

I

II

The Church with which Headlam retained the closest connections was that of Jugoslavia. He continued to write regularly to his old Oxford students and did all he could to help them—particularly through the Jugoslav Society of Great Britain, of which he was one of the original members. In May 1936 mainly in response to repeated requests from his old friend Ireney, now Bishop of Dalmatia, he spent nearly a month in the country. He set off with his cousin, Cuthbert Headlam, and Philip Usher to tour the country by car, but misfortune overtook them in the mountains of Austria. The car absolutely refused to face the hills : after suffering the indignity of being towed through a mountain pass by four oxen, Headlam sent it home in disgust and continued by train. The enforced change of plan proved a blessing in disguise, for his lack of mobility enabled him to see much more of Church life in Dalmatia than he had intended.

He stayed two weeks with Bishop Ireney at Sibennik, a lovely spot on the Dalmatian coast, while Philip Usher went on to Athens and his cousin explored Split and Dubrovnik. Ireney, an able young man in his early forties, had been Bishop for five years, during which time he had worked wonders. On his arrival the diocese had been very poor and depressed, with no organization or institutions : it was now very much alive and organized to a large extent on Anglican lines, with a Diocesan Conference and something akin to a Diocesan Board of Finance. The experiment had been so successful that not only were other dioceses attempting to follow suit but the Roman Catholics had become very jealous. The diocese was territory which had belonged previously to Venice and then to Austria and was still a Roman Catholic stronghold. Headlam sensed a feeling of great bitterness among the Orthodox minority against Italy and the Roman Catholic clergy, who were expert at intrigue. Two things in particular impressed him during his stay. The first was the Sunday morning liturgy at the Cathedral, at which he preached. The service lasted for three hours, but the building was absolutely packed; the congregation stood the whole time—there were no seats—and apart from the Epistle and Gospel they knew the whole service by heart, for they had no books. Their devotion and endurance were remarkable : their like would not be found in England. The second was the Diocesan Conference, attended only by clergy. They showed great keenness, and their interest never flagged during the extremely long sessions : again—'I do not think our English clergy would have stood it.' The main business was finance. Headlam found their enthusiasm most stimulating.

After Sibennik Headlam paid a shorter visit to the Bishop of Novi-Sad, also called Ireney. He was another most able man, of whom

Headlam had a high opinion. He had been one of the delegates at the Joint Theological Commission in 1931 and was a keen supporter of the Faith and Order movement. The tour then finished with a visit to Belgrade and a courtesy call on the Patriarch at Sremski-Karlevsi.

Headlam had sensed Orthodox-Roman Catholic antipathy in Dalmatia during his visit but did not realize its full implications until after his return to England. Serious trouble then broke out. The Jugoslav Government, which was a virtual dictatorship and leaned heavily towards the dictatorships of Germany and Italy, felt that the support of the Vatican might be valuable in furthering this policy. A Concordat had therefore been negotiated and signed secretly by the Papal Secretary of State, Cardinal Pacelli (later Pope Pius XII) and the Jugoslav Minister of Justice, Dr. Auer, as early as July 25, 1935.[4] It was therefore a *fait accompli* at the time of Headlam's visit, but only very few people knew of its existence. No mention of it was permitted in the press; and not until 1937 was any move made to secure its ratification by the Jugoslav Parliament.

Once its terms became public the Orthodox Church protested vigorously. The Roman Catholics were in a minority in the country, numbering about five millions as against the Orthodox six and a half millions, yet the Concordat promised them a dominating position. It was probably more favourable to the Roman Church than any other existing Concordat, and it was said to be opposed even by some of the Roman Catholics themselves. Under its terms Rome was given the right 'freely and openly to carry out its mission,' whereas in Concordats elsewhere it had been only given the right freely and openly to confess its faith : greater freedom was given in the appointment of bishops and in education ; priests were given benefit of clergy ; and lands secularized in the eighteenth century were restored. In November 1936 the Orthodox Synod submitted a declaration to the Prime Minister drawing attention to these inequalities; while Bishop Nicolai of Ochrid wrote a fiery Open Letter—a very brave thing to do—to the Minister of the Interior, declaring that even before its final legislation the Concordat had produced 'the whip, blood, tears, terror and innumerable other physical and spiritual sufferings' for the Orthodox people and clergy.

Bishop Ireney of Dalmatia sent a copy of the Concordat to Headlam on March 18, 1937, denouncing it as monstrous. It contained impossible provisions and represented gross injustice to the Orthodox Church and to all other denominations. Despite their protests the Government was insisting on pressing it through—an action which could only result

---

[4] A previous attempt had failed in 1925 ; cf. pp. 166–7.

in calamity for the country. He appealed to Headlam to bring the matter before the Council of Foreign Relations, to write to the press and, if possible, to send him copies of his articles for distribution. 'Here is an opportunity, a rare but very important one, for the Holy Anglican Church to help us by coming morally to our assistance.'

Headlam rose to the occasion. He ventilated the matter through the Council and wrote a long letter in support of the Orthodox Church. It appeared first in *The Times* on May 4 and shortly afterwards in the Council's *Second Survey on the Affairs of the Orthodox Church.* Copies were distributed as widely as possible, and Canon Douglas— 'really a most effective intriguer'—contrived to have one placed in the hands of the Jugoslav Regent Prince Paul. It was a fine, statesmanlike piece of work—quite devastating yet thoroughly courteous.

'The Jugoslav Government has for some time been engaged on the laudable task of promoting internal pacification within its own territories, and has been pursuing a policy of establishing friendly relations with all its neighbours. For both these purposes, and especially the former, the goodwill of the Vatican would be extremely valuable. Hence negotiations were set on foot for a Concordat which was signed at the Vatican on July 25, 1935, by Cardinal Pacelli and the Jugoslav Minister of Justice, Dr. Auer, but which has not yet been ratified by the Yugoslav Parliament.

'Violent protests against ratification have been made by non-Roman Catholic opinion in Jugoslavia. It is asserted that the Concordat places the Church of a minority, which is not even the largest religious community in Jugoslavia (the Roman Catholics number 37.45% and the Orthodox 48.70% of the population) in a privileged and, indeed, in a dominant position, and examination of the provisions of the Concordat certainly seems to bear out this contention. Some of its provisions are, in themselves, of a kind unknown in a modern state, others give the Roman Catholic minority advantages denied to the other Christian communities.

'We seem to be going back into the Middle Ages when we read Article 13, for it contains the astonishing proposal that where an ecclesiastic is convicted of an offence against public order, and his religious superiors are not in agreement on this point with the civil authorities, the matter shall be referred to a mixed commission of representatives of the Ministry of Justice and of the Episcopate. This privilege is not accorded to the members of other religious denominations, and implies a revival of the mediaeval benefit of clergy, which is, I believe, unparalleled in any other part of the world.

'Equally one-sided is the provision that by Article 32 the civil authorities undertake to enforce the guarantees given by a non-Roman Catholic partner in a mixed marriage. This again is a provision for which there is no parallel in any valid Concordat. It represents a one-sided intervention by the State in a matter hotly contested between the Roman Catholic and other Churches.

'Then there are a series of economic provisions which will have the effect of putting the Roman Catholic Church into a dominant position. Article 16 prescribes that the possessions and institutions of the Roman Catholic Church remain the property of that Church even if the population which these possessions and institutions serve joins another religious denomination. There is no similar legal guarantee for the property of the Orthodox Church. Consequently if the whole population of a Roman Catholic village becomes Orthodox all Church property and Church institutions remain in Roman Catholic hands; but the converse does not apply if an Orthodox population becomes Roman Catholic. All religious bodies in Jugoslavia receive an annual subvention from the State, and it is reasonable that the Roman Catholic Church should receive a subvention proportionately equal to that enjoyed by other Churches, but in addition to that, it is proposed that there should be compensation to the Church for property confiscated at any time in the past, and guarantees are given against expropriation of property which are not enjoyed by any other Church, and there is an unlimited right given by Article 12 for the foundation and support of Roman Catholic institutions from abroad. The result of all these provisions is to place the Roman Catholic Church in Jugoslavia in a position of economic domination over other religious bodies.

'In Articles 24 to 32 there are long series of privileges given to Roman Catholics in education, in the army, and in public institutions. Many of these might be quite reasonable in themselves if they were granted equally to all other religious denominations, but under the circumstances they represent special privileges of the Roman Catholic Church.

'If the Concordat as a whole is examined, it will be seen that it not only grants to a minority Church in Jugoslavia all the privileges accorded to the Roman Catholic Church in countries like Austria and Italy, where the population is overwhelmingly Roman Catholic, but it also contains privileges which are not contained in any other Concordat, and have, in fact, been definitely refused even in a country like Austria. It is perfectly understandable that the Jugoslav Government should be anxious to come to an agreement with the Vatican, and to conciliate the Roman Catholic population of the country, and no one would reasonably complain if the Church, although it represents a minority, should have exactly the same privileges as the Orthodox Church. But the Jugoslav Government has been led into action so discriminatory against the majority of the Jugoslav population as to cause bitter ill-feeling between different sections of the population. The people of Jugoslavia, especially the Orthodox population, are prepared to live in terms of friendship with those of other religions, and are anxious that they should be treated on terms of equality, but the present proposals are having a most disastrous effect, as indeed is natural. They are arousing a feeling of resentment in the Orthodox population, and a *kulturkamp* is threatened. I think too that the Roman Catholic Church has overreached itself, and will transform an easy going acquiescence in its activities into sharp opposition.'

The letter was not without effect. Opposition to the Concordat continued to grow and even within a matter of weeks Headlam received hints of the possibility of the Jugoslav Government not proceeding with its ratification. Finally, on October 26, he wrote triumphantly to his niece, 'You will have seen that the Jugoslav Government have given up the Concordat. I am told that Prince Paul is very much annoyed with the English Bishops, which means I suppose me.'[5] Unfortunately it was a victory for which a price had to be paid. The opposition to the Concordat had aroused strong feelings : people like Bishop Ireney of Dalmatia and Bishop Nicolai, who had led the protests, were regarded as being in disgrace, and differences appeared even in the Orthodox Church itself. Personal feelings undoubtedly played a large part in these differences, which unfortunately existed between some people whom Headlam regarded as personal friends. Despite his pleas to them to 'extend a hand of friendship' to one another, they persisted in their antagonisms. It was a situation which he was helpless to remedy and could only deplore, and its ill effects were manifest when he visited the country again in 1940.

III

The Pro-Synod of the Orthodox Church never met in July 1932—at the last moment it was postponed indefinitely. The chief reason given was the dislocation of ecclesiastical life in the Near East caused by the world economic crisis. There was, however, a further reason. It was still impossible to secure Russian participation, and without it the Bulgarian and Jugoslav Churches were unwilling to act. A fully representative Pro-Synod was therefore out of the question. Further progress towards the recognition of the validity of Anglican orders

[5] Headlam to Miss P. L. Wingfield, October 26, 1937.

could only be made through the independent action of the various Churches—a much more lengthy process. An encouraging start had been given by the Church of Alexandria, which had declared itself in favour of Anglican orders on December 25, 1930—even before the Joint Theological Commission had met. Further encouragement came from the Bonn Agreement between the Anglican and Old Catholic Churches in 1931 : the Orthodox Church already recognized Old Catholic orders, and this Agreement helped to dispel doubts about Anglican orders in Orthodox minds.

The next move came from Roumania, numerically the largest of the Balkan Orthodox Churches. In 1933 the Patriarch, Miron Christea, appointed a Commission to consider Anglican orders. Canon Douglas made the suggestion through an intimate friend, Mgr. Tite, Bishop of Semdria, that it might be useful to have an Anglican delegation to help them with their work. The suggestion was accepted, and a delegation led by Dr. Hicks, Bishop of Lincoln and formerly of Gibraltar, visited Bucharest in June 1935. As a result the Roumanian Commission recommended its Synod to recognize the validity of Anglican orders.

Many people wanted to know why Headlam was not asked to go. The reasons were not hard to find. In the first place the Roumanian Church was the least known of all the Orthodox Churches—her contacts with the Anglican Communion had been slight. Headlam could not boast of the intimate, first-hand knowledge of the country which Dr. Hicks had undoubtedly acquired as Bishop of Gibraltar from 1927 to 1932. As the only Anglican diocesan bishop who knew the Roumanian Church well, he was the obvious person to lead the delegation. Then again, he was much more likely to appreciate the Roumanian point of view than Headlam. The Roumanian Church was very conservative, representing a rigid Orthodoxy of which Headlam was disposed to be critical. At the Lambeth Conference the searching questions on Anglican doctrine had come from the Roumanian delegate ; and Headlam had found him very difficult, to say the least.[6] Finally, there is a limit to what one man can do. It must be remembered that Headlam's work at œcumenical conferences was done at an age when most men have retired : at the time of Bucharest he was approaching his seventy-third birthday. 1935 was the only year between 1930 and 1938 in which he was free from some important œcumenical task or conference over and above his normal work.[7] The break was reasonable and wise.

[6] Cf. p. 209; J. A. Douglas to Mgr. Tite, January 27, 1934.
[7] Apart from the regular work of his diocese, Faith and Order and—after 1932—the Council of Foreign Relations, he attended Lambeth in 1930, the Old Catholics and the Orthodox Doctrinal Commission in 1931, Finland 1933 and 1934, Latvia and Estonia 1936 and 1938, Faith and Order Theological Commission 1936, and Edinburgh 1937.

The Roumanian Commission accepted the validity of Anglican orders, and their decision was ratified by the Roumanian Synod on March 20, 1936.[8] But the Report of their conference with the Anglican delegation suggested some hard bargaining. Evangelical Churchmen were disturbed by what appeared to them to be serious concessions which the Anglicans had made. The Evangelical Group Movement, for example, issued a statement expressing 'grave anxiety in the minds of many Churchmen because of the doubtful presentation of Church of England doctrine' in the Report.[9] On crucial points views were expressed which they were not prepared to accept: there was the statement on the Eucharist—'The Eucharistic Bread and Wine remain the Body and Blood of our Lord so long as these eucharistic elements exist'; or on the Sufficiency of Scripture—'We agree that nothing contained in Tradition is contrary to the Scriptures'; or again, Justification by Faith as expressed in Article XI was sadly watered down in the statement 'Man partakes of the redeeming grace through faith and good works.'

When, therefore, the Bishop of Lincoln presented it to the Upper House of Canterbury Convocation in May 1936 the Evangelical bishops quite definitely refused to accept it: it contained many things with which they found it difficult to agree. The Bishop of Truro (Dr. J. W. Hunkin) then announced that the only person who could help them out of their difficulties was Headlam, who at that moment was in Jugoslavia: they should wait until he returned to hear what he had to say; meanwhile they might find another resolution expressed in a way which was generally acceptable. The Bishops jumped at the suggestion; and at the risk of creating an unfortunate impression in Roumania, the matter was adjourned until January 1937.[10] It was a remarkable testimony to the influence Headlam exerted in œcumenical matters.

In the renewed debate his mastery of the situation was complete. Without a single dissentient he secured approval of a new resolution: 'That inasmuch as the Report of the Conference at Bucharest between the Roumanian Commission on Relations with the Anglican Communion and the Church of England Delegation appointed by the Archbishop of Canterbury is consonant with Anglican formularies and a legitimate interpretation of the Faith of the Church as held by the Anglican Communion, this House accepts and approves of the Report.' He stressed that the Resolution did not mean that the Report was an authoritative statement of the Faith of the Church of England, nor

---

[8] Bell, *Documents*, ser. 3, pp. 48–50.
[9] Cf. *The Guardian*, August 14, 1936.
[10] *Chronicle of Convocation*, May 1936, pp. 57–81.

did it mean that it was the only legitimate interpretation of the Faith. The Roumanian Church had asked whether certain statements of theirs were such as could be loyally held by a member of the Church of England; and the Resolution asked the House to affirm that this was so. For the sake of unity it should be supported: the Balkan Churches had suffered Turkish rule for five hundred years, yet under such conditions they had clung to their Faith. Some had only recently been emancipated and they deserved all the help the Church of England could give them in the difficult task of adjusting themselves to new conditions.[11]

Further developments took place in the following August at the Edinburgh Conference of Faith and Order. Professor H. Alivisatos of Athens informed Headlam that Antioch, Bulgaria and Poland were all likely to ask the Archbishop of Canterbury to send delegations to discuss Anglican orders in the near future. He thought it wise that Athens should take the lead. Its lay Professors of Theology—of which he was one—were scientifically trained experts of repute, and any judgment they might make on Anglican orders would have a profound influence on other Orthodox Churches. Then on February 3, 1938, he informed Headlam that the Archbishop of Athens had decided to raise the question with the Theological Faculty and on its view take a decision with his Synod. In preparation for this he (Alivisatos) was asked to prepare a memorandum on Anglican orders: it was a monumental piece of work and was not completed until May 1939. A month later he wrote triumphantly to Headlam to say that the Faculty had unanimously recommended that Anglican orders should be recognized by economy without reordination. The Archbishop of Canterbury then offered to send out a delegation to discuss matters, but the outbreak of war prevented further action. The Greek Synod met in September and gave a token of their friendly feelings: they would welcome a delegation after the War—meanwhile they were willing to recognize by economy the ordination of any Anglican priest who might wish to join the Orthodox Church.[12]

At the same time advances had been made in other directions. In 1938 invitations came from the Polish and Bulgarian Orthodox Churches asking for delegations to come to Warsaw and Sofia in the following spring to discuss the question of orders. Dr. Lang agreed; and arrangements were made for Headlam to lead a party to both capitals at the beginning of May. By the end of March, however, the political situation in Poland was grave, and on the advice of the Foreign Office the visit to Warsaw was cancelled. It was then agreed

[11] Ibid., January 1937, pp. 5–25.
[12] Bell, *Documents*, pp. 50–1.

that since Professor Alivisatos had almost completed his memorandum and there was every likelihood of a delegation being invited to Athens in the autumn, the visit to Sofia should be postponed until then.[14] Shortly afterwards Canon Douglas reported that the new Patriarch of Jugoslavia had also expressed the desire to meet the delegation when its programme was arranged.

Obviously the outbreak of war changed the whole situation, but it was realized that a visit by English churchmen to the Balkan countries might serve a useful purpose, quite apart from the question of inter-communion. A display of Anglican-Orthodox friendship would have a profound influence on public morale in the face of Nazi intrigue and propaganda. Plans were therefore made—with Government support and approval—for a visit to Belgrade, Sofia and Athens in the spring of 1940. Headlam was quite prepared to accept this modification, but insisted that the cause of Christian unity would still be uppermost in his own mind : if there ever was a time for pressing upon the Churches the need for unity, it was now.[15]

The party which set off at the end of April was composed of Headlam, the Bishop of Southwark (Dr. R. G. Parsons), the Bishop of Gibraltar (the Rt. Revd. H. J. Buxton), Canon J. A. Douglas, the Revds. W. Hannah and P. Usher. Before leaving the Archbishop sent a message of good wishes and warning.

April 27, 1940.

'My dear Bishop,

'. . . I hope all possible arrangements have been made and that you will not find yourselves interned somewhere in the Balkans. Though you may have left the administration of your Diocese in excellent hands you can scarcely supervise it from some prison or monastery in the Balkans!

'I fully appreciate the difficulties of your task. It is on the one hand most important that no impression should be created that you and the rest of your company are agents of British propaganda. On the other hand it would be unreal to say nothing about the true British attitude towards the war. I hope however that at least your visit may foment such friendship as there is between the Anglican and the Orthodox Churches there. I can only wish you good luck and pray that God will guide and bless you and your companions in a very difficult task. . . .'

Yours ever,

COSMO CANTUAR.'

[14] Headlam to Miss P. L. Wingfield, April 23, 1939.
[15] Headlam to Canon J. A. Douglas, March 20, 1940.

They arrived at Belgrade on May 2 and met a committee appointed by the Patriarch under the chairmanship of Bishop Ireney of Novi-Sad. Both Bishop Ireney of Dalmatia and Bishop Nicolai had been invited to come but refused despite all Headlam's persuasive efforts. There was a good deal of personal feeling underlying their absence, resulting from the rift caused by the Concordat trouble : but the Bishop of Dalmatia insisted that non-attendance was the only effective way of registering a protest against the failure of their Church to consider Anglican orders. The Patriarch had asked both Ireneys to discuss the question two years previously, but the Bishop of Novi-Sad had steadfastly refused to make a move. At the conference he explained to Headlam the reason for his inactivity. The Jugoslav Church should not be party to any independent recognition of Anglican orders by the various Orthodox Churches : such action should only be taken by an Œcumenical Synod, and this could not meet without Russian representation. Both Headlam and Douglas pointed out, however, that they were not asking at the moment for full, permanent recognition but for 'economic' recognition—a temporary arrangement until an Œcumenical Synod could meet. The Bishop finally agreed to a resolution which at least left the door open for further discussion : while recognizing that no final decision on Anglican orders could be made without the concurrence of all the Orthodox Churches, the Jugoslav Church was asked to consider the matter and express a provisional opinion which could be presented at the next Lambeth Conference. As Headlam remarked, so far as it went the conference was successful : but in fact little progress had been made. The Bishop of Gibraltar later revealed that the discussions had been rather difficult and at times even heated.[16]

This visit drew a shower of abuse from the German press. The English bishops were a disreputable lot—they had been seen visiting a questionable night club in Belgrade and their behaviour there had been deplorable. But worse than that, they had done their level best to induce the Patriarch—even on their bended knees—to persuade his Government to join the Allied cause. By this time the Germans were in full cry across the Low Countries and France was in a state of collapse. They were not slow, therefore, to point out to the Balkan countries what their fate would be if they were so foolish as to listen to these Englishmen. Despite all this Headlam was deeply impressed with the strong pro-Allied feeling among the people.

On May 11 they went on to Sofia, where their visit was most successful. The conference with the Church leaders was on a far larger

16 H. J. Buxton, 'A War-time Mission in South-Eastern Europe,' *The Christian East*, N.S., vol. 1, no. 5, pp. 136–9.

scale than that at Belgrade and the Metropolitan himself took the
chair. The Bulgarians asked for an explanation of Anglican teaching
on just two points—Apostolic Succession and the sacramental nature
of Ordination—and declared themselves completely satisfied with the
replies. The Metropolitan then promised to present the question of
Anglican orders before a full session of the Synod. Here again
Headlam was struck by the friendly attitude of the people, not least
of King Boris himself. The fact that the king was an ardent botanist
was, of course, a great help!

A week later they reached Athens, where Headlam found Church
leaders far more friendly than he had expected. Since the decision of
the Theological Faculty in the previous year relations had not improved : in fact, there had even been some rather bitter attacks on the
Church of England in Greek theological journals. He had been quite
prepared, therefore, for some coolness but was relieved to find none.
They discussed the doctrine of the Church with the Theological Professors, and Headlam came to the conclusion that their religious outlook was far ahead of their theological expression. Despite their theory
that the Orthodox Church was the only one true visible Church, they
admitted the possibility of other Christians being members of the
invisible Church. It seemed to Headlam that while they did not really
believe the official Orthodox theory, they had no real alternative
theory to put in its place.

The tour now ended rather abruptly. Since their arrival in Athens,
the Germans had overrun the north of France and it was almost certain that Italy would enter the war. The British Minister at Athens
therefore thought it wise for them to return to England with all speed.
Headlam was forced to cancel his plans to return to Jugoslavia ; seats
were found for the party on a plane ; and they left not a moment too
soon—by good luck they passed through Rome airport just before the
arrival of an order from Mussolini to detain them. They passed over
France as the evacuation from Dunkirk was beginning, and they
could see flashes of the gunfire on the horizon.

Headlam presented a full report of the tour to the Archbishop of
Canterbury and to the Foreign Secretary, both of whom were most
grateful for his efforts. Ecclesiastically and politically the results
appeared to have been valuable. All three countries genuinely desired
to be friendly towards England but at the same time wanted to remain
neutral if they possibly could. They realized their inability to resist a
full-scale German advance by themselves as well as the impossibility
of receiving quick and effective help from the Allies. On the other
hand, as Headlam realized, the policy of neutrality had already proved
disastrous to the smaller Northern countries. Bulgaria suffered from

an inferiority complex. 'I would emphasize . . . that when a country like Bulgaria has been in disgrace, any show of friendship and good will is valued, especially if it avoids being too ostentatiously interested.' In this respect England had not helped as much as she might. The fact that the country was represented in Sofia by a minister who had not been given a title and that no effort had been made to provide the Legation with a chaplain were small things in themselves : but with a country like Bulgaria such things did count. On the ecclesiastical side affairs were most interesting. It might appear surprising that although the relations of the Church of England with the Jugoslav Church were closer and more personal than with any other Orthodox Church, little had been done to secure the recognition of Anglican orders. There were, however, reasons for this. In the first place none of the Patriarchs had been theologians or conversant with the problems involved. Then again the seat of the Patriarch was at Karlovci, where there had also been a strong exiled Russian Church. The Russians were very conservative in outlook and their influence on the local Church had been considerable. Finally, the Concordat struggle had had a damaging effect on Church life, and the ablest and friendliest bishops were now in disgrace. Of the Bulgarian and Greek Churches he spoke more optimistically—there appeared to be real hope for closer relations. The Bulgarian Church, which was still regarded by the Greeks as being in schism, was anxious to assert itself ; while the Greek Church had made considerable progress in its spiritual life and efficiency during the past fifty years.

Headlam then described the line he had taken throughout the tour. It speaks for itself. 'I would like to add that in all our negotiations we carefully avoided political issues. . . . Our aim was the restoration of peace, a durable peace for Europe. That must depend ultimately on the substitution of the Gospel of Christ, as the basis of public and private life, for the rule of force. The armies had to do their work, for when an appeal has been made to force, it must be met by force. Statesmen also had to do their work. But unless there was a change of spirit no permanent amelioration was possible. The Christian Church was weak because it was divided. The double duty was incumbent upon us after the war of helping the spread of Christianity, and of doing our utmost to promote the unity of the Christian Church. We appealed to the Orthodox Church to help in the work.'

CHAPTER SEVENTEEN

The Church of
South India

In May 1919 as the result of a conference between representatives of the Anglican Church and the South India United (Presbyterian and Congregational) Church at Tranquebar there appeared the famous Manifesto, envisaging a united Indian Church on what might be called 'Headlam lines.' It was to be based on the Lambeth Quadrilateral and embody episcopal, presbyteral and congregational elements : only the fact and not any particular theory of episcopacy was to be accepted, neither side would be required to disown its past, and the validity of each other's orders was not to be questioned.[1] Both Churches gave the document a favourable reception and a Joint Committee was appointed to undertake negotiations for union. The first meeting was held at Bangalore in March 1920, so that the Anglican bishops concerned could gain a clear picture of the situation before leaving for England to take part in the Lambeth Conference in July.

For members of the South India United Church the 'Appeal to all Christian People' was frankly disappointing. They could not reconcile the acceptance of non-episcopal ministries as owned by the Holy Spirit with the refusal to recognize their validity, and they regretted the disapproval shown towards the practice of intercommunion. They referred the question of ministries to the eminent Congregationalist theologian, Professor Vernon Bartlet of Oxford, and he was insistent that they should all be regarded as equal : all that was required at the inauguration of a united Church was a mutual commissioning of ministers. In 1923 Dr. Foss Westcott, Metropolitan of India, sought advice on the same subject; but the answers he received were conflicting. Cuthbert Turner was definitely opposed to the idea of equality of ministries. 'If the Church of England and the Church of the Province of India does not stand for the assertion that an episcopal ministry has something which a presbyterian ministry has not, I find

[1] B. Sundkler, *Church of South India*, pp. 99–103.

it difficult to see what is the *raison d'être* of its existence at all' : both sides would be compelled to interpret the form of commission in a different sense; it was therefore unsatisfactory and inadequate. Archbishop Lang commented on the same lines; but Headlam was less critical. He considered that mutual commissioning did in fact fulfil the proposal made in Section Three of the Appeal, and any minister so commissioned would fulfil the requirements of a priest of the Catholic Church.[2] By the time the Joint Committee met at Trichinopoly in February 1926, however, the Anglican delegation had devised a new approach which was of fundamental importance in subsequent negotiations. In the conversations between the Church of England and the Free Churches in England after the Lambeth Conference Bishop Frere and Dr. A. E. Garvie had advocated a gradual integration of ministries during an 'Interim Period' in the event of reunion taking place. Dr. E. J. Palmer, Bishop of Bombay, recognizing that union was a living process and not a single dramatic act, now proposed a similar period of fifty years in South India, during which non-episcopally ordained ministers would not be forced upon congregations who were accustomed to an episcopally ordained ministry. The Joint Committee not only welcomed this suggestion but also reduced the period from fifty to thirty years and formulated a Pledge, whereby all parties would undertake to do nothing to offend conscientious convictions or hinder the development of unity during that period. The Proposed Scheme of Union finally appeared in 1929—in time to be considered by the Lambeth Conference of the following year.[3] Hitherto Headlam had played no public part in the negotiations, but his influence had been considerable : the Scheme was very much in accord with his own views, and Bishops Azariah and Palmer and Dr. Banninga, a leading United Church leader, had all kept in touch with him.

At Lambeth he proved to be an able advocate of the Scheme, and the favourable judgment passed on it was in large measure due to his efforts. The Conference pointed out at the outset that the Church

---

[2] 'We believe that for all the truly equitable approach to union is by the way of mutual deference to one another's consciences. To this end . . . if the authorities of other Communions should so desire, we are persuaded that, terms of union having been otherwise satisfactorily adjusted, Bishops and clergy of our Communion would willingly accept from these authorities a form of commission or recognition which would commend our ministry to their congregations. . . . It is our hope that the same motive would lead ministers who have not received it to accept a commission through episcopal ordination, as obtaining for them a ministry throughout the whole fellowship. In so acting no one of us could possibly be taken to repudiate his past ministry.' (Bell, *Documents,* vol. 1, pp. 4–5.) Sundkler, op. cit., pp. 146–53; Headlam to Dr. Westcott, November 6, 1924.

[3] Sundkler, op. cit., pp. 160–75.

resulting from such a scheme would not be a province of the Anglican Communion but of the Universal Church, enjoying at once a restricted union with the Churches of the Anglican Communion. Approval was given to certain fundamental points—the acceptance of episcopacy without any defined theory of it, the gradual unification of ministries over a period of thirty years, and the Pledge; it was also agreed that Confirmation need not be a prerequisite of union, although its use was earnestly recommended. Intercommunion with non-episcopal churches was felt to be an anomaly, but as part of a movement towards union it might be covered by the principle of 'economy': furthermore, by Resolution 42, the Conference undertook not to question the action of any bishop who would use his dispensing power and sanction an exception to the general rule in special areas. Again, the consecration of bishops *per saltum* (i.e. without previous ordination to the priest-hood or diaconate), though normally undesirable, was not invalid and in the circumstances justifiable; while the participation of presbyters in the consecration of bishops was a 'legitimate symbolism' for the inaugural service of consecration, but not afterwards.[5]

Of all these points intercommunion proved to be the most controversial. The non-episcopal members of the Joint Committee in South India were convinced that it was fundamental—without it the whole Scheme of Union was likely to collapse. The Anglican delegation therefore referred the question to their Metropolitan and the Episcopal Synod, who in February 1932 gave permission for it to be practised, on the basis of what had been said at Lambeth. They made it clear, however, that they were not approving of general intercommunion, but only special acts at meetings of the Joint Committee; they also suggested that the method of concelebration should be adopted.[6] One member of the Anglican delegation had serious misgivings about this decision: Father Shore, Superior of the Oxford Mission to Calcutta, was so distressed that he doubted whether he could conscientiously remain in the Indian Church. Nor was he alone—other missionaries of Anglo-Catholic outlook felt the same. He therefore sought the advice of Dr. B. J. Kidd, Chairman of the Oxford Mission, and the latter, impressed by the seriousness of the situation, consulted other interested scholars. As a result, six Anglo-Catholic theologians from Oxford—Professor H. J. Goudge, Professor N. P. Williams, Dr. B. J. Kidd, Dr. K. E. Kirk, Dr. Darwell Stone, Fr. H. B. O'Brien, and Fr. F. W. Puller—sent Fr. Shore a letter, suggesting that he was free to publish it or not as he thought fit.[7] It

[5] *The Report of the Lambeth Conference 1930*, pp. 52, 123–30.
[6] Sundkler, op. cit., pp. 237–8.
[7] Fr. O'Brien to Headlam, August 23, 1932; Professor Goudge to Headlam, August 23, 1932.

expressed grave anxiety at the Church of India's decision, regarding it as in principle a clear violation of Catholic order and going beyond anything sanctioned or suggested by Resolution 42 of the Lambeth Conference.

Matters had not been improved by the action of the Joint Committee, which had met shortly after the decision. Intercommunion had taken place, but the plea for concelebration had been ignored. The situation was, in fact, becoming delicate, and the Oxford Mission to Calcutta had refused to allow any of its members to be included in the Anglican delegation to the Joint Committee.[8] Headlam and Palmer, who had resigned his see in 1929 and was now Headlam's assistant bishop at Gloucester, both deplored what they felt to be a rash action on the part of the Joint Committee, but felt that something must be done to answer the letter of the Oxford theologians. They therefore sent a letter to the Metropolitan of India in August 1932 signed by themselves, the Bishop of Oxford (Dr. T. B. Strong), the Dean of Exeter (Dr. W. R. Matthews) and Professor E. W. Watson. While maintaining episcopacy to be an essential part of the life of the Church, they reaffirmed the contention that other ministries and their sacraments—though irregular—were not invalid, provided the intention to fulfil our Lord's command existed. Intercommunion as a general practice was not to be condoned, but exceptions could be made : Resolution 42 of Lambeth represented a legitimate exercise of the dispensing power of the Church, and the South Indian Churches, where the barriers of separation had been broken down by the all but final acceptance of the Scheme of Reunion, justified the use of this dispensation : it could also be justified by the Orthodox doctrine of 'economy.' At the same time Headlam and Palmer wrote to *The Guardian* and *The Church Times* declaring that the criticisms had arisen from an over-rigid and unsound theology and a lack of spiritual insight : the intolerant partisanship of Rome had wrecked the attempts to secure the recognition of Anglican Orders and now the same spirit was at work ; just as a onesided Evangelicalism had tried to hinder union with the Old Catholics, and equally onesided Anglo-Catholicism was trying to prejudice and hinder the South Indian scheme.[9] These good offices earned grateful thanks from India. The Metropolitan wrote to Headlam on August 25, 'It has greatly lightened the load which I have felt resting upon me at this time ; for whatever my reading may have led me to believe on this particular point, I have felt quite clear as to the correctness of the opinion to which we were led. Yet clearly I have no scholarship to back my opinion or to carry weight with those who hold different opinions.'

[8] Sundkler, op. cit., pp. 241–3.
[9] *The Guardian, The Church Times,* August 19, 1932.

Later in the year, however, the Oxford theologians returned to the attack with a reply to a letter on intercommunion from the Bishop of Colombo. They considered that intercommunion in South India was not covered by Resolution 42, which permitted it only under very strict regulations and in very special circumstances, such as in special areas where the ministrations of the Anglican Church were not available for long periods of time or without travelling great distances. Furthermore, the Constitutions, Canons and Rules of the Church of India stated quite clearly that no one except a bishop or a priest could celebrate the Holy Communion; and they felt that according to Western Canon Law the Indian Church had no right to grant a dispensation. Finally, the appeal to Orthodox 'economy' was tenuous: economy was not universally recognized in the Eastern Church—it was avoided by all except the Greek Church and even Greek theologians were not agreed as to its extent. This letter, which was sent to the Bishop of Colombo on November 16, was published in *The Times* on December 31.

Meanwhile, the Bishop of Worcester had expressed to Bishop Palmer his anxiety at the opposition being aroused in England and its possible harmful effect in India.[10] Palmer consulted Headlam, who felt that it would be helpful if a number of English bishops were to send a letter to their episcopal brethren in India, reassuring them of their favourable attitude towards the Scheme.[11] Between them they made the necessary arrangements, and a letter on these lines appeared in *The Times* on December 28 signed by twenty English diocesan bishops and supported by another letter signed by a large number of influential clergy and laymen.

Headlam's attitude towards this controversy is revealed in a letter to Dr. Banninga on January 5, 1933.

'. . . I have delayed long in answering your letter of September 12. The reason has been that my time has been so much taken up in the affairs of the Church in South India. It has really been very hard work indeed defending the position. I am still sorry that those difficulties have been created by over-anxiety on the part of the representatives of the Churches to have their common communion service before the union was actually completed. I am not sorry in itself, but I think any one would have advised you how much wiser it would have been to abstain from anything of this sort, because it just gives an opportunity and stirs up the people who are opposed to the scheme.

10 The Bishop of Worcester to Bishop Palmer, December 1, 1932.
11 Bishop Palmer to the Bishop of Worcester, December 5, 1932.

'With regard to the Anglo-Catholic opposition, you have to remember that there are two elements in it. There is, first of all, the opposition which comes from a certain number of somewhat narrow-minded, possibly, but very sincere people, such as, for example, the Head of the Oxford Mission to Calcutta. They have been brought up in very strict rules regarding the ministry and sacraments, and undoubtedly what appeared to other persons reasonable concessions seemed to them serious breaches of Catholic Church order. My whole purpose has been to try and conciliate and assure them; but they have of course a position which, up to a certain point, is a very strong one. It is clear, definite and precise, and has been and is held by a wide body of theologians. It would be worth anything to conciliate them. The other side of the opposition simply represents a desire by certain Anglo-Catholics to dominate the Church of England; and a good many of us feel that it will be necessary to come to terms with them and really to make them feel that they cannot do it. . . . They are very clever, and represent ecclesiasticism in its most truculent aspect. What I feel is that this premature intercommunion has seriously disturbed a certain number of devout people, and that the people who are out for dominance are making use of that. So though I am perfectly prepared to defend what has been done, I cannot but wish that there had been a little more wisdom exercised. . . .'

In reply Dr. Banninga expressed great gratitude for all that Headlam had done for the South India Scheme: but, while regretting any inconvenience the joint communion service might have caused, he emphatically asserted his conviction of the rightness of their action.

February 22.

'I can assure you that I am most sorry if anything that I have said or done has caused you any inconvenience or regret. I can assure you that we do most highly appreciate the very fine work that you have done in connection with Church Union. Without your most cordial support I doubt very much if we could have gone on as far as we have done. But with you and Bishop Palmer as our champions in England it has been possible to go forward steadily though slowly and I am most sincerely hopeful that the final consummation will soon be reached. If so, we shall owe much to your wise perseverance in this movement.

'I cannot, however, agree with you that we have made a mistake or have been unwise in pressing for this common communion service before the union. You are naturally looking at it from your standpoint, whereas I am looking at it from the Free Church standpoint and there is a tremendous difference. Naturally, it would have saved you a lot of trouble and there would have been far less opposition could we have left this matter until union had actually been consummated. Looking at it from our standpoint, however, I think it would have been a fearful mistake; for it would have meant that all the opposition that has now been aroused would have been aroused after union within the Church and would have been based upon the charge that we had been false to our promises. The Anglo-Catholic would then have said that it was undoubtedly understood that no Anglican would ever be even invited to a Communion Service celebrated by one not episcopally ordained. Had this happened, our united Church would have been branded at once as having been built on a falsehood. . . . It is well to have the discussion before union and then to enter the union with clear understanding that no man's conscience will be offended as far as he will be concerned, but also that no man may dictate to another man what he shall or shall not do. That after all is the lesson that the Anglo-Catholic must learn if he wishes to have any dealing with the Free Churchman. . . .

'But there is another reason. To me it is a much better and higher reason, namely that this joint participation in the Communion Service has actually led us to higher spiritual things than we have had before. I think every one will admit that the highest peak of our spiritual life in our Joint Committee meetings is these Communion Services, and those of us that have partaken in them will never forget them. . . .

'It is because of my deep interest in the books that you have written on this subject that I have come to my present position and am so convinced that there is a possibility of union between the Episcopalian and the Non-Episcopalian. I thoroughly agree with you that the final authority lies in the Church. . . . Your work will certainly stand as a monument in this connection and we rejoice greatly therein.'

Headlam was unconvinced, however. He considered Banninga's attitude towards the Anglo-Catholics was neither fair nor intelligent: there was all the difference between asking for recognition of the validity of non-episcopal orders and asking for their equality with episcopal orders. Dr. Banninga and his friends were suffering from an inferiority complex, and it might well lead them into difficulties. Headlam's reply was, in fact, a remarkable tribute to his ability to see both sides of the question.

April 4, 1934.

'You seem to look upon Anglo-Catholics as just tiresome people, for whom there is nothing to be said. Now I have made it quite clear that I think their too rigid views are not correct, and that the particular meaning they give to Apostolic Succession is wrong, but that does not take away from the fact that on fundamental points they are right where Nonconformists are wrong. They have preserved the Christian tradition, the Christian creeds, the historic Church order, the ideal of a united Church; and while criticizing the points on which you differ from them, you ought to be prepared to recognize, and recognize fully, what they have done, and the value of what they do. As Dr. Garvie once said : "It is quite true the Congregationalists have got on without a creed, but I don't think they would have done so if they had not been surrounded by Churches with a creed." . . . The real fact is that you have all got an inferiority complex. You are quite right in saying, as I believe, the recognition of ministries must be the basis of union, but you must not be so fussy about it that you demand all sorts of guarantees before the union comes.

'So your whole attitude towards intercommunion seems to me entirely onesided. The position a High Churchman would take up is a perfectly intelligent one. He says : "Intercommunion is to me a sign of real brotherhood and unity. When that is attained I will communicate freely with all the members of the united Church. Until it is attained I prefer to follow the rules of my Church. The fact that a scheme of reunion has been mutually agreed to, and has the authority of the Church to which I belong, will be sufficient for me. Until it has that authority, I do not care to violate the rules of my Church and take part in a ceremony which is to me only partly real. Now you may not agree entirely with that, but it is a perfectly intelligent and fair point of view. You should recognize that a condition precedent to coming together is to try and understand, and be tolerant of the points of view from which you differ. You think yourselves broadminded : you are really quite intolerant.

'So I believe that . . . you are likely to come to grief in the South India scheme because, while you insist upon one side of the pact, you are not prepared to give the other. On the one side you say : "Let it be granted that our orders and ministries are all valid." There I should agree with you. I think you have asked really more than is necessary when you demand that they should all be considered equal. It is quite sufficient that we should all agree to respect one another's orders without going further. . . . Then, on the other side, if the union is to be an effective one, what you have to do is to accept wholeheartedly what I call the Catholic position. That you seem to be continually frightened of doing. Instead of accepting the historic episcopate, you are trying to explain it away; instead of being wholehearted Catholic Christians, you want to be half-hearted Presbyterians or half-hearted Congregationalists. The Anglicans in India have said quite clearly : "We are prepared to give up our Anglicanism to help to build up a united Catholic Church for India." . . . You will have equally to be prepared to do the same.'

Headlam's advice was timely, for opposition to the Scheme was now raised by the London Missionary Society wing of the South Indian United Church on the issue of the equality of ministries. The Joint Committee tried to meet the difficulty in 1935 with a statement that the uniting Churches recognized that Christ had bestowed His grace on all their ministries 'with undistinguishing regard' and had used them all to His glory, but this was not acceptable to all sections of the South Indian United Church. The General Assembly of the latter therefore met in September 1935 under some strain, and the London Missionary Society section even pressed for the abandonment of negotiations for union. This proposal was defeated ; but only at some cost. A resolution was passed stating that it seemed necessary to allow some years more for discussion within the South Indian United Church, with a view to arriving at such a degree of unanimity as would make union possible.[12]

Just at this stage the Church Union in England published a pamphlet *Some Comments on the South Indian Scheme,* written by the Revd. F. Hood, Principal of Pusey House, and addressed primarily to the Diocesan Councils of the Church of India, criticizing the attitude of the Scheme towards orders, intercommunion and confirmation, and encouraging the Councils to reject it. Headlam replied with a vigorous *Open Letter* [13] in which he castigated the Church Union and Hood for 'really bad scholarship,' intolerable arrogancy of language and desiring not reunion but submission to their own point of view.[14] This in its turn brought a strong reply from Hood—*Further Comments on the South India Scheme*—not only justifying his own position, but also suggesting to Headlam that instead of adhering to the views expressed in his Bampton Lectures fifteen years previously, he might be well advised to take to heart some of the comments and criticisms which other scholars had made upon his work. It was a vigorous encounter, but entirely free from malice—as two little incidents subsequently showed. Shortly afterwards Hood, who was a friend of Headlam's chaplain, Philip Usher, was passing through Gloucester and he and Usher lunched together in one of the local hotels. When told of this

[12] Sundkler, op. cit., pp. 269–70.
[13] The original draft of this letter was even more vigorous !
[14] *South Indian Reunion Scheme—an Open Letter addressed to the Revd. F. Hood,* 1935, pp. 2, 4, 14.

Headlam said, 'Why didn't he come and lunch with me? Surely he isn't sulking about South India, is he?' There was, of course, no question of sulks. Later Headlam himself met Hood in the Athenaeum and asked him to come for a walk, in the course of which he asked Hood if he could help him find a new domestic chaplain 'rather more High Church than himself.' [15]

The Church of India was obviously much exercised over the Scheme and early in 1938 sought the advice of the Consultative Body of the Lambeth Conference, asking them whether the modifications which had been made to the Scheme would affect the approval given to it in 1930. Bishop Azariah asked Headlam to prepare a memorandum comparing the 1929 and 1936 editions of the Scheme, and the Archbishop of Canterbury asked the Archbishop of York and the Bishop of Chichester to consult Bishop Palmer and do likewise. Both documents were considered by the Consultative Body—of which Headlam was a member—in July 1938: they both came to the same general conclusion, namely that the alterations made to the Scheme were not such as to give ground for supposing that the Lambeth Conference of 1940 would wish to reconsider the approval given in 1930. On one point, however, they differed—on the rights of bishops. The York-Chichester memorandum expressed concern at the provisions whereby the bishops might be overruled on a matter of Faith or Order: admittedly the procedure was most complicated, and it was unlikely that such action was ever likely to occur; but the danger was there, and it should be removed. Headlam was quite aware of this situation but took a more optimistic line; the danger was so remote that it might well be ignored. The majority of the Consultative Body did not agree with him, but his view was respected in their reply, for while expressing general approval of the Scheme, they were careful to state that a majority of their number were concerned at the danger of the bishops being overridden on matters of Faith and Order. This warning had, in fact, considerable value; for the Joint Committee introduced a safeguard into the Scheme in 1941. The method of voting by Houses, which the Consultative Body had favoured, was not accepted: but the necessity of episcopacy for the shepherding and extension of the Church of South India was emphasized, while it was asserted in the Constitution that the bishop had the responsibility of 'publicly stating as need may from time to time arise, the doctrine of the Church Universal as understood by the Church of South India, and its application to the problems of the age and the country.' [16]

---

[15] Usher was at this time contemplating a move: he finally became Warden of Liddon House in 1937.

[16] Sundkler, op. cit., pp. 299–300.

This question of episcopal rights was, of course, bound up with views existing in the South Indian United Church about the parity of ministries and suspicions about the autocracy of bishops and priests. The position had been exemplified by a request made by the General Assembly of the South Indian United Church in 1937 for the granting of licences to approved laymen to celebrate Holy Communion. The request had arisen partly from practical expediency—the number of ministers was far too small to fulfil the pastoral need, and partly from the desire of certain Nonconformist elements to guard against what they considered to be the dangers of sacerdotalism; lay celebration would provide an essentially Congregationalist element to the Scheme. Dr. Banninga had approved, feeling that the Anglicans would agree by the principle of economy, if nothing else. Headlam, however, supported by Bishop Palmer, had strongly urged him not to support it: there was nothing to say that Holy Communion could not be celebrated except by a priest, but it was a question of order and the rule of order should not be broken; insistence on lay celebration would wreck the Scheme.[17] Finally the whole question had been referred to a sub-committee of the Joint Committee and in September 1940 it had recommended that lay celebration should not be adopted, but that the Constitution should be strengthened by a full statement on the royal priesthood of all Christians—a proposal which had been accepted by the Joint Committee.[18]

The Scheme in its final form was approved by the Joint Committee in 1941 : it now remained for the Churches concerned to make their decisions. The Church of India, although disliking certain details, felt justified in recommending it to the dioceses, but this was opposed by the Bishops of Colombo and Nagpur.[19] They supported a request from the Church Union in England to the Metropolitan of India that he should approach all Metropolitans and Provinces of the Anglican Communion to enquire whether, if the Scheme were adopted in its existing form, they would break off communion with the Province of India, and whether they would refuse to be in communion with the Church of South India.[20] This request set off further controversy in England, in which Headlam played his part by endorsing the Scheme and castigating the Church Union in the press : he was convinced that they lacked the support of the great majority of Anglicans and he doubted whether they wanted any reunion with any one anywhere.[21]

[17] Headlam to Dr. Banninga, December 29, 1937.
[18] Sundkler, op. cit., pp. 291–5.
[19] The Rt. Revd. C. D. Horsley and the Rt. Revd. A. O. Hardy.
[20] Bishop Azariah to Headlam, February 24, 1943.
[21] Cf. *The Guardian*, January 15, May 21, 1943; *The Church Times*, May 21, 1943; *The Times*, March 20, June 14, 1943.

The Metropolitan of India again sought advice from the Consultative Body of the Lambeth Conference and also from the Archbishop of Canterbury. The former replied in July 1943 : the Scheme in its final form contained elements which they did not like, but they were not sufficient to warrant any change in the general approval given by the Lambeth Conference in 1930.[22] Archbishop Temple, after some consultation with the Convocation of Canterbury, gave his reply in January 1944.[23] The Province of Canterbury would not break off communion with the Province of India if it allowed its four dioceses to leave the Province and join the Church of South India, and would permit restricted intercommunion with the Church of South India from the outset.[24] Despite these favourable replies, opposition to the Scheme was still widespread, and the Province of India was urged to delay its final decision until after the next Lambeth Conference, which had been postponed indefinitely owing to the War. This plea was ignored, however; in January 1945 approval was given to the Scheme by seventy-five votes to twenty-one, in order to permit the four dioceses of Madras, Travancore and Cochin, Tinnevelly, and Dornakal to become part of the Church of South India. The Methodist Synod had already agreed to union by an almost unanimous vote in January 1943, and the South India United Church followed suit in September 1946.[25] The Church of South India became a fact with the Service of Inauguration in S. George's Cathedral, Madras, on September 27, 1947.

Headlam failed by eight months to see this day—he had died on January 17 : but at least he had had the satisfaction of knowing that the existence of the new Church was assured by the acceptance of the Scheme by all the participating bodies. The Church of South India was a monument to his œcumenical ideals. Various Christian bodies, including Anglicans, had united to become a distinctive Province of the Universal Church; episcopacy had been accepted as the basis of the united ministry, but the validity of all the existing ministries had been recognized. Whatever misgivings there may have been, the infant Church soon gave ample indication of health and vigour. The following quotation from the United Report of the two Joint Committees of the Convocations of Canterbury and York, which was accepted in 1955, is significant :

'We cannot doubt that the Church of South India has grown in its

---

[22] Sundkler, op. cit., p. 331.
[23] Many people regarded these consultations as quite inadequate. Cf. E. W. Kemp, *The Life and Letters of Kenneth Escot Kirk*, 1959, pp. 156–72.
[24] Sundkler, op. cit., p. 331.
[25] Rouse and Neil, *The Œcumenical Movement*, p. 475.

inner unity and cohesion, and in its sacramental life. There has been a growing appreciation of the office of the bishop in the Church of God, as a bond of continuity and unity; a continuous spread of liturgical worship, as expressed for example in the Services issued by the Synod for Holy Communion, Baptism and Confirmation; and a growing use of the rite of Confirmation administered by the Bishop. In this last matter there is evidence that an institution which is not made obligatory in the Constitution of the Church of South India has been winning its way in circles where it has been unfamiliar, in virtue of its inherent truth and appeal.' [26]

Of particular interest is the comment on Confirmation; for Headlam had written in 1935, 'I believe our Anglican usage (of Confirmation) is wholly admirable. I think that it will prevail, and hope that it will, but I do not think that it is either wise or right to insist upon it as a necessary condition of reunion. . . . I have no doubt that if the South Indian Church is left free, . . . a rule of Confirmation very like the Anglican but perhaps in some ways better will become the rule of that Church.' [27] Events had amply justified his contention.

Further justification for his views on reunion are to be seen in two striking statements by ministers in the Church of South India. On the question of episcopacy the Revd. D. Chellappa, Headmaster of S. Paul's School, Madras, wrote in 1954, 'Unlike the Tractarians, who emphasized the theory of the Apostolic Succession, but failed in their attempts to restore the second-century episcopate in England, the Church of South India, which began with no more definite theory than the Church of England, but only the fact of the Historic Episcopate, seems to be reproducing the second-century episcopate in South India. In other words, there is being hammered out in South India a pattern of episcopacy, not perhaps entirely new in the history of the Church, but largely forgotten since the early centuries.' [28] Finally, on the recognition of other ministries, one of the young Church's most brilliant leaders—Lesslie Newbiggin, Bishop of Madura and Ramnad —wrote in 1958, 'The event which finally made union possible in South India was the publication of a statement by the five Anglican bishops stating that from the date of union onwards they would be entirely willing and happy to receive communion equally from any

---

[26] *Report of the Lambeth Conference 1958*, p. 227.

[27] *Open Letter to the Revd. F. Hood*, 1935, p. 10. Cf. 'I am sure that in any scheme of reunion to make (Confirmation) a *sine qua non* would simply defeat the object we have before us. . . . Leave it free and the merits of the custom and its biblical basis are so strong that I do not doubt that it would prevail universally.' (A. C. Headlam, *Christian Unity*, 1930, p. 112.)

[28] D. Chellappa, 'I believe in the C.S.I.', *Theology*, June 1954, vol. lvii, p. 255.

presbyter of C.S.I. whether ordained episcopally or otherwise. Only such a frank and unambiguous acceptance of one another *at the point of reunion* can provide a basis for unity.' [29]

[29] L. Newbiggin, 'Anglicans and Christian Reunion,' *Theology*, vol. lxi, no. 456, p. 227.

CHAPTER EIGHTEEN

The Northern Churches

I

HEADLAM'S interest in the Scandinavian Churches was of long standing, dating from 1902 when Valdemar Ammundsen—then a young Danish theological student and subsequently a notable figure in œcumenical circles [1]—came to stay with him at Welwyn. This meeting marked the beginning of one of those firm and lasting friendships with foreign churchmen which Headlam seemed to have a genius for making. Many years later at Christ Church, Oxford, he made others, notably with Dr. Nathaniel Söderblom, Archbishop of Upsala, and with two brilliant younger men—Yvnge Brilioth of Sweden and Skat Hoffmeyer of Denmark.[2] These four men were primarily responsible for his first visit to Denmark, Sweden and Finland in the spring of 1927.

In Denmark Headlam's reputation as a theologian was already established and the views on the Church and Ministry expressed in his Bampton Lectures had met with a wide degree of acceptance, as the replies to the questions of the Lausanne Subjects Committee had shown.[3] The official purpose of his visit was to lecture on the origins of the Christian Ministry under the Rask-Ørsted Foundation at the University of Copenhagen, but in addition he saw something of rural Church life in Jutland where Dr. Hoffmeyer was parish priest of Raarup, and he had interesting informal discussions on Church relations with a number of leading clergy, including Hoffmeyer, Ammundsen—by this time Bishop of Haderslev, and Bishop Oestenfeldt of Copenhagen. The Danish Church was episcopal Lutheran but, unlike the Swedish Church, had deliberately given up the Apostolic Succession at the Reformation. Headlam pointed out that this was an obstacle to intercommunion with the Church of England, but in his opinion it could be removed by bishops from both Churches taking part in each other's consecrations. Bishop Oestenfeldt explained that

---

[1] He later became President of the World Alliance for Promoting International Friendship through the Churches.
[2] Brilioth became Archbishop of Upsala, and Hoffmeyer Bishop of Aarhus.
[3] Cf. p. 192.

he had already suggested that Swedish and Norwegian bishops should take part in their consecrations, but the more Evangelical section of the Church would have none of it. Evidence of this attitude was then provided by Professor Jacobson, himself an old-fashioned Evangelical : he considered the Apostolic Succession to be an evil thing, and he hoped that he would not live to see the day when anything like it was restored to the Danish Church. This was not the feeling of most of the people present, but it was evident that although there was considerable interest in the Church of England in Denmark, the time for closer formal union had not yet come : there was a very definite fear of Rome, and the activities of the extreme Anglo-Catholics were viewed with serious misgivings. Furthermore, while many Danes were desirous of having their orders regularized, they were not prepared to do anything that would cause offence or even disunity in their own Church, which commanded the allegiance of ninety-eight per cent of the nation. What was really needed was an extension of contacts between the two Churches, and to promote this Headlam offered to provide hospitality to Danish clergy or students who wished to study the Church of England—a generous offer which was subsequently turned to good account.

In Sweden, where Headlam was the guest of Archbishop Söderblom, the situation was rather different. The first step towards intercommunion between the two Churches had been made at the Lambeth Conference of 1888, and an Anglican Commission under the chairmanship of the Bishop of Winchester (Dr. Ryle) had reported favourably on the validity of Swedish orders in 1911. The Lambeth Conference of 1920 had recommended mutual facilities for communicants, the interchange of pulpits and participation in each other's consecrations—recommendations which had been implemented. Nevertheless, they had never been ratified by the Convocations of Canterbury and York—a necessary preliminary to formal recognition —for the Lambeth Conference had no administrative or canonical authority.

Headlam delivered two lectures on Christian Authority at the University of Upsala under the Olaus Petri Foundation, and there he gained the impression that there was rather less enthusiasm for the Church of England than in Denmark : his audiences were smaller, there was not the same widespread knowledge of English, nor did there seem to be the same strong desire for association with the Church of England. There were no formal discussions with Church leaders as in Denmark, but he had extensive private talks with the Archbishop, whose vigour and efficiency impressed him tremendously—'All the Scandinavian countries feel that he has made their Churches known to the world in a way they were not before.'

By far the most important part of his tour was the visit to Finland, arranged by Dr. Brilioth, who since 1925 had been Professor of Ecclesiastical History in the University of Turku, a free foundation for the Swedish-speaking population of Finland. Here he met the Archbishop of Finland, who, despite his eighty-four years, was full of energy. He was a strong, old-fashioned Evangelical with little sympathy for the œcumenical activities of Archbishop Söderblom, and Headlam felt that he represented a dying generation which was largely out of sympathy with the trends in contemporary Church life. This was made evident in the discussions which he had in Helsinki with Bishop Gummerus of Tampere, Bishop Kaila of Viipuri, Dr. Lehtonen and other Church leaders. They desired closer ties with the Church of England, but were faced with a serious difficulty. Until 1809, when Finland had been annexed by Russia, the Finnish Church had been closely bound to the Church of Sweden : its doctrine and practice had been the same and its bishops had been consecrated in Sweden. After that date, however, Finland had become a separate Church province and in 1817 the Bishop of Turku had received the title of Archbishop. In 1884 all the Finnish bishops had died. The obvious solution had been to invite a bishop from Sweden to consecrate their successors, but this had not been adopted owing to the unco-operative attitude of the Russian Government. In 1870 a Canon had been passed specifically to deal with such an eventuality, by which a consecration might be undertaken by a dean or the senior member of a chapter in the absence of a bishop. Under its terms Canon Professor A. F. Granfelt had consecrated the new Archbishop of Turku, Dr. T. T. Renvall, on October 26, 1884. The episcopal succession had therefore been broken, and an attempt to restore it in 1923 by inviting a Swedish bishop to participate in a consecration had failed owing to illness. Headlam felt that the obvious solution was to arrange for an Anglican bishop to share in a consecration—a suggestion which was acceptable to Finns : but they felt that their Archbishop would be a serious stumbling block and would never approve. They suggested, however, that at their next Church Assembly in 1928 they should propose that if any offers of negotiations were received from the Church of England, the Archbishop should appoint a commission to consider them. Headlam returned to England well satisfied with the results of his journey,[4] and reported to Archbishop Davidson that the prospects of closer relations with both the Danish and Finnish Churches were bright. With regard to Finland, if a Joint Commission could be appointed to discuss closer relations, the initiative might come through the next Lambeth Conference.

[4] Dr. Söderblom wrote (June 1): 'I think your conversations in Finland have accomplished more than I ventured to expect.'

II

Lambeth 1930 saw the next step. Here the sub-committee responsible for relations with episcopal Churches considered a report from Bishop Gummerus of Tampere and also discussed the matter with the Swedish delegate, Bishop Rohde of Lund. He endorsed Headlam's report of 1927; the appointment of a new Archbishop in Finland was only a question of time, and then an English proposal for a Joint Commission would be welcomed.[5] Dr. Lang, who had by now become Archbishop of Canterbury, did not have long to wait. By 1932 Dr. Ingman had become the new Primate of Finland and with his approval a Conference was finally arranged at Lambeth in October of the following year. Headlam was appointed chairman of the Anglican delegation and was supported by the Bishop of Wakefield (Dr. J. B. Seaton), the Bishop of Fulham (the Rt. Revd. B. S. Batty), the Dean of Chichester (the Very Revd. A. S. Duncan-Jones), the Dean of Exeter (Dr. W. R. Matthews), Dr. C. E. Raven, and the Revds. C. B. Moss and P. Usher. The Finnish delegation was composed of the Bishop of Tampere (Dr. J. Gummerus), Dr. A. Lehtonen and Dr. U. Paunu. The basis of discussion was the Quadrilateral as stated by the Lambeth Conference of 1920.[6] On the first three points it was soon apparent that there were no serious differences: the real difficulty was the question of the Ministry. Headlam pointed out that the Quadrilateral, while emphasizing the vital importance of the historic episcopate for the creation of a unified ministry, did not thereby cast doubts on the spiritual efficacy of other ministries. It was then suggested that Swedish or Anglican bishops might participate in Finnish consecrations—a suggestion which the Finnish delegation thought unobjectionable provided that the validity of their existing orders was clearly recognized. Much depended on the meaning of validity, however: it might mean spiritual efficacy or it might mean authorized recognition. In the latter sense their orders were valid as regards Finland, but invalid from a more universal point of view. As a step towards reunion, therefore, it was desirable to remove any doubts as to their validity in this latter sense. The suggestion was then made that 'economic' intercommunion should be established between the two Churches, by which the spiritual efficacy of Finnish orders would be recognized, with the condition that they should be regu-

---

[5] *Lambeth Report,* pp. 148–9; *Lambeth Occasional Reports 1931–8,* p. 154.
[6] The Report of the Finnish Conferences in *Lambeth Occasional Reports 1931–8,* pp. 115–87 is confused: the matter is arranged under subject headings, and the discussions of 1933 and 1934 appear as if they had all taken place at the same time. I am largely indebted to Headlam's own papers and notes by the Revd. C. B. Moss for this section.

larized when an opportunity occurred. This raised the question of the Finnish regulation whereby a dean or the senior priest of a Chapter might act in the absence of a bishop : such a practice would cause great difficulty in England. The Finns pointed out that this was not the normal practice : it was only an emergency regulation which had, in fact, occurred very rarely : it would, however, be a very difficult regulation to change, for the amendment of Church Law was a long and complicated procedure. Both Bishop Gummerus and Headlam were agreed that despite differences on this subject, there was sufficient common ground to warrant hope of a mutual understanding and a satisfactory agreement if the conversations could be continued. They therefore suggested to their respective Archbishops that further discussions should be held in the following year in Finland, where a larger Finnish delegation would be able to take part.

Negotiations were accordingly resumed at Brändö, Helsinki, in July 1934. Both delegations showed changes. On the Anglican side the Archdeacon of Auckland (Dr. A. E. J. Rawlinson) took the place of the Bishop of Wakefield and Dr. W. R. Matthews (now Dean of S. Paul's), while the Finnish representatives were increased from three to seven : Dr. Gummerus had died and had been succeeded by Dr. Lehtonen as Bishop of Tampere, and with him in addition to Dr. Paunu there were now the Bishop of Viipuri (Dr. E. Kaila), the Bishop of Borga (Dr. Max von Bonsdorff), the Dean of Oulu (Dr. J. A. Mannermaa), Dr. M. Tarkkanen and Professor E. G. Gulin. The discussions soon ran into difficulties over the question of Confirmation. The Finnish Church included the imposition of hands in the administration of Baptism, which was regarded as conveying the gift of the Holy Spirit. Their Confirmation did not require the imposition of hands and was considered to involve three things—confession of faith by the candidates, the witness of the elders and prayer for the grace of the Holy Spirit : in the mission field their adult converts were admitted to Communion after Baptism and without Confirmation. Here was an essential difference from Anglican faith and practice, and the Revd. C. B. Moss, having in mind the strong element in the Church of England who regarded Confirmation as a necessary sacrament, and the Anglican assurances given to the Orthodox and Old Catholic Churches of agreement with them over it, felt that attention should be drawn to these facts. Headlam, however, refused to regard this question as of major importance : there was no rite upon which there had been greater difference of opinion, and the Church of England was unique in confining its administration solely to bishops. Furthermore, Confirmation had not been quoted in the Lambeth Quadrilateral as an essential condition to reunion : they were acting

PLATE VI

Diocesan Conference of the Orthodox diocese of Dalmatia, at Sibennik. Jugoslavia, 1936 (Bishop Ireney of Dalmatia on right of A.C.H.)

PLATE VII

Utrecht 1939. The S. Willibrord celebrations

Back row: L to R. Bishop of Haarlem, Bishop of Fulham, Archbishop of Utrecht
A.C.H., Bishop of Deventer

Anglican clergy: L to R. J. A. Coulson, Chaplain at Utrecht, Canon J. A. Douglas
P. Usher

The Balkan Tour 1940. Athens
The Bishop of Gibraltar, The Archbishop of Athens, A.C.H., P. Usher

under the authority of the Lambeth Conference, which for fifty years had omitted it from the essentials for intercommunion. He admitted that the absence of the imposition of hands in the Finnish rite was a defect, but it did contain prayer for the increase of grace, which was the essential thing. There the matter rested, but the Anglican delegation as a whole were far from happy about it.

They then turned to the Ministry. The Dean of Oulu emphasized the difficulties involved in securing a change in Church Law : it would be hard to find a more conservative method of protecting rules of ordination. Furthermore, Finnish presbyterian ordination was analogous to the practice of lay baptism in the Church of England— an emergency measure pure and simple. As evidence of this the three Finnish bishops pointed out that in their joint experience only one such ordination had taken place in the past ten years. Because they could not get rid of the provisions of Church Law, they could not guarantee that there would *never* be any further presbyterian ordinations, but what could be said was that closer unity with the Church of England would stimulate the episcopal principle among them. With this assurance the Anglican delegation was satisfied, and on July 19 the Conference drew up its Report—a task not achieved without a further clash between Headlam and Mr. Moss. The Report as drafted contained the statement that they had reached agreement 'on all fundamental points of doctrine.' With the problem of Confirmation in mind Mr. Moss firmly refused to sign if this phrase were retained. The statement was therefore modified—both Churches were agreed 'on the most fundamental points of doctrine.' It was still not entirely to his satisfaction ; but feeling that disunity would endanger further negotiations and realizing that the Finns needed all the moral support possible against the pressure of Russian Communism, he signed and the Report was published as a unanimous document.

Headlam considered the Conference to have been entirely satisfactory. He thought that the Finns had 'behaved handsomely.' It was no mean achievement to have secured the first formal agreement with the Lutheran Church, and he hoped that the Report would meet with the minimum of opposition in England. After declaring agreement on 'the most fundamental doctrines of the Faith,' it made three recommendations : first that Finnish and Anglican bishops should take part in one another's consecrations; secondly that Finnish communicants should be admitted to communion in Anglican churches—the Finnish Church already admitted to communion the communicants of other confessions, and thirdly that Finnish bishops should be invited to conferences—at Lambeth or elsewhere—between Anglican bishops and the bishops of other Churches, and Anglican bishops should be

K

invited to similar Finnish conferences.[7] The Report was published without the minutes of the two conferences on December 28, 1934, and its reception in the church newspapers gave promise of future trouble. Both *The Guardian* and *The Record* were friendly, but *The Church Times* was distinctly hostile. On January 4, 1935, it suggested that the mischief generated by the South India Scheme was spreading : a 'proposal to effect an infiltration of episcopacy into the Finnish Church' was being recommended on 'naked grounds of utility with no basis of theological agreement on the meaning or necessity of episcopacy.' This was followed by critical letters in the following week from Dr. W. J. Sparrow Simpson and Athelstan Riley, although Mr. Moss wrote a valiant letter of defence, pointing out that apart from the unhappy case in 1884 no Finnish bishop had ever been consecrated by a presbyter, and emphasizing the remark of a Finnish delegate—'We have always valued episcopacy highly, and now we shall value it more than ever.'

In the same month the Report was presented to the Convocations. At York there was no difficulty : both Houses approved and asked the Archbishops to take whatever steps they thought necessary to carry out the recommendations.[8] At Canterbury, however, things were much less straightforward. Headlam presented it in the Upper House on January 23, but too late in the day for consideration. Meanwhile the Dean of Chichester had presented it in the Lower House; here Dr. Darwell Stone had moved an amendment, carried by sixty-five votes to forty-nine, requesting the appointment of a committee to seek for further information and report back in June.[9] When therefore the Upper House met on the following day, they felt bound to fall in line with the Lower House, and asked the Archbishop to appoint a joint committee of both Houses.[10] Headlam was both disappointed and annoyed. Admittedly there was some justification for the line taken by the Lower House, for the minutes of the conferences had still not been published—the absence of English stenographers at Helsinki had caused unavoidable delay : but he felt that religious intolerance was largely to blame, and it was singularly unfortunate that the religious press had poisoned the wells of controversy before any of the members of the delegation had been able to expound or defend their policy. There was every promise of lively exchanges when the names of the Joint Committee were announced : Headlam was in charge, and among the members were Dr. Darwell Stone,

---

[7] Bell, *Documents*, ser. 3, pp. 146–7.
[8] Ibid., p. 147 ; *York Journal of Convocation*, January 1935, pp. 40–3, 79, 81–7.
[9] *Chronicle of Convocation*, January 1935, pp. 34–43, 48–80.
[10] Ibid., pp. 86–110.

Dr. W. J. Sparrow Simpson and the Revd. C. E. Douglas—the leaders of the opposition.

Meanwhile the Report had been well received in Finland. Bishop Lehtonen reported to Headlam on March 12 that all the Finnish bishops were in favour of implementing the proposals. They had in fact hoped that an Anglican bishop would have been able to assist in the consecration of the new Bishop of Viipuri on Ascension Day, but they appreciated the difficulty created by the action of Convocation : nevertheless the Archbishop of Upsala and the Bishop of Estonia had been invited to take part, and their presence would be invaluable in creating a wider œcumenical outlook in Finland. Headlam was loth to see such an opportunity wasted. It then occurred to him that since the Convocation of York had accepted the Report the Bishop of Wakefield might legitimately be permitted to go to Finland for the consecration. At his suggestion both Archbishops considered the idea but reluctantly came to the conclusion that it was unacceptable. Archbishop Temple wrote :

'. . . Action taken by any province, but more especially by that of York, may create an extremely difficult position for the Archbishop of Canterbury if his own Synod opposes that action. My present feeling is that it would not be right to involve ourselves in the tangle that would result, nor can I suppose that our friends in Finland would really welcome it. They could only desire the presence of the Bishop of Wakefield if the Archbishop of Canterbury cordially approved his going; and while *Dr. Cosmo Lang* fully sympathizes, the *President of the Convocation of Canterbury* is not at present free to act.'[11]

By this time the minutes of the conferences had been published,[12] and on March 21 the Joint Committee of Convocation met to discuss them. There were some sharp exchanges and Headlam regarded the meeting as one of the strangest he had ever taken part in.[13] Dr. Sparrow Simpson suggested that the Finnish Church seemed to permit two theories of the ministry—one of episcopal and another of presbyterian consecration. Headlam, however, disagreed. Finnish traditional theory was orthodox : presbyterian consecration had been due entirely to the political and geographical situation of the country. It was irregular, but irregularity was not the same as invalidity; and since the Finns really desired to amend it, it was up to the Church of England to help them to do so.

---

[11] William Ebor to Headlam, March 20, 1935.
[12] *Lambeth Occasional Reports 1931–8*, pp. 115–87.
[13] Headlam to Miss P. L. Wingfield, March 25, 1935.

The Committee had a further meeting on May 2, when discussion was again stormy. Even Headlam—formidable and pugnacious though he could be—confessed to Archbishop Lang, 'It has certainly been about the most unpleasant committee I have ever had to preside over.' [14] No agreement was reached, and the opposition insisted on a Minority Report. The Majority Report was a brief but extremely carefully worded document. It recommended the House to welcome the approach to the Church of Finland and express the hope that in due course complete intercommunion, based on 'a common episcopal ministry,' might be achieved. Then, 'noting that the episcopal ordination of presbyters is the regular practice of the Church of Finland, and assuming that the bishops of the Church will take steps to put the practice of the Church of Finland beyond doubt,' Convocation was asked to approve joint consecrations and the admission of Finnish communicants to Holy Communion in the Church of England.[15] The Minority Report, signed by Douglas, Darwell Stone and Sparrow Simpson, contained six points. Information about Finland was still inadequate for considered judgment; Finnish Church Law permitted the consecration of bishops by people not in episcopal orders; action had been taken under this law in 1884; no guarantee had been given that similar action might not be taken again; such a guarantee should be a necessary preliminary to the equation of ministries; and finally, the Church of England had a unique position of responsibility towards other episcopal Churches and it should be careful not to compromise its position over the question of episcopal succession.[16]

When Headlam presented the Report to the Upper House on June 6 he made a vigorous attack on the minority's objections. He pointed out that the Church of England was in no position to complain about the intransigence of Finnish Church Law, for when the majority of the Church had approved of the revision of the Prayer Book, Parliament had effectively prevented it. The attitude of the Finnish Church towards episcopacy was perfectly consonant with the attitude of the Lambeth Conference, which, while emphasizing the necessity and importance of the historic episcopate, did not deny the spiritual efficacy of presbyterian orders; by inviting the Archbishop of Upsala to take part in one of their consecrations, the Finns had already in fact taken steps to restore the succession. He then referred to a document circulated by Mr. Douglas, which argued that the Finnish Church was essentially Presbyterian. Bishop Lehtonen had examined this and had completely refuted it, pointing out that

[14] Headlam to Cosmo Cantuar, May 6, 1935.
[15] *Canterbury Convocation, Report 610*, p. 2.
[16] Ibid., p. 3.

Mr. Douglas had made mistakes on almost every point of Finnish Church Law. The Bishop had also stated that a Canon permitting presbyterian ordination had existed in the Swedish Church in the eighteenth century, but with the improvement in communications it had gradually become obsolete.

On this occasion there was little difficulty, and after the briefest of debates the Upper House accepted the Majority Report and its Resolutions without amendment.[17] The Lower House, too, was now more amenable, making only one small change—Finnish bishops were not to be invited to share in English consecrations until their succession was regularized.[18] 'Economic intercommunion' with the Church of Finland was therefore formally recognized and with it the Church of England had committed itself to a practical demonstration of Headlam's theories for reunion. It was an arrangement which created much less stir in England than in Finland. Finland undoubtedly valued it greatly; and tangible evidence of the country's gratitude to Headlam for his services was given in October 1938, when the President appointed him a Knight Commander, first class, of the Order of the White Rose of Finland.

The following year was one of disaster. Russia invaded Finland; and Headlam devoted himself to enlisting sympathy and support in answer to Archbishop Kaila's appeal to the Christian Churches of the world for spiritual and material help (December 10, 1939). Then early in 1940 Bishop Lehtonen suggested to him that since a delegation of the British Labour Movement had just visited Finland, a delegation of Churchmen might also come, to see the situation for themselves and to give much-needed encouragement. Headlam's reaction was characteristic—he would secure permission to fly out himself immediately. Archbishop Lang fully approved and expressed both his admiration and astonishment at Headlam's courage and vigour—it was an arduous venture for a man of seventy-five. The journey never took place, however, for before the arrangements could be made, peace was declared. Then came the German invasion of Russia, and Britain's support of the latter caused much bitterness in Finland. It was a distressing situation which Headlam deplored and strove hard to remedy in correspondence with Archbishop Kaila, stressing the urgent need to resist German aggression at all costs.

Happily friendly relations were restored with the end of hostilities. Headlam's retirement in October 1945 began with a message from his old friend, Dr. Lehtonen, now Archbishop of Finland, which made it clear that his labours had by no means been in vain and that his trust in the Church of Finland had been justified.

[17] *Chronicle of Convocation*, June 1935, pp. 364–7, 371–9.
[18] Ibid., pp. 410–23, 425–7.

September 28, 1945.

'Dear Bishop,

'Now that you are retiring from the Chairmanship of the Church of England Council on Foreign Relations, I take the opportunity to thank you for the valuable and long-standing friendship and interest that you have so kindly shown towards the Church of Finland. I still recall vividly our visit to Archbishop Johansson in 1927 at Turku. I am now living in the same house and working for a real friendship and reunion sincerely. Your photograph in my study is to me a daily reminder of you. I owe you very much of inspiring views. A great part of that programme, which aims at a closer union of our Churches, has been fulfilled during the recent years. The historical episcopacy is now a rule in our Church. Only the bishops ordain in Finland. There has no longer been any departure from this principle. The Bishop of Fulham, as you know, has been here lately taking part in my bene-diction, which act concluded the service of my installation as the Archbishop of Finland. Swedish bishops have taken part in almost every consecration here. I hope that the same successful development will continue. . . . Perhaps I too will be able to return the friendly visits of the English bishops before long. . . .

'Great common tasks are waiting and must be solved by our Churches. In my opinion the time is now particularly suitable for the Church of England and the Northern Lutheran Churches to join together. . . .

Cordial and grateful regards,
Yours very sincerely,
A. LEHTONEN.'

III

The negotiations with Finland in 1933–4 were closely followed by those with Latvia and Estonia. These two small Baltic states, pre-dominantly Lutheran in belief, had sought the help and friendship of the other Scandinavian Churches after gaining their independence at the end of the 1914–18 War, and Archbishop Söderblom had con-secrated bishops for both of them. The desire for closer ties with the Church of England had also grown, and valuable lay support had come from Mr. Konstantin Pats, Prime Minister and later President of Estonia.[19] The initiative was taken by the Archbishop of Latvia (Dr. T. Grünbergs), who approached the Archbishop of Canterbury on the possibility of negotiations with the Latvian Church on the

[19] A. Torma, *The Church in Estonia*, 1943, p. 18.

same lines as those just concluded with the Church of Finland. The
Bishop of Estonia (Dr. H. B. Rahamägi) then asked if his Church
might be included too.

Dr. Lang welcomed the proposal, and meetings were arranged at
Lambeth in March 1936. Headlam again led the Anglican delega-
tion, which included the Bishops of Wakefield and Fulham, the Dean
of Chichester, Dr. C. E. Raven, and the Revds. C. B. Moss and
P. Usher. The Latvians were represented by the Archbishop of Latvia
(Dr. Grünbergs), the Provost of Riga (Dr. A. Kundzin) and the Revd.
E. Rumba; and the Estonians by the Bishop of Estonia (Dr.
Rahamägi) and Dr. J. Taul. The discussions followed the same course
as those with Finland : there was a substantial measure of agreement
on the first three points of the Lambeth Quadrilateral, but difficulty
over the question of the ministry. This mainly concerned Latvia. The
first Archbishop, properly consecrated by Archbishop Söderblom, had
retired in 1931 ; but his successor, the existing Archbishop, had been
installed without being consecrated—a situation due entirely to racial
and political difficulties. Dr. Grünbergs had by no means accepted
this willingly—he had in fact stood out for two years against being
installed without consecration, but had finally submitted as an act of
appeasement. It was an incident that the Church of Latvia certainly
had no desire of repeating.[20]

Dr. Grünbergs admitted that in Latvia pastors ordained by general
superintendents had the same rights as those ordained by bishops :
but his Church valued the episcopal office and would value succession
if it tended to strengthen the episcopate. They had to face the fact,
however, that the German minority in Latvia were suspicious of
episcopacy. The Bishop of Estonia pointed out that presbyterian
ordination was also permitted in his Church—if necessary a bishop
could delegate his authority to ordain to a pastor—but it had to be
remembered that there was only one bishop for the whole country,
and in actual practice he himself always performed ordinations. The
discussions then ended with a statement by Headlam on the Anglican
attitude to the question. It was essentially an exploratory conference :
all the delegations were in search of information, which was a necessary preliminary to any attempt at reaching agreement at a subsequent meeting.[21] Headlam was impressed by the leaders of both
Churches, and he was full of admiration for the way in which they
had faced the social, political and economic problems of their countries. He was hopeful of being able to do something to help their

---

[20] *Lambeth Occasional Reports 1931–8*, pp. 218–27; *Chronicle of Convocation*, May 1939, pp. 369–75.
[21] *Lambeth Occasional Reports 1931–8*, pp. 227–30.

Churches, but he felt that they had adopted episcopacy in that half-hearted sort of way which was typical of all Lutheran Churches, regarding questions of ministry as matters of indifference rather than importance.[22]

The discussions were resumed in June 1938, two meetings being held in Riga (Latvia) and two in Tallinn (Estonia), where Headlam took the opportunity of visiting the house in which his ancestor, Peter the Great, used to live. Both the Latvian and the Estonian delegates made it clear that although presbyterian ordination had only taken place in a few exceptional cases, the desire did exist for this provision to be retained—a situation which Headlam thought could easily have been remedied by increasing the number of bishops. At the third meeting, however, in Tallinn, the Latvians put forward a proposal of the utmost value. They stated their belief that spiritual oversight (Episkopat) was rooted in the commission of Jesus Christ, and that in the course of history it had been manifested in various forms. Nevertheless, in the interests of unity they were now prepared to adopt this oversight in the form of the historic episcopate.[23]

It was a great step forward, and Headlam welcomed it as such. There were now no real obstacles to 'economic intercommunion' and on June 24 a Joint Report was signed on the same lines and containing the same recommendations as the Finnish Report.[24] This time there were no difficulties in Convocation, and another official step towards Christian unity was taken.[25] It had been hard work, but Headlam considered it worth while : he wrote to his niece, 'Uniting Christendom demands great endurance, unlimited patience, and a digestion suited to all emergencies.'[26] Once again it was an agreement which caused no great stir in England—the Churches of Latvia and Estonia were after all very small and rather remote : but to them it meant a very great deal and Headlam was a figure of considerable importance. To them, as to many other Christian communities throughout the world, he—with his massive scholarship, his strong character, his understanding of their problems, and his unmistakable passion for unity—truly represented the Church of England. His efforts to bring them a vision of the universal Church and to place them within its context was something for which they were extremely grateful. Dr. A. Roomees, one of the Latvian delegates, wrote to him on December 28, 1938, thanking him for what he called 'the ideology

[22] Headlam to Miss P. L. Wingfield, March 19, 1936.
[23] *Lambeth Occasional Reports 1931–8*, pp. 231–47.
[24] Ibid., pp. 213–14 ; Bell, *Documents*, ser. 3, pp. 154–5.
[25] *Chronicle of Convocation*, January 1939, pp. 129–35 ; May 1939, pp. 369–91 ; Bell, op. cit., pp. 156–8.
[26] Headlam to Miss P. L. Wingfield, June 26–7, 1938.

of the Universal Church' : it was something about which before he had had no clear idea, but now 'the clear, vivifying and fundamental idea of a Universal Church's necessity, professed last summer by Your Lordship, has served me a light in darkness and has shown me the only right way.'

Unfortunately all the high hopes were soon dashed. Both countries suffered from invasion by Russia in 1940, by Germany in 1941 and again by Russia in 1944. As with Finland, Headlam did what he could, keeping in close touch with the Ministers of Latvia, Estonia and Lithuania in London. In the summer of 1944 a correspondent in *The Times* suggested that Russia could easily house these little states within her framework with slight though essential concessions to their peculiar position. Headlam, knowing what they had already undergone, wrote a brief but vigorous reply which was published on August 8. He deplored the suggestion that they would be content under the Soviet regime : such a remark would only make every small nation in Eastern Europe distrust Great Britain, who would certainly not be content with such an arrangement herself : it also suggested that this country was *not* going to be faithful to the promises of the Atlantic Charter. It needed courage to be critical of Russia at that particular time, but of this Headlam had no lack ; and his action earned him the thanks of many people—not least from members of the three states living in exile. Their confidence in him was shown in a remark by the Latvian minister on February 13, 1945, 'If your voice should be heard among the Councils of the Big Three and the other countries, we shall have the possibility of returning to our land and contributing towards mutual peace and understanding among the nations.'

None of these little states have as yet regained their freedom, and beyond giving the Church of England a special responsibility for helping members of the small Churches who were in exile, the arrangements negotiated by Headlam and his delegation have realized little. Bishop Rahamägi of Estonia was deported to Siberia, but Headlam was pleased to renew contact with Dr. Taul and the Archbishop of Latvia, both of whom escaped to the West. They had not forgotten all that he had done for them and Archbishop Grünbergs wrote him a most touching letter on March 26, 1946 :

Esslingen.

'From all the ministers of our Church now in Germany as well as myself I kindly beg you to accept our sincere gratitude for your very kind interest about the fate of our heavily stricken nation and our Church, and for all your efforts in defending us.

'In our memories are still lingering the precious moments of your visit to Riga where you delivered your heart-felt sermon to the Latvian people. Dr. E. Rumba, who on that occasion interpreted you, was in 1941 deported to Russia. According to the information gathered about his fate he has met his martyr's death there.

'We are glad and grateful to you that our nation and our Church is privileged to have such a friend in Great Britain as your eminence. In no other way are we able to reward your kindness than to express our sincere gratitude and to pray for you that God may sustain you and bless you with His Divine Blessing.'

CHAPTER NINETEEN

Faith and Order:
Edinburgh 1937

I

AFTER Lausanne the Continuation Committee undertook two tasks. The first was to discover as accurately as possible just what the different Churches stood for and what they believed. This was done by considering their replies to the Conference Report, a number of which were ultimately published in 1934 under the title *Convictions*. These replies provided a statement of agreements and disagreements existing between the Churches, and they made it abundantly clear that unity could not be achieved by glossing over differences of conviction. The second task was to begin digging down through these statements of faith in search of some underlying common ground of unity.[1] When, therefore, the Committee met at Maloja in August 1929, it appointed a Theological Committee with Headlam as its chairman to examine the doctrine of Grace. For the next two years its sixteen members exchanged papers and memoranda, and finally met for two weeks at Gloucester in August 1931 to write out a report. Here Headlam was at his best, both as chairman and as host. He worked every one hard and positively revelled in it all. He wrote, 'We are having a tremendous time. Our professors arrived on Tuesday, and we have been conferring some five hours a day since then. Our discussions advanced fairly well. The Germans are lengthy and get louder and louder and more emphatic as they go on, until you think they are going to hurl themselves at you—but when they have stopped they are quite calm again.'[2] It is interesting to note the impressions of two men of very different outlook and temperament. Professor W. Manson, a Scottish Presbyterian, wrote. 'Headlam was very patient with the collection of Continental and British theologians who met round the table. He was not a man of many words, but he listened to our verbosity. No one ever showed a better understanding of other communions than his own. He knew his facts and he wanted

[1] *Faith and Order Pamphlets*, no. 74, pp. 4–5.
[2] Headlam to Miss P. L. Wingfield, August 3, 1931.

us to know them : and he took a personal interest in all the members.'
Professor N. Arseniev, of the Eastern Orthodox Church, was similarly
impressed : 'He was admirable. I can vividly remember how brilliant
and how scholarly sound he was. His friendly hospitality and courtesy
as host was closely interwoven with his efficiency as chairman.'

An agreed Report, presented to the annual meeting of the Continuation Committee at High Leigh immediately afterwards, expressed
the conviction that the doctrine of Grace involved no insuperable bar
to unity. 'There are marked differences of emphasis and expression
between different Churches in their formulation of the message of the
Gospel concerning Grace. These differences have arisen in the course
of history, and imply to a certain extent differences of racial temperament, religious experience, and historical environment. We wish,
therefore, to record our conviction that, provided the different
Churches agree in holding the essentials of the Christian faith, such
differences would form no barrier to union between them.' [3] The
results of their labours were finally published in 1932 in a large volume
The Doctrine of Grace. Headlam contributed a survey of the whole
field in a final essay. He concluded with five points :

'1. That our difficulties have arisen from substituting a doctrine of
Abstract Grace for belief in the gracious goodness and loving kindness
of God to mankind.

'2. That a large number of the problems which have been raised
with regard to Grace have arisen from imperfect and onesided
presentations. . . . The cure is not to attempt alternative definition,
but to recognize the value of freedom in the Christian Church, so
that all the different shades of religious truth may be represented.

'3. Therefore . . . there is no need to exclude from a united
Christian society the Calvinist or the Arminian or any of the other
aspects of opinion which have arisen.

'4. That our aim should be not to lay down dogmatic statements
about the constitution of the Christian Church, but to create a united
Church as the great instrument of the Sanctification of the World.

'5. The same must be our method with regard to the Sacraments.
It is not a series of rigid definitions of the Sacraments, but the due
performance of them, that is the important point.' [4]

At this point the whole Faith and Order movement was compelled
to restrict its activities severely in the face of the world economic crisis.
The Continuation Committee did not meet in 1932 or 1933, and the
Theological Committee ceased to operate. The time was not wasted,

[3] Report on the Theology of Grace. *Faith and Order Pamphlets*, no. 66,
pp. 27–8.
[4] W. J. Whitley (editor), *The Doctrine of Grace*, 1932, pp. 395–6.

however, for the Report on Grace and a series of questions on the Church and Sacraments were sent to the Churches, with a request for comments and replies in preparation for the next World Conference in 1937. When the Continuation Committee met again in 1934 a new situation had to be faced. It was evident from the replies received that there was considerable difference of opinion as to what were crucial problems. In England, for example, questions of the Church and Ministry were thought to be vital; on the Continent, however, all the emphasis was on Grace and the Word of God; while in America a most acute problem was presented by divisions based on psychological, social and cultural factors. Changes were therefore made in the work of preparation for 1937, the Theological Committee being replaced by three Commissions, one to consider the Church and the Word, another the Ministry and the Sacraments, and the third the Empirical Approach to Unity—later changed to the Church's Unity in Life and Worship.[5]

Headlam was appointed chairman of the second of these and he adopted the same procedure as before. Some thirty theologians, widely representative and including even two Roman Catholics, circulated papers and commented on them in preparation for a meeting at Gloucester in August 1936. Eventually only twelve members were able to attend, but they were able to produce an extremely valuable Report, which, despite notes and provisos, contained a considerable number of agreed conclusions. They were agreed, for example, that when Biblical criticism had had its say, they were warranted in founding the sacramental and ministerial practice of the Church on a Biblical basis. In the sacraments, Christ was the original and ultimate authority, and the ministers were but His instruments acting on behalf of the Church. God was not bound, however, by His sacraments. Nor was the Church static, but through the Holy Spirit was a living and growing organism. Perhaps the most important point on which there was disagreement was the extent to which God's gifts were limited by the disunity of the Church.

The Report, together with the papers, were published in another volume *The Ministry and the Sacraments*. Headlam contributed two essays, one on the origin of the Christian Ministry, and another which reviewed the whole work of the Commission. Here he made yet another plea for freedom. Unity did not depend on a rigid doctrinal uniformity. 'There will be far greater unity in the Church if it is left free than if an attempt is made to give it uniformity. This absence of definition must be positive and negative. There must be no definition

[5] L. Hodgson (editor), *Faith and Order. Edinburgh 1937*, p. 9; *Faith and Order Pamphlets*, no. 71, pp. 11–12.

declaring what we must believe. There must be no definition declaring
what we must not believe. . . . It will be found that there is little room
for controversy on the devotional side. (For example), we all believe
in the Real Presence of Christ, though how, or in what way, we may
differ. . . . If we could realize that it was not necessary or desirable
that we should have any formula of union, I think unity would begin
to come very quickly, and what would keep Churches apart would
not be dogmatic definitions but different habits of piety.'[6]

The Continuation Committee also decided at its 1934 meeting that
the next Conference should meet in Edinburgh, and should confine
itself to four subjects—the Grace of our Lord Jesus Christ, the Church
of Christ and the Word of God, the Ministry and Sacraments, and
the Church's Unity in Life and Worship. The doctrine of the Church
was not included : it was felt that the time was not yet ripe for a
frontal attack on the problems which it presented. Finally, they agreed
to co-operate with the Universal Council for Life and Work in
reviewing the whole œcumenical movement and in making recommendations for its future organization.[7]

II

The aim of the Edinburgh Conference was clearly set out in the
programme :

'We shall aim at issuing a brief affirmation of our underlying unity
in face of the challenge of the world situation, an affirmation which
bears witness . . . to that *koinônia tôn ekklesiôn* that springs from our
common loyalty to Christ. And then in addition we shall aim at producing a series of as it were confidential Reports to the Churches, in
which we shall record and commend to their consideration such
progress as we shall have been able to make in our joint studies
towards overcoming the obstacles which hinder us from full unity.'[8]

Headlam approached it all with serious misgivings, however, despite
all the effort he had put into the work of preparation. He confided to
his niece, 'I somehow have a feeling that we are not going to make
it a success.' He had expressed these misgivings in an article in *The
Church Quarterly Review* in January 1937. Some powerful force,

[6] R. Dunkerley and A. C. Headlam (editors), *The Ministry and the Sacraments*, 1937, pp. 548–9.
[7] *Faith and Order Pamphlets*, no. 79, pp. 15–16; *Faith and Order. Edinburgh*, p. 11.
[8] *Faith and Order Pamphlets*, no. 74, p. 6.

some strong conviction was needed to overpower the innate conservatism of the religious mind, and it was lacking. A mere utilitarian
aspiration towards Christian unity counted for little against religious
convictions. In Germany, for example, the Separatist tendencies had
been intensified by the influence of Barth; Scotland had been
strengthening its repugnance to episcopacy; the Scandinavian churches
were rather frightened of the Church of England; and the English
movement towards reunion had even been described on the Continent
as another piece of English imperialism. What was really needed was
a belief—a strong conviction in the necessity of the one, Catholic
Church; and it was the neglect of this element which was the great
weakness of so many Christian bodies; there was no antidote against
disunion.[9]

The Conference, attended by 504 delegates representing 123 Churches,
began on August 3, a week after the close of the Life and Work
Conference at Oxford. The method of procedure adopted was different
from that of Lausanne. This time so much preparatory work had been
done, that no introduction and general discussion of the subjects in
full Conference was thought necessary. The Reports of the Commissions were referred at once to their respective Sections, who spent
the first ten days in dealing with them.

Headlam, who was leader of the Anglican delegation, had decided
to devote his energies to the Report on the Ministry and Sacraments,
and at his suggestion Professor W. Manson introduced the Report on
Grace. He warned him that it might be no easy task. 'There is a good
deal of difficulty about this Report. The Anglo-Saxon world seems to
think it a matter of the smallest importance. Someone suggested that
the whole thing could be accepted in half an hour. On the other
hand, our Continental friends look upon it as most vital, and I think
there will be a very strong movement made by some of the Lutheran
representatives to get the Conference to accept the Confession of
Augsburg and the complete formula *"sola gratia, sola fides."* So I think
you may find that you have very difficult work before you, just as
probably we shall have rather difficult work with "Ministry and
Sacraments"—again from the Lutheran standpoint.'[10] Contrary to his
expectations, the work of the Section was remarkably harmonious.
This was in some measure due to an unfortunate circumstance, for
the German Evangelical delegates had been refused their passports by
the National Socialist Government and were absent.[11] On the other
hand much of the credit must go to Headlam and the Theological

[9] 'Faith and Order 1937,' *C.Q.R.*, vol. 123, p. 320.
[10] Headlam to Professor W. Manson, February 19, 1937.
[11] Rouse and Neill, *Ecumenical Movement*, p. 431.

Committee for their fine piece of preparatory work. Professor Clavier, who had been Travelling Secretary of Faith and Order in preparation for the Conference, testified to its value : 'In this last year I have often seen in my travels the effect of hope produced by this preliminary work in many quite diverse audiences.' [12] Professor Manson added his word of praise when presenting the draft Report of the Section : 'We found the Report of Commission I a most valuable preparation for our own work. Without it we could not have done what we have done.' [13] The Section Report was a remarkable document. It was unanimous, with no qualifying footnotes and no reservations; and it began with a stirring statement : 'With deep thankfulness to God for the spirit of unity, which by His gracious blessing upon us has guided and controlled all our discussions on this subject, we agree on the following statement and recognize that there is in connection with this subject no ground for maintaining division between Churches.' [14] The Conference accepted it *nemine contradicente*, and in so doing provided itself with an opening message comparable with the Report on the Gospel at Lausanne.

The work of the Section on the Ministry and Sacraments was not so encouraging. Discussions were long and sometimes heated; and one of the delegates, Dr. Hugh Martin, must have voiced the opinion of many when he wrote, 'One could not help wondering . . . whether after all we were any further forward in this realm of Ministry and Sacraments than at Lausanne ten years ago. It is doubtful if any further agreement has been achieved.' [15] When the chairman of the Section, Professor D. M. Baillie, presented the draft Report on August 13 it was incomplete and bristling with provisos; and he admitted too that without the work of Headlam's Commission to help them, it would not have been before the Conference.[16] Headlam then expressed disappointment at the draft Report, not because it contained anything with which he disagreed, but because he did not think it would be as helpful in the future as he had hoped it might have been. In the first place the Commission's Report had not been as good as their Report on Grace—the subject had been too big and they had not had sufficient time to deal with it properly : it had only been published in May—too late for delegates to give it proper consideration. Secondly, he felt that they had just been trying to do too much in the time allowed : their discussions on the extremely difficult

[12] *Faith and Order. Edinburgh*, p. 121.
[13] Ibid., p. 118.
[14] Ibid., p. 224.
[15] Hugh Martin, *Edinburgh 1937*, pp. 70-1.
[16] *Faith and Order. Edinburgh*, p. 135.

question of the Ministry had only started at 4 p.m. on the last day. There should have been two distinct Sections, one to deal with the Ministry and another to deal with the Sacraments. He then proposed an amendment. He was anxious that something might be done to facilitate the approach of some of the Churches in the next few years. The Commission's Report had stated that the Orthodox Church and the Old Catholics, although insistent on the necessity of episcopal ordination, were not committed to the condemnation of the orders of other churches, while the Anglican Church at the Lambeth Conference had recognized the value of non-episcopal orders. All these Churches believed the historic episcopate to be the one basis of order on which a unified Church could be built. This did not involve any doctrinal teaching concerning the Ministry, and in such a united Church, episcopal, presbyteral and congregational elements would all be included. He would like this to appear in the Report as a suggested basis of union.[17]

When the Report came up for its second revision, however, his proposal had not been inserted. He was persistent and demanded to know why nothing had been done about it. 'On Friday I requested that a certain amendment might be made, i.e. the addition of two paragraphs from page 36 of the Report of Commission III. I asked for these paragraphs because they are the basis proposed for union in South India, and therefore have the support of many, for example the Bishop of Dornakal and Mr. Lucas. Those two paragraphs lay down two principles: the united Church would be based on the historic episcopate but other ministries are not to be excluded and there is to be no condemnation of any Churches who take part in it. I hope that these paragraphs may be inserted at the end of the Report as a practical hint for use in the immediate future.' [18] His plea was in vain, for when the third and final revision of the Report came up, his proposal had still not been included. He again persisted, but Archbishop Germanos did not help matters by claiming that his suggested amendment contained an error, for the Orthodox Church *was* committed to the condemnation of the orders of other Churches.[19] The discussion made it clear that the Conference was not happy about this particular point; so while the rest of the Report was accepted *nemine contradicente*, the section dealing with the Ministry was referred back to a small drafting committee composed of Professor Angus Dun, Professor C. H. Dodd, and Canon O. C. Quick.[20]

[17] Ibid., pp. 138–9.
[18] Ibid., p. 167.
[19] Ibid., p. 177.
[20] Ibid., pp. 175–9.

Headlam's proposal fared no better at their hands, and when they submitted their draft to the Conference on August 18, he again voiced his disapproval. No reason had been given why these paragraphs had not been included and he regretted it. The most fundamental difficulty which the Conference had to face was how to reconcile the authoritative ministry, the historical episcopate and apostolic succession with the orders and sacraments of those churches which did not possess them. To many people it was clear that a united Church was impossible without that historical ministry : yet its acceptance was hindered by the fact that it had been used to deny validity or spiritual efficacy to non-episcopal ministries. He imagined that the omission of these paragraphs was due partly to Orthodox objections ; but he could at least quote one authority in the Orthodox Church, Professor Arseniev, who was not party to them.[21] This statement immediately provoked a short argument between Archbishop Germanos and Professor Arseniev himself. The Archbishop was quite emphatic that the Professor's attitude was a purely private one and was not the opinion of the Orthodox Church as a whole ; whereupon the Professor respectfully but definitely disagreed with him : the Orthodox Church was not bound to say that there was no grace given through sacramental rites in other churches, and he could quote the Metropolitan Philaret of Moscow in his support.[22]

Headlam realized that it was too late for anything further to be done. Although he was convinced that the absence of these paragraphs weakened the Report, he did not oppose it ; and it was accepted by the Conference, *nemine contradicente*.[23] In fact, with the exception of this point, the Report was not one with which he was prepared to quibble, and the agreed findings of his Commission were included : while some response to Headlam's plea for freedom appeared in the section on the Eucharist : 'We all believe that Christ is truly present in the Eucharist, though as to how that presence is manifested and realized we may differ. Every precise definition of the presence is bound to be a limiting thing, and the attempt to formulate such definitions and to impose them on the Church has itself been the cause of disunity in the past. The important thing is that we should celebrate the Eucharist with the unfailing use of bread and wine, and of prayer, and of the words of institution, and with agreement as to its essential and spiritual meaning.' [24] On the Ministry and Sacraments Edinburgh revealed no spectacular advance on Lausanne.

[21] Ibid., p. 187.
[22] Ibid., p. 188.
[23] Ibid., p. 191.
[24] Ibid., p. 244.

III

Much more serious differences of opinion occurred, however, over the plan for a World Council of Christian Churches. The Continuation Committee had agreed in 1934 to co-operate with the Universal Council for Life and Work in reviewing the œcumenical movement as a whole, and this had resulted in the appointment of a joint Committee of Thirty-five to undertake the work.[25] This Committee had proposed the creation of a World Council functioning through a General Assembly meeting every five years, a Central Council meeting annually, and Commissions dealing with special interests and departments : the work of Faith and Order would be carried on by a special Commission.[26] The Life and Work Conference at Oxford had approved of this scheme, and it now remained for Edinburgh to consider the matter. Here it was referred to a large committee, containing representatives of all sections of opinion, which reported favourably at a special meeting on August 11.[27]

Headlam, who had not been a member of the Committee of Thirty-five, was opposed to the whole idea. It meant, too, that he was completely out of sympathy with Archbishop Temple, who was one of its champions. The Life and Work movement appeared to be too closely concerned with political matters and controversy and was in danger of identifying Christianity with Socialism. As it later became clear, his views on the political situation in Germany were misguided, but he felt that the absence of the German delegation from the Conference was largely, if not entirely, due to the interference of Life and Work in supporting the German Confessional Church as against the German State Church. He wrote to Professor Adams Brown, one of the American Presbyterian delegates, 'I look upon Socialism as ultimately disastrous to the development of the individual and only necessary because of the great congestion of population. . . . And I do not approve of Nazi methods, but after all seventy per cent at least of the German Church is irritated with the Confessionals and their theology is intolerable.' [28] It is not surprising, therefore, that when the Conference discussed the Report of Section Four on 'The Church's Unity in Life and Worship' on August 14, Headlam opposed the last paragraph which expressed approval of the creation of the World Council. 'I do not know how many there are who are opposed to it, but there is a definite body of members of the Conference who are

---

[25] Ibid., pp. 192–3.
[26] Ibid., pp. 273–4.
[27] Ibid., pp. 196–7.
[28] Headlam to Professor Adams Brown, August 25, 1937.

opposed to this idea, and many opposed to any definite connection with the Life and Work Movement. If such a Council were to exist, and if it passed resolutions on public affairs, it might do a very considerable amount of harm.' [29]

The statement of approval was modified in the revised draft Report —'If the Churches adopt the proposal to form a World Council of Churches which has been approved in principle by this Conference as well as by the World Conference held at Oxford, we think it should be so designed as to conserve the distinctive character and value of each of the movements represented in the two Conferences' [30] : but Headlam was not satisfied. He moved the addition of the words, 'Some members of the Conference desire to record their opposition to the formation of such a Council.' Temple, who was in the chair, suggested that this might be expressed in a more positive way, to the effect that the plan was approved by an overwhelming majority of the Conference : but Headlam was adamant. 'I want to be perfectly clear. If you do not allow my words to be added I shall move the rejection of the paragraph, and if the paragraph stands I shall refuse to assent to the Report, and by our standing orders it can only be adopted if accepted *nemine contradicente.*' He won his point, and his statement was included. [31]

Headlam was not only opposed to the plan ; he was also annoyed at the way in which it had been handled at the meeting on August 11. The hour was already late when Dr. Garvie, the chairman, had pointed out that since there were at least three more people who wished to speak, the meeting ought to be adjourned to another session. A motion of adjournment had been defeated, however, by 65 votes to 54. Then Principal William Robinson, of the Churches of Christ, had suddenly moved that the question be put, and the Conference had passed it by an overwhelming majority—112 votes to 19. [32] This closure of discussion and snap decision struck Headlam as a piece of 'rigging,' especially as the same sort of thing had happened at Oxford. When, therefore, he reported to the Archbishop of Canterbury, he complained of this as well as giving his reasons for opposition.

September 11, 1937.

'I am afraid I look upon the proposal (for a World Church Council) with extreme suspicion, and a good deal of bitterness has been created. I first heard about it from Bishop Perry, who was very angry at what

[29] *Faith and Order. Edinburgh,* pp. 151, 340.
[30] Ibid., p. 368.
[31] Ibid., pp. 184–6.
[32] Ibid., p. 204.

had happened at the Oxford Conference. He complained and many other people have complained to me, that they were summoned at 4.30 to discuss the proposal, and there was interpolated before it a motion, which again many people objected to, by the Bishop of Chichester about the German Church. The result of which was that the proposal for the World Council was carried without any proper debate. Exactly the same thing happened at Edinburgh. We were summoned at 8.30 to discuss the proposal, but before it came on there were interpolated a large number of purely formal resolutions which lasted till nearly 10. At 10 o'clock I had arranged to go, thinking that the debate was over, and I was not able to stay any longer, and the matter was closured after a very short debate. A good many people thought that this was by design. . . . I don't know anything about that, but, at any rate, great irritation was caused among the minority. When the matter came on again I had the greatest difficulty in getting the amendment inserted stating that some members of the Conference objected to the proposal. As far as I can make out, the whole of the delegation of the Episcopal Church of America are opposed to it, all the Orthodox with the exception of the Bishop of Thyateira, about half or rather more of the Anglican delegation, and a good many scattered people, whom I cannot identify, who talked to me about it. The reasons that we object to it are :

'1. That it associates us too closely with the Life and Work Movement, which has been continually involved in political matters and controversy, and is largely influenced by the passion for identifying Christianity with Socialism. There is no doubt that the Conference at Edinburgh has suffered a considerable amount by the Conference at Oxford.

'2. We think that such a Council, with which it is proposed to associate a sort of bureau at Geneva, may have very dangerous tendencies. The habit of passing resolutions about political matters seems to us very dangerous, and it will be even more futile and quite as provocative as the League of Nations.

'3. It seems to be part of a movement for substituting a Federation of the Churches in the place of a united Catholic Church, and may tend to produce a lower ideal.

'At any rate, I suppose as a punishment for our action, the Archbishop of Dublin, Bishop Palmer, Dr. Macdonald, Canon Douglas and I were all turned out of the Continuation Committee, which, as we were the people who had worked the hardest for the movement, we naturally resented. That has been remedied, but they have still kept out Dr. Gavin, who is quite the ablest of the American theologians. Throughout it seemed to some of us that the Conference was in danger of getting into the hands of the Student Christian Movement and of the American Protestant Churches, who, for the most part, seem to take no interest in theological questions at all. I think the representatives of the American Episcopal Church were very much disgruntled altogether, as the Conference had really emanated from them, and they found themselves with very little voice in anything.

'I have written to you very frankly because I think it is desirable that these reactions ought to be known to you. Of course, I am quite definitely putting forward my own view of things, and you might very likely hear different opinions from other people, but still I think this point of view ought to be put before you.'

The Archbishop referred the matter to Temple, who wrote to Headlam : although denying that there had been any suggestion of 'tactics,' he admitted that even he had been disappointed at the rather unexpected trend of events.

October 8, 1937.

'. . . I must urge that the word "tactics" is inappropriate as it suggests a deliberate desire to stifle full discussion. It is quite true that the reading of messages which was taken first on the evening of August 11 occupied far more time than had been anticipated, and the Arrangements Committee certainly did not contemplate the crowding of the other proposal into the second part of a single session. We had expected an adjournment of the debate. My own part in the proceeding consisted of urging that the time limit should not be applied to the first speakers in opposition, and to suggest to Dr. Garvie in the chair that he should recommend an adjournment. He did the latter, but a private member proposed the closure—not at all because he was eager to rush the thing through, as he was not deeply interested in it one way or the other. He thought it most unlikely that we should hear anything further to alter the opinions the delegates had already reached. This purely unofficial and quite unexpected motion was carried by a large majority, and then the question was put with the result stated. I was myself disappointed because I thought the way things had been done at Oxford gave some colour to the idea that this proposal was being officially pushed through, and I was most anxious to avoid that at Edinburgh. This aim was defeated by what was the clear opinion of the greater number of the delegates who were still present when the closure was moved. You will, of course, state your opposition at any time when you think fit, and will criticize as severely as you consider appropriate the actual course of events, but I hope you may feel able to avoid any phrase likely to suggest that you think there was a deliberate intention to burke discussion.'

IV

A much more encouraging feature of Headlam's report to the Archbishop was the résumé of his unofficial discussions with the Orthodox delegates. He had been asked to sound them on the possibility of further approaches betweeen the two Churches; and despite the official Orthodox statement to the Conference on August 16, emphasizing their united and conservative outlook,[33] he was able to reveal a much more flexible and promising state of affairs.

September 3, 1937.

'. . . First of all I would say that there was a good deal of dissension amongst the Orthodox at Edinburgh. The controversy being between the rigidly Orthodox and those with a more moderate and critical outlook. Some of the former wished I think to leave the Conference and have nothing to do with it. One or two of them were severely critical of things that I said, but others thanked me for what I had done, and apologized for the narrow Orthodoxy of some of their people. There is throughout the Orthodox Communion this same contrast between those who simply adhere to their inherited Orthodoxy and those who are trying to adjust it to the facts of the modern world.

'I had a long talk with Professor Alivisatos, who is by far the ablest and I think the most influential of the Professors (He was Chairman of the recent Conference of Orthodox Professors which was held in Athens), and he suggested to me that he thought it would be best that you should write to Archbishop Chrysostom of Athens, sending a copy of the Roumanian Agreement, and saying that we should wish to have the opinion of the Greek Church about it. . . . Alivisatos would talk the matter over with the Archbishop, and suggest that we should send a delegation to Athens. It is really most desirable that this should be done. I understand that the Poles, the Bulgarians, and the Patriarch of Antioch have all suggested that we should approach them, but the status and knowledge and position of the Greek Faculty of Theology is on such a far higher level, that it would be better that we should discuss all these questions with them rather than with those other Churches. . . . What I shall try and press upon Alivisatos is that we should try and avoid definitions, which have no authority and are

[33] Ibid., pp. 154–8.

often very crude, and should agree on accepting the theology and Church order of the Undivided Church. That would be a far better basis for any form of unity than an attempt at redefining. Professor Alivisatos, I know, like Professor Arseniev, recognizes that definitions are contrary to the spirit of the Orthodox Church.'

These discussions ultimately bore fruit in the Anglican delegation to the Balkan countries in 1940; though unofficial they were one of the most important pieces of work which Headlam did at Edinburgh. His main contribution to the Conference itself was his work on the two preparatory Commissions : but he was no longer the dominating figure that he had been at Lausanne. He could not reconcile himself to the enthusiasm shown for the World Council and, it would not be far wrong to say that his heart was no longer in the Movement. When the Continuation Committee met at Clarens in the following summer, he again expressed his doubts—the World Council would mean the end of Faith and Order as they knew it. He was, however, keenly interested in the proposal to appoint a Commission to consider the doctrine of the Church, although he himself had no desire to head such a Commission. It was at his suggestion that the distinguished Methodist scholar, Dr. Newton Flew, was appointed chairman. At the end of the meeting he said, 'I think we may congratulate ourselves on a very admirable discussion; I think it is the best we have ever listened to in our Movement.' [34] On this happy note, Headlam's work with Faith and Order ended. He did not go to the Continuation Committee in 1939; he wrote, 'I think that I shall shirk the Faith and Order meeting at Clarens this summer. I shall be giving up the whole thing shortly, and it does not seem to me to be really worth while.' [35] His intention was made effective by the outbreak of war a few months later.

The last task which Headlam undertook in connection with Faith and Order was to act as chairman of a committee appointed by the Archbishops of Canterbury and York to prepare a Report on the Edinburgh Conference for the proposed Lambeth Conference of 1940. This Report, which was published in 1939, noted some interesting advances on Lausanne. It was becoming increasingly apparent that many difficulties hitherto regarded as insuperable were no longer found to be so : the remarkable Report on Grace bore witness to this. Theological differences now cut across confessional differences, and the differences between Fundamentalists and Modernists could be found in most religious bodies. There had also been a great change

[34] *Faith and Order Pamphlets*, no. 91, pp. 35–7, 50.
[35] Headlam to Miss P. L. Wingfield, June 4, 1939.

in the general attitude towards the sacraments: great differences in doctrine still existed, but a new atmosphere was apparent—a stronger interest in the sacramental side of religion among Protestants, and less rigidity in teaching.[36] Then there was the attitude towards Apostolic Succession: this subject had not been dealt with at Lausanne, but at Edinburgh, although different churches meant different things by it, the conception of continuity with the Apostles was gaining ground and was being treasured by all Churches.[37] The Report on the Communion of Saints indicated another interesting advance: in the past, although this subject had meant much to some churches, to others it had meant little or nothing. The very presence of the Report meant the breaking of new ground, and the opening of new avenues of thought requiring discussion.[38]

The most disappointing result of the Conference was the Report on the Ministry and Sacraments. The trouble had really begun with the Commission, of which Headlam had been chairman: although their Report had made a considerable advance towards unity and mutual understanding, it had been spoiled by the undue complexity of the subject and by the lack of time for study. All this was reflected in the Conference itself: the subject was too wide for a single Section and the time allowed too short.[39] One particularly unfortunate feature was the increasing desire for some form of federation, as distinct from union, and a corresponding reluctance to accept episcopacy.[40] The root of such troubles lay in the different conceptions of the Church which prevailed. Indeed, it was not too much to say that there was not a single Section which has not felt itself hampered at every turn by the fact that this essential problem of the Church had not received thorough preliminary consideration. The Edinburgh programme had, in fact, been unbalanced, and, if the right inference was now drawn by the Continuation Committee, and the problem of the Church was given a primary place, the work of the Faith and Order Movement might still be brought back into the right line.[41]

As we have seen, the Continuation Committee did draw the right inference, and Headlam himself had hinted at the same point in his article on the Conference in *The Church Quarterly Review*.[42] Perhaps without being fully conscious of it, he seems to have realized that the

---

[36] *Report of the Archbishops' Committee on the Edinburgh Conference of Faith and Order*, 1939, p. 32.
[37] Ibid., p. 19.
[38] Ibid., p. 14.
[39] Ibid., pp. 6–7, 18.
[40] Ibid., pp. 20–2, 32.
[41] Ibid., pp. 15, 32.
[42] 'Faith and Order 1937,' *C.Q.R.*, vol. 123, pp. 305–21.

doctrine of the Church was not quite so simple and straightforward as he had imagined twenty years before.

This Report made no reference to the proposed World Council of Churches, as it was agreed to deal with it separately : but Headlam remained firmly opposed to it to the end. He had already opposed Archbishop Temple's motion in the Church Assembly in February 1938 to appoint representatives to attend a provisional Conference in May 1939 to consider a draft constitution for the World Council,[43] and he again opposed him in June 1940 when he asked the Assembly to approve its establishment and to accept the invitation to be represented. On this occasion both Temple and Headlam circulated Memoranda before the debate setting out their respective points of view, and it was typical of them that they assisted one another in their preparation with the utmost friendliness. Headlam reiterated his view that the Council would substitute a form of federation for real reunion : admittedly it was easier of attainment, but it constituted an acquiescence in a lower ideal and if anything would tend to stereotype disunion. The Federal Council of the Free Churches in England was a shining example of this. Furthermore, the Federal Council showed a propensity for passing resolutions with a political or semi-political flavour, and he was afraid the World Council would do the same : Dr. J. R. Stevenson, who had been chairman of the Edinburgh Committee which had studied the recommendations of the Committee of Thirty-five, had in fact stated that he wanted a body which would condemn the totalitarian states. He was also very much afraid that the Council would also divide Christendom into two camps—Roman and non-Roman : had not Dr. Temple himself said, 'If the new organization were to win the confidence of the Churches, it would do something to provide a voice for non-Roman Christendom'? Two such camps would do great dis-service to the cause of Christian unity.

In his speech before the Assembly Temple expressed sorrow that Headlam, after all his untiring labours in the Faith and Order movement, should now be compelled to disagree. The objections he raised against the World Council could hardly be justified, however. It was not true that federation would replace reunion : the constitution of the Council did not point to a federal solution, and it would not destroy the freedom of individual churches. Nor would it divide Christendom into two camps : the Roman Church had in fact been invited to join, but had refused most courteously.[44] Finally, the

---

[43] *Proceedings of the Church Assembly*, vol. 19, pp. 197–205.
[44] The Vatican had also assured Temple in the previous year of the possibilities of unofficial consultation with Roman Catholic theologians and scholars. (F. A. Iremonger, *William Temple*, 1948, p. 412.)

danger of the Council issuing pronouncements was remote : in any case its main topics would be evangelistic.[45]

Headlam was completely unconvinced by the Archbishop's assurances. He stuck to his objections and told the Assembly of his suspicion that the whole scheme possessed what he called a somewhat 'anæmic Socialism.' It was also an unfortunate moment to deal with such a motion : the Council could not possibly function effectively until after the War, and they had no idea as to what conditions would be like then.[46] Lord Hugh Cecil suggested that in view of the authorities ranged for and against the proposal, the debate should be adjourned until after the War : but both he and Headlam failed to win the support of the Assembly. For better or for worse, the Church of England committed itself to membership of and support for the World Council.[47]

Headlam was by no means alone in his fears, and it must be admitted that indications were not entirely lacking at the time to justify them. Events since then, however, and particularly the great Conferences at Amsterdam in 1948 and Evanstoun in 1954 have shown that he was perhaps too pessimistic. Was this not perhaps due in some measure to his imperfect conception of what the Church really was? As Dr. W. A. Visser 't Hooft remarked nearly fifteen years later, the problem of 'the Church being the Church' could not be met by a demonstration of social activity or by the presentation of the historic confessions and creeds. It cut deeper than either ; and it transcended the problems on which both Life and Work and Faith and Order had mainly concentrated hitherto.[48] Faith and Order was incapable of solving such a problem by itself ; and this was what Headlam did not fully see.

---

[45] *Church Assembly Proceedings*, vol. 21, pp. 21–3.
[46] Ibid., vol. 21, p. 35.
[47] Ibid., vol. 21, pp. 38–9, 43.
[48] Rouse and Neill, *Ecumenical Movement*, p. 701.

CHAPTER TWENTY

The Council on Foreign Relations

I

THE years following the 1914–18 War saw a marked and steady growth of the desire for friendship and intercourse between Christian bodies throughout the world. The work of promoting closer relationships was, however, for the most part haphazard and unofficial. In the case of the Church of England, with the exception of the Archbishops' Eastern Churches Committee, it was undertaken by such voluntary bodies as the Society of S. Willibrord, the Jerusalem and the East Mission, the Anglo-Continental Society and the Anglican and Foreign Church Society. Praiseworthy though their efforts were, they were inevitably limited in scope and appeal; and the feeling developed among interested Churchmen that relations with foreign Churches should be the concern of the whole Church and not merely of certain societies within it. Headlam first raised the point at the private Bishops' Meetings : then after some discussion it was brought to the attention of the Church Assembly. In November 1925 the Dean of Canterbury (Dr. G. K. A. Bell) moved the appointment of a 'Commission on Relations with Foreign Churches' to develop the interest of members of the Church of England in the life and work of foreign Churches and to promote mutual knowledge.[1] A small committee with Headlam as chairman was appointed to consider the matter,[2] and it presented a unanimous report in the following November recommending the appointment of such a Commission, which should operate within well-defined limits.[3] Since the Archbishop of Canterbury was absent from the Assembly with a chill and elucidation was needed on a number of points, a decision was postponed until the next session. Meanwhile Headlam sent him an interesting report

[1] *Church Assembly Proceedings,* vol. 6, pp. 543–4.
[2] Headlam (Chairman); the Bishop of Winchester (Dr. F. T. Woods); the Dean of Canterbury; Athelstan Riley; Arnold Mitchell.
[3] *Church Assembly Proceedings,* vol. 7, pp. 418–32; *Report Church Assembly 210* (1926), pp. 1–4.

on the situation, revealing that at this juncture, at least, he did not contemplate taking the lead himself.

November 23, 1926.

'My Lord Archbishop,

'. . . It seemed to me, as a result of the discussion which was a very good one, that the great body of the Assembly was very much interested in the proposal and would welcome it, but that it was more important than I had thought it, and that on certain points we must guard the action of such a Council very carefully. What we must avoid above all things is that it should be thought that we have political objects in view, or that we are going to take any side in religious controversy. I am equally opposed to any idea that we should put ourselves at the head of the Protestant Churches of the Continent, or that we should attach ourselves to the Catholic Churches of the Continent. What we want is to obtain knowledge and information and to cultivate Christian relations. Personally I detest much of the policy of the Church of Rome, which I think absolutely deplorable, but I am sure that the best way of meeting it is so far as possible to treat the Roman Church as we should like them to treat us. . . .

'May I make one suggestion? It has been proposed that the Chairman of the Council should be the Archbishop of Canterbury acting, of course, through a Vice-Chairman, and I should very much like to suggest that the Vice-Chairman should be the present Dean of Canterbury. If such an arrangement were made it would put the Council completely in touch with your Grace and enable it to fulfil the functions that I have suggested. Moreover, if the present Dean of Canterbury were the Vice-Chairman, we should have someone at the head who had both the leisure and the ability to manage the Council properly. When I first brought the matter forward at the Bishops' Meeting, I stated that I thought it would be most advisable, at any rate to begin with, that the Chairman should not be a bishop. . . .'

Dr. Davidson, in expressing his views to the Assembly in February 1927, counselled caution. He thought the Council should be regarded as experimental: in the first instance it might be appointed for a period of three years, which would bring them to the Lambeth Conference of 1930; the whole question of Church relations would then certainly have to be considered. It might also be dangerous to require such a Council, involved perhaps in private and delicate negotiations, to report to the Assembly and therefore to the public every year: in this matter there should be some elasticity. His advice was taken, and the Assembly unanimously requested the Archbishops to appoint a

Council for three years, which should issue such reports as it might from time to time considerable desirable.[4]

A chain of circumstances—some unforeseen—then delayed further action for over four years. First the Prayer Book controversy occupied every one's attention : this was followed by Archbishop Davidson's resignation in November 1928. His successor, Dr. Lang, was ill for the first part of 1929, after which it was time to prepare for the Lambeth Conference of 1930. He was again ill in the early part of 1931 and it was not until the late autumn that he asked Headlam to reopen the question in the Church Assembly.[5] Headlam did so on February 5, 1932, whereupon the Assembly asked the Archbishops to proceed with the appointment of the Council.[6]

In the following months Headlam was actively engaged in its formation and in drawing up its terms of reference ; for the Archbishop, regarding it as very much his own child, was content to leave the initiative with him. By the end of the year all necessary preliminaries were complete. There was now no question that Headlam, with the triumphs of Lausanne, Lambeth, Bonn and the Anglo-Orthodox Conference behind him, should be chairman. The Revd. J. A. Douglas, with whom he had already established an effective working partnership in œcumenical affairs was appointed honorary general secretary, and the Revds. C. B. Moss and Philip Usher honorary assistant secretaries. Over forty nominees had agreed to serve. At the first meeting on February 2, 1933, the Archbishop defined their terms of reference. They were to be engaged on 'the survey and promotion of the relations of the Church of England with Foreign Churches' subject to certain limitations : other Churches in the British Isles, other provinces of the Anglican Communion, and missionary dioceses in his direct care were not their concern ; nor could they take his place by conducting negotiations on their own initiative. He then suggested the appointment of four sub-committees to deal respectively with the affairs of the Roman Catholic Church, the Orthodox Church,[7] the lesser Eastern Churches, and the Continental Churches. To these were added a little later a further sub-committee

---

[4] *Church Assembly Proceedings,* vol. 8, pp. 49–52.

[5] Cosmo Cantuar to Headlam, November 30, 1931. In the same letter the Archbishop told Headlam that in view of all his other œcumenical activities, particularly the conferences with the Orthodox and Old Catholic Churches, he would not be expected to take a leading part in the renewed discussions with the Free Churches. While, therefore, Headlam continued to be a member of the Anglican-Free Church discussions and attended the meetings as often as he could, he was no longer a member of the sub-committee which did so much of the spade work.

[6] *Church Assembly Proceedings,* vol. 13, pp. 168–86.

[7] This took over the work of the Archbishop's Eastern Churches Committee.

to arrange the interchange of students. Without further delay the Council then settled down to work.[8]

Its activities obviously covered a vast field—far wider than the reports which Headlam presented periodically to the Assembly sometimes indicated. The Report of May 1934 did, however, give an interesting picture of its early activities. It began by establishing regular contacts with other Churches through recognized correspondents—in some cases Anglican chaplains serving abroad, in others members of foreign Churches themselves. Largely on the basis of their reports the Council was able to publish a number of Surveys, the first two of which appeared in May 1934—one on the affairs of the Orthodox Church and another on the Continental Churches with special reference to Germany. The interchange of students also began with the acceptance of an offer from the Œcumenical Patriarch to receive an Anglican student at the Theological College of Halki. In return the Council received one of the Patriarch's deacons, who went to S. Stephen's House, Oxford. Shortly afterwards, at the request of the Catholics of the South Indian Syrian-Orthodox Church two priests were accepted for one year, one going to King's College, London, and the other to Mirfield. The Council also decided to experiment with a magazine in French to diffuse information on the Continent about Anglican thought and activity and to further the cause of reunion. The first number appeared in April 1934 under the title *Œcumenica—a Review of theological synthesis*, not as an official organ of the Council but published with its support and consent. Finally the Report drew attention to the Assyrian Church and its need of help, and to the Russian Orthodox Academy in Paris, where Orthodox students were trained. A Russian choir had toured the English cathedrals under the Council's auspices, not only to raise funds for the Academy but also to introduce Russian Church music to people in England.[9]

With the passage of time the Council's activities developed and extended. In the scheme for the interchange of students, for example, almost all the English theological colleges expressed their willingness to accept foreign students either free of charge or on very nominal terms, and the Council received more requests than it could cope with. On the other side a number of English students were able to study abroad as guests of some of the Continental and Orthodox Churches. In 1938 the scheme was extended to include foreign clergy who wished to gain some insight into English parochial life.[10] A

[8] *Report Church Assembly 426* (1933), pp. 2–5.
[9] *Report Church Assembly 454* (1934), pp. 1–3.
[10] *Report Church Assembly 611* (1938), pp. 1–10.

further venture was the creation of a Periodicals Bureau for the dispatch of theological and general literature abroad. This work was entirely voluntary and by 1938 current issues of some forty-six periodicals were being sent to over thirty foreign Churches.[11]

Between 1933 and the outbreak of war in 1939 the Council also published seven valuable Surveys—five on the affairs of the Continental Churches and two on the affairs of the Orthodox Church. In the former the ecclesiastical situation in Germany was given pride of place, and of this more will be said subsequently : but reports of activities in the Old Catholic Churches, Holland, the Northern Churches, France and Czecho-slovakia were also described. The article on Czecho-slovakia in the Second Survey appeared under Headlam's signature and was the result of a visit which he paid to that country in May 1935.[12] The creation of the Republic had created serious problems for communities who were predominantly Roman Catholic : it had resulted, for example, in the secession of nearly two million people from the Roman Church between 1919 and 1930 and also in the creation of a new Czecho-Slovak National Church. The situation had aroused Headlam's interest and in particular he wanted to see exactly what the new National Church, with its nucleus of seceded Romans, was really like. He therefore spent two weeks in May 1935 in visiting the headquarters of the different Churches in Prague and Bratislava and in discussing the situation with their leaders. He found every one—including the Roman Catholics— extremely co-operative and friendly. It is interesting to note that he found the theological position of the National Church to be one of extreme Modernism and almost Unitarian. He made the interesting comment on this, 'They were most anxious to be friendly and described themselves as real Christians and anxious to be considered Christians. I think the right way to treat such people is to accept them for what they want to be. Their present position is quite illogical. They must ultimately cease to be Christian, or become more really Christian, and if we were to treat them as simple Unitarians, which we might, they would soon become so.'[13] This charitable point of view was one which he invariably adopted in promoting friendly relations with other Churches.

The two Surveys of Orthodox Church affairs were equally valuable. The first, published in 1934, gave a brief description in a dozen pages of recent events in the various individual Orthodox Churches. The

[11] Ibid.
[12] *Second Survey on the Affairs of the Continental Churches*, 1935, pp. 45–52.
[13] Headlam to Miss P. L. Wingfield, May 16, 1935.

second, published in 1937, was a much longer document. After an Introduction describing the constitution of the Orthodox Church, it gave an account of the Conference of Orthodox Theological Professors at Athens in 1936—the first of its kind for two hundred and fifty years, another short account by Headlam of the proposed Jugoslav Concordat with the Vatican, and finally a long article on the recent history of the Russian Patriarchate—all providing information not easily obtainable elsewhere.

Inevitably with Headlam and Douglas playing a leading part in the work of the Council as well as in the reunion conferences of the thirties, it was not always easy to define precisely where 'Council' work ended and 'reunion' work began. The Balkan tour of 1940 was a case in point: but Headlam was always careful not to assume responsibilities which rightfully belonged to the Archbishop. So, for example, when presenting the tenth Report to the Church Assembly in June 1939 he pointed out that while it referred to the negotiations with Latvia and Estonia, it should not be thought that the Council had been interfering in reunion work : the responsibility for the negotiations had been in other hands; the Council was merely recording what had happened in those two countries, just as it recorded ecclesiastical events in other countries.[14] But with the help of the Council's machinery Headlam displayed an interest in ecclesiastical affairs which was literally world-wide. Any worthy cause which would promote the well-being of any part of the Church Universal was sure to receive his attention and support. He was quite prepared to take time and trouble over any Church, no matter how small or how remote. He realized far more clearly than most people how much some of these weaker brethren valued Anglican help and sympathy. So, for example, when he tried to encourage necessary reforms in the Coptic Church and to restore friendly relations between it and the Egyptian Government in 1935, Canon Ibrahim Luka wrote, 'We, the Copts, are longing for life and we hope to find in the men of the English Church a great help for attaining this life.' Or again, a little later, when he interested himself in the internal differences of the South Indian Syrian-Orthodox Church—to the extent of offering to go to India to discuss matters, the Revd. K. M. Simon wrote, 'Whether peace is established or not, your name will go down to posterity in the history of the Syrian Church, as a great soul who once worked for it sincerely.' There was also his continuous pleading of the cause of the Assyrian Christians in Iraq, who, despite supporting the Allies with great bravery and at considerable cost in both World Wars, were left year after year without a permanent home to live in hostile

14 *Church Assembly Proceedings,* vol. 20, p. 342.

L

Moslem surroundings—a discreditable situation for which he did not
hesitate to lay much of the blame at the feet of the British Government.[15] Or again, there was the case of the tiny Lutheran Church
in Iceland, which found itself in a position of isolation when the
island declared itself independent of Denmark in 1944. Despite his
eighty years, Headlam would have gladly travelled there to see what
help he could give them had not his doctor firmly refused to let
him go.

All this work frequently brought him into contact with members
of governments at home and abroad, and particularly with members
of the British Foreign Office and Colonial Office, some of whom—
men like Sir John Simon, the third Viscount Halifax and Leo Amery
—had been his contemporaries at Oxford or Fellows of All Souls. The
surprising thing is that although he never hesitated to make repre-
sentations to them or even to the Prime Minister himself on behalf
of individuals or communities, he never played an active part in the
life of the House of Lords. This may have been partly due to a strong
desire not to convey the impression that the Church was meddling in
politics, for this was something he felt that the Church should not
do : but he himself confessed to Hensley Henson shortly before he
died that his silence in the Upper House was due to a lack of courage
—a weakness which no one would ever have dreamt of attributing to
him. 'One of the failures in my episcopate is that I had not the
courage to use my position (in the House of Lords). I had a great deal
that I might have said there, which in my opinion would have been
useful as a contribution to the national thought.' [16]

Be that as it may, Headlam's work for the whole state of Christ's
Church militant here in earth through the medium of the Council on
Foreign Relations was one of the great achievements of his life and
one for which, perhaps, he received less credit at home than he did
abroad.

II

Headlam's attitude towards the religious struggles in Nazi Germany
was by far the most controversial element of his work with the Council. Subsequent events proved his estimate to have been mistaken :
but it must be remembered that throughout he was dominated by
two fundamental ideas—a firm conviction that a united national

[15] Cf. *Report Church Assembly 454* (1934), p. 2 ; *Report Church Assembly
538* (1936), p. 1 ; *Church Assembly Proceedings,* vol. 25, p. 143.
[16] E. F. Braley (editor), *Letters of Herbert Hensley Henson,* p. 194.

Church was a highly desirable institution for any country, and a fear of Russian Communism as the real enemy to be faced. There was undeniably a great deal to be said for both of them, but he erred in refusing to see that the Church in Germany was not an independent Church and in failing to take the dangers of National Socialism sufficiently seriously.

Hitler came into power in January 1933, and very soon afterwards, as part of his plan for the unity of all German people, called for the creation of a single Protestant Church. It was a call which the numerous Churches of the Reich were willing to support, although they had no intention of throwing away their independence in the process. Their representatives, in consultation with Hitler's representative, Dr. Ludwig Müller, agreed on the outlines of a new constitution, embodying a system of titular bishops under a Reichsbischof.[17] They then chose Dr. Friedrich von Bodelschwingh as the first holder of this new office on May 27. This by no means satisfied Dr. Müller, who himself aspired to the office, or the extreme Nazi group who wished to bring the Church into complete subservience to the State. They successfully persuaded Hitler that the Church was rent by a conflict, which would only be resolved if he intervened and assumed control. He thereupon appointed Müller as his personal representative in charge of Church affairs and laid down the constitution of the new united Evangelical Church, giving in fact dictatorial powers to the Reichsbischof, although in theory he was to be advised by a spiritual cabinet and assisted by an elected National Synod.

Two parties contested the election for this National Synod—the Gospel and Church or Confessional Church party standing for religious freedom, and the German Christian party desiring to assimilate the Church with the Nazi movement. It was a most unfair and unequal election. The Gospel and Church party were forbidden to hold meetings or to use the press and radio; thousands of non-Church people enrolled as German Christians simply to vote; and on July 22 on the eve of the election Hitler broadcast a speech in which, although not giving a direct order, he gave the broadest of hints that every one was expected to vote for the German Christians.

This, briefly, was the situation about which Headlam felt the need for first-hand information. At the beginning of July, before the election campaign had begun, he asked the Dean of Chichester, the Very Revd. A. S. Duncan-Jones, to fly to Berlin on a fact-finding mission. During his brief visit the Dean met Hitler as well as Müller

[17] Not a bishop in the Anglican sense, but in the sense of a general superintendent.

and other Church leaders, and on his return produced a very tendentious report, expressing views which he subsequently regretted.[18] It conveyed an impression which was guaranteed to convince Headlam that all was well and that reports of disturbances should not be taken too seriously. Many people who believed in the independence of the Church also firmly supported Hitler, who had himself stated that he had no wish to interfere in the internal working of the Church. The only alternative was Communism. Christ, in fact, was often regarded as the leader in a battle against Communism rather than as a Saviour from sin. Many people, too, were impressed by what Hitler had done for Germany : they felt that God had worked a miracle. Admittedly there were some people undergoing persecution and oppression, but the Dean felt that any public expression of sympathy with them from England would be disastrous. They should be assured of our prayers and sympathy, but it should be done through personal and private channels. These impressions were supported by Dr. A. J. Macdonald,[19] who also visited Germany a few weeks later. Support for Hitler was widely-spread and deeply-rooted ; and criticism would be resented, not by a single party but by a majority of the German people.

Meanwhile the situation became increasingly critical. The German Christians won a resounding victory in the elections; Müller was appointed Reichsbischof ; anti-Jewish restrictions began to bear hardly on many ; and it was feared that the Confessional Church clergy were almost certain to be dismissed or retired. The British Chaplain in Berlin, the Revd. R. H. Cragg, suggested to Headlam that if the German Church authorities realized that the eyes of the rest of Christendom were on them, they might well modify their actions : a letter from the Council wishing them Godspeed in their efforts to bring the Church to the people, and expressing the hope that the rumours of repressive measures were not true might therefore do some good.[20] Headlam agreed; and on September 27 he wrote to Müller congratulating him on 'the formation of a united German Church, free from State control,' and asking him at the same time for some assurance on the sinister and untrue rumours, which, if not repudiated, would damage the reputation of the German people and impair good Church relations.[21] The Archbishop of Canterbury considered the letter far from wise and certainly not strong enough. Freedom from State control, instead of being assured for the German Church, was something about which many people had serious mis-

---

[18] The substance of the report appeared in a letter which he wrote to The Times on July 6, 1933. Cf. S. C. Carpenter, *Duncan-Jones of Chichester* (1956), pp. 85–6.

[19] The Revd. A. J. Macdonald, Rector of S. Dunstan-in-the-West, a member of the Council, and regarded as an authority on German affairs.

[20] The Revd. R. H. Cragg to Headlam, September 17, 1933.

[21] Headlam to Reichsbischof Müller, September 27, 1933.

givings : while some sinister rumours, far from being untrue, were in fact matters of common knowledge.[22]

Headlam felt, however, that the Archbishop was being less than fair. Confirmation of his own point of view came shortly afterwards from an interview with Dr. Hossenfelder, the new Bishop of Branden-burg and a leader of the German Christians, who was visiting Eng-land. He assured Headlam that they were extremely anxious to be on good terms with the Church of England, that they had been very unfairly judged, and that the reports of events in Germany were very one-sided.[23] Without delay Headlam wrote a letter to *The Times* deploring the censorious tone adopted by the rest of Europe towards Germany and commending her courage in facing up bravely to diffi-culties and in restoring order from chaos. This letter, which appeared in *The Times* on October 24, was welcomed by the supporters of National Socialism and was reproduced in many German newspapers : on the other hand it brought him many letters of criticism and abuse. He was accused of being a superficial observer who was deceived by appearances, and of refusing to see things—concentration camps, atrocities and the like—which spoke for themselves. Truth to tell, Headlam was not sure of his ground. He was, of course, absolutely right when he said that the censorious attitude would stir up the worst elements in the German character : but he could not really make up his mind whether in fact Germany merited censure or not. On the very day that his letter appeared in *The Times* he wrote to Mr. Cragg for information. 'We get all sorts of information in this country which is very detrimental to Germany and the German Christians, and *we really don't know what is true.*' Mr. Cragg promised to do what he could but pointed out the difficulties.

'It would be a simple task to pick out the good that has resulted from the new movement . . . and to draw a discreet veil over everything else. . . . It is really information on what is not published in the press here that is valuable. . . . I quite agree with what you wrote in *The Times* which incidentally gave much satisfaction here, but I do feel that unless the other side of the question is also known to those in authority at home they have not a fair view of the situation. It is all very well for the Germans to complain that they are wrongly represented in the foreign press, but one knows that their own press gives a very false and entirely one-sided view. In the main the programme of the New Church movement is excellent and needs little criticism. The idea of bringing the Church into closer touch with

[22] Cosmo Cantuar to Headlam, October 11, 1933.
[23] Headlam to Miss P. L. Wingfield, October 22, 1933.

the people and instilling life and energy into the methods of work are after all those of our own National Mission. It is the method that is at fault. A movement that can dispense with the help and guidance of men like Deissmann, Dibelius and scores of others in Church and University life and replace them with untried and untrained men opens itself to criticism. Officially pronouncement after pronouncement has been made to the effect that no one shall be interfered with on account of his beliefs, but the fact remains that there are many instances where people have been removed and many others where they have been and are being interfered with. This, it is true, is not always from or by the Church itself, but by the local political group who take steps to make it impossible or difficult for clergy who are not of the party to continue in office. . . . There is a considerable and very justifiable anxiety as to what the future may have in store and by what methods the party may seek to control the Church.'

Support for these remarks came in Müller's reply to Headlam's letter of September 27. The first part was effusive—full of thanks for the good wishes and of pious hopes for friendly relationships : but on 'the sinister and untrue rumours' Müller was evasive and non-committal. Reorganization inevitably involved personal changes, but he suggested that instead of dismissals, the departures should be regarded as voluntary : he referred to 'the ecclesiastical leaders who *have given up* their former office in connection with the present reorganization of the Church.' On the question of repressive measures against Christians of Jewish origin, he merely stated that they 'absolutely remain our brethren in Christ' : but he did not deny their persecution. He also admitted that 'some regional churches, above all the Old Prussian Churches, had issued special ecclesiastical statutes concerning the clergymen of non-Aryan descent' : and he went on rather significantly, 'The German Evangelical Church cannot fully exercise its service for the people to-day, to which service it was called upon by God, *if it would ignore the race problem.*'[24]

By the spring of 1934 Headlam was toying with the idea of going to Berlin to see if he could help resolve these differences. He sounded a number of people—Archbishop Lang, Archbishop Temple, Duncan-Jones—but they all were unenthusiastic, and he gave up the idea. A few months later, however, he was invited to Berlin as a guest of the Nazis. It was evident that they regarded him as a useful ally—a supporter from the Anglican episcopal bench would be a distinct feather in their cap and of untold value for propaganda purposes. Dr. A. Rosenberg, the Commissioner for the Supervision, Instruction

[24] Reichsbischof Müller to Headlam, November 30, 1933.

and Education of the National Socialist Movement, pressed him to come. But Headlam, after seeking the advice of Mr. Cragg and the British Ambassador in Berlin, refused, telling him that it would be quite useless for him to come to Berlin while the Church was being treated as it was. Rosenberg acknowledged Headlam's refusal with every courtesy—it was quite evident that he was taking pains to create a good impression and cultivate his friendship. The two men corresponded on a number of occasions during the next year, and Rosenberg produced all the well worn arguments—the Party desired a united German Evangelical Church; opposition came from those who feared a diminution of their clerical and personal authority; the Party had no desire to be involved in ecclesiastical disputes; the Third Reich was a great barrier against Communism; the foreign press misrepresented them; the Roman Catholic Church had allied itself with Communism in opposition. But Headlam did not mince his words in reply.

'Let me say that there has been a great desire on the part of many Englishmen to be on terms of friendship with Germany, and this is especially true of the religious world. . . . But this has been very much disturbed by the treatment of the German Church, and the accounts that have come to us about the confinement of clergy in concentration camps and of other forms of violence. . . . I am sure that for every one's sake a change of policy and action would be wise. . . .

'Most of the recent troubles have arisen through the autocratic action of Reichsbischof Müller. . . . Almost all the divisions among Christians have arisen mainly through the interference of the secular power in religious matters. . . .

'News has come to us that a new policy of censorship has been introduced, and that religious periodicals, and especially those of the Confessional Church, will be subjected to the control of a State censor. Will you allow me to say that it is difficult to conceive a more foolish policy at the present moment? . . .

'We think that nothing can excuse the anti-Semitism of Streicher and his paper. Moreover we believe that the whole Aryan theory is entirely unscientific and baseless. . . . The policy by which clergymen, for example, of some Jewish descent, are turned out of their livings, seems to us equally stupid and cruel. . . .

'I am afraid all these things that I have mentioned have had a most unfortunate effect on public opinion in England.' [24a]

By October 1935 it had become apparent that the struggle between Müller's Church Department and the Confessional Church, as it was

[24a] Headlam to Dr. A. Rosenberg, February 25, 1935.

now called, was incapable of internal resolution. Hitler himself therefore intervened. The Reichsminister for Church Affairs, Herr Kerrl was appointed with full powers to clear up the situation. On October 3 he announced the creation of a Church Committee under Dr. Zöllner, the General Superintendent of the Protestant Church in Westphalia, and a deeply respected man. This Committee appealed to the German people to be loyal to the State and announced that its purpose was to settle the dispute and prepare the way for a self-governing Church. Some people, particularly in the Confessional Church, viewed this development with caution and even accused Dr. Zöllner of truckling with the State, but many regarded it as a sincere and honest attempt at conciliation. Headlam was inclined to agree.

'The Germans are most anxious to get the support of this country, and we really can do a great deal for German Christians, as the Government wish to stand well with us. They have now put an end to all the rules and regulations and are making a new start which we hope will be more intelligent. . . . They have issued an Appeal in which they speak of self-government being given to the Church soon. . . . They have had to put in one paragraph about "national race and soil," but that was unavoidable in Germany at the present time. We hope very much that this will mean that the days of persecution will come to an end and that the German Church will be allowed to work out its own salvation.' [25]

Unfortunately this hope was soon shattered. The new policy was unacceptable to some members of the Party and to the German Christians. They brought influence to bear on Kerrl, who began violent and coercive measures. Headlam considered this to be evidence that behind Hitler were forces which he was unable to control.

By the beginning of 1937 Dr. Zöllner found it impossible to continue. Promises made to him were not kept, his work was hindered, and access to Hitler was denied him : finally he himself fell under suspicion and his house was raided by the police. He and his whole Committee therefore resigned on February 7. Headlam did not deny the difficulties, but he refused to regard Hitler himself as in any way responsible for them : nor did he feel that the Confessional Church was wise in its militant opposition to State policy. He drew up a note on the situation in March 1937.

'1. I do not believe that Hitler is simply playing tricks to try and destroy the German Church. I think that he would very much like

[25] Headlam to Miss P. L. Wingfield, October 28, 1935.

to have a united Church and he expects all people to accept the National Socialist policy. But I do not believe that his policy is simply to destroy the Church.

'2. Even if it were, it is not wise always to treat a person in Hitler's position as if he were a criminal. It does not seem to me diplomatically wise. It is much better to ascribe to him good intentions. His actions on several occasions have seemed to suggest it.

'3. It has seemed to me that there was an underground conflict between Hitler, who after all in the position in which he now is, must look at things from a wider point of view than the extreme Nazis and the extreme Nazis themselves.

'4. I am sure that it is wiser for the Confessional Church to join with all the other Orthodox Lutherans and not to stand out. I think that the Church as a whole may be quite able to make reasonable terms; but if the Confessional Church stand out they will be playing into the hands of the people who are trying to induce Hitler to take extreme steps. That has seemed to me the weakness of their policy throughout. As long as their congregations remain intact, if they found at any time the new conditions were being used to the detriment of Christianity, they could go back to their old policy of opposition.'

This point of view was supported by Dr. Macdonald, and he and Headlam prepared a report on these lines for incorporation into the Council's proposed *Fourth Survey of the Affairs of the Continental Churches*. Their desire for a policy of appeasement was not one which commended itself to other members of the Council, however. At the Council's spring meeting, when approval was sought for the report, there was a battle royal, with Headlam and Macdonald on one side and the Bishop and Dean of Chichester on the other.[26] The minutes give no indication of the struggle and Headlam's papers reveal nothing; but with men of such fiery temperament as Headlam and Duncan-Jones in conflict, sparks must have flown. Headlam was beaten. His report was not accepted and Duncan-Jones was asked to prepare a less tendentious document in its place.

Despite his defeat, Headlam still managed to have his say. He wrote a Preface to the Survey expressing his own point of view, and he endorsed what he wrote in presenting the Report to the Assembly on June 22. He contended that people in this country made too much of the conflict. The Confessional Church was much smaller than most people imagined and it was getting still weaker. The majority of German pastors were living quietly in their own parishes doing good work, faithful alike to the Christian religion and to the German State.

[26] The Bishop of Chichester—Dr. G. K. A. Bell.

It was also quite untrue to say that National Socialism was anti-Christian. Dr. Fabricius, a learned and respected theologian, in his book *Positive Christianity in the Third Reich* clearly demonstrated that it was based upon positive, orthodox Christianity and was the great moral and spiritual force in Germany. The State did not persecute Confessional pastors who confined themselves to preaching the Gospel truths : it was only when the pulpit was used for criticism of the Government that difficulties arose. He was quite convinced that the opportunity existed for the Church to establish itself on a sound basis of self-government free from State interference.[27]

The Preface brought a shower of criticism and abuse on Headlam's head from many quarters, not least from the Archbishop of Canterbury. He considered that Headlam had contradicted himself : at one moment he wrote of the cessation of police interference and the freedom 'at any rate to a certain extent' of the Church after the appointment of Dr. Zöllner; yet later Dr. Zöllner's own letter basing his resignation on State interference in Church affairs was appended to the Report. Again, if Dr. Zöllner found himself obliged to protest against attacks on the Christian faith by the State and Party, how could he (Headlam) endorse the claim of Dr. Fabricius that Hitler was fulfilling the word of God and guaranteeing the further spread of the Gospel?

Despite the criticisms Headlam stuck to his guns when presenting the Survey to the Assembly. Canon Douglas rallied to his support, claiming that the Preface contained no bias and saw both sides of the question, but both the Bishop of Chichester and the Archbishop of Canterbury were critical. Dr. Bell claimed that statements made by Hitler, Rosenberg and Goebbels painted a very different picture from that of Dr. Fabricius, who was little known in Germany and had little influence : nor should persecution be interpreted merely as physical captivity—it meant depriving Churchmen of freedom of speech, assembly and print and systematically attempting to capture the young.[28] The Archbishop insisted that the Preface must not be regarded as having the authority of the Council or the Church Assembly or the Church of England as a whole : it had only the authority of Headlam himself, and he rather wished that his views had been expressed in an appendix rather than in a preface.[29]

The Bishop of Chichester placed a resolution before the Upper House of Canterbury Convocation, asking the Bishops to express their grave concern over the sufferings of Christians in Germany. Headlam

[27] *Fourth Survey of the Affairs of the Continental Churches* (1937), pp. 3–6 ; cf. *Church Assembly Proceedings,* vol. 18, pp. 269–73.
[28] *Church Assembly Proceedings,* vol. 18, pp. 274–80.
[29] Ibid., p. 289.

took exception to this. While the situation in Germany was grave, it would not be helped by any resolution which the House might pass : it was also unfortunate that the House should get into the habit of expressing judgments on political matters for which it was not appointed. He therefore moved the Previous Question. The Archbishop again answered him sharply : there was no question of politics being involved and no one in the House would agree to such a resolution if it was in fact or in intention political. Headlam stood quite alone—he could not even find a seconder and his motion fell to the ground.[30]

On his way home from the discussions in Latvia and Estonia in June 1938 he spent a week in Berlin, and accompanied by his niece, Miss A. Headlam-Morley, met a great many people—leaders of the Confessional Church and the official National Church, newspaper editors and even the Foreign Minister, von Ribbentrop. It can only be said that his views did not appear to be much affected by his experience—the Confessional Church was still making a lot of fuss over small matters and it should not be encouraged to do so. But truth to tell, he hardly knew what to believe. On his return he confessed, 'Really I am in a maze. Things are reported differently by different people, and there is a good deal of false witness. It is very difficult to distinguish between the actions of the Government and the actions of the Party. . . . There is none of that anti-Church friction in England which you get in the Hitler Youth. . . . A Nation that submits to such a foulmouthed speaker as Göring and allows its press to disseminate such atrocious lies deserves to suffer.'[31] Fundamentally, however, he was absolutely convinced that Germany wanted friendly relations with England. In spite of persecution, callousness and brutality, that desire existed : it was something good, and despite all the difficulties involved, it should be fostered and encouraged.

'I continue to get a great many letters from Germany—all dwelling on their thankfulness for peace, all saying they want an alliance with us and friendship or more than friendship with the English Church. I am sure that that is the best way to deal with the situation, but it is difficult. The great body of the German people do not in the least know what is done in their name. . . . But all the same there is a callousness about them, and a complete incapability to see the other side. They are prepared to bully any minority they do not like, but complain bitterly when they are in a minority that they are not allowed to direct the policy of the country. And they are not shocked

[30] *Chronicle of Convocation*, 1938, no. 1, pp. 110–12.
[31] Headlam to Miss P. L. Wingfield, July 10, July 17, September 24, 1939.

at brutality when it is done by their own side. But the only way to correct all this is to be friends with them, if possible. The method of scolding adopted by the Archbishop of Canterbury and others is purely futile. It justifies their own self-righteousness, and irritates them and makes them worse.' [32]

Again, on the question of persecution and repressive measures, he was convinced that they were primarily the result of German temperament and should not be taken too seriously. He himself had experienced this explosive temperament in Germans at theological conferences, and events in Germany could be reasonably attributed to this cause. The following extract from a letter written to him by a lady who had been brought up in German clerical circles before marrying an Englishman illustrates the point.

'I was born and brought up in just those circles, and remember endless strife, even within the family, over politics and religious differences. My uncle, who was practically Landesbischof of Mecklenburg-Schwerin, was always in trouble, as he was a strict Orthodox Lutheran who would not allow cremation, nor remarriage of divorcees of any kind, while he ruled in Mecklenburg. It was extraordinary to see him with his five pastor sons, three pastor sons-in-law, and my brother, also a pastor, plunge into argument. If they did not actually come to blows the uproar was alarming at times. My mother, who hated this warlike behaviour, used to remind them that by one of the first paragraphs of the Reichsgrundgesetzbuch the Jesuits had been excluded from the Reich because of their political activities and constant preaching on secular topics as well as secret machinations. These pastors did the very same thing *and* gloried in being "had up" for it. I remember well when one of the pastor cousins had tackled, as he called it, the German Government for not starting a war with Turkey who had ill-treated the Armenian Christians. He always spoke of it as his "martyrdom" when he was given "Stubenarrest" for his indiscretion, and secretly regretted that no more came of it.'

It was in the light of a situation such as this that he thought the action of Dr. Niemöller should be considered. He did not pretend to defend the treatment that Niemöller had received; but he did feel that his behaviour had been far from wise. He had used the pulpit to attack Hitler consistently and he had disobeyed certain regulations which the State had made. He had made Hitler angry, and to make a person of Hitler's power and temperament angry was simply asking

[32] Headlam to Miss P. L. Wingfield, October 9, 1938.

for trouble. It would have been better for him and his friends to have followed the command to be wise as serpents and harmless as doves. To quote his correspondent again :

'I do not wish to belittle Pastor Niemöller's courage or speak lightly of his sufferings, but the whole thing sounds entirely familiar to me. . . . When I first came to Germany I was struck by the words "church militant," which I thought described the good pastors in Germany to perfection. I have never known them to do anything but fight, with each other or with the Powers that be, but only now does the press see fit to use Pastor Niemöller's case as anti-Nazi and war propaganda.'

Finally, right up to the outbreak of war, Headlam was an optimist. He still felt that although the rights and liberties of the Church in Germany were not the same as they had been before Hitler came to power, the Christian position could still be regarded with some hope and confidence. The great mass of clergy—Protestant and Catholic alike—who confined themselves to their pastoral duties and did not undertake political action, could work uninterruptedly. The difficulty, of course, was to know exactly where political action began : as Headlam himself asked, 'Can praying for peace be legitimately called a political action?' But the fundamental fact still remains that he did not take the German religious situation sufficiently seriously. He seemed to base his judgment on what many Germans *wanted* to believe about National Socialism, and on their own personal and private faith, which, so long as it was kept personal and private, was free from interference, but as such was debarred from influencing the course of events.

III

During the 1939–45 War the Council continued to function under an Emergency Executive Committee with Headlam as chairman. When the Council met on October 19, 1939, it had to decide precisely what its policy should be. Much of its work would obviously be curtailed ; but one question which had to be settled was whether such an organization with wide connections overseas should be harnessed in any way to the war effort. The Council clearly decided that it should not indulge in political propaganda : apart from having an inadequate staff, it was felt that such activity was quite outside its legitimate sphere. It should confine itself to religious and friendly contacts with the various Churches within its purview, and members were encouraged to maintain contacts wherever possible by private correspondence. This did not mean, however, that members were blind to the fact that much good might be done in putting the British case before other Churches and particularly before the Orthodox Churches in the Balkans. Headlam therefore wrote to the Minister of Information (Lord Macmillan) suggesting that this work might be profitably undertaken by his department and mentioning possible people—Philip Usher was one who would be useful.[33] The Minister welcomed the suggestion. A special section of the Religious Relations branch was established to deal with the Orthodox and Old Catholic Churches and Usher was placed in charge.[34] Archbishop Lang fully approved of this arrangement, but was most insistent that the Council and the Ministry should remain completely distinct : the Council should not utilize the Ministry as a convenient medium through which to circulate its documents.[35]

As the war developed, one important task of the Council was to send messages of comfort and encouragement to Churches suffering from aggression and to care for clergy and congregations who found themselves displaced. In this work Headlam was indefatigable, particularly in the case of the Baltic states and Jugoslavia. The value of his efforts is shown in the following letter which he received from the Latvian Minister in London in March 1944 :

'It is difficult for me to express in words how deeply I appreciate your interest in my country and the goodwill towards my people which you have shown both in the past and in your recent letters. . . . I have written to my colleague in Stockholm emphasizing that he should do all possible to bring your goodwill to the knowledge of our Archbishop and to those from among the "intelligentsia" who are working by underground means for our country's integrity.'

One of his most notable services was on behalf of his old friend Bishop Ireney of Dalmatia. For six months after Jugoslavia had been occupied he had been permitted to live in his palace at Sibennik. The Blackshirts then deprived him of all his possessions, imprisoned him for two months and finally interned him in a concentration camp near Florence. He was freed when the Allies liberated Rome in the summer of 1944. Headlam had already attempted to secure his release

[33] Headlam to Macmillan, October 20, 1939.
[34] Macmillan to Canon J. A. Douglas, November 14, 1939.
[35] The Revd. A. C. Don (Archbishop's Chaplain) to Headlam, November 27, 1939.

from concentration camp without success. He wrote to his niece, Miss P. L. Wingfield, on July 8, 1943 :

'I am starting an intrigue, the progress of which may interest you. The object is to get Bishop Ireney out of a concentration camp in Italy, and if possible get him to this country. I started with getting the Archbishop to write to the Foreign Secretary. Then to-day I went to see Miss Christich, who is head of the Jugoslav Red Cross. . . . I found her very sympathetic and friendly. She will obviously help, and is going to bring the matter before Queen Marie. . . . Then at the Athenaeum I had the good fortune to meet Bishop Mathew. He is Assistant Bishop at Westminster Cathedral and belongs to the Cardinal Hinsley party who desire friendly co-operation. I found him most sympathetic. He thinks the Vatican would help, as they want to correct the impression which has been caused by the many rumours which have been spread about their action. I was interested to find that he thought the Concordat a great mistake. To-morrow I am going to see Sir George Rendel, who is now Minister in Jugoslavia and try to get his help. If we can get the Foreign Office to agree for an exchange of prisoners, then we will approach the Vatican through the Apostolic Delegate. We have plenty of important Italians among our prisoners—Generals etc. : but the Italians don't seem in the least to want them back.'

In June 1944 after the Bishop's release, Headlam again intervened to get him brought to England : Ireney was a figure of some standing and his presence in London would be a great asset to the Jugoslav cause—or as Canon Douglas expressed it in his own inimitable way, 'The presence of Ireney in Great Britain would be like an onion in the mince and might well change all the imponderabilia of the internal Jugoslav situation.' Once again pressure was brought to bear —the Archbishop of Canterbury, the Foreign Secretary, King Peter were all approached—this time with limited success. Bishop Ireney was permitted to travel, not to London, but to America : but Headlam saw to all his wants until he was settled there. Unfortunately Ireney was quite unaware of all this kindness : although Headlam and other friends had written to him constantly, their letters had always been either confiscated or mislaid. Consequently he had become very embittered—these so-called friends were no friends, who could not bother to help him or even answer his letters. It was not until after his arrival in America that he received his first letter from Headlam on August 28, 1945—their first contact since Belgrade 1940. The letter explained a great deal—Headlam had written without fail in spite of no replies, to Sibennik, to Florence and to Rome. Ireney was overwhelmed and poured out his thanks and his apologies in an immediate reply.

On February 9 Headlam presented the eleventh Report of the Council to the Church Assembly—the first since 1939. Surprisingly enough it contained not a single reference to the Council's activities during the war years: it was devoted entirely to an account of the visit of the Bishops of Albany and Southern Ohio to this country in 1944. In his speech, however, he did refer to the work which had been done in maintaining contacts and in helping those who had suffered, expressing the hope that it would all further that great cause—Christian unity. 'We cannot but hope that all these contacts, and the fact that different religious bodies have been drawn together in opposition to anti-religious totalitarianism may mean some steps towards Christian unity after the war.' [36]

IV

When Dr. Temple became Archbishop of Canterbury in April 1942, he expressed the hope that Headlam would carry on as Chairman of the Council for as long as he could: but Headlam knew that he would soon have to go. At a meeting on July 30 the Archbishop congratulated him on his approaching eightieth birthday and expressed their indebtedness to him for all his work. Headlam, well aware that some people felt that it was high time for him to resign, deliberately remarked in the course of his reply that he hoped to continue in office for some years to come: but he did not really mean it. He confessed to his niece on the following day, 'Whenever people begin to talk like this, I always feel the unreality of it all.' He did, in fact, continue for another three years, but by September 1944 he had already made up his mind to retire. He wrote to the Archbishop on September 12:

'. . . Apart from the fact of my excessive senility there are two motives which impel me (to retire). The one is, that I wish to live—if I go on living for a few years—in my own home; and the other, that there are two or three literary works which I want to finish, although it seems very presumptuous to talk of producing literary works at my age.'

[36] *Report Church Assembly 767; Church Assembly Proceedings*, vol. 25, pp. 143–4.

Dr. Leonard Hodgson, Regius Professor of Divinity, had been suggested as his possible successor as Chairman of the Council, and Headlam went on :

'I certainly think highly of Leonard Hodgson, and I hope he may have a sound and stabilizing influence at Oxford. . . . When I became a bishop and was congratulated, I pointed out that there was only one Regius Professor of Divinity at Oxford, and that there were over a thousand bishops in the world, and I have never made up my mind whether it was a mistake to become a bishop. If I had been told that I could remain Regius Professor and carry on what is called the œcumenical work, and become Chairman of the Council on Foreign Relations in that position, I think I should have hesitated very much. I should probably have decided to remain at Oxford. . . .'

On June 21, 1945, Headlam announced that he would resign as chairman at the end of September, at the same time as he resigned his see. Canon Douglas also announced his resignation as secretary : he too was now an old man and he felt it wise to go, so that Dr. Fisher, the new Archbishop of Canterbury, could start with a completely fresh team. It was a difficult decision for both men to make. They were well aware that it was time to go : but the Council as it then existed was their creation and there were very few—if any —people who really knew what they had given in care, time and money during the first twelve years of its life. For Headlam the work of the Council was a necessary step on the road to Christian unity. History had shown the Church of England in the past to have inclined towards exclusiveness, but this was a danger which should be avoided. After the issue of the historic Appeal to All Christian People by the Lambeth Conference of 1920 he had said, 'The Church of England is at the parting of the ways ; she is called, I believe, to take her place in building up the religious unity of the world, but she will fail in her mission unless she is prepared to lay aside her exclusiveness and is ready humbly to meet all other Christians.' [37] While the Church of England was national and should be prepared to look at things from a national standpoint, it should also be international : the national Church should always have its international relations.[38] The Council on Foreign Relations, in making Christians of different Churches aware of one another and in bringing them closer together, played an important part in establishing a wider belief in the Catholic

[37] A. C. Headlam, *The Building of the Church of Christ* (1928), p. 136.
[38] *The Church of England*, p. 196.

Church—the Christian ideal of the oneness in Christ which represented the one wholesome form of internationalism.[39]

So then Headlam stepped down from the stage, relinquishing the role by which he was best known by Christians of many races. After his death in 1947 his successor as chairman, the Bishop of Chichester (Dr. G. K. A. Bell) paid tribute to him in the twelfth Report of the Council [40]:

'In 1945 Dr. Headlam, formerly Bishop of Gloucester, resigned the chairmanship which he had held with such distinction since the formation of the Council in 1932. He died on January 17, 1947. The work done by Dr. Headlam in the fields of theology and religious education and Christian unity, as well as in his own diocese and as an eminent member of the Anglican episcopate are well known. The Council would, however, desire to pay a special tribute to his leadership, and his range of achievement, in the relations between the Anglican Church and foreign Churches. He was tireless in his efforts to secure a deeper understanding of, and a closer relationship with, other Christian communions and their different traditions. It is with a deep sense of personal loss that the Council records its gratitude to him as their chairman and guide over many years.'

---

[39] *What it means to be a Christian*, 1932, p. 160.
[40] *Report Church Assembly 821* (1947), p. 1.

CHAPTER TWENTY-ONE

The Bishop in his Diocese

I

AT his enthronement Headlam had stressed the importance of administrative efficiency in a diocese. It did not take him long to discover that in this respect Gloucester was not lacking—a reflection, he thought, of the great interest taken by the diocese as a whole in the work of the Church. He was very conscious too of the enormous amount of work that was being done for very little financial reward. In the Report of the Board of Finance for 1931 he compared Gloucester with St. Albans—a diocese of approximately the same number of livings but with a much larger population.

'I notice that whereas St. Albans pays £250 a year for its Assistant Bishop, this diocese pays £200, of which £100 is paid by myself, only £100 being paid by the Board of Finance. A salary of £200 a year scarcely pays the expenses of an Assistant Bishop in going about the diocese. It has to be recognized how much gratuitous work is being given to us. The next item I find is that of Archdeacons' and Rural Deans' expenses, which in the St. Albans diocese comes to £305 and with us to £11. Not only does the diocese contribute nothing to the expenses of the Archdeacons, but it gets the whole of the services of the Archdeacon of Cheltenham for the sum of £300 a year, which is paid by the Ecclesiastical Commissioners to Archdeacons. . . . We have expressed our willingness to contribute to the expenses of the Rural Deans. They are not wealthy men, but they are ready to do their work and pay all the expenses themselves. For the support of the Canon Missioner St. Albans has to pay £561. Gloucester, in its Budget this year, pays only £360. In this case we are helped by an endowment. St. Albans pays £543 for its Director of Religious Education, Gloucester pays £285. . . . The Sunday School Organizer in the St. Albans diocese receives a stipend of £200 a year and £48 for her expenses including her car. In Gloucester we pay £100 a year, and we get in return for that the most enthusiastic and competent work.

'If we turn to officials, the St. Albans expenses are £1,763, ours £700. That arises from the fact that so much of the work of the Diocesan Board of Finance is done by an Honorary Secretary, to whose enthusiasm and capacity we owe an immense debt. . . . The cost of administration is only about 2% of our turn-over.

'I think any one who studies this record will feel how much the Church is indebted for all this unpaid or slightly paid work which is done with so much efficiency and so much enthusiasm, and I hope that many Church people in the diocese, when they read this record, will feel moved to contribute more generously to the work of the Church.'[1]

There was a limit to unpaid or poorly paid work, however, and above all Headlam was acutely aware of the need to supplement clergy stipends. When the Board of Finance had begun its work in 1913 it had only been able to help a few incumbents in a small way; and it was only in 1918 that the Ecclesiastical Commissioners had begun the long series of gradually increasing grants to supplement incomes. Furthermore, this help was offset by the effects of the Tithe Act and the Older Incumbents Pensions Measure. Headlam fully approved of the ideal of every village having its own priest—'My aim is to preserve, as far as possible, the country parson as we know him in the history of the Church'—but at the same time it was important that every man should have an adequate income and an adequate sphere of work. It was a grave waste of the resources of the Church to employ the full time of an able-bodied man in a parish with a population of under two hundred : unless he had interests and resources of his own a clergyman should reasonably be expected to be able to care for at least five hundred people. Two policies were therefore initiated—the uniting of benefices wherever this was practicable, and the supplementation of lower benefice incomes.

Under Headlam's direction the Maintenance Committee of the Board of Finance, in consultation with all interested parties, considered some forty or fifty cases of union, most of them before 1930. He illustrated the value of this policy in 1927. In one week he had instituted five new incumbents, four of them to united benefices : the five benefices, which now had an average income of £470 a year, had originally been nine small separate parishes with an average income of £167 a year. Under this policy the number of benefices in the diocese were reduced from 315 in 1923 to 280 in 1943.

[1] *Report of the Diocesan Board of Finance 1931*, pp. 13–14.

For the augmentation of poorer stipends, over and above help given from central sources, he successfully appealed to the generosity of the diocese. As early as 1925 the stipends of all livings with a population of under three hundred were being made up to £268 and all over three hundred to £307. There was also a characteristic touch—grantee clergy also received a free gift of books. By 1935 the figures had crept up to £320 and £372, and by 1945 to £350 and £400 exclusive of Easter offerings and grants made by Queen Anne's Bounty towards the cost of dilapidations.[2]

Headlam was, of course, often attacked about his own large stipend, but he always had his answer. The money was given to him, not for his own personal advantage, but to enable him to do his work in the diocese. Quite apart from the administrative costs of his office he considered it his duty to spend a considerable sum on hospitality.

'A wise and considerate hospitality is of the greatest advantage in knitting together the frame-work of any society—it substitutes the personal for the official relationship—and I am sure it is a wise tradition that looks on hospitality as one of the duties of the episcopal office, and has provided the opportunity for exercising such hospitality. It is not, as some people seem to think, money wasted, and I can assure them that it is not done for the sake of the Bishop but for the sake of the diocese.'[3]

He was also most generous : the lead he gave to his own diocesan appeals was exemplary, and no worthy cause or clergyman in genuine need was ignored. Spending little on himself, it gave him real pleasure to spend money on others : he loved giving presents and the number of books he gave away must have numbered thousands. The Palace, too, was a great drain on his finances,[4] and despite a private income as well as his episcopal stipend, he often found it difficult to make ends meet. 'I have £500 to pay for my dilapidations, and then I shall have to subscribe to my own appeal. I have too much to do and I am nearly bankrupt.' This remark, made in 1928, had a familiar ring. In a review of his financial situation just before resigning he estimated that during his episcopate he had spent the whole of his episcopal stipend, the whole of his private income and some £2,000 to £3,000 of capital besides. But he had no regrets : the money was well spent.

He had little sympathy, however, with any drastic schemes for reforming the Church's financial system. In 1937 a group of clergy

[2] *Diocesan Board of Finance Report 1945,* pp. 15–16.
[3] *Diocesan Magazine,* December 1930.
[4] When he gave it up during the 1939–45 War, he estimated that he saved between £1,000 and £2,000 a year.

and laity led by the Ven. L. Hunter, Archdeacon of Northumberland,[5] produced a document entitled *Men, Money and the Ministry* in which they suggested that Church endowments should be pooled and distributed equitably; all clergy, from the Archbishop of Canterbury downwards, should be paid from this central source according to needs and circumstances; the parson's freehold would inevitably suffer, but it would be replaced by the guarantee of economic security. Headlam criticized it severely—he had seldom read a book which caused him greater irritation; and he saw nothing to justify either the drastic proposals or the spirit in which they were put forward. Here, as in other spheres of life, he was opposed to over-centralization: the salaries of bishops, archdeacons and other officials might well be paid from a central source, but at the parochial level the diocese and its Board of Finance should be the authority. As for the parson's freehold, despite certain disadvantages, it should on no account be taken away: it provided a parson with that security and independence which allowed him to speak and act freely, not only as against his parishioners, but as against his superiors.[6]

II

Headlam had informed his clergy at his first Diocesan Conference in 1923 that a bishop was to be regarded as a commander and a leader, not as a regimental officer.[7] It was a conception to which he was always faithful. He never went around the diocese to see what his clergy were up to. They had been given a job to do and he trusted them to do it—in their own way and to the best of their ability. This did not mean, however, that he neglected them. He was interested in the welfare of every one; sick priests were visited diligently; and those in trouble or in need were sure of his help. His kindness, too, could reveal itself in unexpected ways. He was very careful about Confirmation records, having them carefully cross-indexed and bound, so that it was possible in a very few moments to find the date and place of confirmation of any particular person. One clergyman made a mistake in his returns and sent in the wrong list. Before long he was informed of his error. He hastened to write a letter of apology: there was no excuse, it was just carelessness. He soon received a reply. Headlam was glad that he had made the mistake, for it indicated that he was overworking in his large parish and obviously needed secre-

---

[5] Bishop of Sheffield from 1939.
[6] 'Parochial Endowments,' *C.Q.R.*, vol. 125, pp. 247–64.
[7] Cf. p. 170.

tarial help; if it was a question of money, could he possibly be of
assistance?

He was always on the alert, too, for signs of any clergy who were
being treated unjustly. He had never forgotten the sad case of
Dr. J. B. Dykes, his father's predecessor at S. Oswald's, Durham, and
the slightest suspicion of clerical persecution was abhorrent to him.
On one occasion some parishioners came to him to complain about
certain extra devotional services which were being held by their
Anglo-Catholic vicar, who was in fact a very devout and devoted
priest. Headlam listened to their complaints and then dismissed them
abruptly : 'I have often been compelled to reprove people for praying
too little, but I will never reprove them for praying too much.' He
expected, however, that clergy should be able to stand up for themselves, and if necessary to stand up against him. He answered a young
clergyman with the words, 'I have one piece of advice to give to you.
Never be subservient to any one, not even to me.' He admired a man
who would stand up to him, and he never bore malice. On one
occasion he summoned a well-known priest to the Palace to give an
account of some action of which he disapproved. An extremely violent
interview took place, which ended with the priest storming angrily
out of the presence of an equally angry Bishop. Not long afterwards
one of the most attractive livings in the diocese fell vacant. Headlam
consulted one of his staff, who told him that the best man for the job
was one whom he would never appoint. He pressed for the name
and after some hesitation was told that it was the priest with whom
he had so recently quarrelled. 'I am glad you have mentioned him,'
he replied, 'I also thought him the best man for the job.' To the stout-
hearted man who did his job faithfully all was forgiven.

Nor did he resent criticism, although his critics always had to face
the fact that he was not likely to take their remarks lying down. On
one occasion the clergy of a rural deanery felt that something should
be done about his confirmation addresses : their substance was undeniably sound, but they tended to be too long and above young people's
heads. Something shorter and more inspirational was needed. It was,
however, no easy matter to convey this opinion to the Bishop. Finally
the Chapter did it in what was considered a tactful manner by suggesting that it might be a relief to him if one of their number were
occasionally to preach for him. Headlam was not deceived.

'I hope you will realize that I do *not* resent any criticisms, or any
proposals. If they are good, I shall adopt them; if they are bad, I
shall neglect them; if they are improper, I shall refute them; but I
shall always like to hear and to know them. I am not particularly

inclined to the giving of addresses by a parish priest. I do not lay any particular stress on the merits of anything I do myself, but I am sure that the addresses by the Bishop have a good deal of weight; nor am I inclined to encourage the reduction of the didactic element, and I am not altogether sympathetic with those people who are so anxious for what they call the inspirational. From time to time I have heard what I would describe as the inspirational, and I think it has a tendency to be wordy. I shall be glad to hear from you if there are any more points you are likely to suggest.'

Needless to say, the Chapter made no further suggestions.

He was particularly impressed if an ordinand or a priest stood up to him when being interviewed for the first time; it was usually something of an ordeal. Canon J. B. Goodliffe, for many years Rector of Cheltenham, has described his first meeting, which, though formidable, was not without its humour.

'My first meeting with this remarkable man was unusual. After an incumbency in Liverpool, I was offered the post of Rector of Cheltenham. There had been no rush on the part of others to accept, as there had been some bother in the town about the post. We were invited to stay at the Palace. I was somewhat overawed by the stern, austere aspect of my host, whose piercing blue eyes missed nothing. He invited me into his study and wasted no time on preliminaries. "Do you know any Hebrew?" I replied equally tersely, "Golgotha, the place of a skull, is the limit of my knowledge." "I am glad," said Headlam. "Only Baptist Ministers and Regius Professors know Hebrew—and both are slightly mad." He went on inexorably, "Can you preach? If not, you'll starve." I replied cautiously that I thought I should grow neither fat nor thin.

'He then suggested a walk. He saluted no man by the way, and led me to a muddy stream with an upturned boat. "Behold Gloucester docks. I would not have you think my diocese is in any way behind yours of Liverpool." I took the hint. After a silent return, I saw I had passed the test. "I have decided to make you Rural Dean." I thanked him. "The reason is that I don't know you, and I do know the others." I began to like my new Bishop. This was refreshing. We went to Evensong in his chapel. The singing was hearty, as a small army of maids, daughters of miners of the Forest of Dean, made up the choir. The Bishop was a stickler for liturgical accuracy, yet I could not but wonder about the apt coincidence of the lesson. The Bishop, casting glances at me, read how the trees had decided to choose a king. I gathered that after the noble trees had been discarded, a bramble bush was chosen.'

Headlam was always most careful in his appointments, taking infinite pains to consult people who were interested or affected or who could help him : and he much preferred to reward his own men rather than import people from outside the diocese. Actually he did not think that too much patronage should be in the hands of the Bishop—'I can conceive nothing worse for the diocese than a system under which I appointed all the clergy'—and while he promoted the creation of the Diocesan Board of Patronage, he considered that for the most part private patrons carried out their duties efficiently and conscientiously. His one rooted objection was to party trusts, which gave preference to men of particular theological opinions and often demanded conditions which he thought unjustifiable.

Despite his reputation as a theologian and an ecclesiastical statesman Headlam failed to attract many really first-class ordination candidates. Some, of course, may have been frightened off by his brusque and formidable manner : but it was largely due to the fact that his views on candidates were thought by most people to be rather unorthodox. His well-known dislike of theological colleges, for example, was hardly likely to attract men who had been trained in them; and the fact that he did not require residence at them as a necessary qualification for ordination did open the door to many people whose training may have been rather indifferent, to say the least. The legend existed that any one who had taken the Oxford Ordination course, which he himself had instituted, was accepted without further question. His willingness to ordain Nonconformist ministers and men about whom other bishops had grave doubts was also well known. But some of these rather unorthodox candidates did prove themselves to be astonishingly successful and devoted parish priests.

One of Headlam's most important achievements at Gloucester was to give the diocese a sense of unity. When he arrived early in 1923 the parochial and diocesan machinery created by the Enabling Act of 1919 was not yet in smooth-running order, communications and public transport were far below their present standards of efficiency, and the inherent sense of conservatism in isolated country parishes was still strong. In a variety of ways he strove to encourage every one to look beyond their own parochial boundaries and to realize their responsibilities to one another as well as to the diocese as a whole. So, for example, when he launched his great £120,000 Appeal for Churches and Schools in January 1929, he stressed the importance of having one big fund rather than a number of smaller parochial funds competing for offerings. It was with this end in view that he arranged a week of self-denial for the whole diocese in Advent 1929 culminating in a great Service of Offering at the Cathedral, to which all the individual parishes brought their gifts. He appealed too for what he called 'parochial unselfishness' : parishes were asked to set aside their own needs and schemes until the Appeal was over : any who were rash enough to ignore the request could take warning. 'I shall not lightly give my approval to any expenditure on decoration, ornaments, organs etc. ; nor shall I feel inclined until our bigger work is accomplished to take part in the dedication of such work.'[8] The Appeal raised £63,000—very much less than was hoped for : but at least it was sufficient to secure some spiritual provision in every new district which had been created : but over and above this Headlam felt that the effort had increased the unity and corporate interest of a very large section of the diocese. In the same way he hoped that the other Appeals—for Church Schools, for Clerical Stipends, and for Re-endowment—would all help foster the spirit of diocesan unity.

Another means to this end was the holding of large Confirmation services at big centres. He did not object to visiting country parishes where the number of candidates was very small, but he felt that there was a great deal to be said—especially in the case of young people— for letting them share in a great service, either in the Cathedral or in one of the large parish churches such as Tewkesbury, Winchcombe or Cirencester. Such services enabled people from small and often isolated parishes to realize that they were not just entities in themselves, but essentially parts of a greater whole. In this category might be mentioned the service which he himself had instituted in the Cathedral on Easter Eve, when he held a Baptism of Adults followed by Confirmation. This return to primitive custom appealed to him and he encouraged people to come.

This corporate spirit did develop during his episcopate in quite a remarkable way : by and large Gloucester was an efficient, happy and united diocese. In his Charge delivered at his fourth Visitation in 1937 Headlam paid some well-deserved compliments. 'Speaking of the diocese as a whole, I am impressed by the loyal and conscientious way in which the work, alike of clergy and laity, is carried out. . . . I am always impressed by the loyalty and fidelity of the Churchwardens of this diocese. . . . I am impressed with the way in which the great majority of the clergy do their work. . . . In all matters which concern the obedience of the clergy, to the best of my knowledge, there is no disobedience and no disloyalty among them.' These were no mere platitudes : if Headlam said that he was impressed, he meant it. Much of this efficiency and fine spirit was really due to Headlam's policy of holding regular visitations. Every four years the whole diocese had to render him an account of its stewardship, parish

[8] *Diocesan Magazine,* November 1930.

by parish, and his enquiries were searching and comprehensive. There was in fact no real opportunity for any one to sink into lethargy. But more than anything it was due to Headlam himself : he was a born leader. 'He knew how to rule,' said the Bishop of Tewkesbury, 'and we appreciated it.'

III

Many people felt that Headlam's stay at Gloucester could not possibly be a long one and that his translation to London or even the primacy was only a matter of time. Speculation was therefore rife when Archbishop Davidson resigned in 1928 : but Headlam himself had no real desire for promotion. 'Many people wish me to be Archbishop of Canterbury. However gratifying all this is to my vanity, and however gratifying to my ambition it would be to be Primate, it is really much more comfortable for me to be living quietly here (in Gloucester), and I believe I shall do much more good.'[9] Gloucester was not a large diocese and now that he had got its measure, he had enough time for his œcumenical work. Then, after 1930, he had the benefit of help from his old friend Bishop E. J. Palmer, who came to live in Cheltenham on retiring from the see of Bombay. His arrival was not only a great asset; it was providential; for twice in the early part of 1931 Headlam was ill with blood pressure. He was now approaching his seventieth year and it seemed to him that perhaps it might be best to retire. 'When you get to seventy people don't want you. If I had been anything but a bishop I should have been pensioned and put on the shelf long ago.' Retirement would, of course, be pleasant : it would mean a return to Whorlton as well as complete freedom for theological work. Then, in the spring of 1932 the see of Winchester fell vacant on the death of Dr. F. T. Woods. The suggestion was made to him that he might like to move there, and this too had its attractions. Winchester was a lovely diocese, offering an opportunity of renewing contacts with the College, while it could legitimately be regarded as a promotion. On the other hand, he felt far too old to move and start all over again. Three possibilities were therefore open to him—to remain at Gloucester, to move to Winchester, or to retire. For several weeks he simply could not make up his mind. 'For the first time in my life I feel really perplexed about myself. I have no doubt often made mistakes, but I have never had any hesitation as to what seemed the right thing to do and a path has seemed to open : now it is all quite hazy. No doubt this is one of the symptoms of old

[9] Headlam to Miss P. L. Wingfield, November 19, 1928.

age, or someone might say that it was presumptuous in me to have a future at my age.' [10]

The advice of some of his friends brought him no nearer to a decision. Sister Lavinia Smith, for example, encouraged him to retire : there were plenty of lesser men who were quite capable of running Gloucester; he should be free to give himself to the whole Church. Canon Maynard Smith, on the other hand, advised him to stay : Gloucester was *not* a difficult diocese to run and it did *not* demand his full attention; retirement would deprive him of the right to attend the Bishops' Meetings and would in consequence seriously restrict his ability to influence the policy of the Church of England. He was still hesitating when he fell ill again—this time far more seriously. A complete rest for two months was ordered and Archbishop Lang declared that he owed it to the Church to make a complete recovery : until that was achieved any decision as to his future could wait.

July 29, 1932.

'My dear Bishop,

'I have read your letter of the 27th with very real distress and concern. I am sincerely sorry to hear of this tiredness of the brain, and I most earnestly hope that two months' complete rest will thoroughly restore you. Your health is of so great importance to the work of the Church at the present time that it is your duty to take every possible care of it. I shall have so often to appeal to you for service and help that I cannot contemplate your not being able to respond. . . . As to your thoughts about the future, I must not allow myself to express any opinion. I think everything must depend upon how you are and feel after your time of rest is over. I most fully appreciate your wish to have some time to bring out your book on Christian Theology, and even if you resigned your diocese I know that you would still be available for the work of promoting union especially with these Foreign Churches. So far as the obligation of continuing diocesan work is concerned let us have some talk about it when you are less tired and your mind is fresh and clear after your time of rest.

Yours ever,

COSMO CANTUAR.'

Headlam therefore went off for a cruise in the Mediterranean—at first rather reluctantly. 'I shall be doing all sorts of things which are considered nice but nothing that I really want to. However, it is all

[10] Ibid., May 5, 1932.

very good for me morally and I hope physically.' But once he arrived off the coast of Asia Minor and was able to visit old haunts, he thoroughly enjoyed himself; and Philip Usher was an ideal companion. At the beginning of October he returned to Gloucester completely recovered. He had also made up his mind to stay there and take life a little more easily. 'I really think that I am very much better and have got over just about all my troubles. Henceforth I propose to live the leisurely life of an eighteenth century bishop.' [11]

There was, however, little opportunity for a more leisurely life. Diocesan demands grew no lighter, while to all his œcumenical work there was now added the responsibility of the Council on Foreign Relations. He was now over seventy; and his breakdowns had indicated that even his iron constitution had its limitations. Bishop Palmer, too, was far from fit: the assistance he was able to give grew less and by 1935 ceased altogether. Headlam realized the urgent need of regular episcopal help—occasional duty from any retired bishop who might be free was neither satisfactory nor sufficient. He therefore instituted proceedings to secure the appointment of a Suffragan Bishop. The procedure was inevitably lengthy, but approval was finally secured. On February 24, 1938—the Feast of S. Matthias—the Archdeacon of Gloucester, the Ven. A. J. Hodson, was consecrated the first Bishop of Tewkesbury, with the Forest of Dean as his special care. It was an excellent appointment, for the Archdeacon had served the whole of his ministry in the diocese and was deservedly popular with his fellow-clergy: his love and admiration for Headlam was deep—although he was by no means uncritical—and Headlam was indeed fortunate to have the benefit of his help and wisdom during the difficult years of the War.

IV

Headlam was not one of those people who considered war with Germany inevitable: to the very last moment he still thought that Hitler would get what he wanted by chicanery and not by fighting. When war did finally come he realized that England was ill-prepared. 'A wave of sentimentalism, of pacifism, and love of economy had made us forget our duty as guardians of a great empire and the inheritors of the command of the sea.' [12] Ever since 1931, when he had refused to take the chair at meetings to discuss the 1930 Lambeth Conference resolutions on peace and disarmament, he had held the

[11] Ibid., October 3, 1932.
[12] 'The War,' *C.Q.R.*, vol. 131, p. 102.

unpopular view that the Empire should be kept strong. Despite the ill-preparedness, however, he encouraged men to face the struggle with determination and as best they could. He himself had intended to carry on as Bishop of Gloucester until the Lambeth Conference of 1940 and then retire : but now he felt that he must carry on if possible until the end of the War. It was a sad prospect, for it meant the non-fulfilment of so many things on which he had set his heart— he was far too old to look forward to picking up the threads again when peace came. 'The War means the failure of all one's plans for the organization of the diocese, for senior schools, for further visits to the Balkan countries, for reunion at home and abroad, for the Lambeth Conference, and for Missions.' [13] There was, however, one small crumb of comfort! It meant the suppression of many committees, meetings and time-wasting activities, and he could at least get on with his own work.[14] He immediately gave up the Palace as an economy measure, let it with the exception of his study to the local College of Domestic Science, and went to live with Canon Maynard Smith and his brother.

As in the first World War Headlam traced the course of events in *The Church Quarterly Review* under the initial 'X,' still aided by the expert military knowledge of his cousin, General John Headlam. Here he noted with satisfaction the country's steady growth in strength : but if there was a weakness in the war effort, it was in the munition factories. The standard of work and output was not always what it might have been, while there was too great a difference between the lot and pay of the soldier and that of the munition worker : in total war they should all be under military discipline and receive the same rates of pay.[15] Such opinions did not, of course, reach a very wide public in *The Church Quarterly Review*; but Headlam chose to express them to a large congregation in the Cathedral on a National Day of Prayer in September 1941. The nation had not been prepared at the beginning, and it still showed no signs of being able to defeat Germany if Russia were defeated. There was too much complacency : it could be seen, for example, in the slackness among munition workers. In the face of such failure the nation was called to penitence—penitence for the corporate sin of the country—and to prayer.

The sermon, which was widely reported, aroused considerable resentment among the munition workers of Gloucester. Much of this slackness was not the result of complacency but was caused by bottle-

[13] Headlam to Miss P. L. Wingfield, September 22, 1939.
[14] Ibid., October 28, 1939.
[15] Articles on the War. *C.Q.R.*, vol. 131, p. 257; vol. 133, pp. 219–20; vol. 135, pp. 87–8.

necks in the delivery of materials. Headlam was inundated with protests and abusive letters. Many clergy felt that even if he were right, the occasion had been ill-timed and the denunciation too one-sided : they wished to dissociate themselves from his remarks. A clerical deputation headed by the Bishop of Tewkesbury and the Dean lodged a protest. Throughout it all he remained quite unmoved. Shortly afterwards he met a deputation from the workers themselves. He recorded the interview as being 'very pleasant.' 'They listened attentively and they stated their own case extremely well.' It was clear that there was in fact very little to quarrel about. Headlam stuck to his guns and the deputation admitted that there had been some slackness. He then pointed out that he was not accusing *all* workers of slackness but only some : the remarks in his sermon were to the advantage of good workers if they would only recognize it. Finally he promised to issue a statement to clarify the situation. The delegation were willing to accept this and the meeting ended amicably. Headlam commented on the incident in the next issue of the *Diocesan Magazine.* He believed it was his duty to condemn what was wrong in any class of society ; and to hold up the work of the country for the sake of higher wages was to him a serious moral wrong. Despite temporary unpopularity the work of the Church would not be injured because they had the courage to denounce what was wrong.

Headlam, of course, was not without his supporters, even in quite unexpected places. There was an old coalman who worked in the poorer quarters of Gloucester, a great character given to scolding people to whom he delivered coal—usually in strong language—but dropping in sacks of coal surreptitiously when he knew there was real hardship. He was heard to make the remark, 'He didn't put it half strong enough. I'd like to shake hands with the old b— !' When Headlam was told, he was very thrilled and said that he would like to do the same with him.

In 1943 he aroused further controversy by denouncing the destruction of historical monuments in Germany and Italy. Again he received a stream of protests, many of them abusive. 'They addressed me as a "little livered weakling," a "poor fool," a "beastly German friend." These literary embellishments do not matter. What does matter is the brutality they exhibit.' Again he refused to retract. Such destruction could have no value in winning the War ; and to be glad about it put people on the level of the Nazis themselves. These buildings were part of the common culture of Europe, and as such their loss should be deplored. Failure to do this showed not only a lack of culture but implied the evil in men's hearts which would make them think wrongly after the War. The spirit of vengeance was dangerous : it made the last peace ineffective, and it might well do so again.[16]

In January 1945 yet another batch of 'fan mail' arrived—'as unintelligent as they were uncharitable'—after he had stated that what was needed was not the destruction of Germany but its liberation—liberation from Nazism and Prussianism. The Germany which had made such great contributions in the past to literature, philosophy, science and art should be restored.[17] It would be a good thing, although he doubted whether it were possible, for Germany to be divided again into its original small states under their own rulers. She did not understand democracy; and kings were better than tyrants. Our own parliamentary system suited the national character of this country, but when transported to other countries whose people had not been trained for it or were temperamentally suited to it, it was found to be most unsuitable. There was nothing particularly Christian or holy about it. Peace and prosperity would not be secured by imposing any particular form of government on other nations but by changing the hearts of men; it could only be done by Christianity.

Headlam clearly did not believe that the Church was concerned with political or economic ends. Its duty was simply to make men good Christians. A good Christian cared for his fellow-men; and if, for example, he was a politician, his politics would be devoted to their well-being. Christianity gave him the end : his political or economic science taught him the means. No particular brand of politics was exclusively Christian, and any suggestion to the contrary was to be deplored.[18] He considered Archbishop Temple's ventures into Socialism to be a grave error : any attempt to identify Christianity with a system of national or state socialism was untrue to our faith and disastrous to the country.[19]

He was equally opposed to any idea of the Welfare State. When the War Agricultural Committee came into the Palace in 1941 he wrote :

'I am beginning to be more and more distrustful of the bureaucratic methods of bringing prosperity. I think it is not a way which is in the least likely to be effective. We want to make our farmers effective by giving them a good and suitable education, and to create the economic conditions under which they will get a fair profit, and then leave them to themselves. All the would-be reformers want to impose

[16] *Diocesan Magazine.* September 1943, December 1943, February 1944.
[17] Ibid., January 1945, February 1945.
[18] 'The Church and Politics,' *The Church of England Newspaper,* October 16, 1942.
[19] 'A New World,' *The Guardian,* February 28, 1941.

on us state-direction and control. All the people who are most intent on the denunciation of totalitarianism are doing their best to make us totalitarian. I believe the road to prosperity is free initiative and individual enterprise; and the state should create the conditions which will bring that about. . . . What we want is to be allowed to live quietly without being bothered, and to be free to do our own job. We don't want social reform which means taking all the initiative out of people, and the government doing badly what families ought to learn to do for themselves.'[20]

But how was this freedom and prosperity to be achieved? Headlam had been giving an answer throughout his life. It would be achieved by a sound educational system based on religious freedom and equality; by the reunion of Christendom, whereby the Church became the great bond of union between the nations; and by missionary activity, whereby men devoted themselves with strength and earnestness to spread the Christian religion throughout the whole world.[21]

v

Despite his original intention to try and remain at Gloucester until the end of the War, by 1942 he was beginning to doubt his ability to do so. He celebrated his eightieth birthday with a sense of increasing weakness. 'I used to be able to manage a twelve hour day, but cannot now. I really don't like having two sermons a day, and am tired after a long meeting.' There were, however, practical difficulties. 'I don't see how I can resign. I have no home to go to,[22] and I could not possibly afford to pay my income tax, as the first year after a man resigns he has to pay his income tax on his previous year's income.' He was greatly affected too by the loss of people on whom he had relied for so many years. The first to go was Brown, his chauffeur—a Whorlton man whom he had known all his life and who had been in his service since 1910. He was a great character, *persona grata* in the vicarage kitchens of the diocese, and perfectly ready to put Headlam in his place in true North country manner. He was a family institution and his return to Whorlton with heart trouble was a sad blow. Then in the summer of 1941 Philip Usher died in the Middle East shortly after becoming an R.A.F. chaplain. He had been closely connected with Headlam ever since his undergraduate days immediately

[20] Headlam to Miss P. L. Wingfield, July 31, 1941.
[21] *Our Religious Duty,* sermon preached at All Souls' College, November 3, 1940.
[22] Whorlton was occupied by a school evacuated from Stockton-on-Tees.

M

after the first World War. Though completely dissimilar in temperament, there was a bond of deep affection between them. Canon Douglas remarked that no pupil ever won Headlam's heart so much as Philip Usher. Early in 1944 he lost another prop—one which was well-nigh irreplaceable for a man of his age : after twenty-one years efficient and devoted service, his secretary, G. H. W. Jones, died suddenly. Shortly afterwards another old friend and trusted helper— Sister Lavinia Smith—died from a stroke. Small wonder that he confessed to becoming not only senile but incompetent. By the summer of 1944 there was a good prospect of recovering possession of Whorlton and he decided that, come what may, he would resign in the following year.

In the spring of 1945 he announced that he would retire on October 1, giving four reasons for doing so.

'First of all, being well over 80, I may be naturally considered unfit by reason of my age for continuing the somewhat strenuous work.

'Secondly, my medical attendant is anxious that I should do so. That would not move me in the least if there were not other reasons.

'Thirdly, my deafness is a very considerable bar to the usefulness of much of my work. I cannot really take part in Bishops' Meetings or Convocation, and find attendance at them very much a waste of time as far as I am concerned. I hear very little of what other people say, and it makes it difficult for me to intervene in debates.

'But there is a further reason in addition to these, and it is this : I have two theological works I wish to complete, the Book on Christian Theology and the Life of our Lord. I believe that if I resign now I may have sufficient strength for the next few years to complete them, and I believe I should be doing more good work in that way and in perhaps some other smaller literary work, than continuing as a Bishop.'

His last important work before leaving the diocese was to launch a Diocesan Re-endowment Fund. He felt that the whole diocese should be systematically surveyed and reorganized in order to adapt it to the needs of the day. To finance such a scheme he launched this new Fund, which was to be devoted to three purposes—the Cathedral, the needs of particular parishes or districts, and clerical stipends. He intended it to be a long-term campaign—'a consistent policy carried out quietly for twenty or thirty years would enable us to accomplish this task' : and he hoped that much of the money would be given by regular giving—every parish was asked to give one Sunday's collections every year. In May he announced that he would visit every rural deanery on behalf of the Appeal ; it would also give him an opportunity of saying good-bye to the whole diocese. By August 27 he had the gratification of knowing that £16,570 had been given or promised. A statement on this effort which he wrote to *The Times* contained an indication of the very high regard he had for the work of the parish priest with more than a hint of his own sense of inadequacy in that respect. 'It must be remembered that the work of a parish priest is very difficult. I have been, besides a parish priest, Principal of a University College, and a Professor in more than one University, and have had a good deal of important work to do; but I have no manner of doubt that the work of a parish priest was the most difficult of all, to do it well. It demands gifts, personality, character *such as most of us are unable to attain to.*'[23]

His last few days were strenuous. He preached in the Cathedral and in S. Matthew's, Cheltenham, held a Synod of Clergy and a meeting of Rural Deans, gave a course of addresses to ordination candidates, took two institutions, spoke to the clergy of Cheltenham, dedicated a Red Cross Centre and opened a World Christian Exhibition. On his last Sunday (September 30) he held an ordination in his Cathedral. When it was all over he remarked, 'I have managed in a fortnight to say most of what I thought. Now I can be silent.'

The official farewell took place at the Diocesan Conference on Friday, September 22, when he was presented with an illuminated address, a toy car and a cheque with which to buy a real one. All the speeches testifying to the appreciation every one felt for his ministry were summed up in the remark of the Bishop of Tewkesbury, 'Under your shepherding we have indeed been a happy and contented diocese and we wish to thank you most sincerely for your leadership during these difficult and critical years.' In return Headlam thanked them all for their great kindness over twenty-three years. 'One thing I can assure you of is that I have tried to do my best, and I think I may honestly claim that I have worked fairly hard, in excess of eight hours a day.' He recalled that when he first spoke to them at his enthronement he had mentioned the threefold duty of a bishop—his work in his diocese, his work in the Church as a whole, and his work as a scholar and theologian. 'I have tried to carry out those three duties. I have given most of my time to my diocese, but I have been able to do a certain amount of work for the Church as a whole, and in later years I have had the good fortune to travel to most of the Churches on the Continent, and to do something towards creating greater unity in the Christian world.' He ended, 'I am conscious of my failures, but in spite of that I am glad you are willing to accept me as a friend, earnestly concerned for the well-being of the people of this diocese,

[23] *The Times*, February 2, 1945.

and forgiving many of the harsh things which I may appear to have said. After all, there are many things which a Bishop ought to say, but which are not very pleasant for every one to hear. Good-bye.'

Headlam may justifiably be reckoned to have been a good diocesan bishop, who made a far greater impact and had more success than he himself probably realized. He wondered, of course, whether he had been really wise in accepting a bishopric, but there is no doubt that by and large Gloucester regarded him with a pride tinged with genuine affection. As with Hensley Henson at Durham, people felt that with his going they were losing someone whose like they would probably never see again : despite all his brusqueness and gaucherie he was a man apart, and the diocese had no regrets at having had him as their Bishop. So it was, that after his departure a man was heard to say, 'Ecclesiastically Gloucester is empty.' But he was the first to admit that any credit for what had been achieved was not entirely his : he wrote to the Bishop of Tewkesbury, 'Ever since I have been in the diocese, I have had an extraordinarily loyal and efficient body of colleagues and assistants, and the work of the diocese has owed very much to them. I hope between us that we have been able to do some good in our generation.'

CHAPTER TWENTY-TWO

Education

I

HEADLAM'S Primary Charge in 1924 made it quite clear to the Diocese that he was an uncompromising champion of church schools and a firm believer in freedom—freedom from undue control by the authorities and freedom for denominational religious teaching. He deplored the results of a bureaucratic method of organization in which the unimportant things were looked upon as the most important. 'Buildings, uniformity of system, carefully kept statistics are all of very secondary importance compared with intellectual and spiritual aims. . . . If your education is to be of value it must be definitely spiritual and therefore in close association with the religious life of the country. . . . We want to have the full influence and power of religious reality in education, we want to have a system which gives complete freedom. . . . I am convinced that there are two movements, both dangerous to freedom, which have to be strongly resisted at the present time. The one, the attempt to make our education more bureaucratic, to get the schools more and more into the hands of the local authority or the central authority, to take away the initiative and freedom of the teachers and of the local governors. The other is the attempt to introduce anything like a uniform or systematized system of religious teaching.'[1] Religious education should be given as far as possible in accordance with parental wishes, while the Cowper-Temple clause requiring the teaching of undenominational religion in council schools should go. It should be dogmatic and denominational, given by teachers who were sincere and knowledgable Christians, who had been properly trained and who had a respect for those whose religious beliefs differed from their own. Such ideals should permeate the whole educational system from the universities to the elementary schools.

---

[1] *The Church of England*, pp. 148–52. Headlam expressed his views in fuller form in an article in *C.Q.R.*, vol. 104, pp. 122–47, which was also published as a booklet entitled *Religious Education*.

At the universities it required the establishment of religious centres not only for theological research but also for the training of clergy, ordinands and teachers : in training colleges opportunity and encouragement should be given to students to secure a qualification in religious knowledge : while secondary and elementary schools should possess independent bodies of managers to ensure as far as possible freedom for denominational teaching.

To further such aims Headlam asked the Church Assembly on July 10, 1924, to appoint a Commission to enquire into the whole question of religious education and its relation to the development of national education and to formulate suggestions.[2] The Assembly agreed to do so, but nothing was done for nearly two years—a delay for which Archbishop Davidson was mainly responsible. He did not sympathize with all Headlam's views, preferring instead to secure by agreement a single national organization of elementary schools in place of the dual system of provided and non-provided schools[3] : furthermore, with the recent advent of a Labour Government he felt that the whole education question was in the melting pot, and he was reluctant to do anything which might hamper rather than further its cause.[4]

Towards the end of 1925 Headlam began to press the Archbishop, who finally asked him to suggest a scheme of work and draw up a list of possible members. In reply he proposed that they should survey the whole field of education with four main lines of enquiry—

1. The co-operation of other religious bodies in securing religious instruction in all schools.
2. The provision of qualified teachers of religious instruction.
3. The fair treatment of all religious educational institutions.
4. The replacement of the Cowper-Temple clause by a regulation permitting religious instruction in accordance with parental wishes.

He also put forward the names of some twelve people, most of whom were appointed to form the nucleus of the Commission. Sir Henry Hadow (Vice-Chancellor of Sheffield University) was appointed chairman, and among its members were Dr. Temple (Bishop of Manchester), W. H. Moberley (Vice-Chancellor of Manchester University), Sir W. R. Buchanan Riddell (Principal of Hertford College, Oxford), Sir Cyril Cobb (member of the Education Committee of the L.C.C.), Dr. T. Loveday (Vice-Chancellor of Bristol

---

[2] *Church Assembly Proceedings*, vol. 5, pp. 187–90.
[3] Bell, *Randall Davidson*, p. 1132.
[4] Randall Cantuar to Headlam, November 26, 1924.

University), Canon B. H. Streeter, Athelstan Riley, Captain Harold Macmillan and Miss Lilian Faithfull (Principal of Cheltenham Ladies' College). A later addition was Spencer Leeson (Headmaster of Merchant Taylors' School), who proved to be a veritable thorn in Headlam's flesh. At their first meeting on July 23, 1926, they agreed to follow Headlam's suggested lines of enquiry and undertook to present a report at the end of two years.

Meanwhile Headlam was grappling with the educational problems in his own diocese. In July 1924 he expressed concern at the future of their church schools. Two had recently been given up and in neither case did this action appear to him to be justified. He felt that pressure was being brought to bear upon the managers by the Gloucestershire Education Committee to give up their schools on the grounds of economy or efficiency—a dishonourable thing for a public body to do. These remarks, which appeared first in the *Diocesan Magazine* and then in *The Times* caused considerable resentment among members of the Committee : some regarded it as a declaration of war, while the chairman strenuously denied that any pressure had been brought to bear. Headlam sought the views of some leading Churchmen who were members of the Committee, and they succeeded in convincing him that the Church schools were in fact being treated with fairness and justice. He therefore withdrew his accusations. He was prepared to accept that the Committee itself had behaved fairly and justly : nevertheless the fact remained that the administration of the existing regulations created irritation and resentment.

This irritation and resentment coloured all Headlam's dealings with the Board of Education and with the local authorities—he made another attack at the Diocesan Conference in 1925—and his uncompromising and rather belligerent attitude did not always make things easy for his own diocesan education officials. In 1925 he created a Federation of Church School Managers to help them with all their difficulties and to further a united diocesan policy and action. It was a timely move, for on October 1 the Board of Education issued its 'Black List' of schools, condemning some as incapable of improvement and unsuitable for further recognition, and demanding of others extensive alterations, additions or reorganization to bring them up to the necessary requirements. This list hit the diocese hard, for although there were no schools in the first category, there were nearly twenty in the second and in almost all cases the requirements were quite beyond the means of the parishes concerned. Headlam, of course, regarded this as yet another device on the part of the authorities to secure control of church schools. In *The Times* of November 26 he strongly condemned the whole scheme as unjust. This evoked a spirited reply from Lord Eustace Percy, the President of the Board of Education : far from being unjust, it simply laid down an orderly, definite and agreed programme of improvements which could be spread over a period of years in accordance with the means available. Headlam welcomed the statement, but pointed out that whatever might be the desire of the Board, the result of its action was to put schools in a difficult position. He met the situation by creating a Loan Fund, subsidized by the Diocesan Board of Finance, from which managers could borrow money at a very low rate of interest to set their schools in order.

The following year, however, brought the prospect of further heavy demands with the publication of the Hadow Report, recommending the end of all elementary education at the age of eleven, after which children would go to secondary schools, technical schools or senior schools. This plan seriously affected the existing arrangement of single schools, and especially church schools, in villages throughout the diocese, but Headlam refused to be beaten. He was determined to keep his schools if at all possible, and he was indefatigable in raising money for repairs and improvements. Between 1926 and 1929 he spent £23,857 on this work, and in September 1929 he proudly announced the opening of All Saints' School, Cheltenham, as a senior church school—the first in the diocese to be organized in accordance with the Hadow Report. It was a co-operative effort by three parishes —Holy Trinity, S. John's and All Saints—which had pooled their buildings and resources to create junior schools in the first two parishes and a senior school for all three in the third.

The Education Act of 1936 gave considerable help towards the building of denominational senior schools, empowering the authorities to grant fifty to seventy-five per cent of the total cost if they considered such schools to be necessary. Headlam immediately took advantage of this. In July 1937 he issued an Appeal for £60,000 to build seven new church senior schools,[5] to recondition existing elementary schools and to create a Repair Fund. The response was most encouraging. In the first year nearly £35,000 was received or promised, and before the outbreak of war in 1939 the acquisition of sites and the preparation of plans was well under way.

II

Headlam had also encountered difficulties on the Commission on Religious Education, notably on the thorny question of religious

[5] The authorities agreed to contribute three-quarters of the cost.

education and the State. Most of the members, led by Spencer Leeson, were evidently in favour of coming to terms with the State on the lines previously favoured by Archbishop Davidson. Headlam was entirely opposed to the idea. He wrote to the chairman on June 16, 1928 :

'I have been thinking for some time about the tendency of our Commission on Religious Education. In many ways its work is very good, and a great deal that it will produce will be of great value : but there are certain tendencies which, personally, I think are imperfect in themselves and also, if allowed to prevail too much, will prevent our work being effective. The majority of the members of the Commission, quite rightly no doubt, are educational in their outlook more than definitely ecclesiastical, and I cannot help feeling that a good many of the memoranda take perhaps a too optimistic view of the merits of undenominational and undogmatic education. Now I am quite sure that if that tendency prevails it will have an unfortunate effect. In the first place may I say that the result of my experience is that religious teaching on such lines is ultimately ineffective. If a man's moral principles are not built up on a real religious faith, he has nothing strong to rely upon when he faces some of the deeper realities of life. What I may call the ordinary school religion does not really touch a man's deeper nature. If the real religious instinct has been given elsewhere, then it is valuable ; otherwise it is nothing he will be able to rely upon when he comes against the sterner realities of his future life. Then again, a religion which is undenominational does not bring him into contact with the religious life of the country, and he does not get the help which he otherwise would get from being a member of and in close association with the Christian Society. This is very marked indeed, I believe, in our country villages. Further, speaking from the point of view of the Church of England, if he has not had any wise instruction as to the status and position of the Church to which he belongs, he cannot defend it against the sort of attacks that may be directed against it in after life. Let me take an illustration. Many people, men and women, later in life feel strongly the need for religion. If they have been properly taught it will come to them naturally through their own Church, but if not they may be at the mercy, for example, of a skilled Roman controversialist ; and they will have very little in themselves to meet him. A certain amount of vague Protestant prejudice is a very unsubstantial basis on which to defend the teaching of the Church of England against a skilled controversialist.

'Now I cannot but notice that there is a tendency, especially in relation to secondary schools, to say that all is going on well and in the best way. That is certainly not the case. Some schools, as we have found, are very good, and there is a great deal of original thought being given to religious education; but we want great freedom and opportunity besides a somewhat different ideal.

'Not only is this necessary in itself but still more if our report is to have any influence. Our business is to produce a solution of the religious education question which will have some chance of becoming law, and will also commend itself to the Church Assembly. I know pretty well the temper of the majority of that body, and I do not think you will carry it with you unless you make it quite clear that the position and demands of the Church are to be met. It is all very well to be conciliatory to local Education Authorities and the Board of Education, though they are neither of them very popular in the country; but after all the Church of England has, in the opinion of the Church Assembly at any rate, still some rights and some ground to have its opinion considered.'

Headlam failed to move the majority of the Commission. In June 1929 when they voted on their attitude towards the Cowper-Temple clause, eighteen members opposed any recommendation for its repeal and only six, including Headlam, supported it. When therefore the Commission produced its Report C.A. 301 at the beginning of 1930, although Headlam agreed with most of its proposals, including the creation of a central Educational Council for the Church Assembly, he was quite opposed to those relating to religious education and the State. He thought the idea of developing religious teaching within the limits of the Cowper-Temple clause failed to meet the needs of the case for Church people : nor was it just to make people pay for schools which they did not want, and then make them pay extra for schools which they did want : it involved building up a system of religious education in the interests of one part of the community only. He therefore produced a Minority Report C.A. 301A, which was signed by five other members—Sir Cyril Cobb, Dr. Loveday, Captain Macmillan, Sir Walter Riddell and Athelstan Riley, expressing this point of view and recommending that Parliament should pass a one clause Bill, empowering local education authorities to arrange for the religious instruction of all children in accordance with parental wishes notwithstanding the Cowper-Temple clause.

The fact that the Church Assembly heavily endorsed the Majority Report on February 6, 1930, left Headlam quite unmoved.[6] He wrote in the *Diocesan Magazine* in March, 'I was beaten on the Commission

[6] *Church Assembly Proceedings*, vol. 11, pp. 119–50.

for Religious Education; I was beaten again on the Assembly. I am afraid that I remain quite convinced of the inadvisability of the action which has been recommended.' In implementing the other recommendations of the Report, however, he was wholehearted. He played a large part in the reorganization of the National Society, whereby it received a new Charter in 1934 to become the Central Council for Religious Education.[7] He followed this up by reorganizing all the educational activities of the diocese under a Diocesan Council of Religious Education with a Director at its head.[8] He also tried to promote a scheme for founding and endowing a theological hostel in the University of Bristol, which might ultimately form part of a Faculty of Theology. Two houses were in fact offered and some £6,000 promised, but the project came to nothing largely through lack of support in Bristol itself. Headlam was quite prepared to launch yet another appeal for funds, but his brother diocesan at Bristol would have none of it.[9]

On the Government policy towards education he had profound misgivings. The White Paper of Mr. R. A. Butler, President of the Board of Education, entitled 'Educational Reconstruction' and published in July 1943, forecasting the lines the proposed Educational Bill should take, filled him with gloom. He told his Diocesan Conference in October 1943 that if such a Bill were passed, it would mean the death of all church schools. An undenominational system of religious education and a unified system of national education were quite deplorable. When the Bill received its first reading in December he thought of organizing an all-out attack on it, but the Bishop of Tewkesbury persuaded him to change his mind. His suffragan wisely pointed out that nothing was likely to be gained and much might even be lost: the National Society had agreed in principle to the Bill, the Church Assembly had accepted this decision, and it was impossible to deny strong opinion throughout the country in favour of the abolition of the dual system. Unpleasant though it might be, it would be wise to accept the inevitable. Headlam was compelled to agree, but with great reluctance. 'This megalomaniacal Education Bill,' he wrote, 'is a very evil thing. It gives the Government a monopoly of education, and all monopolies are evil. It is really totalitarian. It is very curious, that while we are supposed to be fighting totalitarianism, we should also be initiating it.'[10]

This measure, which became law on August 3, 1944, unquestionably demanded a great deal of church schools. Managers were

[7] Ibid., vol. 11, pp. 519–34.
[8] This scheme did not become fully operative until 1943 owing to the War.
[9] Headlam to Canon L. E. Parsons, March 30, 1939.
[10] Headlam to Miss P. L. Wingfield, January 3, 1944.

required to meet half the cost of improvements or alterations necessary to make their schools conform to Ministry regulations and also
had to meet half the cost of internal repairs. Inability to do so would
result in their schools becoming controlled : two-thirds of the managers would be appointed by the local authorities; and denominational instruction would be limited to two periods a week, the rest of
the religious instruction being based on an agreed syllabus. In
addition to all this, costs had inevitably soared owing to the War.
Headlam had to face the bitter fact that all his earlier hopes for
senior church schools were shattered : under the new regulations only
one such school would now cost £90,000. The original scheme was
therefore abandoned : the Appeal Fund Committee felt they could do
little more than explore the possibilities of building two or three
junior schools with Government help.

It was a sad end to Headlam's efforts. He wrote to the Bishop of
Tewkesbury, 'It is sad that our work together has been spoilt by the
Education Act. I am really very bitter about it. It seems to me absolutely wrong, and the action of the church authorities equally wrong.
. . . I don't trust the Board of Education. I have had more than fifty
years' experience of them; and it is not that they care for Education :
it is that like all bureaucrats they want to get everything in their own
hands.'[11] He was quite sure that the National Society, led on by
Spencer Leeson, Archbishop Temple and Mr. R. A. Butler, had 'sold
the pass' and if only the Bishops, like the Roman Catholic Bishops,
had had the courage to stand together, things might have been very
different.

He took the opportunity at his final Diocesan Conference on
September 20, 1945, of delivering one last broadside—what he himself called 'a very portentous address.' Their original plans for senior
schools were shattered—and the Board of Education were guilty of a
definite breach of faith : 'to encourage one to raise a large sum of
money and then when the money is raised, to make new conditions
which it is impossible to fulfil, seems to me the sort of dishonourable
proceeding which I expect from a Government department when it
thinks it has public opinion on its side.' The diocese would need to
raise something in the region of £1,350,000 to bring up all its schools
to required standards—a complete impossibility. It was obviously
intended for their destruction.

'I have often seen it stated that the aim of our educational system
is that every one is to have the opportunity of getting on in the world.
That is, of course, a wrong ideal. The object of education is not
that we may get on but that we may live rightly. . . . It is quite right

[11] Headlam to the Bishop of Tewkesbury, August 6, 1945, August 21, 1945.

that our educational system should be such that a really clever boy can obtain a scholarship and in due course become a Cabinet Minister, but the many thousands who will have to be agricultural labourers will be much better trained by learning to do their work properly than by any amount of book-learning. Nor need they complain of their lot. A good agricultural labourer is much more useful than most cabinet ministers and leads a happier and healthier life.'

CHAPTER TWENTY-THREE

The Bishop in his
Study

I

In his Primary Charge Headlam had deplored the decrease in the
supply of learned clergy and the tendency to despise theological
learning. 'It seems to be forgotten that unless there continues a supply
of learned clergy ready and able to grapple with the questions of the
day, the Church, especially in a time of movement like the present,
will inevitably be out of touch with modern thought.' [1] He therefore
did all he could to encourage sound learning among his clergy. The
poorer incumbents, for example, were given not only grants to supplement their incomes but also gifts of books which otherwise they
would never be able to buy. He also took infinite trouble over his
Clergy Schools and Diocesan Conferences, inviting as speakers a long
succession of ecclesiastical scholars and statesmen such as few other
dioceses could have equalled. These men were drawn from a very
wide field, for he had no desire to encourage an outlook that was
parochial or even insular. [2] He wanted the diocese to be alive to issues
and movements which were not necessarily its own immediate concern. So, for example, on one occasion Archbishop Germanos of
Thyateira was asked to speak on Anglican-Orthodox relations; on
another occasion the South Indian scheme was surveyed from opposite points of view by Bishop Palmer and Dr. Sparrow Simpson; and
on another the Oxford Group Movement was debated by a noted
advocate, London Hamilton, and a stern critic, Canon Frederic Hood
of Pusey House.

By far the most notable of all these gatherings was the sixty-third
Church Congress at Cheltenham in October 1928. Headlam as its
President was the guiding genius and produced a wonderful array of
speakers from this country and from overseas to discuss the Church
of England and its relations with the State, with other Christian bodies
and to modern thought. He surveyed the whole field in his Presiden-

[1] *The Church of England*, p. 199.
[2] Ibid., p. 205.

The Bishop in his Study

tial Address : it was Headlam at its best—a masterpiece of compression and lucidity, containing his views on the Prayer Book controversy, disestablishment, finance, education, party spirit, modern thought and reunion.[3] The Congress did not meet without a conflict. Dr. H. D. A. Major, Principal of Ripon Hall, who was invited to speak on 'The Anglican Interpretation of the Faith,' had just created a stir in the July number of *The Modern Churchman* by claiming that although the Modernist believed in the supernatural, it was a non-miraculous supernatural; and that Christ was a perfectly non-miraculous Christ, who was God's son in the moral sense in which all human beings are the sons of God. His invitation to speak was resented by the Church Union, which announced that it would not support the Congress and would feel impelled to discourage its members from attending. An Open Letter of protest bearing nearly a thousand signatures including that of Lord Halifax was also sent to Headlam. His offer to discuss the matter with the organizers of the protest was refused—the matter was not one which would admit discussion, nor were they prepared to change their minds. Headlam, regarding such an attitude as intolerable, ignored them and addressed his reply to Lord Halifax, for whom he had a great respect. His letter appeared in *The Times* on October 2, the opening day of the Congress. It was an effective answer to the critics : although he was prepared to admit his disagreement with Dr. Major in more than one respect, the quest for truth was not served by condemning him as a heretic and by stifling discussion.

'I often do not agree with Dr. Major : I dislike the tendency he shows to build up what may be called an Unorthodox Orthodoxy : I think sometimes he is nearly as dogmatic as his opponents : some of his language is precarious : but I have found no evidence that he does not really believe in the truth of the Incarnation. . . . What I am in effect asked to do is on the ground of a number of passages divorced from their context to condemn Dr. Major without giving him the opportunity of stating his case . . . (I believe that Dr. Major) as we all do, feels the difficulty and urgency of the many problems created by the new thought of the day; that he is anxious to defend the truth that he believes; and that he is attempting to build up an apologetic and a philosophy of his faith which is in accordance with modern thought. I do not entirely agree with his method or his statements : but the way to meet them is by open and free discussion. If that is allowed the result will be that those things which are true will be established and those things which are false will gradually be for-

[3] H. A. Wilson (editor), *The Anglican Communion*. Report of the 63rd Church Congress, Cheltenham 1928, pp. 3-35.

gotten. . . . It is a far better way than that of forbidding discussion and condemning those who differ from us as heretics.'

Another method by which Headlam encouraged his diocese to avoid a narrow outlook was by making good use of his monthly *Diocesan Magazine*. Here, in brief and extremely simple articles, he kept people informed of his own extra-diocesan activities—tours and conferences, work with the Faith and Order Movement and the activities of the Council on Foreign Relations, and at the same time gave his views on the issues of the day—wages and unemployment, strikes, taxation, education, war and so on. He often made these deliberately provocative, simply to get people talking and thinking. 'I am very glad when my utterances, whether on theological or other topics, are criticized, if the criticism is done in an intelligent way. In fact I sometimes state things in a more or less aggressive fashion in order to elicit criticism or stimulate thought.' [4] The criticism which was sometimes aroused was, in fact, a source of embarrassment to his clergy ; while the letters which he himself received were at times hostile and abusive. These he liked to keep ; and among his papers there is a file bearing the title 'Fan Mail.' 'See how wicked I am,' he would say, producing some of the more violent specimens. 'That is what makes me feel that I am right.' No amount of criticism would make him change his views. 'It is, of course, to a certain extent uncomfortable to be exposed to such a violent criticism, but my experience has been that it is generally those statements for which I have been criticized which I am afterwards able to look back to as being justified.' [5] Indeed, such was his fearlessness and integrity that many people came to feel that perhaps he knew a great deal more than they thought, and that after all there was some grain of truth in his vigorous remarks.

II

Despite the fact that Headlam continued to read on a prodigious scale, he wrote little that was really new after becoming a bishop. There was no decrease in his theological output ; but most of his work dealt with ecclesiastical events and issues of the moment, many of which have been discussed elsewhere. He had no high opinion of these productions—they were 'fugitive writings' and 'poor stuff' ; and although he undoubtedly enjoyed putting pen to paper, it was evident that they had been written largely from a sense of duty. The

[4] *The Diocesan Magazine*, June 1934.
[5] Ibid., October 1941.

longing was always there to get down to 'that Big Work,' which was in fact never completed.

The Church Quarterly Review continued to play a large part in this literary activity. Indeed, if it had not been for his efforts, the magazine would probably have ceased to exist. By 1926 its position was precarious : the circulation was small and liabilities were mounting. The company was therefore wound up and Headlam became sole proprietor with personal responsibility for the debts. At the same time he transferred the whole undertaking to Gloucester. The printing was undertaken by a local firm, while Canon Maynard Smith became editor in the place of 'the Members of the Faculty of Theology, King's College, London,' who had been responsible since 1921. Four years later Philip Usher took over the editorship and held it until his death in 1941. Headlam finally disposed of the magazine to the proprietors of *The Guardian* for a nominal sum on his retirement in 1945. Claude Jenkins estimated that over the years Headlam must have lost well over £1,000 in keeping it going : but Headlam regarded it as money well spent. From a personal point of view it gave him constant access to new books and international periodicals and also provided him with a convenient means of expressing his own views. At the same time it was unique, and the Church of England would have been very much the poorer for its passing. Canon Maynard Smith described as being 'the organ of a sober but very definite Anglicanism—intended for educated people who were not necessarily specialists. It aimed at being for Churchmen what *The Quarterly Review* was for the world at large : and it preserved that width of culture which was once the glory of the Church of England.'

Another venture which Headlam backed was the new edition of the Greek New Testament. The eighth and last edition of Tischendorf's great work, which had appeared in 1869 and 1872, was now quite out of date. A new work to replace it, published by Professor H. von Soden of Berlin in 1913, had then failed to gain general acceptance among scholars. The need for a new edition with a modern critical apparatus was therefore as great as ever. Headlam became increasingly impressed by this need when working on *The Life and Teaching of Jesus the Christ*. At the end of 1925, therefore, he discussed with a few friends—Sir F. J. Kenyon, Dr. B. H. Streeter and Dr. J. H. White among them—the possibilities of a joint undertaking. He felt that while such experts on the Versions as Professor F. C. Burkitt on the Syriac, the Revd. G. Horner on the Coptic and Dr. White on the Vulgate were still alive, it would be a grave error not to make use of them. As a result a committee was formed with Headlam as chairman and including the Bishop of Oxford (Dr. T. Strong), Sir F. J.

Kenyon, Professor A. Souter, Dr. B. H. Streeter, Dr. J. H. White, and Professor A. Nairne, with the Revd. S. C. E. Legg as secretary and editor. Help was also promised from America and Germany, and later from France : it was therefore an international and an interconfessional undertaking. The cost of such a work was high—perhaps as much as £10,000, and Headlam devoted a great deal of time and energy in appealing for funds. Progress was slow—the task was much greater than Headlam had at first realized : but at least he had the satisfaction of seeing the Gospels of S. Mark and S. Matthew published before the War brought the work to a temporary close.

III

Headlam did much of his actual writing away from Gloucester. The library of the Athenaeum was a favourite retreat; and if he possibly could, he would shut himself away for several days at a time. 'The Library of the Athenaeum is one of the best places I know for concentrated work.' There he would write as much as a hundred pages in a week. The fact that he wrote at speed is obvious. His English was always simple and clear; but it was not polished and could be slovenly, containing such elementary errors as 'different to' instead of 'different from.' His spidery and almost illegible handwriting, too, gave the impression of hurry and speed. It was, of course, a family failing—both his father and his brother, James, were deplorable writers. But Headlam's pen always appeared to be struggling rather unsuccessfully to keep up with his thoughts which were flying on ahead. At times his writing could be thoroughly exasperating, causing misunderstandings and wasting valuable time : but it could also be diverting. There was, for example, his note from Scotland which apparently read, 'Plenty of *sin* here, but it's rather nice,' when in fact he really meant *rain*. The stories of his writing are legion, and he could be rather sensitive about them; but two remarks dating from the period when he was Domestic Bursar of All Souls stand out above all others. One was by Henson and the other by F. E. Brightman. Henson, whose own hand was immaculate, used to say that Headlam's writing was undoubtedly influenced by his study of Coptic ; and on one occasion, after receiving an unusually illegible letter, he replied, 'After the necessary probation (when intellect ruled and vision grew dim before the weird hieroglyphics, which yet were dictated by kindness and charged with friendship), I discovered at least a plausible theory of their meaning. Though this theory has necessitated some bold, and—as some might think—unwarranted emendations of the text, I have sufficient confidence in its substantial accuracy, as to base my present epistle on that supposition, feeling that even if I be in error, the author of the misty uncials which deceived me is as generous as he is (occasionally) unintelligible.' Brightman's description of his writing very cleverly brings in his office at All Souls : 'It is very difficult to give even an approximate date to a composition evidently from so rude and illiterate a hand : but it is clear that it must have been written before the ordinary principles of cursive writing were at all understood. Probably it is the composition of some slave, who being attached to a school of letters in some menial capacity, as for instance to look after the food, had picked up a few words, which he is unable to write correctly.'

After this digression it now remains to consider briefly the more weighty writings of Headlam's episcopate, particularly those which have not been discussed elsewhere. Mention might first be made of the William Belden Noble lectures delivered in America in 1925 and published under the title *'Jesus Christ in History and Faith.'* They continued the work begun in *The Life and Teaching of Jesus the Christ*, which dealt with the first part of our Lord's earthly life. A certain amount of recapitulation was necessary to make the lectures a cohesive whole, but they were primarily concerned with the later events of our Lord's life and with certain theological questions—the relation of the Christ of History to the Christ of Faith and Christ and the Church. Headlam was not too happy about them. He confessed to Professor Nairne, 'I really do not think the lectures are very good though they contain good stuff in them. For instance, the lecture on the Death of our Lord is rather a poor performance.' Nevertheless they were interesting and revealed considerable learning. In his preliminary study of the Gospels, for example, he suggested a four document theory in preference to the current two-document theory which was very much in line with the view expressed by Dr. Streeter, whose book *The Four Gospels* appeared shortly after the lectures were delivered.[6] He also provided weighty support for the orthodox point of view just at a time when it was most needed, particularly in America, where Foakes Jackson and Kirsopp Lake were then busy producing their massive and radical *The Beginnings of Christianity.* So, for example, the Transfiguration was a truthful account of a real spiritual experience[7]; the Virgin Birth was an early belief of the Christian Church, harmonizing with the Biblical conception of our Lord[8]; and the combination of strong and good evidence with the

[6] *Jesus Christ in History and Faith,* pp. viii–x.
[7] Ibid., p. 65.
[8] Ibid., p. 170.

series of events which followed the Resurrection might reasonably bring conviction to men's minds.[9] Dr. C. A. Alington summed it all up effectively : 'It is a great comfort when pundits like Kirsopp Lake and Company go about airily declaring that nothing is true and very little probable to find someone who will soberly state the orthodox case from the point of view of sound scholarship.' Although this was the smaller of the two books which Headlam wrote on our Lord, it was certainly the more valuable.

Headlam, of course, was proud of being a solid, orthodox, middle-of-the-road Church of England man. Nowhere is this clearer than in his Primary Charge *The Church of England*. It revealed him as one who was supremely proud of Ecclesia Anglicana : it had a character of its own which corresponded to the national character of the people; it had had a glorious history in the past; it met the needs of the present age; and it should have a great future. Firmly rooted in the fundamental principles of the Christian religion, it was both adaptable and comprehensive : and because it was the great *via media,* he felt that it had a vocation to a wider witness. 'Originally it was a national Church which had certain characteristics of its own, it is true, but was simply important as being the Church of the English nation. Now it is more and more outgrowing that characteristic, and coming to stand as representative of a special type of Christianity. It is not only an Episcopal Church, but is developing in its Theology and Order certain features of its own which it would present as the contribution of its life and thought to the religious life of the world. This type that it aspires to present may be described as Free Evangelical Catholicism.' [10]

If his Primary Charge proclaimed a firm belief in the Church of England, Headlam's Third Charge *What it means to be a Christian* proclaimed a firm belief in the fundamentals of the Christian faith. It was an attempt to answer in simple language the question so often asked, 'What is the *faith* in which I believe?' This in itself involved two other questions—'What is the Christian message which we have inherited?' and 'How can we express it so that others can understand it and accept it?' An answer involved three things—a correct knowledge of what Christianity is, an intelligent statement of it, and finally a philosophical defence of it.[11] This is what he attempted to provide in this little book. It contained a great deal of what was the common creed of Christendom : in fact he was deliberately suggesting a basis on which the different Churches might well agree—belief in God,

[9] Ibid., p. 169.
[10] *The Church of England*, p. 47.
[11] *What it means to be a Christian*, p. 8.

Jesus Christ, the Holy Spirit, the Trinity, the Christian Life, the Church, the Sacraments and the Hope of Immortality. The line of thought was quite logical. Avoiding the academic approach he constantly appealed to reason, conscience and experience. The Charge was really his own apology for the Christian life. 'I have written what I can in accordance with my knowledge—I have tried to solve my own difficulties and to express my own faith—I can only hope that these may seem to some of those to whom I write to be helpful.'[12]

A great deal of this was given much more fully in his unfinished *magnum opus*, the first volume of which appeared in 1934—*Christian Theology: the Doctrine of God*. It was a text-book—he stated quite frankly in the Preface that it was intended as a manual of theology for those who desired to enter the Christian ministry in the Church of England[13]—and it was based on the lectures which he had given both at King's College, London, and at Oxford. It also embodied a great deal of what he had written in earlier books, while six chapters had appeared as articles in *The Church Quarterly Review*. Headlam's purpose, as he explained in the Introduction, was 'to formulate and to expound systematically and intelligently our theological knowledge.'[14] So far, this had not been done in English theology: there was nothing to compare with S. John of Damascus *On the Christian Faith*, the *Summa Theologica* of S. Thomas Aquinas, or the *Institutio Christianae Religionis* of Calvin. 'English people do not love system or order or completeness.' The only modern work which approached the subject with any degree of intelligence was Dr. Strong's *Manual of Theology*.[15] Gore's massive *Reconstruction of Belief*, which had appeared between 1921 and 1924 was not even mentioned: but it is interesting to notice a striking difference between the work of the two men. Gore's trilogy presented a man wrestling with his thoughts, thinking things out and not quite sure of his conclusions. With Headlam, however, there was no wrestling with thoughts or working perhaps rather laboriously towards a conclusion: he was quite clear in his own mind and proceeded from start to finish with majestic ease. He was master of the situation and his own learning did not oppress him.

His approach to the subject was historical, and his point of view conservative. In some respects he was so conservative as to appear out of date. Some of the problems which he discussed and the books to which he referred were old-fashioned and even forgotten: the Sanday-Williams discussions of 1916 on the infallibility of the Church, for

[12] Ibid., p. 11.
[13] *Christian Theology: the Doctrine of God*, 1935, p. v.
[14] Ibid., p. 1.
[15] Ibid., p. 4.

example, were no longer a live issue in 1934.[16] He was not unaware of this, for he stated in the Preface, 'Some of the difficulties raised may appear obsolete to the student of the present day, but I do not think that an acquaintance with the problems of twenty or thirty years ago will really be harmful.' [17] He believed in the traditional statement of belief and was not seriously moved by the questions of the moment. The present period was one of transition, and many of the current thoughts and controversies were likely to be ephemeral and of no consequence. It was therefore extremely wise to have one's feet on firm ground. 'Church History shows that progress is made not by plunging into new ideas any more than by clinging obstinately to tradition, but by the thoughtful moderation which steadily sifts new and old truths.' [18] Headlam had already made up his mind on essentials of the Christian faith by the time he had gone to King's College, and nothing had happened since which made him feel that any change was necessary.

The second volume on Creation, Redemption, Grace, the Church and the Sacraments, which was promised in the Preface never appeared, although a glance at the articles in *The Church Quarterly Review* will show that he had done a great deal of work on it: between 1939 and 1942 ten essays appeared on Creation, Redemption and Grace. He also published a small book on *The Atonement* which was of considerable interest. It contained the Frederick Denison Maurice Lectures for 1935 delivered at King's College, London, and was regarded by Professor Nairne as one of his best pieces of work. He was inspired by the appearance in English of two Continental works—*The Mediator* by Emil Brunner and *Christus Victor* by Gustav Aulen—to consider the evidence of the Atonement afresh. As a result he came to the conclusion that redemption was not accomplished by any sort of transaction : there was no question of appeasing an angry God, but of reconciling sinful, selfish men to God. The relations of men to God were changed because God changed them. Man was saved, not from the penalty of sin, but from sin itself; and the only thing that could overcome sin was love. This was revealed in the redemptive work of Christ, which meant not simply the Cross but the whole of His life and teaching—a sacrifice of love and obedience. This redemptive work was to be continued by His followers. Man's salvation came through himself—God accomplished something in men and through men.[19] But this salvation involved sacrifice by the reconciled as well as by the Saviour. Sacrifice was

16 Ibid., p. 135.
17 Ibid., p. v.
18 Ibid., p. 473.
19 *The Atonement*, 1935, p. 188.

self-sacrifice, and was part of the ultimate nature of God Himself.[20]

There are two important points to notice about Headlam's view of the Atonement. In the first place it denotes a change from the position expressed in the Commentary on *Romans*. There the view was expressed that the Atonement involved a change of attitude or relation on the part of God as well as of man, although it was doubtful what was involved. 'There is frequent mention of the Anger of God as directed against sinners. . . . When that Anger ceases to be so directed there is surely a change on the part of God as well as of man. . . . We are obliged to use anthropomorphic expressions which imply a change of attitude or relation on the part of God as well as of man; and yet in some way which we cannot wholly fathom we may believe that with Him there is "no variableness, neither shadow of turning." '[21] But now Headlam was quite sure that there was no change in God but only in man : Christ's atoning work revealed God's love for mankind that was always there : man's conscience was cleansed and his life could be transformed.[22] Headlam had changed his mind on this point and he did not say why. Secondly, there was the significance of the Atonement in Headlam's views on reunion. Self-sacrifice is the true bond of union : perfect love and obedience must be offered in Christ's members. But such sacrifice of love and obedience cannot possibly be offered by a Church which is divided and in the sinful state of schism.[23] The effective work of man's redemption was therefore closely bound with the unity of the Church. Reunion was necessary to complete the atoning work of Christ.

[20] Ibid., pp. 174–6.
[21] *Romans*, pp. 129–30.
[22] *The Atonement*, pp. 12, 187.
[23] Ibid., pp. 174–6; *The Doctrine of the Church and Reunion*, pp. 223–4.

CHAPTER TWENTY-FOUR

Retirement

On October 1, 1945, Headlam returned home to Whorlton immeasurably relieved to be free from diocesan responsibilities and to feel that 'it does not matter to any one but oneself whether one does anything or not.' Nevertheless, there was no question of a life of slippered ease. 'Starting again at Whorlton and the dealing with my furniture present to me a very formidable task, but I want to get everything properly arranged. I hope to be really straight by Christmas. It is obvious that having attained the age of eighty-two, I cannot expect to live long and I do not want to leave things in a mess, which they clearly are at present.'[1] He was irked too by the numerous war-time regulations still in force, a state of affairs for which he was not slow to blame the recently elected Socialist Government. 'It is difficult to be anything else but indolent and self-indulgent. I cannot get on with anything that I want to do. Whenever I want to do anything, there is a government regulation, or the necessary person is not procurable. So one just does not do it. And when there is one thing one wants to do and cannot do it, one is not good enough to think of something else one might do. The fact is we are suffering from a government which thinks it is much cleverer than all the governments have been before, and is going to show how much better it is than the silly aristocrats who never had a plan; and they have to learn that they really are stupid people. And they are always talking about the splendid things they are going to do and never do them. If you leave the people of this country alone, they will do things as well as is possible.'[2] Despite the difficulties, however, he was settled in by Christmas: he was blessed with a good cook and could report that he was living in 'wicked comfort.' His attentions were now turned elsewhere.

First there was the garden. 'If there is no further war, and if there is no revolution at home, and if my land is not nationalized, and if I

[1] Headlam to Miss P. L. Wingfield, October 3, 1945.
[2] Ibid., October 20, 1945.

live to the age of ninety, and if I preserve my mental capacity, and if I don't go bankrupt, I may be able to get my garden straight.' Here he was fortunate in securing the help of two German prisoners of war who proved to be cheerful and interested workers. By the summer of 1946 he was again able to arrange open days in aid of various charitable causes. He also entered wholeheartedly into the life of the village. It gave him great delight to drop in on his tenants for a chat and a cup of tea beside the fire and he gave his support to all the local functions : at one sale of work he spent all his money on dolls and toys, to give away to the most unruly children in the room —'It is a great thing to make these occasions promote moral well-being.' He attended Church most regularly and rarely missed the parish breakfast after Holy Communion on Sunday mornings. If the Vicar needed help he was ready to give it, but he made no attempt to interfere with the running of the parish : nor did he often go away to preach.

Then there was his vast collection of books and papers—'the accumulations of an ill-spent life. If, instead of being a bishop and that sort of thing, I had lived intelligently at Oxford, I might have produced something worth while : but all these ephemeral productions are very poor stuff.' There were three things he wanted to do. The first was to complete the Life of Jesus Christ, prefaced by a new survey of the New Testament evidence : the second was to write the second volume on Christian Theology : and the third was to collect some of his 'fugitive writings' of the past twenty-five years for a book which he proposed to call *My Stewardship*. He settled down to the Life of Christ with a will, agreeably surprised to find that mental activity came to him much more easily than it had done for many years. 'My powers of locomotion grow less : on the other hand I am very vigorous mentally and write with greater ease than I used.'

It was not long before he was submitting sections of the work to various friends for comment and before the end of the year some half dozen chapters were in various stages of completion. One essay, 'The Historical Value of S. Mark's Gospel' opposing Form-criticism in general and Dr. A. E. J. Rawlinson and Professor R. H. Lightfoot in particular, appeared in *The Church Quarterly Review* for October 1946[3] ; while another, 'Jesus' Last Journey to Jerusalem' appeared in January 1947.[4] Most of his time was devoted to a study of S. John's Gospel—'a rather complex but engrossing problem.' He wrote to his

---

[3] *C.Q.R.*, vol. 143, pp. 1–22. Cf. A. E. J. Rawlinson (later Bishop of Derby), *S. Mark* (Westminster Commentaries), 1925 ; R. H. Lightfoot, *History and Interpretation in the Gospels,* Bampton Lectures 1934.
[4] *C.Q.R.*, vol. 143, pp. 162–79.

niece, 'I am really extraordinarily wicked and unintelligent. I believe that a statement made in the New Testament is generally correct, and that the Fourth Gospel was written by S. John the Apostle. Can you imagine anything more out of date? I am sadly reactionary. I do not know what will happen to me. I think at any rate my writings will be put on the Index.' [5] This section of the work was completed at the beginning of January 1947. Only three days before his death he sent drafts of two chapters to the Dean of S. Paul's (Dr. W. R. Matthews), together with his own comments on certain suggestions which the Dean had previously made. Some of these suggestions evidently did not meet with his approval; one was even considered 'unintelligent.' The Dean remarked, 'The years faded away, and I felt that I had shown up an essay.' [6] This by no means constituted the whole of his literary activity during retirement, however. There was a long review of Dr. E. G. Selwyn's massive Commentary on the first Epistle of S. Peter in *The Church Quarterly Review;* an article on 'Jesus Christ' for Hutchinson's *Pictorial Encyclopedia*—a masterpiece of clarity, simplicity and compression; a short biography of his old friend, Alexander Nairne, who died in 1936, for *The Dictionary of National Biography*; and an essay on 'the Duty of the Christian Church' in Sir James Marchant's symposium *Has the Church Failed?*

Of particular interest was his strong indictment of Communism in another article 'The Iron Curtain,' which appeared in the July 1946 number of *The Quarterly Review.* [7] It was inspired mainly by his concern at the trend of events in Jugoslavia, where General Mihailovitch had been supplanted by General Tito and where so many of his friends were suffering severe hardships. Bishop Nikolai of Ochrid, who had been imprisoned at Dachau, met Headlam in London at the end of 1945 after his release. He wrote later : 'Bishop Headlam came to see me. He was an aged man, disturbed because of the terrible change in Jugoslavia from bad to worse. He asked me with anguish whether I knew anything of his old students over there. He asked me of each one of them by name. He had forgotten none. I knew that many of them had met a martyr's death : but I left his question unanswered in order not to add more pain to the pains of an old man and friend.' Shortly afterwards Headlam wrote to Miss Christich, secretary of the Jugoslav Association in London, 'I am very distressed about the Jugoslav situation and feel that there is so little that I can

<hr />

[5] Headlam to Miss P. L. Wingfield, December 14, 1946.
[6] The five chapters on S. John together with the essay on S. Mark's Gospel and a biographical study by his niece, Professor Agnes Headlam-Morley, were published after his death under the title *The Fourth Gospel as History.*
[7] The Iron Curtain, *The Quarterly Review*, vol. 284, pp. 257-71.

do. Now that I have retired I have neither position nor money.'[8] He did, however, write a letter to *The Times*, which appeared on April 17, protesting against the detention of General Mihailovitch, whom he considered to be genuinely pro-Ally and the victim of Communist aggression, and pleading that he might be given a fair trial—if possible by an international tribunal. A month later he wrote again, urging that a petition for such a tribunal might be sent to the Allied nations. A group of American airmen who had been rescued by General Mihailovitch then undertook to organize a petition; but in the face of Russian intransigence their efforts were doomed to failure. It was in the light of these events that Headlam wrote his article. In it he discussed Russian activity in those countries which he knew best— Jugoslavia, Latvia, Lithuania and Estonia—describing graphically their plight from evidence which he had obtained at first-hand. He then pleaded for firmness in dealing with the Russians : there should be no concealment of opinion, no silent acquiescence, no subservience —simply from considerations of expediency. Russia wanted war no more than any one else. What was needed was peace based on freedom and respect, and a firm adherence to the principles of the Atlantic Charter and of the United Nations. The article, which was as much a condemnation of weak Allied leadership as it was of Russian aggression, was not devoid of all effect. Copies were sent to Sweden and from there distributed as widely as possible throughout the Baltic states to reassure their people that their friends in Great Britain had not completely forgotten them.

On the subject of education, too, he expressed himself with vigour —he still felt very bitter about the fate of his plans at Gloucester. 'It is the want of courage that prevents people saying what they think, and the want of intelligence which prevents them thinking things out, that has got us into this mess. All the time I was Bishop I was a rebel at Bishops' meetings, especially on the Education Question. . . . (Choir schools, for example,) are just the special schools that any one who really understands would want to preserve and improve; but what can you expect when the people who control education are politicians whose only idea of it is a machine for turning farm labourers into clerks and dairy maids into typists and then wonder that we have not enough to eat.'[9] He delivered his final broadside only a week before he died in the journal of the anti-Socialist body, the Durham Municipal and County Federation. Education was something spiritual, requiring an atmosphere of freedom to be healthy : schools should be autonomous self-governing bodies, controlled neither

[8] Headlam to Miss A. Christich, January 11, 1946.
[9] Headlam to The Bishop of Tewkesbury, January 23, 1946.

by the central nor the local authorities, both of which were incompetent. Teaching was a vocation, and thanks to the National Union of Teachers it had been degraded into a career : teachers with a vocation were what mattered, not fine buildings and fat salaries. Finally, religious education demanded freedom and toleration, for all children should have the right to be taught according to the beliefs of their parents.

Headlam was not tied to his study, however, nor even to Whorlton. He went to London a number of times ; and the love of foreign travel was still there. In the spring of 1946 the University of Oslo decided to confer upon him an honorary doctorate of divinity. Professor Einar Molland wrote, 'The reason why we wanted to bestow this honour upon him was that we admired his learning, his sound judgments and his independent views. We were thinking of his books on Romans, the Church of England, and Reunion ; and we were thinking of his vote at Edinburgh in 1937—without agreeing with him.' He was determined to receive the degree in person and called up his old chaplain, Edward Prichard, from Gloucester to travel with him. The trip was brief and thoroughly enjoyable, but rather a strain. 'I am beginning to find adventures like this too much for my old age. . . . I used to be a good courier myself, but now my senility and deafness make me very helpless.'

His last trip took place in the autumn. After preaching in Durham Cathedral at the annual Commemoration Service of Founders and Benefactors on October 23, he spent a fortnight in Oxford to attend the opening of the new Bodleian by the King and to preach the Commemoration Sermon at All Souls and a further fortnight at the Athenaeum in London. These sermons at Durham and All Souls were his last two public utterances and both referred to influences which had counted for so much in his own life. At Durham he spoke of his great hero—Joseph Barber Lightfoot. There were only two men in his lifetime whom he was prepared to call really great : one was Robert Cecil, Marquis of Salisbury, and the other was Dr. Lightfoot. Lightfoot possessed great intellectual power and learning combined with a great simplicity and sincerity of character. His edition of the Apostolic Fathers—the greatest patristic work of the century—brought an element of sanity and scientific method into the study of the origins of Christianity. He had done more than any one to restore the authority of the Scriptures from the effects of that learned, acute but wrong-headed criticism which had been such a potent factor in Germany. To stand for and to attain historical truth was a great quest ; and all who desired to follow it would do well to take Lightfoot as their guide and mentor. A great teacher at Cambridge, he had also been a great diocesan bishop and a wise ecclesiastical statesman.

But with all this he had also been a great spiritual power : the simplicity, the sincerity, the profundity and the dignity of his character had made a tremendous impression.

Eleven days later he spoke in the more intimate atmosphere of All Souls' Chapel of the College he loved so well. He reminded his hearers that they should aim not only at being a learned society with certain duties to fulfil but also at achieving a certain corporate friendship. Twice within a generation they had been called to duties which had sadly depleted this circle of friends, cutting off prematurely many whose lives would have been great. He then paid tribute to three great members of the College who had died recently. First there was Archbishop Lang. 'I do not think that he was . . . a great ecclesiastical statesman ; but for the work of a clergyman, for the personal work of an archbishop he had every gift; eloquence—a mellifluous and persuasive eloquence, great social gifts, and above all an absolute conviction of the truth and beneficent power of the Christian religion and complete confidence in the position of the Church of England.' Then there was Sir Charles Oman : 'an historian in the truest sense. He had an intense interest in the past life of the world in both small and great things, and he told the story of the past with great knowledge and accuracy, without any pretension, without dwelling on its importance, without any desire to emphasize its lessons. . . . We learn from history by reading the true story and not by listening to the comments of the historian.' Finally there was George Geoffrey Dawson [10]—'he had a deeper sense of duty than any one else I have known.' As he looked back on his many friends, one definite thought came to his mind. All those who had impressed him by their character and for whom he had felt affection and admiration were those who had possessed a real hold on spiritual realities. In this sense the affairs of the world had sadly lacked wisdom in recent years. ' "Where shall wisdom be found? and where is the place of understanding? . . . The fear of the Lord, that is wisdom, and to depart from evil, that is understanding." ' Headlam had spoken his last word.

After four weeks' absence it was a great relief to get back to Whorlton. He confessed to the Bishop of Tewkesbury that he had been away too long : he was conscious of his infirmities, and it was high time for him to retire into private life. In addition to his deafness, which prevented him from taking part in general conversation, he was now troubled by a cough which made him feel a nuisance. He had consulted a specialist in Oxford, who had diagnosed fibrositis of the lungs : his heart was in order and the only thing to do was to

[10] George Geoffrey Dawson. Elected Fellow of All Souls 1900, Estates Bursar 1919–23 ; Editor of *The Times* 1912–19, 1923–41 ; died November 7, 1944.

refrain from exercise of any sort. It was a far from pleasing prospect. He was also saddened by the sudden death of his cousin, General Sir John Headlam. They were exactly the same age, had roamed Teesdale together as small boys and had gone to Reading School together. They had been extremely fond of each other and had kept in close touch throughout their long lives, for like Headlam, Sir John was a first class correspondent. He had come to Whorlton for a holiday that summer, and the two old men had thoroughly enjoyed their few weeks together in their old haunts. His death on October 14 after a stroke was undoubtedly a great shock.

Headlam lived quietly until Christmas, showing no signs of getting worse. He then felt well enough to invite a number of friends to come and see him during the holidays and would have invited even more had not his housekeeper pointed out that food rationing made catering on such a scale quite impossible. He gave way—'It is extraordinary how many things seem to need fat for their construction.' But he was not convinced—he had not been Domestic Bursar of All Souls for nothing : after his death a cookery book was found in his desk—he had begun to look into the problem himself.

In particular he looked forward to a short visit from his nephew and heir, Kenneth Headlam-Morley on January 3. The weather became bitterly cold, but he insisted on going to Darlington station to meet him. The train was an hour late, and although he did not complain of any undue ill effects, the long wait undoubtedly did him no good. Apart from a visit to his doctor he never went out again. He went on working as usual and was in good spirits. The final sections of his work on S. John's Gospel were completed : he wrote a cheerful letter to his niece, Miss Wingfield, with his views on Agatha Christie's latest detective novel, and another to his old friend, Hensley Henson, condemning a recent book edited by the Bishop of Oxford under the title *The Apostolic Ministry,* which severely criticized his own views, as 'a very bad book.' [11] On January 15, however, his sister Rose began to feel rather anxious. The doctor ordered him to bed, insisting on absolute quiet : his cough was not so bad but his breathing was laboured. The household regarded it as a bad sign when he obeyed without a murmur. Two days later, early in the morning, he asked his housekeeper for a calendar and a pencil. She produced them and left him satisfied that he was comfortable. On her return, however, he was dead, having passed away quietly in his sleep. The calendar was by his side, with the days marked off to January 25 : he had been counting the days to the anniversary of his consecration on the Feast of the Conversion of S. Paul twenty-four years before in Westminster Abbey.

[11] E. F. Braley, *Letters of Herbert Hensley Henson,* pp. 193–4.

Three days later he was buried quietly and simply by the Bishop of Durham (Dr. A. T. P. Williams) beside his wife in the little village churchyard adjoining the house in which he had been born. A large congregation filled Gloucester Cathedral on January 24 for a memorial service at which the Bishop of Tewkesbury paid a moving tribute to him as a great man. 'There is no need for me to lay stress on his greatness. Like Saul, he was head and shoulders above his fellows. And whatever the world may think, his place is secure in the history of the Christian Church. It is not of what he did, but what he was—that I want to try and speak. And of one aspect in particular, his simplicity. He was so great, because he was so simple. . . . It may be truly said of him, as of another great champion of the Faith sixteen hundred years ago :—"He planted trees, that other men in later days might sit under them." '

In 1949, on January 25—the twenty-sixth anniversary of his consecration, a memorial to him was dedicated in the North Quire of the Cathedral. It bore the words :

In memory of
Arthur Cayley
Headlam C.H. D.D.
Bishop of Gloucester
1923–1945

Who when men's hearts were
failing them for fear and for
looking after those things which
are coming on the earth bade
us take courage and seek anew
the vision of the City of God.

A true friend to his clergy and
a wise counsellor to the Church
of God : a great scholar and a
great patriot : he ever did his
duty, generously, courageously,
with integrity and simplicity.

He entered into the fuller
service of his Lord on the
17th day of January 1947.

Now I saw in my dream that they
went on and Great Heart went before them.

CHAPTER TWENTY-FIVE

Arthur Cayley Headlam

A TALL, clean-shaven figure with a silk top hat tilted on the back of his head, a slightly upturned face and both hands brandishing in the air behind him at a downward angle a stick or an umbrella, Headlam presented a striking appearance. He was thick-set but never fat, and with his strong jaw, pugnacious chin and thick neck looked every inch a fighter. His large and prominent 'Bentley' nose, thin lips, high cheek bones, surmounted by piercing blue eyes and rather thin fair hair all contributed to give him a remarkable resemblance to Holbein's drawing of Erasmus. It was not unfitting, for he was a wholehearted admirer of that great man—he had what Archbishop Brilioth called 'an Erasmian rationality.' Archbishop Söderblom once wrote to him (April 11, 1922), 'My wife observed your personal resemblance to Erasmus; and indeed also spiritually the Erasmian part of the Church has in our day, as far as I know, no more authentic and authoritative representative than you. I have defined Anglicanism as the only true continuation of Erasmian details in its comprehensiveness and in its sympathy for an older and wider type of the Church, in contrast to the violent differentiations operated by Luther with Calvin and Loyola in the sixteenth century.'

When this striking figure spoke he compelled attention. Devoid of graces of gesture and eloquence, he was always lucid and audible—despite certain habits of speech which nothing on earth would induce him to change. He always referred, for example, to Dr. Rashdall as Dr. Rashd*ale,* although he knew full well that that was not the pronunciation which the owner of the name used. His appeal was always to the intelligence rather than to the emotions, and he cared little whether his remarks were conciliatory or not. He was prone to express himself with rather an air of defiance, but he could also do so with his tongue in his cheek. He loved shocking people. There was the occasion when he received an honorary degree at Trinity College, Dublin. Dr. Bernard, the Archbishop of Dublin, recalled that at dinner afterwards he caused some stir by remarking in a loud voice, 'I have often heard of Irish wit and humour, but I have never come across it.' But outrageous remarks, particularly when they referred to people, could hurt. Headlam judged people by an abstract rather than a personal standard and expected others to understand this : when a judgment was true, the question of its expediency in kindness was therefore, strictly speaking, irrelevant. From a human point of view, of course, such an attitude is completely defective. Judgments made on this basis could have serious consequences—far more serious, perhaps, than he sometimes realized. A clergyman who had seceded to Rome saw the folly of his ways and decided that he should return to the Church of England. He came to see Headlam and gave his reasons for wishing to return. There was a terse reply. 'Mr. X., your reasons for returning to the Church seem to me as bad as your reasons for leaving.' Headlam told the story himself ; and his hearer taxed him for not taking into account the unfortunate effect such a remark could have on the man, to which he merely replied, 'Well, it was true anyway.'

Not that Headlam was by nature unkind. Beneath the rugged and forbidding exterior there was a nature that was essentially kind. Hensley Henson's remark was apt—'I have compared him to a Brazil nut, repulsively hard in the shell, and admirable in the kernel.'[1] Only rarely and with difficulty could this shell be penetrated. In public his clergy might appear to be regarded with indifference as a mere collection of units : yet when he spoke of them in private he obviously knew them all—their parishes, their families, their problems : they had become distinct personalities for whom he had a great care. On one occasion he took the funeral of an incumbent who had just died. He went through the service quite impassively, addressing no word of comfort to the mourners. The congregation was disappointed. Yet in the vestry afterwards the Rural Dean had to turn the other way so as not to intrude upon his grief. He found it almost impossible to show publicly those deep feelings which did in fact exist. His wife's death in 1924 completely devastated him—he was intensely and inarticulately lonely : yet the merest handful of people really knew. He once confessed to his niece, Miss P. L. Wingfield, 'People think me hard, and I suppose I have rather a hard exterior, but *really I want affection very much and feel it.*'

As an old man of nearly eighty he could write of his wife, 'I used to love to make Evelyn look nice, and I think that I very often succeeded. People used to tell me how much her good looks had come out, and I love still thinking and dreaming of her, and I see her just

---

[1] E. F. Braley (editor), *Letters of Hensley Henson*, p. 250.

N

as plainly as I used to do, and the things we used to buy together. You know, one's love and affection shows itself in these frivolous things and I always feel glad to have cared for them. It seems to me a right sort of worldliness and does a great deal to make life happier.'[2] These are not the words of a man who was fundamentally hard. Or again, there is the letter he wrote when his brother James died of tuberculosis after a brilliant career both as scholar and as diplomat.[3]

September 8, 1929.

'My dear Persis,

'You will see from the papers that Jemmie died on Friday afternoon.

'It is a very great loss to me. We did everything together until I went to Winchester and then afterwards in the holidays, and he was one of the few people for whose judgment and approval I cared.

'As one's old associates and friends pass away, one begins to take less interest in life. One goes on doing things but it is not with the same interest. As long as Evelyn was with me, I really cared whether I "got on" or not. Now there is not the same interest and thrill about life. And really I think that it was the pleasure and approval of Jemmie for anything that I did that gave me the greatest zest in my work.

'He developed in some ways rather late. When he was quite small he took things easier than I did, and although he had obviously plenty of intellectual power, he did not seem to care. But as he got older his power and love of work seemed to grow, and in the later years of his life he worked with all and more than all his strength. He had an extraordinary sense of duty, great intellectual honesty, and very great unselfishness. He was one of the most unselfish men that I knew—a little too indifferent to his own welfare.

'Well, we have to go on doing our work, and I have about the most important and interesting work to do there is. I may be able to do something (if I live) but I doubt it; but I think some seed has been sown which will bear fruit when we are gone.

'You do not know how grateful I am for all your kindness to me. There is no one else to whom I can write frankly. And I do very much

[2] Headlam to Miss P. L. Wingfield, January 2, 1941.
[3] James Headlam-Morley, Fellow of King's College, Cambridge 1890–6; Professor of Greek and Ancient History, Queen's College, London 1894–1900; Inspector of Schools 1902–14; the Foreign Office 1914–29, of which he was Historical Adviser; he did a great work in the Royal Institute of International Affairs at Chatham House. He received the royal licence to assume the name and arms of Morley in 1918.

want some-one to love, who does not mind my saying that I love her.

Your loving uncle,

A. C. GLOUCESTR :'

Kindness must have been there, because he could deplore the lack of it in other people. One incumbent was misguided enough to upset his parishioners very badly, and the matter was reported to Headlam. The unfortunate man was summoned to the Palace for an interview. The excuses which he made were of no avail, and finally his conduct was condemned in a single sentence. 'Mr. X., you have been very unkind to your people.'

There was about him a rugged gentleness and he undoubtedly mellowed with age. Archbishop Lang used to attribute the change to his consecration as bishop—'I never knew a man in whom the grace of consecration made a more marked difference.' He grew less irritable and more patient. When visiting older people, as he enjoyed doing in his later years, he would take trouble to talk about things that would interest and amuse them. Young people were always a source of delight to him : not that he would unbend sufficiently to romp with them, but their company always gave him pleasure especially when roaming the country-side. Somehow children could pierce through his hard shell and see what was inside much more easily than their elders. Many wrote to him regularly, and from their contents the letters were obviously spontaneous and not written at the behest of parents. His papers contain large numbers of little notes and cards, mostly from children of the vicarages in the diocese ; they were carefully preserved in the files marked 'Private Letters' treated with no less regard than the missives of scholar and statesman. He cherished them all.

To this regard for people must be added his great love for two places above all others. The first was All Souls. After the death of his wife in 1924 he was re-elected to a category of Fellowship which did not admit married men to it. Nothing could have given him greater pleasure. He stayed there whenever he could, rejoicing in the masculinity of its company : it was 'the most comfortable club in Europe.' The personnel of the College had, of course, changed considerably from his earlier days, and many of the younger Fellows were impatient of restrictions, particularly those of institutional religion. But, as he once remarked in a Commemoration Sermon, he still considered the College was being faithful to the aim of its founder—the provision of learned clerks for the public service. While regretting the halfhearted loyalty to religious ideals, he could not see, on the whole, any sign of deterioration, despite the considerable changes in custom and outlook. Men now seemed to work harder, they had pleasanter and easier manners, and they certainly had earnestness and strength of purpose.

His second great love was, of course, his real home, Whorlton. Nothing pleased him more than to roam the river Tees or to work in his garden. He rarely went out when he was there on holiday—perhaps a trip to Bishop Auckland to see Hensley Henson, a visit to Bowes for the Agricultural Show, or a day at Langdon Beck to see the gentians in bloom : but very little more. He was unashamedly completely selfish. If visitors were staying at the house they were expected to amuse themselves : people who came to see him had to come into the garden if they wanted to talk : and if he did go out, an overcoat over his gardening clothes was considered sufficiently respectable. In his old Norfolk jacket, knickerbocker trousers and big grey hat, he did not care how dirty he became. When his sister remonstrated with him for coming in to tea with dirty hands, he replied, 'Rose, I am on holiday. You cannot expect me to wash for tea when I am on holiday.'

His gardener, Hudson, served him for nearly twenty years, and they knew each other's ways perfectly. There was a time-honoured ritual when he arrived home on holiday. The first day was spent in the house—often in bed : on the second day there was a detailed inspection of the garden : then on the third day operations began, and they continued daily from 10 a.m. to 5 p.m. He gathered seeds from all over the world—primulas were his great interest—and his methods of collection were varied. On occasions it was known for seeds to be sent home to him with the diplomatic mail : overseas bishops were approached for supplies at the Lambeth Conference : and œcumenical conferences abroad were a fruitful source. When King Boris of Bulgaria died in 1943 he was heard to remark, 'That is a nuisance. He promised to send me some primulas!' It all must have cost him a fortune, but it was his recreation in the fullest sense of the word. 'I am working steadily in the garden—it means long hours, but I hope conducive to health and sanity : the latter particularly it seems desirable to cultivate, as a very large part of the world seems to me mad ; and it is very hard to keep one's head in all this turmoil.' Or again, 'My garden is a wilderness, but it is a beautiful wilderness, and will give me plenty of opportunity for resting my brain.' There was no question of creating a showpiece or even something that would last. It was simply his hobby to have an interesting garden. 'As long as it flowers in your time and mine,' he used to say to Hudson, 'it will do.' He was a 'proper gardener' : not one who merely kept a smoothly mown lawn and a herbaceous border, but one who gathered rare plants, cultivated his own seeds and knew all their Latin names. Of necessity Hudson was left to carry on by himself for the greater part of the year, but Headlam insisted that he received his due meed of praise. When the garden was thrown open for an 'At Home' not only was Hudson invited to come : Headlam refused to sit with any one else but him for his tea, for it was his day as well.

Apart from gardening Headlam had few relaxations. He did not fish or shoot or play golf. He enjoyed walking, striding along at a killing pace with a springy step which made him appear to be constantly bobbing up and down : he smoked occasionally : and he enjoyed a good dinner—'a good dinner if often very good for one both physically and mentally.' He had no special tastes in literature —neither poetry nor foreign literature seemed to attract him ; but he loved detective stories. When Miss Dorothy Sayers forsook detection for theology he was disappointed. 'Why should she? I can write all the theology that is necessary, but I can't write detective stories.' He also loved animals, especially dogs, although he was singularly unsuccessful in controlling them. Miss Le Bailly recalled that one of the very rare occasions on which she caught him completely off his guard was when she found him in the Palace drawing-room romping on the sofa with James, his cousin Maud's fox terrier : both were having a glorious time—the dog was all over him while he chuckled away with his own peculiar crowing chuckles.

Despite his firm belief in the value of hospitality he found it difficult to engage in small talk on social occasions. One topic on which he could wax enthusiastic was, of course, gardening ; and then he really could let himself go. At a luncheon party he once disconcerted every one by suddenly getting up to demonstrate how to weed an onion bed : but then, it was not unusual for him to be disconcerting. He was quite prepared to defy convention if necessity demanded, even at the risk of appearing rude. If his tea was hot and he was in a hurry, he would drink it from his saucer : if he was compelled to listen to speakers who were tiresome, he would give vent to prodigious yawns : and if he could not escape a concert—and music bored him completely—he would slumber unashamedly.

It was not surprising, therefore, to hear him say in his later years that deafness had its advantages, for it saved one from listening to a great deal of nonsense especially in Convocation and the Church Assembly. He was certainly critical of his fellow bishops. He once went so far as to say that the company of other bishops at Lambeth was for him the most uncongenial aspect of the episcopal office. Much of this dissatisfaction stemmed from his distrust of Temple as Arch-

bishop, attractive though he found him as a man. He disagreed with
him over the Education Act of 1944, he disagreed with him over the
creation of the World Council of Churches, and he disagreed with
him over his attempt to commit the Church to a Socialist policy. 'I
am getting myself involved in controversies. I think the Archbishop's
attempt—somewhat hesitating—of committing the Church to supporting a political programme is very dangerous. . . . I may also get
involved in the Education controversy. It is a great misfortune that I
find myself more and more at variance with a great many Bishops—
especially the Archbishops.'[4] Then, when Temple died, he wrote,

'He was a very good Christian. We always got on well together personally, but I often differed from him, and opposed what he wished
to do, and was defeated. All the same I think he was often wrong, and
I had little respect for his judgment. . . . He was a man of very considerable intellectual powers, but not the highest wisdom. He was a
great Christian, but I should find it difficult to take him as my
leader.'[5]

As far as he was concerned the Church of England of his own generation had produced only one man who was really great and who possessed religious genius, and that was Charles Gore. 'He had a power
which none of his contemporaries possessed, and that means that he
will leave a bigger mark on his generation than any one else. There
are only few men who really have religious genius: Wesley had,
Newman had, Luther had, Ignatius Loyola had. It does not mean that
they are great theologians. They may have many of the mental and
moral defects of imperfect men, but they have a power which others
have not. Gore belonged to that class and that is why he was greater
than his contemporaries.'[6]

What, then, of Headlam himself? Henson conceded his massive
learning but was not prepared to accept him as great. Others disagreed with this judgment. Canon J. A. Douglas wrote, 'Headlam
had his weakness but he was intrinsically among the greatest clerics
and the greatest Christians—if not the greatest—whom it has been
my happy inspiration to know. Verily he had a great and tender heart
as well as a great and creative brain.' Canon Claude Jenkins was
quite sure that if Headlam had ever become Archbishop of Canterbury, he would have been a great Archbishop: despite what was said
about his rudeness, he was not ruder than Frederick Temple. He had,

[4] Headlam to Miss P. L. Wingfield, October 26, 1942.
[5] Ibid., October 29 and November 2, 1944.
[6] Headlam to Sister Lavinia Smith, January 28, 1932.

in fact, many of Frederick Temple's finer qualities, and he was certainly a better judge of men and affairs than William Temple. He was essentially a big man : others might disagree with him or dislike him, but they simply rested in his shade. After the Lambeth Conference of 1920 his greatness was recognized in more than one quarter and he was mentioned as a likely successor to Archbishop Davidson. The stature of a man who is thought worthy to move straight from a professorial chair to the Primacy of All England is hardly small. There was certainly nothing small or petty or artificial in his make-up. 'He was just big,' wrote the Bishop of Tewkesbury, 'and one cannot judge such a man by ordinary standards.'

Dr. Bright said of Leo the Great that people tended to think of him only as a great public person—he did not seem to need an interior. The same might truly be said of Headlam. None the less the interior life was there and was very real. He was, of course, by nature shy and reserved about spiritual things : but in any case the prayer life was not a matter for display. 'The religious man is one who has faith, that is one who believes in the reality of spiritual things and is therefore in harmony with the spiritual world . . . and because he thus lives in harmony with what is the ultimate reality, he attains the greatest satisfaction possible on earth. And the means whereby he attains this is prayer. . . . It is, (our Lord) tells us, something secret. There must be no ostentation about it.' [7] Nevertheless, those who knew him could recognize on occasions an outcrop of his life of prayer. It could shine through when he prayed at the bedside of someone who was sick : it could shine through when he laid on hands at an ordination : and it was there when he pronounced the name of God in a Blessing. In keeping with this lack of ostentation was his love of simplicity in worship. He did not object to the use of vestments and elaborate ceremonial, but his preference was for something simpler— the surplice had a 'dignified simplicity' and he felt that 'the simpler service harmonizes better with the genius of the English people.' [8] He loved a plain celebration of the Holy Communion at an early hour— 'It is the only sort of service I really like.' He did not attend weekday celebrations except on very special occasions, but he never missed on Sundays. He knew his Prayer Book through and through. For his private devotions he was content to rely mainly on an old Victorian book of prayers, but he certainly knew S. Augustine and Thomas à Kempis well.

What might be called his apologia for the devout life was to be found in the Charge delivered at his third Visitation in 1932 and

[7] *What it means to be a Christian*, pp. 104–5.
[8] *The Church of England*, p. 86.

published under the title *What it means to be a Christian*. The Christian life could be summed up in four words—service, duty, sacrifice and love—words which characterized the life of Jesus Christ.[9] They expressed obligations which had no limit—the limit was as wide as humanity and man's opportunity.[10] The ideal Christian was one who fulfilled his duty in the world, who had learned to live in Christian charity and peace with all men, and who could present a strong and courageous front to the troubles and vicissitudes of human life because his life was based on the Reality transcending the world.[11] He was helped to lead this life by means of divine grace—the loving kindness of God exhibited by the influence of His personality.[12] The happiness of life consisted in love—not in passionate love, but in brotherly love, the pleasant relationships of man and man which were the richest possessions of life.[13] On the other hand the true Christian needed something more than happiness : adversity played its part too. 'I suppose that every religious man . . . would readily admit that if his life had been one of continued happiness, well-being, prosperity or bodily health, he would have failed to learn the lesson of life.' [14]

All this was manifested supremely in his work for Christian unity. Dr. Matthews has remarked what a curious paradox it is that a man who found it so difficult to get on easy terms with people in normal social intercourse was able to do so much for the promotion of better understanding between Christians throughout the world. His friendships with foreign Churchmen—Söderblom, Brilioth, Batiffol, Ireney, Nicolai and Alivisatos to name but a few—were certainly among the richest possessions of his life. They had a tremendous mutual love and respect. With them he had a gentleness, courtesy and patience that was quite astonishing : his coldness of manner disappeared and he was transfigured. Philip Usher used to say that one had to see him in an international environment to realize the true stature of his greatness. While there was not necessarily a general agreement with all that he said and did, there was at least a wide recognition among other Churches of the debt they owed him in the œcumenical movement. 'If it had not been for him,' said one of the Orthodox delegates at Edinburgh in 1937, 'we should never have been here.' His work was dominated by four fundamental principles.[15] In the first place, it

---

[9] *What it means to be a Christian*, p. 135.
[10] Ibid., p. 139.
[11] Ibid., p. 106.
[12] Ibid., p. 101.
[13] Ibid., p. 43.
[14] Ibid., p. 49.
[15] These four principles appear in J. G. Lockhart's biography of Archbishop Lang. They originally appeared in a memorandum on reunion drawn up by Canon J. A. Douglas at the Archbishop's request, and which was submitted to and approved by Headlam.

had to be recognized that there were no short cuts to reunion—the work must proceed without remission and without hurry. Secondly, no one was to be excluded from the process of 'growing together.' Thirdly, there were to be no party or sectional approaches to other Churches—the work must always be done by the Church of England as a whole. Finally, negotiations with one Church should not prejudice or even be inconsistent with negotiations with another Church.

A dominating feature of his work was his insistence that agreement on broad principles was all that was necessary for reunion : agreement on details or on the interpretation of the fundamentals of faith and order were not necessary. Many scholars have considered this to be a mistake ; and admittedly it has produced difficulties. Here is the judgment of the Russian theologian, Professor N. Arseniev : 'His great gift, his great instrument wherewith to serve the Church of God was his scholarship and his fine power of organization and of uniting intellectual efforts of different people for a great common work. He found admirable well-adapted words to summarize the opinions of others, to propose a common formula, an intellectual bridge. And here perhaps was a weak point of his : his love for synthetical unifying formulae, for conciliatory overbridgings of differences, that were sometimes premature and could sometimes conceal the deeper issues behind them. But how clear-cut, how lucid was his interpretation of the problem and of the different approaches thereto, and how he knew and respected the spiritual independence of others. This made him an ideal chairman, full of lucidity, of sense for order and of tolerance.' It was, of course, a fact that he was an admirable chairman of conferences on reunion. By virtue of long experience he knew exactly what procedure to adopt, how to treat the issues, and what resolutions a conference was likely to accept. But his too liberal approach could lead to inconsistencies. To assure both Orthodox and Lutheran theologians, for example, that the Church of England was in general agreement with their respective views on Confirmation, when both those Churches did not themselves agree, solved nothing. It bred doubt. It certainly bred doubt in the minds of some of the more rigid Orthodox theologians. 'If he is so inconsistent, how can we trust him?' some of them once asked.

But to Headlam there was no real inconsistency. He was doggedly determined to follow a policy : it may have appeared as a rather rough and ready policy to some, but it was a policy inspired by a vision. 'A Church which produced Clement of Alexandria and Origen, Athanasius and the Alexandrian school, Chrysostom and the Antiochene school, the great Cappadocians, the two Gregorys and Basil, the African school, Tertullian, Cyprian, Augustine, Leo and Gregory the Great, shows no narrowness and no failure in spiritual power. It conquered the ancient world; it subdued the untrained vigour of the barbarians. A Church which was based not on confessions but on such a tradition would embrace within its fold evangelists and those we wrongly call Catholics, modernists and pietists, Lutherans and Calvinists. There would be a home in it for all that is true in Romanism or Orthodoxy or Anglicanism. It would be a free home for the working of the Spirit.'

So then we leave Arthur Cayley Headlam—that 'fascinating blend of dignity, ferocity and humour,' as Sir Michael Sadler once described him : a great man, who made no attempt to seek the limelight, but on whom, for a variety of reasons the limelight played. As a very old man he summed up his own life—'On the whole my life cannot be said to have been uninteresting and I ought to be content. Of course, I am not; which shows how wicked and unholy I am !' Preaching in Gloucester Cathedral on January 25, 1949, at the dedication of his memorial, the Dean of S. Paul's ended, 'The type of bishop of which Dr. Headlam was an outstanding example is a rare one, and, I think, much rarer to-day than it was a generation ago. I am thinking of the type of a man who has few of the ordinary popular gifts, but has a mental grasp and a wide outlook of the world of thought and the world of history; one who can speak with the learned in the tongue of the learned, and with statesmen in their language, and in all these languages speaks of Christ. Unless we can enlist such men among our leaders, the Church will suffer. We thank God for the labours and example of Arthur Cayley Headlam.'

APPENDIX

1887. Shelley and the Shelley Society. *C.Q.R.*, vol. 25, pp. 51–77.
1888. Tudor's Philosophy of Church Life. *C.Q.R.*, vol. 26, pp. 407–22.
Professor Harnack's History of Church Doctrine. *C.Q.R.*, vol. 26, pp. 447–68.
1889. Mark Pattison, *C.Q.R.*, vol. 28, pp. 371–90.
Contributor to *Appendices ad Novum Testamentum Stephanicum*, edited by W. Sanday, Oxford.
1890. Farrar's Lives of the Fathers. *C.Q.R.*, vol. 29, pp. 400–24.
1891. *Notes on the Study of S. Paul's Epistles*, Oxford.
The Council of Ephesus. *C.Q.R.*, vol. 33, pp. 91–115.
1892. *Ecclesiastical Sites in Isauria*. Supplementary Papers No. 1, Society for the Promotion of Hellenic Studies.
Recently Discovered Early Christian Documents: the Gospel and Apocalypse of Peter. *The Guardian*, pp. 1883–4, 1929.
Professor Ramsey's 'Historical Geography of Asia Minor.' *The Quarterly Review*, no. 349, pp. 211–34.
1893. Harnack on Early Christian Literature. *The Classical Review*, vol. 7, pp. 62–4.
The Akhmim Fragments. *The Classical Review*, vol. 7, pp. 458–63.
1894. Contributor to the 4th Edition of *A Plain Introduction to the Criticism of the New Testament* by F. A. Scrivener.
1895. *A Critical and Exegetical Commentary on the Epistle to the Romans*, with W. Sanday.
The Church of the Apostolic Fathers. *The Quarterly Review*, no. 364, pp. 369–98.
The Theology of the Epistle to the Romans. *The Expository Times*, vol. 6, pp. 57–60, 103–6, 152–5, 206–8, 263–8, 355–7, 491–4, 547–50.
Recent Discoveries and Research. *Report of the Church Congress*, Norwich, pp. 262–5.
1896. The Canons of Hippolytus. *The Guardian*, pp. 243, 699, 991.
1897. *The Teaching of the Russian Church*.
Methods of Theology—the Historical Method. *Report of the Church Congress, Nottingham*, pp. 69–74.
1898–1902. Contributor to Dr. Hastings' *Dictionary of the Bible*.
Articles on Acts of the Apostles, Gnosticism, Herod, Book of Jubilees, Julius, Sergius Paulus, Prisca, Province, Rufus, Sceva, Simon Magus, Tertullus, Theatre, Theudas, Tryphena, The Unknown God.
1899. Methods of Early Church History. The Birkbeck Lectures. *The English Historical Review*, vol. 14, pp. 1–31.
Contributor to *Authority and Archaeology: Sacred and Profane*, edited by D. G. Hogarth.
1900. Contributor to *Church Problems*, edited by H. H. Henson.
1901. Criticism and the Acts of the Apostles. *C.Q.R.*, vol. 53, pp. 1–22.
Abbé Loisy and Biblical Criticism. *Journal of Theological Studies*, vol. 2, pp. 622–4.

1902. The Church and Education. *C.Q.R.*, vol. 53, pp. 456–69.
The New Education Bill, *C.Q.R.*, vol. 54, pp. 204–14.
Education and Religious Liberty. *C.Q.R.*, vol. 55, pp. 169–200.
The Editions and Manuscripts of Eusebius. *Journal of Theological Studies*, vol. 4, pp. 93–102.
Contributor to *The Criticism of the New Testament,* edited by H. H. Henson.
The Education Act 1902. A Church Policy. *The Guardian*, pp. 1860, 1891.

1903. *The Sources and Authority of Dogmatic Theology.*
The Credibility of the Acts of the Apostles. *C.Q.R.*, vol. 55, pp. 388–405.
Church Worship and Church Order. *C.Q.R.*, vol. 57, pp. 1–28.
The Clementine Literature. *Journal of Theological Studies*, vol. 4, pp. 93–102.
The Education Act 1902. A Church Policy. *The Guardian*, pp. 25, 69.
Contributor to *Critical Questions,* edited by James Adderley.

1904. The Education Acts and after. *C.Q.R.*, vol. 57, pp. 396–413.
The Christian Society 1. The Jewish Community. *C.Q.R.*, vol. 59, pp. 29–58.
The Vatican and the Abbé Loisy. *The Times Literary Supplement*, January 15, 22, 29.
The Authenticity of the Pastoral Epistles. *Report of the Church Congress, Liverpool*, pp. 117–23.

1905. The Christian Society 2. The Teaching of our Lord. *C.Q.R.*, vol. 59, pp. 257–87.
The Christian Society 3. The Earliest Christian Community. *C.Q.R.*, vol. 60, pp. 317–33.

1906. The Christian Society 4. The Development of the Church. *C.Q.R.*, vol. 61, pp. 241–78.
Education and Politics. *C.Q.R.*, vol. 62, pp. 403–30.

1907. *Universities and the Empire.*
The Church Quarterly Review: Past and Present. *C.Q.R.*, vol. 64, pp. 1–12.
The Gospel History and its Transmission. *C.Q.R.*, vol. 64, pp. 169–97.
The New Theology. *C.Q.R.*, vol. 64, pp. 409–35.
Contributor to *The Practice of Instruction,* edited by J. W. Adamson.

1908. The Education Bill. *C.Q.R.*, vol. 66, pp. 1–23.
The Athanasian Creed. *C.Q.R.*, vol. 66, pp. 40–71.
The Lambeth Conference and the Union of the Churches. *C.Q.R.*, vol. 66, pp. 257–84.
Some Notes on Sicilian Coins. *Numismatic Chronicle*, ser. 4, vol. 8.
The Church and the New Universities. *Report of the Church Congress, Manchester*, pp. 565–9.

1909. *History, Authority and Theology.*
The Pauline Theology in relation to the Records of our Lord's Life and Teaching. *Report of the Church Congress, Swansea*, pp. 329–33.

1910. The Christ of History. *C.Q.R.*, vol. 69, pp. 257–81.
The Eucharist in History. *C.Q.R.*, vol. 70, pp. 29–62.
The Training and Examination of Candidates for Orders. *C.Q.R.*, vol. 71, pp. 119–40.
Contributor to *The Church of the Nativity at Bethlehem,* edited by R. Weir Schultz.

1911. The Odes of Solomon. *C.Q.R.*, vol. 71, pp. 272–97.
The Value of the Establishment of the Church. *C.Q.R.*, vol. 73, pp. 1–24.

The Religious Training of Teachers in Elementary Schools. *Report of the Church Congress, Stoke-on-Trent,* pp. 294–8.

Christian Miracles. *The Guardian,* pp. 1460–1, 1500–1. Reprinted in *Miracles. Papers and Sermons contributed to The Guardian,* edited by H. Scott Holland.

1912. Episcopacy; and Apostolic Succession. *The Prayer Book Dictionary,* edited by G. Harford and M. Stevenson.

John Henry Newman. *C.Q.R.,* vol. 74, pp. 257–87.

Christian Miracles—the Evidence. *Report of the Church Congress, Middlesborough,* pp. 185–91.

Contributor to *London Theological Studies* by Members of the Faculty of Theology in the University of London.

1913. *S. Paul and Christianity.*

Foundations. *C.Q.R.,* vol. 76, pp. 1–30.

Some Books on S. Paul. *C.Q.R.,* vol. 76, pp. 165–75.

Montenegro and the Eastern Question. *C.Q.R.,* vol. 76, pp. 257–86.

Degrees in Divinity. *C.Q.R.,* vol. 76, pp. 357–70.

The Epistle of Priesthood. *The Times Literary Supplement,* December 4.

Oxford. *The Burlington Magazine,* vol. 24, no. 127.

1914. *The Miracles of the New Testament.*

The Emperor Constantine and the Edict of Milan. *C.Q.R.,* vol. 77, pp. 257–81.

Notes on Reunion: the Kikuyu Conference. *C.Q.R.,* vol. 77, pp. 405–23.

The Ecclesia Anglicana. *C.Q.R.,* vol. 78, pp. 137–59.

Nature Miracles and the Virgin Birth. *C.Q.R.,* vol. 79, pp. 1–36.

The Outbreak of War. *C.Q.R.,* vol. 79, pp. 157–73.

The Church in Australia. *The Challenge.* July 17, 24, 31, August 7, 14.

1915. The Ezra Apocalypse. *C.Q.R.,* vol. 79, pp. 288–317.

Our Duty. *C.Q.R.,* vol. 79, pp. 426–47.

Sir William Ramsey on the New Testament and Recent Discovery. *C.Q.R.,* vol. 80, pp. 181–7.

Kikuyu: the Archbishop of Canterbury's Statement. *C.Q.R.,* vol. 80, pp. 321–47.

The War: Our Danger. *C.Q.R.,* vol. 80, pp. 435–55.

Nestorius and Orthodoxy. *C.Q.R.,* vol. 80, pp. 456–64.

The Issues of the War. *C.Q.R.,* vol. 81, pp. 174–99.

Mr. Pullan's Doctrine of the Catholic Church. *C.Q.R.,* vol. 81, pp. 199–206.

1916. The Holy Catholic Church. *C.Q.R.,* vol. 81, pp. 322–51.

The Conduct of the War. *C.Q.R.,* vol. 81, pp. 408–28.

The Religion of Syria. *C.Q.R.,* vol. 81, pp. 433–41.

The Russian and the English Churches. *C.Q.R.,* vol. 82, pp. 92–106.

The War: the Task before us. *C.Q.R.,* vol. 82, pp. 157–71.

The Crisis of the War. *C.Q.R.,* vol. 82, pp. 380–95.

The Virgin Birth. *C.Q.R.,* vol. 82, pp. 395–401.

The National Mission: Where does the defect of the Church lie? *C.Q.R.,* vol. 83, pp. 1–19.

The War and Religion. *C.Q.R.,* vol. 83, pp. 81–110.

The War. *C.Q.R.,* vol. 83, pp. 155–73.

1917. *The Revenues of the Church of England.*

What is Catholicism? *C.Q.R.,* vol. 83, pp. 292–329.

The War: a new Crisis. *C.Q.R.,* vol. 83, pp. 359–90.

The War. *C.Q.R.,* vol. 84, pp. 154–68.

Authority. *C.Q.R.,* vol. 84, pp. 201–22.

The War and Peace. *C.Q.R.,* vol. 84, pp. 323–44.

The War. *C.Q.R.*, vol. 85, pp. 135–51.
Essays in Orthodoxy. *C.Q.R.*, vol. 85, pp. 151–7.
Introductory Essay to *A Study in Christology* by H. M. Relton, pp. vii–xxiv.

1918. *The Study of Theology*, Oxford.
The Teaching Office of the Church in relation to the Universities; and The Training of Candidates for Holy Orders—in *The Teaching Office of the Church*, Report of the Archbishops' First Committee of Enquiry on the National Mission.
Church Reform: the Church and the Nation. *C.Q.R.*, vol. 85, pp. 281–301.
The War: the Great Onslaught. *C.Q.R.*, vol. 85, pp. 328–42.
The Bishopric of Hereford. *C.Q.R.*, vol. 86, pp. 99–118.
The War: the Dismemberment of Russia. *C.Q.R.*, vol. 86, pp. 130–9.
The Training of the Clergy in Oxford. *C.Q.R.*, vol. 86, pp. 146–50.
Recent Work on the Gospels. *C.Q.R.*, vol. 86, pp. 269–304.
The War. *C.Q.R.*, vol. 86, pp. 333–44.
Ancient Coinage. *C.Q.R.*, vol. 86, pp. 354–61.
Church Reconstruction: the Administrative Reform. *C.Q.R.*, vol. 87, pp. 1–22.
The War: a Turn in the Tide. *C.Q.R.*, vol. 87, pp. 127–44.

1919. Eastern Christianity: Reform and Reunion. *The Quarterly Review*, no. 458, pp. 112–26.
The Reorganization of the Financial Resources of the Church of England. *Report of the Church Congress, Leicester*, pp. 241–7.
Belief and Creed. *The Guardian*, March 21.
Church Reconstruction: the Worship of the Church. *C.Q.R.*, vol. 87, pp. 279–302.
The War: Peace and After. *C.Q.R.*, vol. 87, pp. 329–44.
The Situation at Home and Abroad. *C.Q.R.*, vol. 88, pp. 123–38.
Folk Lore in the Old Testament. *C.Q.R.*, vol. 88, pp. 139–44.
The Ecclesiastical Commission. *C.Q.R.*, vol. 88, pp. 193–216.
The Terms of Peace. *C.Q.R.*, vol. 88, pp. 310–20.
Unrest. *C.Q.R.*, vol. 89, pp. 131–42.

1920. *The Doctrine of the Church and Christian Reunion*, Bampton Lectures.
The Economic Situation. *C.Q.R.*, vol. 89, pp. 321–36.
Reunion and Theories of the Ministry. *C.Q.R.*, vol. 90, pp. 104–22.
Comprehension. *C.Q.R.*, vol. 90, pp. 251–64.
The Lambeth Conference. *C.Q.R.*, vol. 91, pp. 139–56.

1921. *Theological Education at the Universities*, Oxford.
Three Sermons on the Atonement.
Union with the Orthodox Church. *The Christian East*, vol. 2, no. 2, pp. 91–7.
The Beginnings of Christianity. *C.Q.R.*, vol. 91, pp. 301–30.
The Problems of Peace. *C.Q.R.*, vol. 91, pp. 331–51.
Divorce. *C.Q.R.*, vol. 92, pp. 209–35.
Arabia. *C.Q.R.*, vol. 92, pp. 325–35.
Hugh James Rose and the Oxford Movement. *C.Q.R.*, vol. 93, pp. 86–102.

1922. The Gospel and the Person of our Lord. *Report of the Church Congress, Sheffield*, pp. 112–16.
The Modernist Christology. *C.Q.R.*, vol. 93, pp. 201–32.
Report of the Royal Commission on Oxford and Cambridge. *C.Q.R.*, vol. 94, pp. 322–51.
The Christian Belief in God. *C.Q.R.*, vol. 95, pp. 1–13.

1923. *The Life and Teaching of Jesus the Christ.*
Little Bishoprics. *C.Q.R.*, vol. 97, pp. 146–63.

1924. *The Church of England.*
Preface to *The Anglican Revival* by Y. Brilioth, pp. v–x.

1925. *Jesus Christ in History and Faith.*
The Book of Common Prayer (pt.). *The Encyclopedia Britannica,* vol. 18, pp. 420–3.
The Four Gospels. *C.Q.R.,* vol. 100, pp. 1–26; vol. 101, pp. 136–64.

1926. Economics and Christianity. *C.Q.R.,* vol. 103, pp. 64–95.
The Present State of the Serbian Church. *The Christian East,* vol. 7, no. 2, pp. 49–55.
The Lambeth Conference and Reunion. *The Congregational Quarterly,* vol. 4, pp. 19ff.

1927. *The New Prayer Book.*
Religious Education. *C.Q.R.,* vol. 104, pp. 122–47.
A Defence of the New Prayer Book. *C.Q.R.,* vol. 104, pp. 199–218.
The Lausanne Conference and the Orthodox Eastern Church. *The Christian East,* vol. 8, no. 4, pp. 184–9.
Contributor to *The Future of Christianity,* edited by Sir J. Marchant.

1928. *The Building of the Church of Christ.*
Presidential Address. *Report of the Church Congress, Cheltenham,* pp. 3–35.
An Appeal to Presbyterians. *C.Q.R.,* vol. 107, pp. 1–25.

1929. Two Lives of Christ. *C.Q.R.,* vol. 109, pp. 1–18.

1930. *Christian Unity.*
The Christian Ministry. *C.Q.R.,* vol. 110, pp. 89–119.

1931. The Lambeth Conference and Reunion. *C.Q.R.,* vol. 111, pp. 205–26.
Christian Theology. *C.Q.R.,* vol. 112, pp. 175–218.
Christian Theology. The Bible. *C.Q.R.,* vol. 113, pp. 71–107.
Contributor to *Why I am not a Catholic,* edited by Sir J. Marchant.

1932. Christian Theology. The Church. *C.Q.R.,* vol. 113, pp. 263–82; vol. 114, p. 1–26.
Christian Theology. Authority. *C.Q.R.,* vol. 114, pp. 185–211.
The Doctrine of Grace: a Statement of the Problems. Essay in *The Doctrine of Grace,* edited by W. T. Whitley.
Bishop Lightfoot's Place as a Historian. Essay in *Lightfoot of Durham,* edited by G. R. Eden and F. C. Macdonald. (Cambridge.)

1933. *What it means to be a Christian.*
What the Church as a whole owes to the Oxford Movement. *C.Q.R.,* vol. 116, pp. 167–86.

1934. *Christian Theology* (Oxford).
The Doctrine of God. *C.Q.R.,* vol. 118, pp. 1–22; 163–87.

1935. *The Atonement.*
South Indian Reunion Scheme. An Open Letter to the Revd. F. Hood.
Formgeschichte. *C.Q.R.,* vol. 119, pp. 280–95.
Preface to *The Gospel of S. Mark,* edited by S. C. E. Legg. (The Critical Greek Testament.)

1936. Church and State. The Real Issues. *C.Q.R.,* vol. 123, pp. 15–24.

1937. *The Passing of the Glory of Hailes.*
Faith and Order 1937. *C.Q.R.,* vol. 123, pp. 305–21.
The Origin of the Christian Ministry; and a Review of the Problem. Essays in *The Ministry and the Sacraments,* edited by R. Dunkerley and A. C. Headlam.

1938. *The Proposed Scheme of Union for South India.* Notes on the Schemes for 1935. 1936 compared with that of 1929.
Parochial Endowments. *C.Q.R.,* vol. 125, pp. 247–64.
The Report on Doctrine. *C.Q.R.,* vol. 126, pp. 83–94.
Christian Unity and Freedom. *Christendom,* vol. 2, pp. 534–43.

1939. *A Policy of Honesty, Faith and Love.*
Creation. *C.Q.R.*, vol. 127, pp. 185–226.
The Doctrine of Man. *C.Q.R.*, vol. 128, pp. 1–39.
The Doctrine of Sin in relation to Modern Thought. *C.Q.R.*, vol. 129, pp. 1–45.
The War. *C.Q.R.*, vol. 129, pp. 116–23.

1940. The War. *C.Q.R.*, vol. 129, pp. 314–27; vol. 130, pp. 101–16; 290–305; vol. 131, pp. 102–18.
The Atonement. *C.Q.R.*, vol. 130, pp. 1–27.
The Atonement—the work of Christ—the Apostolic Church. *C.Q.R.*, vol. 130, pp. 193–213.
The Atonement in History (1). *C.Q.R.*, vol. 131, pp. 1–30.

1941. *Our Religious Duty.*
The War. *C.Q.R.*, vol. 131, pp. 253–70; vol. 132, pp. 78–93, 238–58; vol. 133, pp. 55–70.
The Atonement in History (2). *C.Q.R.*, vol. 131, pp. 167–91.
The Doctrine of Grace: the Biblical Basis. *C.Q.R.*, vol. 132, pp. 1–25.
Grace in Church History. *C.Q.R.*, vol. 132, pp. 149–73; vol. 133, pp. 1–20.
A New World. *The Guardian*, February 28.

1942. *Our Duty.*
The Task of the Christian Church.
The War. *C.Q.R.*, vol. 133, pp. 208–25; vol. 134, pp. 68–85, 220–39; vol. 135, pp. 78–92.
The Theology of Grace. *C.Q.R.*, vol. 133, pp. 127–58.

1943. The War. *C.Q.R.*, vol. 135, pp. 234–51; vol. 136, pp. 95–112, 221–34; vol. 137, pp. 89–107.
The Historic Mission of Jesus. *C.Q.R.*, vol. 135, pp. 175–205.

1944. *The Holy Catholic Church.*
Why I am satisfied. An Open Letter to Professor Joad.
The War. *C.Q.R.*, vol. 137, pp. 205–22; vol. 138, pp. 99–111, 224–31; vol. 139, pp. 78–93.

1945. *Education.*
The War. *C.Q.R.*, vol. 139, pp. 204–17; vol. 140, pp. 61–76.
The War and the Peace. *C.Q.R.*, vol. 140, pp. 180–93.
The Future: War or Peace? *C.Q.R.*, vol. 141, pp. 86–97.
The Epistle of Polycarp to the Philippians. *C.Q.R.*, vol. 141, pp. 1–25.
The Christian attitude to the War and the Peace. *The Quarterly Review*, vol. 283, pp. 16–28.

1946. 1 Peter. *C.Q.R.*, vol. 142, pp. 98–118.
The Historical Value of S. Mark's Gospel. *C.Q.R.*, vol. 143, pp. 1–22.
The Iron Curtain. *The Quarterly Review*, vol. 284, pp. 257–71.
Alexander Nairne. *Dictionary of National Biography 1931–40*, pp. 644–5.
Jesus Christ. Article in *Hutchinson's Pictorial Encyclopedia*.
Contributor to *Has the Church Failed?*, edited by Sir J. Marchant.

1947. Jesus' Last Journey to Jerusalem. *C.Q.R.*, vol. 143, pp. 162–79.
Education. *Journal of the Durham Municipal and County Federation*, no. 2, pp. 4–7.

1948. *The Fourth Gospel as History.*

INDEX

INDEX

Acts of the Apostles, 45, 69
A.K.C. Diploma, 82, 85–9
Alivisatos, Prof. H., 156–8, 233–4, 279–80, 360
All Saints' School, Cheltenham, 328
All Souls' College, Oxford, 29, 33–47, 66, 72, 102, 131, 214, 290, 338–9, 348–50, 355–6
Amélineau, M., 38
American Episcopal Church, 156, 178–9, 192, 198–9, 212, 277–8
American Missions, 52–4
American-Orthodox Conversations, 1918, 156–8
Amersfoort, 215, 218
Ammundsen, Dr. V., Bishop of Haderslev, 252
Amsterdam, 283
Anglican and Eastern Orthodox Churches Union, 61
Anglican and Foreign Church Society, 284
Anglo-Catholics, 188, 191, 196, 199, 222, 240–1, 243–4, 253
Anglo-Continental Society, 284
Anglo-Finnish Conversations, 211, 255–8
Anglo-Free Church Conversations, 150–4, 162
Anglo-Latvian Estonian Conversations, 262–5, 289
Anglo-Old Catholic Conversations, 210, 215–19, 286
Anglo-Orthodox Conversations, 208, 222–5, 227, 286
Anson, Sir William, 34, 47
Apadna, 51
Apostolic Succession, 113–14, 117–20, 141, 145–6, 148, 150, 162, 206, 236, 245, 250, 281
'Appeal to all Christian People,' 150, 152, 154, 203, 207–8, 238–9, 305
Appendices to the Oxford Greek Testament, 38
Armenian Church, 54, 164, 204, 211, 300
Arseniev, Prof. N., 225, 268, 274, 280, 361
Asia Minor, 49–55, 317
Assyrian Church, 287, 289–90
Athenaeum, 338, 348
Athens, 40, 53, 55, 233–4, 236, 279, 288

Athos, Mount, 52, 54
Atonement, The, 342–3
Auer, Dr., 227–8
Australian Church, 101–2
Authority and Archaeology, Sacred and Profane, 70–1
Azariah, Bishop of Dornakal, 239, 247, 273

Bacon, Prof. B. W., 132–3
Baillie, Prof. D. M., 272
Bailly, Miss G. le, 174, 357
Balkan tour 1940, 233–7, 280, 289
Baltic, 262, 302
Bampton Lectures 1920, 111, 140–7, 155, 160, 192, 203, 205, 246, 252, 343
Bangalore, 238
Banninga, Dr., 243–4, 248
Baptist Church, 195
Barbour, Dr. H., 42
Barbour, Dr. R., 42, 198
Baring, Dr. C., Bishop of Durham, 25
Barker, Sir E., 79, 96
Barnes, Dr. E. W., Bishop of Birmingham, 182
Bartlet, Prof. V., 238
Bate, Revd. H. N. (later Dean of York), 68–9, 146
Batiffol, Mgr., 131, 360
Batty, Rt. Revd. F. S., Bishop of Fulham, 215, 219–20, 222, 255, 262–3
Bebb, Revd. Ll. J. M., 72
Belgrade, 134, 165–7, 227, 234–6, 303
Bell, Dr. G. K. A., Bishop of Chichester, 163, 247, 277, 284–5, 297–8, 306
Bentley, Richard, 21, 23
Berends, Mgr. J. J., Bishop of Deventer, 215–16, 220
Berlin, 291, 294–5, 299
Bernard, Dr. J. H., Archbp. of Dublin, 101, 353
Birkbeck, W. J., 55
Birkbeck Lectures, 71
Bitolj (cf. Monastir), 165–6
Black, Dr. Sutherland, 70
Blyth, Dr. G. P., Bishop in Jerusalem, 55, 57